Masculinity and Male Codes
of Honor in Modern France

Oxford University Press

Oxford   New York   Toronto
Delhi   Bombay   Calcutta   Madras   Karachi
Kuala Lumpur   Singapore   Hong Kong   Tokyo
Nairobi   Dar es Salaam   Cape Town
Melbourne   Auckland

and associated companies in
Berlin   Ibadan

Copyright © 1993 by Oxford University Press, Inc.

Published by Oxford University Press, Inc.,
200 Madison Avenue, New York, New York 10016

Oxford is a registered trademark of Oxford University Press

Library of Congress Cataloging-in-Publication Data
Nye, Robert A.
Masculinity and male codes of honor in modern France / Robert A. Nye.
p. cm. — (Studies in the history of sexuality)
Includes bibliographical references and index.
ISBN 0-19-504649-8
1. Honor—France—History.
2. Men—France—Conduct of life—History
3. Masculinity (Psychology)—France—History.
4. France—Social life and customs.
I. Title. II. Series.
BJ1533.H8N84   1993   305.31′0944′0903—dc20
92–22151

1 3 5 7 9   8 6 4 2

Printed in the United States of America
on acid-free paper

Masculinity and Male Codes of Honor in Modern France

Robert A. Nye

New York   Oxford
OXFORD UNIVERSITY PRESS
1993

For Mary Jo

PREFACE

If honor is dying in the modern world it is not for want of rhetoric. Honor is still invoked when the integrity, prestige, or dignity of an individual or corporate entity has been called into question, though none of these terms adequately captures the word's elusive meaning. We think we know what it means when we are told that a military unit has fought honorably, or that a nation's honor has been besmirched, or that a presidential nominee to high position is "a man of honor," because we can see in these instances honor's ancient origins in knighthood and oaths of loyalty. But the term is also applied to a number of other phenomena, from sexual propriety to sports performance, to business ethics, where the historical link to pre-industrial values is scarcely so evident, and the meaning of the term seems vague. How and why did these modern concerns and activities come to share in the aureole of honor?

I hope this historical investigation of honor codes in France—where honor has flourished as nowhere else—will illuminate some of these questions and issues, and explain, furthermore, why we are presently living through the twilight moments of honor in the West. Honor is a masculine concept. It has traditionally regulated relations among men, summed up the prevailing ideals of manliness, and marked the boundaries of masculine comportment. Its codes sprang from the social and political arrangements of male-dominated warrior societies in which the possession of honor, together with its wealth and its perquisites, was essential for elite status. With time, the company of honorable men expanded to accommodate worthy individuals of non-noble blood; but, even though the criteria for the possession of honor had broadened sufficiently at the threshold of the twentieth century to include most men, the connection between honor and masculinity remained intact and was affirmed, I hope to show, more self-consciously than ever before.

Women had no real place in this system of honor. They were only permitted to safeguard their sexual honor, which in truth belonged to their husbands, fathers, and brothers, who were ultimately responsible for its integrity and defense. As I will argue, women's ineligibility for honor was affirmed on the authority of both cultural tradition and modern medical science; without honor they could not, any more than a dishonored man, participate in most aspects of public life. The decay of honor has coincided with the gender revolution that has gradually opened to women most former bastions of male monopoly and privilege. Although honor systems

successfully assimilated new male recruits from non-noble social strata
without drastically altering their values or operations, they have failed to
do the same with women. Honor has accordingly been in full-scale retreat
from the public arena into the men's clubs, the boardrooms, the war rooms,
the locker rooms, and other places where exclusively masculine society
still survives. My history concludes two decades into the twentieth century,
at the high-water mark of modern honor. Depending on your point of
view, it has been all downhill or all uphill since then.

The idea for this book grew out of a friend's reproof that I had given
short shrift to sexuality in my previous book on the medicalization of
deviance in modern France. I decided to concentrate on male sexuality,
but quickly found that the concept of sexual identity was more useful
analytically than thinking about sexuality in either its narrow sense as sexual
behavior or as a category of intellectual history. Thinking about sexuality
in terms of identity led me in turn to think about sex as a category of being
and about the relation of male sex and female sex in a larger system of
sexual and cultural meanings. It also made me consider the way that male
sexual identities have been constructed and maintained by inheritance and
reproductive practices, by a legal order that has legitimized them, and by
social rituals in which men have expressed and confirmed their masculinity.
Honor codes are the conceptual bridge I use to link together private sexuality and the public domain of male sociability. Readers may find that
this historical study is also a useful think piece for trying to understand
contemporary issues of sexual identity. I certainly have.

I am indebted to several colleagues and institutions for support and advice.
I wish to thank the National Science Foundation, the Harry Frank Gug-
genheim Foundation, the Rutgers Center for Historical Analysis, the National Endowment for the Humanities, and the University of Oklahoma
Research Council for generous financial aid. In the course of working on
this project I benefited from the use of the collections and staffs of several
libraries, among them the Bibliothèque Nationale, the British Library,
Widener Library at Harvard University, Firestone Library at Princeton,
The University of California at Berkeley library, Rutgers University library, Bill Ford of Cornell University library, and the University of Oklahoma library.

Friends and colleagues have provided help in various forms: advice and
encouragement, references or insights passed on in discussion or correspondence, or reading and criticism. In the first two categories I wish to
thank Jim Allen, John Anzalone, Ed Berenson, John Biro, Martin Button,
Gary Cohen, Arnold Davidson, Steve Englund, Sharif Gemie, Jan Goldstein, Robert Griswold, John Hoberman, Jim Johnson, Nancy and David
Kitts, Judy Lewis, Dave Levy, Robert Mayer, Lesley Nye, Karen Offen,

Katie Park, Iain Pears, Kris and Guido Ruggiero, Vern Rosario, Bob Shalhope, Henry Tobias, and Joyce Zonana. A number of people read and criticized drafts of portions of this book. I owe particular debts to Emily Apter, George Chauncey, Jim Fisher, John Hoberman, Gregg Mitman, George Mosse, Bonnie Smith, the late Robert Stoller, and especially Chris Williams. I extend special thanks for editorial help to Anne Dutcher, Lorrie Flint, Rich Nye, Karen Hervey, and Sally Ragep.

I must single out for particular gratitude the members of the 1989–90 seminar at the Rutgers Center for Historical Analysis, which was devoted that year to the "Historical Construction of Identities." Mary Jo and I passed a splendid year in this wonderful interdisciplinary company, and I mean interdisciplinarity in the best sense: scholars from different disciplines working toward a common understanding of the same problem. I benefited from the very candid criticism my work received from the group and perhaps still more from the sense of intellectual adventure and camaraderie the seminar displayed all year under the incomparable leadership of its *magister ludi,* John Gillis. I wish to thank Roger Bartra, Sey Becker, Rudy Bell, Steve Cagan, George Chauncey, Deborah Cornelius, Linda Dowling, Tamas Hofer, Marcia Ian, Jerma Jackson, Ron Nieberding, Uffe Ostergard, Barbara Sicherman, Neil Smith, Jack Spector, Dorothy and Edward Thompson, Jackie Urla, Pam Walker, and Linda Zerilli. A special thanks to Jill Stahon.

I owe a special debt to four people. I am grateful to Guido Ruggiero, who asked me to publish this book with Oxford University Press and had the patience to wait until I could deliver it. John Gillis read an early draft and provided useful comments from his vast reservoir of learning and humanity. Elizabeth Williams, once my student, now my teacher and friend, gave a very close and invaluable reading of the chapters on medicine and sexuality. Ruth Harris read carefully through the whole manuscript and offered criticism and advice on matters of fact, logic, and interpretation. Her support and encouragement have been very important to me.

Once again, Mary Jo did all the above and more. This is the third book I have dedicated to her, but it will not be the last. She has inspired me, restrained me, and taught me, always at the right time and with the right words. She has made my love, work, and life all of a piece.

Norman, Okla.   R.A.N.
April 1992

CONTENTS

Masculinity and Male Codes
of Honor in Modern France

1

Introduction: Sex, Society, and Identity

After having spent a long day in the Bibliothèque Nationale reading disintegrating old sex manuals, I was browsing through the wares of a quayside stall and came upon a popular French text on sexual virility published in 1971 that reiterated almost word for word the beliefs about male sexuality I had encountered earlier that afternoon. Young women on the lookout for virile lovers, I read, should consider men with dark and abundant body hair; they should pay special attention to their hands, because the hand was a reliable indicator of the size and shape of the penis, and a weak handshake a dead giveaway of impotence. The "primordial element" of a happy marriage, according to the author, was the husband's ability to maintain an erection and sexually satisfy his wife. If he should fail in this task, he will set in motion both a "psycho-pathological inversion" of his natural dominance and her "instinct to feel herself dominated," which will end in "neurosis, adultery, and divorce."[1]

In light of apparent advances in the twentieth century in sexual enlightenment and a gender revolution in social and economic life, the persistence of popular literature linking sexual anatomy and character with biological sex seems odd, even sinister. Indeed, many of us have grown accustomed to using the socially inflected term *gender* in place of *sex* to signify the difference between men and women, and we generally accept the post-Freudian notion of our sexuality as libido, which we may bestow in the manner we please on a person or object of our own choosing. When we use the word *sex* nowadays, it is in reference to sex *acts,* or to denote the sex of beings lower than ourselves in the phylogenetic scale. Our postmodern consciousness encourages a distrust of all determinisms and stimulates in us the conceit that we may reconfigure our selves infinitely, select new identities, slip in and out of roles in protean fashion. For those engaged in contemporary sexual politics, it seems perversely old-fashioned to consider sex, as our recent ancestors did, to be something that entails preordained economic, social, and familial roles, and dictates desires and personal comportment in keeping with biological sex.

Inevitably, these changes in the outlook of our culture on sex and sex

3

difference have profoundly influenced the way we theorize about these concepts when they become objects of historical or anthropological study. Perhaps because we regard our sexual beings as something we may, at least in part, shape to a design of our own, we are able to imagine in turn the various ways the sexual natures of individuals in other societies or in earlier times were constructed in particular social and cultural circumstances. Our ability to think of sex as a constructed *identity* therefore provides us with a valuable analytical tool for understanding sex as a historical artifact furnishing individuals with particular kinds of self-awareness and modes of social self-presentation. As many theorists have noted, by historicizing sex we can escape the bind of thinking about it as an adamantine and transhistorical category of being.[2]

Recently, the lines of influence have begun to move the opposite way, from history back to politics. The current debate between "constructionists" and "essentialists" that permeates feminist, gay, and lesbian politics is as much about historical epistemology as it is about political strategy. Constructionists have argued that because essentialist definitions of sex have been used in the past to justify oppression, women and sexual minorities will benefit from a conception of sex based on social rather than biological categories, on the grounds that the former admits of change and makes discrimination based on "type" less likely. On the other hand, some contemporary essentialists—to distinguish them from the old tradition of biological essentialism that is the subject of this book—have indicated that the best foundation for long-term understanding lies in acknowledging the existence of an unchanging substratum of sexual being. Women, gays, and lesbians, the argument goes, must base their politics on their "real" natures and needs and compete for rights with other interests in a plural society.[3]

Some feminist theorists have tried to reformulate this debate along more fruitful lines by considering the merits of constructionism and essentialism in historical context. Diana Fuss has argued that essentialism is not in itself either progressive or reactionary, nor is it a necessary feature of patriarchal societies. We must ask about each "essence" we encounter, "How does the sign 'essence' circulate . . . and what motivates its deployment?" Moreover, she cautions, just as the critic or historian should regard all essences as constructions, so should they realize that constructions are merely essences that have displaced their essence onto the concept of sociality.[4] Denise Riley writes in a similar vein that instead of veering between these two categories, the meaning of *woman* must be assembled historically, through an "awareness of the long shapings of sexed classifications in their post-1790's upheavals." An identity that threatens "to be dissipated into airy indeterminacy" may be "referred to the more substantial realms of discursive historical formation."[5] The historical turn in recent feminist theory clearly illustrates that the epistemological caveats and desiderata that characterize contemporary sexual politics have a direct connection to new ways of studying sexual identity in the past.

There is, however, one aspect of the close relation between politics and history that poses a problem to understanding sexual identity in the past or in societies different from our own. I refer to the use of the term *gender,* which, for reasons I have mentioned, has begun to supplant *sex* in current discourse. Gender is a concept borrowed from grammar that connotes "a socially agreed upon system of distinctions rather than an objective description of inherent traits."[6] We may readily appreciate the contemporary attraction of a distinction between men and women that seems less determinate than one based on "inherent" biological sex, but, despite the clear analytical value gender possesses, we risk misunderstanding how individuals and societies constructed or experienced sexual identity in the past if we substitute gender for the older category of sex or use gender and sex interchangeably as though they were the same thing. As I hope I am able to demonstrate in this book, our ancestors were much more likely than us to regard sex as destiny, an *amor fati* that swept them along in its powerful currents.

It may also be the case, as I will later argue, that because of its historical experience French culture has developed a particular bias in favor of biological sex as a primordial category of being that has persisted into the contemporary era. Perhaps no modern French text better exemplifies this notion of sex than Georges Bataille's meditation on the sources and expressions of erotic excitement, *Erotisme* (1957). Bataille defines eroticism as a quest independent of the "natural" goal of reproduction, but he insists that the energy and direction of erotic feeling are determined by the fact that sexual reproduction makes each of us "discontinuous" (sexed) beings seeking to re-establish continuity with the natural order, even though death is our reward for achieving it; this fate makes us akin to all other species on the "scale of organisms," all the way down to the sperm and egg. We differ from them only in our ability to exploit this irresistible drive for our own erotic satisfaction.[7]

None of this should lead us to conclude that sex was not a socially constructed mode of being in French culture, but it does remind us of the need to consider sex and gender dialectically, as Joan Scott does when she speaks of gender as "a social category imposed on a sexed body."[8] The anthropologist Harriet Whitehead has made a similar distinction this way: "When I speak of cultural construction of gender, I mean simply the ideas that give social meaning to physical differences between the sexes, rendering two biological classes, male and female, into two social classes, men and women, and making the social relationships in which men and women stand toward each other appear reasonable and appropriate."[9] A considerable part of my aim in this book is to discuss how these biological classes were constituted in particular orders of meaning in modern society. As Ortner and Whitehead have argued, though men and women have assumed a wide range of gender roles in different societies, these roles are invariably subject to an ideological reinterpretation in terms of a rigid sexual hierarchy where men occupy the dominant and most prestigious positions.[10] When a woman performs a traditionally "masculine" activity, her work is nonetheless considered to be less prestigious in the sexually inflected value system of the group; she remains a woman in the prestige hierarchy and a female in her own sexual identity.[11]

Sex thus appears to have operated ideologically or normatively to ensure the maintenance and reproduction of the social order by disciplining individuals who have stepped outside or challenged the boundaries of their gendered roles. Until recently in European society, *charivari* enacted boisterous shaming rituals to reprove nagging or domineering women, henpecked or cuckolded husbands, by recalling to them, and to the whole community, their "true" sex, thus setting right a world which inappropriate behavior threatened to turn upside down.[12] Words were coined for men who helped their wives in the kitchen or did stitch-work, a woman's task. In the Burgundian village of Minot, one scorned such a man as a "fanoche," that is, "a man who behaves like a woman, 'femme-fanoche' suggests the assonance. In a word, he is no longer a man."[13]

But what was "true" sex? As these examples suggest, traditional societies possessed some collective understanding against which individual sexual identity was measured, invariably some form of the binary opposition, "male–female." But how is this identity constituted? What is the relation between the "individual" and the "social"? Pierre Bourdieu has argued persuasively in his *The Logic of Practice* that sexual identity is not based on formal rationality; it is a "practical belief," "not a 'state of mind', . . . but a state of the body."[14] It is "social necessity turned into nature," in which " . . . the most fundamental social choices are naturalized and the body, with its properties and its movements, is constituted as an analogical operator establishing all kinds of practical equivalences among the different divisions of the social world—divisions between the sexes, between the age groups, between the social classes. . . . "[15]

A major contention of my book is that sexual identity has been largely experienced and regarded in the past as a *natural* quality, expressed in and through the body and its gestures. This is so, as Bourdieu indicates, because the acquisition and reproduction of this practical sense is not imitative or consciously learned, but is an *embodiment* which takes place

> below the level of consciousness, expression, and the reflexive distance which these presuppose. The body believes in what it plays at; it weeps

if it mimes grief. It does not represent what it performs, it does not memorize the past, it *enacts* the past, bringing it back to life. What is "learned by body" is not something that one has, like knowledge that can be brandished, but something that one is.[16]

The gestures and practices of sexual identity are thus as corporeal in their lived reality as the sexual anatomy and the secondary sexual characteristics with which they are correlated, replicating in uncanny fashion the sexual divisions in the greater social world, "as if it produced a biological (and especially sexual) reading of social properties and a social reading of sexual properties. . . . "[17] As Bourdieu states, "It is not hard to imagine the weight that the opposition between masculinity and femininity must bring to bear on the construction of self-image and world-image when this opposition constitutes the fundamental principle of the division of the social and the symbolic world."[18]

Anthropologists or sociologists who study the continuum of sexual meanings that link the body and the social order can observe in their fieldwork the precise relation of physical appearance and movements to the social context in which they are expressed. Historians, however, cannot see their human subjects in this lived relation to their world but must try to reconstruct it as best they can from the evidence that survives. It is a subtle and difficult task for the anthropologist to accurately observe and interpret sexual identity in a small and relatively undifferentiated culture at a particular moment in time; it would be a labor of inconceivable difficulty for a historian to fully reconstruct the relationship of all bodies—male and female—to the social order in a complex, multitiered society over an extended period.

Although I have limited my topic in this book to the study of upper-class masculinity in France from the end of *l'ancien régime* to just after World War I, I hope to demonstrate how it will illuminate a remarkable part of the social, political, and cultural terrain of modern French history. I am in part concerned here with social structure and lines of cultural cleavage. My study reveals in particular how the bodies and sexuality of upper-class males and their modes of sociability and conflict were related to their elite social and political status. Women and femininity are not the subject of this work, but because French culture in this period continued to conceptualize male and female as a binary opposition, women are always in the field of focus as the "other" sex with which male sexual identity was in a persistent state of complementary equilibrium. Since the sexes were culturally defined in terms of one another, changes in one sex provoked adjustments in the other, producing moments of crisis and negotiation of great analytical interest.

I am also interested in how male sexual identity changes over time. I address in this book the transition experienced by all European societies from a feudal world shaped over centuries by the values of noble warriors to an industrial order dominated by the commercial and professional bourgeoisie. What I learned, surprisingly, is that although the language and empirical basis constituting what it meant to be a man changed radically with the production of new formal knowledge about the body, the primordial qualities of manliness exemplified in the noble gentleman were adopted with minimal revision by middle-class men. The instrumentality that facilitated this process of adaptation was a male code of honor that survived the destruction of the Old Regime in 1789 by accommodating its practices and usages to the unique sociability and legal arrangements of bourgeois civilization. As it had done from the early Middle Ages, this honor code worked to both shape and reflect male identity and ideals of masculine behavior. It did this chiefly by regulating the social relations of men in groups and by providing a basis for adjudicating private disputes between them. The duel was only the most spectacular representation of this function of the honor code; on a more prosaic level, honor codes informed the day to day relations of men in professional life, sports, the political arena, and other areas of public life.

It is the remarkable endurance of this ancient code of honor that provides me with my principal problem of explanation: why did a code that sustained a military and landowning *race* (the term used by nobles themselves) appeal to their bourgeois successors who believed all careers were open to talent? There are three answers, I believe, to this question. One is well known to historians; it concerns the process of assimilation beginning well before the French Revolution wherein *roturiers* (commoners) intermarried and intermingled socially with the old nobility, appropriating along the way some of the usages of honor. Because the nobility retained much of its social, political, and economic power well into the nineteenth century, the prestige of the old aristocratic code continued to work its magic on successive generations of ambitious bourgeois, for whom noble savoir faire remained the ideal of fashion.

The threads of the second answer may be located in the structures of manners and sociality woven into the patterns of the middle-class social and political order. In these domains honor provided bourgeois men both with the basis for claims of individual distinction and a collective warrant for certifying the superiority and exclusiveness of their class. The code thus played the same role in bourgeois culture as it had played in the court society of the Old Regime, where, in the words of Norbert Elias, "Court society represents itself, each individual being distinguished from every other, all together distinguishing themselves from non-members, so that each individual and the group as a whole confirm their existence as a value in itself."[19]

The third reason for the endurance of honor was suggested to me in a passage from Foucault's *The History of Sexuality*. In discussing the difference between the old nobility and their successors, he wrote:

> The bourgeoisie's "blood" was its sex. And this is more than a play on words; many of the themes characteristic of the caste manners of the nobility reappeared in the nineteenth-century bourgeoisie, but in the guise of biological, medical, or eugenic precepts. The concern with genealogy became a preoccupation with heredity; but included in bourgeois marriages were not only economic imperatives and rules of social homogeneity, not only the promises of inheritance, but the menaces of heredity.[20]

Because their fortunes were dependent not simply on inheritance, but on viable and talented *inheritors,* there was much more at stake in marriage and reproduction for bourgeois families than there had been for Old Regime nobles. A nobleman had only to produce or designate an heir who could serve as an appanage to an entailed estate, but a bourgeois *paterfamilias* needed a successor who would preserve and augment a legacy built with the energy and skill of his forebears. In the course of the nineteenth century, doctors and scientists produced a body of rules and precepts governing the hygiene of reproduction that reflected and shaped in turn the practical requirements of bourgeois inheritance. By the logic of these rules, the sexuality of an individual was subsumed in his or her sex and judged by a consistent standard of reproductive capacity. A man's sexual identity was thus revealed in his physical sex and manly character, a view that, for a number of geopolitical and demographic reasons, may have been more deeply rooted in France than elsewhere in the West. In effect, honor was *embodied* in bourgeois men as a set of normative sexual characteristics and desires that reflected the strategies of bourgeois social reproduction. A man who deviated from these standards by choice or by "nature" dishonored himself and brought shame to his family—a judgment applied with equal severity to both the bachelor and the homosexual.

We may gain an appreciation of the effects of this process of embodiment by considering honor codes in modern Mediterranean societies. Around the rim of the Mediterranean, honor and shame have operated primarily to regulate the relations between the sexes, families, and clans; to distribute prestige (and therefore status) among them; and, finally, to promote cohesion in the whole society through the "shaming" of individuals who have forfeited their honor. But honor is also an ideal, providing "a nexus between the individuals of a society and their reproduction in the individual through his aspiration to personify them."[21] In honor and shame societies men are regarded as the "active" and women the "passive" principle. Both sexes are attributed a measure of honor at adolescence, but women's honor is primarily sexual in nature and consists first of her virginity and later her strict marital fidelity. Women can only lose their honor, but men are permitted to accrue to theirs by seeking glory and distinction in the public arena. Men, however, may also lose their honor in a variety of ways, suffering a kind of annihilation and social death. They might act in a cowardly or fearful manner, commit civil crimes, break a betrothal, engage in unprovoked violence, or fail to oversee and protect the honor of the women in their family.

Because the profound connections between sexuality and identity encourage a man to aspire to a manliness "that subsumes both shame and masculinity," his sexual identity becomes a key element in his social identity as a man of honor, legitimizing his claims to the worldly honors he may have won.[22] The criteria of male identity may take graphically material form. A cuckold is assumed to be lacking in the usual marital authority because he is in some sense deficient as a man, that is in his genital endowments. Various insults in rural Andalusia locate willpower in the genitals, and among the Sarakatsani, a man "must be well-endowed with testicles and the strength that is drawn from them."[23] Effeminacy is deplored, especially when linked to cowardice, and there is widespread fear in honor and shame societies of impotence. The irony of male authority in such societies is that the considerable power males possess by virtue of their masculinity is exceedingly fragile, is open to constant challenge, and produces keen feelings of vulnerability in men.

I do not wish to argue that one may directly apply the concepts of honor and shame derived from the study of modern Mediterranean cultures to historical societies, even those, like France, with an important Mediterranean heritage; modern cultures and the codes that regulate them are themselves the product of a long historical evolution and deserve study in their own terms.[24] But acquaintance with the codes that regulate honor and shame offers the historian an insight into the crucial relationship between a man's sexual and social identity. As David Gilmore has written, ideals of masculinity "are not simply a reflection of individual psychology but a part of public culture, a collective representation."[25] We cannot easily penetrate the veil that cloaks private sexual experience and identity in the past, but the representations in the surrounding culture to which they are dialectically bound have left abundant traces in the public record. As several observers have noted, since codes of honor operate like systems of informal law, the rules, and the sanctions and rewards that compel submission to them must circulate openly, where they may be read by all, including the historian.[26]

In advanced societies, the rituals, gestures, and ceremonial occasions that are the data for Bourdieu's notion of personal identity as "practical sense" exist alongside systems of formal law, pictorial images, and innumerable forms of discourse that may either reinforce or oppose these informal practices. As Michel Foucault and the school of cultural history he has inspired remind us, the cultural sphere is the site of power struggles between competing representations that may not be reduced to, but must somehow be correlated with particular interests and social groups. But because representations have a kind of independent and fluctuating status, the truths they assert and the dominion they seek may be tailored to a multitude of ends. They may serve as markers of collective identity and similitude or they may undermine community in alliance with discrete factions or individuals. Cultural representations are thus both structures of meaning and discursive practices that are employed in contingent ideological strategies.[27]

If we are to successfully understand the meaning of representations, including the evidence they reveal about forms of individual and social identity, we must read them carefully in historical context. As Roger Chartier has written, "Cultural history is able to reflect usefully on social questions, since it focuses its attention on the strategies that determine positions and relations and that assign to each class, group, or milieu a perceived being which constitutes its identity."[28] We must not forget, however, that in the past these identities have assumed forms that entailed a high degree of fixity and determinism. We may be misled by the enthusiasm that postmodern critics have for speaking of the instability of identities, their evanescent forms and degrees of "density." Though the social origins, assumptions, and purposes of those in the company of honorable men varied between the Old Regime and World War I, the men who submitted themselves to the sexual prescriptions and the social rituals of the honor code felt themselves enmeshed in a fatally narrow circle of alternatives. The forms and content of the code changed markedly in the course of the centuries, but its power to command obedience remained intact.

Compared with the extraordinary growth in the history of women and femininity, the history of men and masculinity is a comparatively underdeveloped field. Inspired as much by political as by scholarly concerns, women's history has sought to bring to light not only the contributions women have made to our civilization, but also how they have suffered, often silently and invisibly, in the thrall of patriarchal culture.[29] This does not mean that only men have been well-served in the history written prior to the growth of women's studies; it could well be argued that men have been written about only as politicians, diplomats, generals, tycoons, and the like and not *as men*. Because feminists and historians of women have provided most of the methodological tools historians are now using to write the history of men and masculinity, there has been a temptation to continue the tradition of treating men and male sexuality as less problematic than the *vita sexualis* of women. Peter Gay, for example, has written that the bourgeois erotic experience is "inseparable from the nineteenth-century debate over female sexuality." Gay quotes as justification for this emphasis the early twentieth-century sexologist Iwan Bloch, who argued that "expressions of male sexual desire and lust" are "fairly unequivocal," while the "old controversy" over the nature and strength of women's sexual appetites has "not been resolved even today."[30]

The conviction that men have imposed various forms of subjugation on women has helped establish the idea that the category "woman" has been historically unstable and that men have construed women's bodies and sexuality more or less as they pleased, making them by turns wanton or passionless, domestic angel or promiscuous tramp. There is certainly some truth in this view, but it seems odd to conclude, as Tom Laqueur has done in *Making Sex. Body and Gender from the Greeks to Freud,* that men have constructed women from the archimedean point of "a generally unproblematic, stable, male body," leading him to the pronouncement that "it is probably not possible to write a history of man's body and its pleasures. . . ."[31] One wonders why Laqueur does not consider a point made years ago by Alain Corbin, to wit, that if men have constructed an amatory and familial regime that has brought suffering to women, the historian would do well to also regard these regimes as "signs of masculine suffering," in the sense that "the emotion of the partner, wife or concubine, cannot be isolated from the forms of expression or inhibition, or the satisfaction or frustration of masculine desire."[32] It brings little credit to men to say that their constructions of women's "nature" have been designed to cover a variety of masculine anxieties or shortcomings, but it does suggest that there is something in the history of men's experience that has provoked periodic reassessments of both women's nature *and their own.* How could it be otherwise if "man" and "woman" have been yoked together as complementary if fluctuating terms from time out of mind?

I hope to demonstrate in this book that men have also constructed their bodies and sexual nature, but perversely, in the form of ideals that few men have been able to realize in practice. The psychoanalysts Robert Stoller and Nancy Chodorow tell us that the mother's predominant responsibility for child-rearing in our society makes it necessary for a boy to break violently at some point from the orbit "child–mother" and forge a new oedipally oriented masculine identity.[33] Because his quest is premised on an impossibly exaggerated fantasy of a powerful father or a rigid cultural standard of male ideals, a man's sense of self will be invariably partial and provisional, subject to endless revisions and fresh efforts. As Walter J. Ong has put it, a man can never wholly interiorize his masculinity, but is always seeking it "in some way outside of himself."[34]

As I have already suggested, we can only exceptionally reconstruct the private, oedipal experiences of French males, but we can try to recover from the historical record the surviving traces of what French culture decreed men *should* be. Honor codes, with their exacting and often brutal exigencies, afford us a chance to glimpse the challenge that faced any man who aspired to honorability. The "problem" of honor, as I hope will emerge in this book, is that it was never secure, required constant reaffirmation, and was always open to challenge. Ironically, in a society governed by honor, masculinity is always in the course of construction but always fixed, a *telos* that men experience as a necessary but permanantly unattainable goal. A man was in greatest danger of dishonoring himself at the very moment he most expressly affirmed his honor. Though the metaphor may seem imprecise, even gratuitous, the French ethnologist Michel Leiris has caught the sense of this dilemma in his autobiography, *L'Age d'Homme* (translation, *Manhood*), in which he equates the writer's requirement to tell the truth to the code of the *torero,* which was to his mind far worse because of its physical danger:

> I have already spoken of the fundamental rule (to tell the whole truth and nothing but the truth) to which the writer of confessions is bound, and I have also alluded to the precise ceremony to which, in his combat, the *torero* must conform. For the latter, it is evident that the code, far from being a protection, contributes to his danger: to deliver the thrust under the requisite conditions demands, for instance, that he put his body, during an appreciable length of time, within reach of the horns; hence there is an immediate connection between obedience to the rule and the danger incurred.[35]

My plan in this book is to trace the evolution of male honor codes from the Old Regime through the second decade of the twentieth century. As I have suggested, there were two domains of male honor in modern France: the honor embedded in the sex of the male body and its sexual hygiene, and the public rites of honor expressed in male sociability and the duel. My aim is to show how these two domains of honor stood in relation to one another over time. For analytical purposes I devote most attention to the body in chapters 3 through 6 and stress the public forms of honor in chapters 7 through 10. In chapter 2, I discuss the earliest forms of the honor code in France, including the duel, and the relation of the code to Old Regime society, politics, and noble inheritance. Chapter 3 concentrates on the process of social integration that led bourgeois males to adopt certain usages of noble honor, but I focus in particular on the development of a conception of bourgeois patrimony that included a distinctive set of inheritance practices and a related ideology of sex and sexual behavior. In chapter 4, I show how the French Revolution institutionalized and normalized bourgeois inheritance and the family order that depended on it. This is the era when men and women were first identified in law and medicine as opposite but complementary beings whose unequal social status was expressed in their bodies and sexuality.

In chapter 5 I trace the effects of this "embodiment" process on theories of biological inheritance and reproductive fertility that arose in the mid-nineteenth century. I discuss how these theories, in conjunction with a "depopulation" crisis and France's threatened fall from great power status, brought unusual pressure to bear on men to conform to new cultural standards of manliness. Chapter 6 deals with the "discovery" of the perversions by fin de siècle psychiatrists. I explain how these forms of non-reproductive sexual behavior, particularly male homosexuality, operated ideologically as negative counterpoints to the period's conventional cultural norms of masculinity, and I compare French medicine, which had an unusually intolerant view of these sexual aberrations, with the more progressive psychiatric outlook elsewhere in Europe.

In chapter 7 I backtrack to the revolutionary era to discuss male bourgeois sociability and its relation to dueling practices in the first half of the nineteenth century. Chapter 8 is concerned with the rediscovery of the manly rituals of fencing and the real and symbolic links between the culture of the sword and the political culture of the early Third Republic. I examine at length the varieties of the duel that prospered from 1860 to 1914 in chapter 9, which is divided into six appropriate sections. I conclude by considering courage—the most splendid adornment of the man of honor—in its various pre-war and wartime manifestations. As I hope my conclusion will show, the legacy of honor to the twentieth century has been far from positive. Honor was invented to sustain order in a patriarchal and violent world, but it has ended by perpetuating both violence and patriarchy in ours.

2

Honor and Male Identity in the Old Regime

In this chapter I discuss the formation and maintanance of male codes of honor in the Old Regime. I believe this will not only provide us with an understanding of the ways upper-class male identity was constructed in that era, but also with a model for the way this process worked after 1789, which is the primary focus of this book. I hope to show here how the concept of honor originated in an ideology of noble military service and became associated, on account of strategies of inheritance, reproduction, and power with the idea of noble *race*. Though the notion that honor was a birthright was far from the only meaning it possessed at the end of the Old Regime, the close connection honor assumed between "nature" and "culture" is in a certain sense characteristic of the entire tradition of codes of honor, both ancient and modern. Men of honor chose their fate in a way that suggests both determinism and free will: a "destiny" that "invited" men to joyfully "conform" to its strictures.[1]

This typical and rather mysterious blending of the "natural" and the "cultural"—one might easily substitute the "biological" and the "social"— in definitions of honor and honorability is remarkably analogous to the way that nineteenth-century French medicine and science later conceived of sexual identity, a topic I address in chapters 4–6. In the modern era, honor was embedded more palpably in anatomical sex than had been common in Old Regime discourses of honor. Thus, maleness (and femaleness) were qualities with which one was normally born; but, like honor, they could be "lost" in a variety of ways, so that one could become both "unsexed" and "dishonored," as I will argue, at once. The pathetic aspect of this process is that it did not work in reverse. The "unsexed" or the "dishonored" could not easily re-attain sexual wholeness or honor through short-term efforts; at the very least one needed to be born with some "disposition" for them, which a regime of moral and physical rigor might usefully cultivate.

I can illustrate briefly the evolution honor codes have followed by looking at how etymological dictionaries define the changes in the meaning of "honor" over the sweep of the centuries. In its very earliest incarnation, from the ninth to perhaps the twelfth century, "honneur" was not a quality one possessed, but referred to a noble man's *biens* (worldly goods) in the form of fiefs or benefices. The reverence or respect he enjoyed in the world depended on these "marks and attributes of his dignity."[2] A man's wife was one of these possessions, and the term appears to have acknowledged her only in that capacity.

By the sixteenth century honor attaches more closely to the noble individual himself, to his reputation, beauty, and personal character. It was a "natural" quality of noblesse, however, because it slipped away from those who sought it, while adhering to those, secure in their nonchalance, who appeared least concerned with it.[3] By this time the words *honte* and *honteux* had developed from the same root, meaning, essentially, "modest" or "chaste," and applying to women for the first time as individuals. It is clear that *honneur/honte* have not yet been organized in a binary meaning "honor" and "shame."

The Littré of 1863, drawing its examples from the seventeenth and eighteenth centuries, recognizes "honor" as applying wholly to personal characteristics, including virtue, courage, and the desire for distinction, terms reflecting largely aristocratic preoccupations. The *point d'honneur,* which governed personal combat, resolved disputes pertaining to the possession of these qualities. The obligation for a man to defend a woman's chastity is assumed, and honor and shame have now become a binary, the latter meaning "dishonor" and "humiliation", or the fear of that condition. It is clear that both sexes may possess and lose honor, but a woman's honor is included within the larger sphere of a man's, which it is his duty to superintend.[4]

Modern usages drawn from the period after 1800 acknowledge the rise of bourgeois society. Honor now refers to the "sentiment one has of one's moral dignity as it depends on the consideration of others," and meanings denoting notions of contractural or personal integrity now fall within the range of the term: thus, *parole d'honneur* dates from 1806, and *sur l'honneur* dates from 1835.[5] *Honte* is now not simply the mere absence of honor, its negation, but a quality in itself with considerably more salience, inviting "disdain, scorn, mockery, dishonor . . . indignation." It is a "bitter sentiment of weakness, indignity, baseness, according to one's own conscience and in the eyes of others."[6]

This etymological evolution suggests the principal themes I will develop in this book. First, honor became an increasingly important feature of *individual* identity. Second, though honor has become more clearly spiritual or moral in nature, it is base action that earns scorn, and the old association of honor with the martial virtues of strength and courage is still intact, if less in the foreground. Third, it is apparent that by the turn of the eighteenth century the male members of the bourgeoisie have gained the capacity to possess honor and to lose it; judging by the range of usages pertaining to its loss, it would appear this loss was keenly felt. Finally, its etymological history makes it clear that honor was not *merely* a sentiment. Though one could have feelings about the condition of one's honor, or that of others, honor was a *quality* that inhered in individuals but which radiated out from them, producing signs that could be read by those who knew the code.

There are two historical sources of noble honor. One of these sprang from a set of related inheritance practices, the other from the public military vocation of the nobility. Though I discuss these sources of honor separately here, they were in fact connected to one another in theory and in practice, as I hope my account will make clear. It was very early in the Middle Ages that diffuse kinship patterns began to "crystallize into patrilineal dynasties, that is, into lineages."[7] The emergence of such systems among the early noblesse presupposes that a noble controlled an adequate amount of land or claim upon fiefs to make heirship strategies worthwhile. These noble families were invariably endogamous, seeking marital alliances with propertied individuals of their own class which would enable them to expand or at least perpetuate their holdings through blood kin. There were no formal rules for how property was to be transferred, but rather a set of what Pierre Bourdieu has called "implicit principles" of considerable flexibility, whose aim was to "reproduce" the family.[8]

Bourdieu argues for an understanding of *reproduction* in the broadest sense as the whole body of inheritance, fertility, and educational strategies "by which any group endeavors to pass on to the next generation the full measure of power and privileges it has itself inherited."[9] The preferred system of heirship was devolution to the eldest son, but when a son was either lacking or unfit, the integrity of the property could only be maintained if a daughter could be designated heir. By the early Middle Ages the inheritance patterns characteristic of Eurasian (as opposed to African) society had already emerged in Western Europe. This "vertical," rather than "collateral" system transferred property *down* the generations rather than *across* nuclear family lines to brothers, uncles, or nephews.[10] To preserve this system, therefore, primogeniture was occasionally set aside. Moreover, in the interest of expanding family power, all children received a dowry or settlement to compensate them for not being the principal heir, enabling them to marry as favorably as possible.

To illustrate how reproductive choices were maximized, Bourdieu offers us the distinction between a hand of cards and the way it is played. The hand of cards the patriarch is dealt is the result of the fertility strategy he has adopted and his luck in the lottery of child mortality. The way it is played includes the marital and inheritance strategies he chooses in order to make the most complete use of his "hand."[11] The overall success of his "reproduction" is based on his ability to assess and control his own family capital, *and* to correctly appraise the material and the symbolic capital in the lineages which offer him marriage alliances.

As we learned from the etymological dictionaries, in the eleventh century honor referred to goods, land, and its inheritance.[12] When inheritance strategies designed to keep this wealth intact began to emerge, the "honor" that inhered in land became identified with the family which possessed it, and, by extension, with the effectiveness of its strategy of reproduction. If a family was unusually successful in this process, retained its land *and* married all its offspring handsomely, it could accrue to its power and to its honor. As an insurance against the danger of no male heir, and to avoid claims on his land by a daughter's bastards, the patriarch was well-advised to keep his wife loyal and his daughters chaste.[13] It also behooved him to educate his sons to their responsibilities, especially the heir whom he expected to manage the reproduction of the family after his demise. We might thus most profitably think of family lineage not as a genealogical tree but as a strategically adaptable "concept of caste, which means simply purity or honour."[14]

Because the family's honor was dependent on the education of the heir to his duties and the building and maintanance of useful kinship ties, its members were obliged to fully mobilize their moral and material resources in behalf of these aims, and likely developed a deep and perhaps unconscious commitment to their worthiness.[15] The internalization by family members of the goal of assuring the integrity of their assets imbued honor with an ethical dimension that James Casey has likened to a kind of premodern "civic responsibility" governing the affairs of the caste.[16] Despite this expression of collective effort, the system worked to assure male and patriarchal dominance and to favor male offspring generally. If a male heir married too low, it was regarded as simply a bad business bargain. But if he married too high, to a woman who brought more resources to the union, he ran the risk of losing his authority in the domicile; being "embarrassed" in this way exposed him to the danger that his wife might be unfaithful to him, in which case the family line and its assets could be lost by the claims of her son.[17] In any event, too many female offspring threatened the integrity of the property by forcing the patriarch to go into debt to dower his daughters.

At the same time as these *private* inheritance practices were taking root in the eleventh-century noble family, French noblemen were exercizing a *public* function as military commanders and dispensers of justice. These duties, as much as their role as heads of patriarchal households, "accentuated the masculine nature of this social class."[18] The right to maintain a castle, a mission to command, a familiarity with arms, were the "honors" of the knightly vocation. Historians of chivalry have emphasized the distinction in medieval thinking between nobility and lineage on the one hand, and the "virtue" of the knightly profession on the other. The inner qualities that inspired a man to demonstrate his courage and prowess at arms deserved a recognition separate from the acknowledgement of his noble birth, but they were nonetheless inseparable from it. As Maurice Keen summarizes the medieval debate between the relative merits of "birth" and "worth,"

> ...the debate and verdict were directly related and relevant to a complicated system designed to provide for the social recognition of virtue, in practice. It was an object of that system to bring out at the same time the exemplary role that theorists assigned to public honours, privileges, and insignia.... The chivalric system was related to a reasoned and reasonably coherent social ideology, which had acquired a full measure of literary expression. It used the same sort of methods to denote distinction of birth on the one hand and distinction in martial prowess on the other because the relation between the two...was consciously understood.[19]

The heraldic *blazon* which a knight carried into battle was a sign of the warrior's valor, a visible measure of "the social respect that honourable acts could earn."[20] But it was also the symbol of his lineage, which reflected glory on the whole of his noble ancestry and bestowed honor on his descendents. Virtue and lineage were thus altogether enmeshed. A good heritage was insufficient warrant of status unless a man fought with enough courage and skill to gain renown (*rénommée*) in the chivalric order. Still, as Duby writes, "It is this common [military] vocation that undoubtedly explains how...it was so easy to move from the notion of nobility, supported by the image of antiquity of race combined with the idea of native authority and power, to the notion of 'chivalry', so closely bound to the notion of military power."[21]

The specific virtues a good knight needed in the system of chivalry were of a narrowly military sort. Properly cultivated, however, they helped him thrive in an atmosphere of danger and in the company of a hierarchy of fellow warriors. Keen summarizes these virtues using the original French words, signifying the preponderant contribution France made to the culture of chivalry: "*prouesse, loyauté, largesse* [generosity], *courtoisie,* and *franchise* (the free and frank bearing that is visible testimony to the combination of good birth with virtue.)"[22] Individual mastery of these traits helped guarantee the survival of the fighting unit by ensuring group solidarity, a kind of natural selection for collectively advantageous sentiments. Generosity toward a fellow knight might earn a reciprocal gesture; an enemy treated generously in defeat might return the favor in victory. The unvarnished honesty the unit required in dire circumstances for the evaluation of individual skills or for tactical decisions demanded frankness, but fighting morale could flourish only when frankness was tempered with a courtesy that respected the dignity of individuals. A company of knights was a company of equals in lineage, of individuals in valor; the virtues required of the chivalrous man ensured that fiercely courageous men could nonetheless coexist in harmony.

With the coming of the crusades a distinction arose between the knights who fought at home to defend their "honor and heritage" and those who undertook the "voyage lointain" to the Holy Land. The fourteenth-century *L'Arbre de batailles* of Honoré Bonet summed up the outlook of crusading knights, whose experiences supplied an exotic quality of striving to the ethic of native chivalry. The crusader learns

> ... to feel himself well led, to count on the aid of companions in the case of difficulty or to save a friend in danger. The habit of fighting explains a valorous comportment, but also a certain blindness, a passion and fury, the love of booty and women, the desire to surpass all others, the fear of being suspected of cowardice, the fidelity to ancestors and lineage, scorn for an adversary, the sense of honor, the desire to increase his renown or expunge a previous fault.[23]

The cult of chivalrous love operated to reinforce these qualities. The knight who sought worldly honor in behalf of a woman followed an incentive that sustained and spurred him on; her acknowledgement of his deeds was a worthy supplement to the esteem of his comrades in arms.[24] The discretion of his relation with her, idealized in the medieval romances as a love concealed from the world, was the counterpart to the closed societies of chivalric orders, where secrecy forged bonds between men of proven valor. However, the loyalty which inspired the knight to self-sacrifice in behalf of his lady was a merit on the battlefield, and a gallant and self-effacing modesty in a lover's company was an excellent school in courtesy for a company of querulous men readily given to affront.[25] The chivalric quest for love as an ideal end was in actuality a poetry of soldierly decorum, a means for tightening the bonds between men living in danger.

My argument is that the kind of self-regulating behavior that helped noble families perpetuate their lineage in the early Middle Ages was complemented by the virtues demanded of noble knights. These different influences conspired to create a "calling" for the males of the household that "was both a function and a moral quality, ... not only an occupation but a showing forth of traits of character which fitted one for the occupation in the first place."[26] Though the logic of social reproduction and knightly virtue worked in tandem, the distinction between them was maintained throughout the Old Regime in the form of an ideology of military profession that remained the special province of the nobility, and which allowed the nobility to continue to lay claim to qualities not possessed by *roturiers*.[27] However, the chief expression of this ideology was a remarkable sixteenth-century apologetics for the natural superiority of the nobility, which further reduced the chasm between nature and culture and effectively naturalized noble "qualities."

Arlette Jouanna has documented the extent and power of this body of "social myths" in sixteenth- and seventeenth-century noble culture. The apologists for these views argued that men were born with an "unequal aptitude to virtue."[28] These aptitudes were inherited *en bloc* from ancestors who had exercized them long enough in successive generations for them to have become hereditary. As Jouanna writes, this was a genuine biological theory of "acquired characters," *avant la lettre,* fully buttressed by references to the biological ideas of the era.[29] This body of myths served the purpose of guaranteeing the preeminence of individual noble lineages, but also gave to "the orders of which they were a part, a personality at once biological, moral, and social; thus it made [nobles] socio-natural types, kinds of mythical beings."[30]

These myths still formally preserved the old distinction between nature and culture. Thus, a noble man was born with an aptitude for virtue, but he must nonetheless behave in a way that will allow him to *realize* his aptitude. Failure to do so, through laziness or vice, would provoke a "degeneration," a kind of noble derogation that brought dishonor to the lineage.[31] Being "without race," the *roturier* could never attain to the level of noble virtue, though he might approach it through "steadfast application."[32]

A man born to a noble line was thus faced with an obligation to present himself in public in a manner that conformed to the expectations of his peers. Hence the extraordinary emphasis in this era on "notoriety," the ceaseless need for men to affirm and reaffirm their noble natures in the trivial and the heroic alike. The trivial consisted of modes of dress, of noble bearing and demeanor, an affability and courtesy to men and women of all classes, and even body shape, which, like "race" in equine stock, signified ancestry.[33] Heroic action in military life, or willingness to engage in duels, averted the "ignoble" fate of dying without achieving renown. The persistent regularity with which nobles in this era endorsed the ideals of noble virtue suggests the fragility of a set of "natural" qualities that "nonetheless had to be regularly reasserted."[34]

By the end of the sixteenth century, the rise of a permanent court society encouraged new emphasis on the manners and comportment that would enable noblemen to get on in a highly refined atmosphere where every act was saturated with political meaning.[35] An unusual number of "courtesy" books, many modeled on Castiglione's *Il Cortegiano,* began to appear, whose ostensible aim was to educate rough and battle-hardened country gentlemen to a more exacting regime of personal comportment.[36] There was certainly an explosion of terms that could designate a noble in this era, in addition to "gentilhomme," or "homme d'honneur," one could name him an "honnête homme," "homme de bien," "homme de qualité," even "homme habile." The remarkable polysemy inherent in "honneur" should not delude us into thinking that a new stress on cleverness or on moral goodness was an invitation to the bourgeoisie to join ranks with a nobility of birth. "Honnêteté" at the end of the sixteenth century, was still a long way from "honesty," in its modern moral or economic sense. The new valorization of ideals of internal moral worth, of learning, and of courtly worldliness was another variation on the theme that high birth alone did not guarantee noble rank.

The courtesy books make it clear that men who lived and worked for gain could not aspire to a noble "honnêteté," as their economic activity was "an infallible sign of a cowardly, low, and vile nature."[37] Merchants could be "honnête" in their own sphere, but the bourgeois consideration of profit as a goal meant they could neither grasp nor experience the pure bonds of "loyauté" that marked men of gentle birth.[38] The contrast between the classes is underscored in a passage from an early seventeenth-century courtesy book:

> Whoever wishes to join the Court of Emperors, Kings, Queens, Dukes, Duchesses, Marquis, Marquesses, Counts, Countesses or other illustrious persons must be a noble by birth, and of ancient nobility; for it is less reproachable for a *roturier* not to act virtuously or perform virtuous works than for a nobleman, who, if he does not follow the path his predecessors have taken shames the name and the honor of his race.[39]

There is a positive way to look at this point. Far from retreating from the battlefield to an impotent realm of moral reflection, the "honnête homme" was simply adding weapons of sociability to his quest to overtop his rivals and achieve renown. The energy he now invested in self control, in mastering the techniques of courtly savoir faire, were new means he could use to drive his rivals from the field, not by a display of rage or an aggressive *mien,* but through a subtle exercise of concealment, discretion, and graceful manners. As Stanton has summed up this development, "To dominate the self is to dominate the other."[40]

Alluring though it might have been, the life of a peaceable courtier did not yet satisfy all the requirements of the man of honor in the sixteenth century. He still felt the need to engage in acts of valor to assure his claims to honorability. Alas, chivalry was in woeful and irreversible decline. The crusades were long concluded, knightly orders had ceased to be the focus of a sociability of honor, and knight-errantry had become, in Cervantes' usage, quixotic. But the medieval jousting tournament, which had itself grown out of the earlier collective *melée* of fighting knights, had evolved a number of forms of individual combat in which men might display their resolution and prowess at arms. Such combats remained in fashion throughout Europe in the sixteenth century, though increasingly under the supervision of kings and their representatives.[41]

In the French *pas d'armes,* a contest designed to display the courage of an individual knight, and in combat *à outrance* (with sharpened weapons of war rather than *à plaisance,* with blunted arms), men could still risk their lives and honor. By the sixteenth century, however, these fields of honor bore little resemblance to fields of battle. The weapons they used were outmoded, and they had become preoccupied with the *forms* of combat rather than with effective results *tout court;* the joust had evolved, as Keen says, from "a skill into an art."[42] In some degree, all these survivals of knightly combat served as exemplars for the emergent duel of honor.

The most important of these variants of individual combat may have been the *duel judiciaire.* This duel had been widely practiced in medieval Europe as a way of establishing guilt or innocence in a dispute between two noble individuals. It was a formal judicial proceeding akin to the notorious "ordeals" of fire and water that survived into the seventeenth century as tests for witchery. Originally favored by the church as a secular representation of divine justice, these combats were generally to the death, in the absence of intervention by the prince or monarch who presided over the ceremony. The presumption of innocence fell to the victor, ostensibly favored by God's grace, no matter how weak his case or how much greater his skill at arms.

Repudiated by the church, the legal status of such proceedings ended by the fifteenth century, but in France the combats themselves persisted as *private* duels of honor presided over by the king, not in his capacity as first magistrate, but as first gentleman of the realm. These combats were apparently as bloody as before, but they differed from the medieval trial in recognizing no winners or losers, attributing no innocence or guilt.[43] Instead, such occasions put a premium on valor; the blood that was shed was said to "wash" the stain of an affront from an insulted man, and to erase the charge of "liar" from his accuser.

In the last of these bastard combats presided over by a French monarch, that of the *sieurs* Jarnac and La Châtaigneraye in 1547, the latter was killed—by the famous "coup de Jarnac"—but was deemed to have preserved his honor.[44] Billacois devotes a brilliant chapter to the analysis of this duel, arguing it was the last public duel in France and the first duel of the *point d'honneur.* Henri II, who had just assumed the throne, presided. He refused either to conciliate the two or to hurl his baton into the dueling terrain to end the conflict before its bloody conclusion. He thus abdicated royal intervention in a genre of dispute that thereafter became wholly private and unregulated by the state.[45] Despite periodic efforts at state repression, the duel never lost, from this time, its character as a legal proceeding at private law for resolving differences between men of honor.[46]

For the balance of the sixteenth century, and until the reign of Louis XIV began, the duel became a "total social phenomenon": an institution, a criterion of social differentiation, a political manifestation, an esthetic, and a desacralized religious ritual.[47] It was a kind of touchstone for the multiple significations of a system of honor that regulated social and political relations within the French nobility. The growth in importance of the duel coincided with the religious civil wars, which divided Catholic and Protestant nobles, and with the expansion of the power of the French monarchy, which promoted further cleavages by pitting aristocratic clients of the king against intransigent defenders of local autonomy.

The grid of personal loyalties that developed in this era was predictably complicated and unstable, and alliances were unusually ephemeral. The system of honor that undergirded these alliances made of each man a power unto himself, so that any claim nobles made to political autonomy was made "by virtue of their personal identity."[48] If one man swore loyalty i ⁄ the cause of another, his steadfastness was dependent not so much on the fortunes of the other's cause, or even his skill as a leader, as on his patron's formal and personal demonstrations of gratitude and the reciprocal acknowledgement of his client's dignity and independence.[49] In Kristen Neuschel's words, "Some of the events of great significance to nobles were seemingly trivial moments of personal insult or self-aggrandizement. The importance attached to such incidents was, in turn, simply one expression of a general tendency to weight moments of action—personal arguments, triumph in battle, and other incidents of honor and shame—as the building blocks of political life."[50] In this largely oral culture, gestures, formulas of polite expression, and displays of generosity and hospitality were burdened with an especially heavy political significance; no action escaped scrutiny, and no affront, however slight, went unchallenged.[51] Political alliances, even those reinforced by the solidarity of co-religionnaires, foundered with ridiculous ease, and duels between gentlemen became universal.

The situation was further complicated by the campaign of the French crown to limit the political and juridical authority of the regional nobility, an effort that spawned a violent and dangerous resistance until the majority of Louis XIV. As part of this effort to bend nobles to the will of the monarchy, Richelieu and his successors issued a series of edicts punishing dueling, which they rightly understood to be an expression of the nobility's challenge to royal claims to a monopoly of violence. These edicts were largely ignored, despite the willingness of the crown to carry out the death sentence.[52] An ideology of "aristocratic romanticism" developed in the face of this repression, reflecting the contradiction between the "situation" of the nobles, who were at the summit of society, "but who felt themselves to be strangers there. The recourse to the duel was thus for them a return to a state of nature, a nature that was both edenic and conflict-ridden. . . . "[53] As we shall see, this nostalgia for a time when men could settle their differences in personal combat remained an important component in the rhetoric of modern honor.

As had been true for the model of the courtier, the earliest models of the French duel were imported from Italy, in the form of translated *codes duello*.[54] Written dueling codes were a more or less concerted effort by champions of the duel to subject the spontaneous violence of dueling combat to legal usages. These efforts were not in vain. By the seventeenth century, the monarchy, despairing any absolute prohibition, began to focus its legal repression on the half-way measure of prosecuting those who violated the (private) "laws" of the duel, thereby helping to legitimate the duel as a convention of legal norms.[55] Transgressions of the most authoritative codes became the source of challenges by interested parties who believed themselves enforcing a legal right.[56]

The earliest codes encouraged an offended man to submit a written *cartel* to his opponent in which he listed accusations, ceded or demanded choice of weapons, and in general pressed his suit for redress. Cartels were eminently public documents, widely circulated and evaluated in noble circles. But in this era they were less a device for ensuring an orderly duel than for satisfying the fantastic obsession of contemporaries with issues of right and precedence. Indeed, the codified criteria of choice for seconds, for weapons, and for comportment were often ignored in the heat of the duel itself. Even gross inequalities in weapons or the number of seconds—matters of cardinal legal importance in the nineteenth-century duel—were overlooked, lest a protest be interpreted as cowardice. Indeed, when one gentleman brought his entourage to witness his combat with another, gestures of support could accelerate into threats, until everyone was involved in the fray. If an enemy was quickly dispatched, a sword was freed to help an ally, even if that meant unfair odds.[57]

The weapon of choice was the épée, another Italian refinement, often supplemented by the *poignet,* which was held in the opposing hand. The preference for the épée was both practical and symbolic: practical because it was light in weight, could be worn at the side, and could inflict wounds either with its sharp point or an edge of its triangular blade; symbolic because it was a descendant of the broadsword of intrepid crusaders and the representation, par excellence of justice in human society. An elaborate ritual of gesture and word grew up around the proper forms to observe in the duel when an opponent was disarmed or a sword broken, which became occasions for gentlemen to show a gallant generosity to one another and a respectful reverence for the instrument of justice.[58]

Above all, the épée became the sign of democratization *and* of hierarchy in seventeenth-century society. The wearing of a sword, which became universal among noblemen in this era, erased distinctions between gentlemen. As Billacois has written, "More than either esteem or respect, the adversary should inspire a sentiment of *fraternité*. Not only after he has manifested in the duel a valiance equal to his noble rival, but in the very moment that he accepts his challenge."[59] Therefore the sword operated simultaneously as a visible symbol of a collective monopoly, discouraging the *vile* from social pretense.

But swords also killed. Because it was often conducted in semiprivate circumstances to avoid monarchical surveillance, accurate figures do not exist on the number of duels that may have been fought in this era. A huge number, however, were fatal. The best guess is that as many as 10,000 deaths were the result of affairs of honor in the twenty years between 1589 and 1610.[60] The mortality rate tailed off in the 1620s, but until mid-century it was common to fight to the death or to cease only after inflicting deep wounds, from which victims often succumbed in any case.

The blood that was let in these battles was also an object of ritual veneration. It was said to be a "sacrifice," a "purification," and a sign that "vengeance" had been wrought.[61] It was a symbolic and a literal "baptism," a rite of passage for a class of men whose blood was the precious mark of their distinction, but who must shed it negligently to prove they were worthy to have it course in their veins. In theory each duel was a *duel au premier sang* (duel to first blood); the symbolic power of blood as a sacramental element was such that its flow "washed" clean the offense that blotted a noble soul. But in practice it did not behoove two men anxious to prove their courage to fall into fraternal embrace at the appearance of the first scratch; tongues would wag, and to assuage "opinion," rivers of blood were made to flow. The close connection between honor and noble blood in the metaphysic of the early modern French duel was one of the features that distinguished French honor from honor elsewhere. In Spain "Old Christian" blood took precedence over nobility per se. In Italy, despite Italian invention of the forms of the "affair of honor," the single duel of combat was never as popular as collective vengeance, which favored murder and abduction in behalf of family and clan. In Germany, duels were few in the seventeenth century, little more than an exotic import from across the Rhine.[62]

The most illuminating contrast may be that with England. In the mid-sixteenth century, the system of English honor closely resembled the French. Great lords commanded political allegiance on the basis of personal oaths of loyalty; as in France the alliances forged on these bonds were unstable and ephemeral. English gentlemen dueled to protect their honor and enjoyed a monopoly of the practice, as did their Gallic brothers. There was an intimate relation in England between blood and lineage, which "predisposed to honorable behavior."[63] And there was the same urgent drive that required men of honor to affirm their status in violent deeds of renown.

Yet, more effectively than their Valois and Bourbon cousins, the Tudor monarchs managed to capture for the English state the loyalty men of honor once felt for regional political communities. They did this by championing a unifying dynastic religious credo, so men could serve God *and* country, and by their patronage of a humanist and cosmopolitan education, which made learning virtuous and honored service to the state. Tudor absolutism may have been short-lived, but it succeeded in crushing in a few generations the noble "honor communities" that had comprised the chief resistance to the state-building process. The French nobility not only took much longer to subdue, but absolutism left untouched its feudal, regional, and military prerogatives.

England also experienced in this era a degree and quality of social and economic change that largely bypassed France. A vigorous capitalism and a prosperous gentry encouraged English nobles to cultivate marital and business alliances with their lesser brethren, which both watered down "blood," and made it and the life it sustained more dear.[64] In his celebrated attack on the duel, Bacon advanced an argument that "It is in expense of blood as it is in expense of mony. It is no liberality to make a profusion of mony upon every vaine occasion, not noe more it is fortitude to make effusion of blood except the cause bee of worth."[65] Summing up these developments, James has argued,

> Against these winds of intellectual mutation and social change, some aspects of honour stood relatively firm. There could be no whole-hearted rejection of blood and lineage in a society for which this was still a central concept. But uncertainty about the status of heredity in relation to other aspects of honour increased, with a proneness to present honour, virtue and nobility as detachable from their anchorage in pedigree and descent.[66]

In France the bond between heredity and honor was closer, more hotly defended, and remained so into the eighteenth century. In matters of honor and the marks of dress and precedence by which honor was recognized, the French *noblesse d'épée* conspired to make honor and pedigree identical in the course of the seventeenth century, deemphasizing the vocational aspect of their rank.[67] Though a vigorous noble lobby developed which hoped to gain a monopoly of offices and honors for birth in place of merit, access routes to aristocratic culture and its perquisites remained open throughout the Old Regime. The right to wear the sword and engage in duels was claimed by many young robe nobles in the last years of the Sun King, as many observers have noted.[68] If recently elevated robe nobles were successful in having their dueling challenges accepted by nobles of older lineage, they could rightly claim to possess honor themselves. But, as we shall see, before a man could even reach that crucial threshold, he needed an impressive combination of wealth and legal standing, the fruit of generations of family discipline and achievement. As the assimilation of robe and sword nobility took place, the cultural forms and usages that signified the possession of noble honor underwent a progressive elaboration and refinement, a gatekeeping function designed to bar access to all but the most qualified.

Despite the efforts of old nobility to protect its monopoly of honor, some of the concepts and practices of honor were proliferating among the humbly born. A universally accepted explanation for how high culture passes into lower social realms does not presently exist. The "trickle-down" theory has its problems for the history of popular culture, as has been pointed out recently.[69] Our choice seems to be the same one that anthropologists have confronted since the end of the last century: are similar cultural forms better understood as a consequence of dispersion across class or cultural boundaries, or can we explain them more effectively by a theory of independent and parallel evolution?

The best solution may be to combine both approaches. There is good reason to believe, as I will argue in the next chapter, that a systematic implementation of inheritance practices by any families possessing sufficient goods or property eventually created the values of an honor culture. But there is also evidence that court and noble models penetrated far into the non-noble countryside. Yves Castan has found considerable proof of this in his study of "honnêteté" in eighteenth-century Languedoc. He found that, within certain limits, the models of popular civility in the rural and small-town South were those of the court and urban "polite society".[70] This development sustained the social hierarchy, Castan argues, by creating an ironic equality of manners in which anyone with pretensions to "honnêteté" was obliged to behave the way the "honnête" class behaved as a "constant proof of their merits."[71] The forms of courtesy exchanged between rich farmers or between merchants and their clients were not as refined as those of the elite, but needed to be signaled in a conventionally "open and pleasant manner," lest offense be taken.[72]

In the matter of the duel, Castan found numerous examples which closely followed aristocratic models. But he also found non-noble men defending their honor in a rough and ready way that made a mockery of the ritual practices. Indeed, whenever a dispute was especially grave—a situation that would inspire an unusually punctilious observance of propriety in cultivated men—Castan's "dueler" delivered what amounted to a "declaration of war," claiming his right to avenge himself on his rival's person, his property, or his relatives. He might lie in ambush for his enemy or hire a gang of cutthroats to avenge an unpaid debt or a slight. But, as Castan reveals, though a man's honor was at stake in such conflicts, it was not a refined *courtoisie* or noble "generosity" that he sought to display, but his sheer "determination," a much more useful trait in a subsistence society.[73]

A crucial feature of Castan's small-town honor was the different regime it decreed for the sexes. For women, honor consisted of chastity; a woman's chastity was not *natural* to her, but was a quality "on deposit" that she defended with her piety, and for which she was accountable "to her parents, her husband, and her children."[74] Castan found that the situation in which judgments about female honor arose most frequently was when a young woman slept with a suitor before extracting from him a promise of marriage. Her "dishonor," it would appear, was the potential danger her bastard posed to the integrity of her patrilineal inheritance, and thus to her whole family. By contrast, a man's dishonor consisted of his failure to carry out a promise of marriage in the wake of a seduction, a situation that the courts addressed by requiring him to make good his vows.

In cases where the marriage "promise" was a matter of dispute and legal right was vague, community-sanctioned violence took over. Fathers and brothers sought vengeance in behalf of their jilted female, and the male relations of her paramour mobilized in his behalf. These battles involving clan honor were mostly disputes over imminent property transfers, where terms of dignity and reputation served as metaphors for each family's struggle to accumulate and maintain the means to survive. When a "dishonored" girl gave birth, she often felt the weight of family opprobrium so keenly that she felt obliged to kill her child, as happened with terrible frequency elsewhere in the historic Mediterranean.[75] The close relation between family honor, patrilineality, and marital strategies in rural eighteenth-century Languedoc and elsewhere seems to bear out the argument that there is a general connection between honor and inheritance practices that has assumed a number of local and historically specific forms.[76]

Battles over honor also erupted in the cafés and streets of eighteenth-century Paris. In this milieu of business and work, a man's honor was very much a matter of his reputation for honesty, skill, or good work habits. He also might react violently to a slander on his profession or his guild, which he saw, by implication, as an assault on his own integrity.[77] The claim to have been acting in the defense of honor was less often used by salaried workers than by craftmasters and merchants, in effect those with a greater *investment*, both psychological and economic, in their occupation.[78] Though it took a back seat to professional honor, virtually all Brennan's brawlers were willing to defend the reputations of their wives or daughters, because a "man's ability to control his wife's sexuality...

counted heavily in their definition of honor. . . . "[79] We are very far here
from the ritual usages of the noble duel. Challenges were often issued,
occasionally by men who wore swords, but rivals rarely observed the lapse
of time between insult and combat required by the dueling code, with its
demands for sangfroid and self-mastery, but sprang directly to the fray,
using weapons that came to hand, or fists and boots.

Though the differences between the noble duel and the guildsman's
barroom fight were many, reflecting the social distance of the Parisian café
from the habitats of the elite, the similarities are remarkable. There is no
doubting the close relation between a man's honor and his *estate,* whether
that be his title to land, or the occupation that put bread on his family
table. Both guaranteed his place in the social order; in both *milieux* a man
lost honor by failing to defend the reputation of his womenfolk, even when
he knew the insults to be untrue. Whether these dramas of honor originated
in the café or the salon, the primacy accorded to appearances was central
to all, because, as Brennan points out, "Reputation is a public trust, a
public persona, and it is dealt with publicly by others."[80]

Though it seems likely that the honor societies of the recent Mediterranean are the descendants of these eighteenth-century variants, we can
only speculate on how and why rural- and urban-working cultures like
these and countless others developed their honor systems. Did rich farmers
and merchants in a particular locale mimic the customs and manners of
the local aristocracies, themselves in thrall to the model of courtly life? Or
was there a deeper logic in the fabric of values that knit sexual identity,
marriage, and inheritance so tightly together? In the next chapter I examine
how both these influences appear to have worked on the French bourgeoisie
to cultivate in them a culture of honor.

3

The Roots of Bourgeois Honorability

In a story set some years after the fall of the Napoleonic regime, Balzac declares through a character that "there is no nobility anymore, nothing more than an aristocracy."[1] In the first half of the nineteenth century, Balzac and many other writers of fiction made a nice living exploring in their works the composition of this successor class of the pre-revolutionary elite. It was a subject of endless fascination for contemporary readers, who became adept at sorting out the subtly inflected contrasts in dress, speech, and manners that were the acknowledged markers between those who had been born to high status and those who had earned it. The enthusiasm for discerning cleavages in the social elite had, and continues to have, a remarkable appeal in French culture and everywhere French upper-class life is taken as the last word in taste. In the preface to the American edition of his *Distinction. A Social Critique of the Judgement of Taste,* Pierre Bourdieu tenders an ironically disingenuous apology for emphasizing "the particularity of the French tradition, namely, the persistence through different epochs and political regimes, of the aristocratic model of 'court society', personified by a Parisian *haute bourgeoisie* which, combining all forms of prestige and all the titles of economic and cultural nobility, has no counterpart elsewhere. . . . "[2]

My aim in this chapter is to consider the historical roots of this "aristocracy." As a result of the process of social amalgamation with the noblesse that began in the Old Regime, the post-revolutionary bourgeois elite combined aspects of noble culture with traits typical of the upper levels of the European bourgeoisie. The mentality that resulted from this cultural synthesis was marked by the blend of dependency and opposition which has characterized the historic relations of the European bourgeoisie with noble elites. The French bourgeoisie felt a peculiarly deep ambivalence toward their fellow notables, which was reflected in the complex dynamics of the honor culture they shared. In the most harmonious of times, a mutual sense of honor was one of the conceptual justifications for intermarriage, political alliance, and mutually respectful social relations, but in troubled

31

ones—the revolutionary era in particular—a distinctive bourgeois honor emerged that revealed the historic fault lines between noble and *roturier*.

I will argue here that the formation of a modern culture of honor was not a simple matter of a newly rich middle class imitating its social superiors, adopting a ready-made model of comportment from the medieval past. The synthetic honor codes that emerged in post-revolutionary society bore the unmistakable stamp of bourgeois values; they were deeply influenced by the historic struggles of a vigorous urban elite to establish its independent claims to precedence; they reflected the bourgeois preoccupation with moral discipline, inner values, and with the control of reproduction and sex. But these codes also preserved elements of the feudal past in their requirement that men of honor display personal courage, loyalty, prowess in combat, and gallantry in love. The historical circumstances in which these codes were first shaped will occupy us here.

The complexity of the bourgeois outlook on honor was most clearly revealed in the eighteenth-century debate on the *point d'honneur* and the duel it sanctioned and regulated. Bourgeois jurists had long applauded the trend toward less bloody combats, and hoped to exploit the growing legalism of the duel as a means of bringing it under state control. *Philosophes* engaged in a broad frontal attack on monarchical injustice attacked the "scandal" of the *point d'honneur* as "one of the worst running sores of *féodalité*."[3] The existence of this form of private justice was a vestige of a barbarous past, an intolerable symbol of class distinctions, and an affront to the well-ordered state. Even Montesquieu, the foremost theorist of the role of honor in monarchy, deplored the conflict that the *point d'honneur* engendered between private and public law. In the *Lettres Persanes* he wrote that "If one follows the laws of honor, one dies on the scaffold; if one obeys those of justice, one is banished forever from the society of men: there is thus only the cruel alternative of dying or being unworthy to live."[4]

This concern about the duel was imbedded in a far more profound debate about the relative merits of honor and virtue in modern society, which had formed into rival discourses attacking and defending monarchy. Montesquieu was the principal apologist for an aristocratic monarchy in which "Honor sets in motion all the parts of the political system; it links them through its action so that each contributes to the common good, while believing to follow his particular interests."[5] By pursuing glory in war, seeking offices and preferences in peace, and defending personal honor in private life, the nobleman both animated the state and established moral standards for civil society.

Bourgeois critics of the feudal order hoped to replace honor with virtue, which evoked for many of them both the grandeur of the classical republic *and* the virtuous bourgeois, "who was a worker and useful to the nation."[6]

Rousseau became the spokesman for and the personal exemplar of virtue in the last quarter of the century. Under the aegis of his self-lascerating *Confessions,* the gallantry of kings and nobles looked like licentious cupidity when set in contrast to the personal virtue of sexual continence and the public virtue of *civisme.*[7]

In the last decades of the century noble robe magistrates endeavored to discover a legal principle that would clearly distinguish between noble and *roturier,* in order to defend the elite privileges they felt to be under attack. They settled on the idea of legitimating the concept of noble *race,* reversing the old principle "virtue makes the noble" into the notion that nobility, particularly the inherited kind, produced virtue.[8] This strategy had two signal disadvantages: it made honor more vulnerable to attacks from those who regarded virtue a consequence of high-minded action, and it facilitated the future liquidation of a class of people whose *nature,* it could be said, disposed them to tyranny. In the radical phase of the Revolution, it was commonplace for writers like Louis Sebastien Mercier to contrast the principle of "public virtue" with "the feudal concept of honor,"[9] and for Robespierre to proclaim a new regime "where distinctions arise only from equality itself. In our country, we wish to substitute morality for egoism, probity for honor, principles for conventions, duties for propriety, the role of reason for the tyranny of fashion."[10]

It is misleading, however, to take the rhetoric of this phase of the Revolution as emblematic of the fate of honor in the Revolution as a whole. The much maligned duel, which had become the very symbol of the decay of honor, was denounced from the tribunes of the revolutionary assemblies, but it was not outlawed by name in either the penal code of 1791 or the Napoleonic Code that followed a decade later; there were even a few sensational duels in the first year or so of the new regime.[11] If the number of duels in the 1790s dropped well below the figures from the previous decade, it was because of the extraordinary sense of agreement in this era that patriots should not draw their weapons except in defense of the fatherland, the so-called nationalization of honor that Norman Hampson and others have remarked upon.[12]

This powerful new religion of the fatherland was constructed, at least in part, out of symbolic materials that had played a traditional role in the old system of honor. The concept of "loyalty," which had bound liegeman to lord and soldier to soldier was "reconstituted" as loyalty to the nation.[13] Images of men in fraternal union were enormously popular in revolutionary iconography, and the pre-revolutionary concept of Hercules as a king and father was replaced by Hercules the "militant revolutionary brother" accompanied by his sisters liberty and equality.[14] To contemporaries it must have seemed that family honor was inseparable from this stirring love of country. A father wrote these lines to a son fighting on the republic's frontiers: "When you suffer, know that it is for your parents and for your fatherland. When you march into combat, do not forget that you do so for your father, your mother, and your sisters, and know how to prefer death to dishonor [*ignominie*]."[15]

The Revolution was unsuccessful in stamping out honor because pre-revolutionary social developments had helped ensure its prosperity. Despite the reformist rhetoric condemning honor and the duel, most rich bourgeois seemed bent on living nobly. They abandoned "dishonorable" trades, bought fiefdoms and ennobling offices, and took up the sword and all the responsibilities this entailed.[16] As Colin Lucas has written, in this effort to achieve social integration, "life style" was of paramount importance because, in the absence of the legal "proofs" of nobility, or while waiting to acquire them, "appearances were the first step toward reality."[17] Once ennobled, the bourgeois gentleman was difficult to distinguish from nobles of old extraction in things both great and small: dress, the splendor of their *equipages,* the magnificence of their homes, or their sensitivity to the point of honor.[18]

To become "annoblis" the rich bourgeois could buy outright an office or title bestowing noble rank, or opt for a career in the army, administration, or the courts because "there was something noble about them, and second, that they offered at some stage [usually three generations of possession] concrete opportunities of ennoblement."[19] Such practices had been traditionally considered a *savonette à vilain* (washing away of vile birth), a mystical transformation of nature, but by the eighteenth century the old nobility began to acknowledge the advantages of this sort of upward mobility for their caste, in the form of advantageous marriages and a fresh reservoir of talent and savoir faire to supplement their hereditary qualities and savoir vivre.

Guy Chaussinand-Nogaret has argued that this upwelling of new blood so transformed the traditional definition of noble status that

> from 1760 onwards the notions of worthiness and honour, which had defined what was special about nobles, were overtaken by a new notion: merit, a middle-class value, typical of the third order, which the nobility took over, made its own, accepted and officially recognized as a criterion of nobility. From that moment on there was no longer any significant difference between nobility and middle classes. A noble was now nothing but a commoner who had made it. This notion of merit admittedly took on a certain number of noble criteria, such as military worth, but these blended with middle-class virtues like work, assiduity, competence, utility, benevolence. And so the standards implied by noble status were turned upside down.[20]

Indeed, so long as the gateway to social advance was not blocked, ambitious bourgeois did not call for the abolition of the noble order or its legal privileges. In their *cahier de doléance* of 1788 a group of Burgundy lawyers argued that "the privileges of the nobility are truly their property. We will respect them all the more because we are not excluded from them and because we can acquire them: great actions, gallantry, courage, personal merits, offices, fortune even, all these are paths that lead us to them."[21] That gallantry and fortune enjoy equal billing here as qualities deserving of ennoblement is powerful testimony that on the eve of the Revolution many members of the bourgeoisie believed noble qualities were already within their purview. The historic process of venal ennoblement was so firmly established in France that even the antifeudal outburst of the Revolution could not entirely disrupt it. Napoleon I took up the practice of ennobling worthy men where it had left off under the Bourbons, and later regimes continued it as a means of ensuring the support of a loyal "meritocracy."[22]

If, however, we focused only on the *blend* of features that composed the makeup of this elite of wealth and blood, we would fail to understand how important the differences between them remained. While there is some evidence that nobles in the nineteenth century learned to live in a bourgeois manner, valorizing the qualities of work, thrift, and merit, a far more powerful case may be made that most of the descendants of Old Regime noble families sought to preserve their distinctiveness, even while engaging in "shameful" trades.[23] Noble families practiced endogamy to a far greater extent than did those of the bourgeoisie, and, by living more on the land than in towns, and limiting social life so far as possible to their noble relations, they kept alive a set of cultural ideals and manners that were still more or less unique to their class.[24]

However much they might have craved noble rank, the upper strata of the bourgeoisie, for their part, possessed certain qualities and engaged in particular practices that linked them more closely to their humble brethren in the middle classes than to titled lords. These qualities derived from the legal status of *roturier* property and from the reproductive and inheritance strategies that were required to defend and expand it. In enacting these strategies, those characteristics that permitted bourgeois property to prosper became rooted in the bedrock of family *mentalité*. A specifically bourgeois notion of family honor emerged from the repetition of these strategies; this concept remained at the fundamental core of bourgeois outlook throughout the Old Regime. The acquisition of a noble title was only, in certain respects, a glittering veneer that did not replace, but rested on, the bourgeois honor that earned it and preceded it.

In Old Regime noble families the eldest sons were entitled by law to two-thirds or more of the family property; together with the law of entail, which preserved the unity of noble lands, these rights usually allowed for a smooth transfer of property and minimized the danger of an alienation of family heritage. All that was required was a viable, preferably male, heir. If the estate was rich enough, daughters could be comfortably dowered; if not, there was no disgrace in their taking the veil. Honorable careers in the church or army awaited younger male siblings. However, by the eighteenth century the nobility no longer played the role of a juridico-military service elite on a dangerous frontier. It no longer needed to combine public and private motive to produce an heir who was both valorous and fertile, who would bring honor to the family *and* perpetuate the line. The decay of the service function of the nobility—rhetoric to the contrary notwithstanding—meant a noble patriarch needed *only* to sire an heir; legal mechanisms then switched on to ensure an orderly succession. By the eighteenth century the need for warrior-heirs to defend castle and fief had long disappeared; noble reproductive strategies tended to consist of minimal agenda unmoored from collateral cultural imperatives.[25] Barring mishap, honor followed blood as a river falls to the sea.

The situation for commoners was quite different. Honor had to be first won and then held in the face of a swarm of legal obstacles. In the various mix of customary and Roman law that regulated *roturier* inheritance, there were two potential disasters for the non-noble family: too many heirs or no heirs at all. In the first case, especially in the considerable areas governed by *lois coutumiers,* the law required the more or less equal division of the property among the heirs, threatening the heritage with irreversible fragmentation. In the second, the property of a childless couple reverted to collateral lines in proportions governed by law. The tight controls over the disposition of property in France was a consequence of the fact that most forms of property were regarded as "lineage" property, belonging to the family instead of its particular members. Even in Languedoc, where Roman law gave the patriarch greater control of his patrimony, testators were still not free to dispose of property en bloc in the forms and to the persons they pleased, but were obliged to follow formulas ensuring an equitable distribution.[26] In contrast to French practices, the English legal system recognized property as an individual asset, inherent in individual rights, and freely disposable. It would be difficult to exaggerate the importance of this difference.[27]

An English father could bestow his property on whomever he deemed the worthiest of his heirs. By extension of the "natural" rights of individual property, his children were free to marry whomever they wished whenever they desired; marriage strategies were not legally bound to inheritance strategies. A French father, by contrast, had little control of the heritage over which he presided as guardian. In compensation for this testamentary impotence, the *patria potestas* of Roman law provided the father considerable control over the marriages of his children. Not surprisingly, a number of strategies developed which made use of this power of paternal guardianship to enhance the family's control over inheritance, in which a child's freedom to marry was sacrificed to the patriarch's increased control over family assets.

For a French bourgeois family that aspired to crown its rise to wealth with ennoblement, four things were required: an investment strategy that would permit the accumulation of wealth surely and not ignobly; an inheritance strategy that would maintain most of the wealth as a *bloc;* marital strategies that would enhance its growth and smooth transmission; and fertility strategies that would neither fragment the heritage nor arrest its progress. All these strategies were *family* strategies in the sense that they required family members to act as a unit and to sacrifice their individual interests in behalf of the prosperity of the group. Ralph Giesey reminds us that in earlier, harder times,

> 'Caring for one's own' meant transmitting a heritage that would make certain that those of one's blood would escape starvation and likely survive the ravages of war and pestilence. In that age the state could not even promise survival, let alone an adequate livelihood, to its subjects. A reasonable family heritage was a life-and-death proposition, . . . hard to imagine in modern, affluent societies. Apologists for perpetuating family fortunes generally stressed the motive of family glory, but the basic motive was simply that of survival.[28]

The ancient device of partitive inheritance—dividing the heritage between all the children—was designed to maximize the chances of their survival. What was needed in later times was a smooth coordination of the four strategies just outlined to allow that device to be partially overridden in practice, so that the overall heritage could grow. A favored investment strategy was long-term *rentes,* which payed a small but reliable return in forms that were recognized as *propres,* or "lineage" wealth that belonged to the family. Another, of course, was the purchase of an office that, if repurchased by three successive generations, would become hereditary. Both strategies brought "honor" to the bourgeois families that practiced them, not just because they were undertaken to attain noble status, but because they required family solidarity and delayed collective gratification to be wholly effective. The amassing of the requisite capital to purchase nobility was a multigenerational task which assumed "that each generation will play an active role in the family's rise to wealth," the precise opposite of noble entail, which automatically "guarantees the integrity of the family heritage by placing it beyond the control of any one generation."[29]

In the matter of inheritance strategies, various legal methods existed for settling the bulk of the family wealth on one individual, usually the eldest male, or, in the event of his incompetence, a sibling or male collateral. There was usually a "disposable" quantity of varying proportion that could be freely leagued; to this might be added the inheritances that were officially "renounced" by siblings in the interest of the chief heir. Fathers implemented other semilegal devices to diminish the legal shares of the chief heir's brothers and sisters, and urged their other sons into self-supporting careers.[30]

Marriage strategies designed to enhance bourgeois fortunes included the obvious need to marry sons to families willing to dower with most generosity, while marrying daughters well but cheaply. These aims required a paterfamilias who was an apt negotiator; they also required children to subordinate their desires to those of the family interest. In the most extreme sacrifice of all, the children of the poorest, or perhaps the most avaricious families, were pressured not to marry at all, eliminating at one stroke an expensive marriage settlement and possible future legal claims against the principal heir by the offspring of his siblings.[31]

Fertility strategies dovetailed with marriage strategies designed to keep patrimonies intact: fewer children meant less division of resources and the liklihood of more lucrative marriage contracts. There were two principal ways bourgeois families could achieve this end: late marriages, which reduced the span of a woman's marital fertility, and contraception. The first of these strategies was much in evidence until at least the end of the eighteenth century. Indeed, in the French population as a whole, the population pressures in rural areas and fear of further land parcelization led to a continued rise in marriage age throughout the 1700s.[32]

During the eighteenth century contraception became an increasingly important way to limit births, particularly among the elite. As the popularity of and confidence in *coitus interruptus* spread, marriage age began to decline and nuptiality increased. This confidence was not misplaced; despite more and earlier births, both legitimate and illegitimate fertility declined in the course of the 1700s.[33] This meant that bourgeois families in particular had successfully managed to bring an enhanced control over fertility into their arsenal of strategies for controlling their economic future. The *social* reproduction of the family was no longer a hostage to its *biological* reproduction; rather, as we enter the nineteenth century, the reverse had become true. Biological reproduction now *served* the family's grand agenda for attaining honor. As André Burguière has noted about this development, "Sexual asceticism plays the same role in the spirit of matrimonial enterprise that the sense of thrift played in the spirit of capitalist enterprise." Whether late marriage or contraception, " . . . we remain in the same cultural logic: the instinctual life must be inhibited in order the better to serve reality."[34]

We are now, perhaps, better able to see the reason for the characteristic blurring of the "natural" and the "social" in the matter of honor. The four strategies I have discussed were deployed by bourgeois families in the Old

Regime to gain honor for themselves and their descendants. To reach this goal, these strategies demanded varying degrees of self-denial of family members, from the self-discipline of thrift and the control of sexual impulses to the more serious sacrifices of celibacy and the renunciation of heritability. As we have noted, the course bourgeois families charted to reach the pinnacle of society was slow but sure, requiring the efforts of several successive generations. When the patents of nobility were finally delivered, the family had, in a certain sense, already attained a kind of honorability through the transgenerational practice of self-denial, behavior that had doubtless become "second nature" to individual family members. Thus the claim to honor became, over time, inseparable from the honorable behavior through which families strove for honorability, not unlike the personal self-conviction process of Protestant predestination. In honoring their *roturier* ancestors, which they did in a variety of ways, old bourgeois families were paying homage to the qualities that had permitted their social advance.[35] How could it have been otherwise? A society which recognizes a close bond of *race* and class, will not validate the case of a man who argues his personal worth at the same time as he deplores the quality of his *souche* (stock).

The irony in this development lay in the fact that while only those who lived nobly could qualify to purchase patents or offices, just to arrive at that stage required a bourgeois aspirant to exercise to the utmost the bourgeois qualities that would carry him there. No one really expected this middle-class asceticism to disappear overnight; that is why the "three-generation" rule generally applied to an ennobling office. As Ralph Giesey has put it, "Wealth is the necessary basis, but acculturation requires manners and bearing which only the third generation of the rising family acquires from infancy."[36]

By the end of the eighteenth century, the lines distinguishing the character traits of the "noble" and "bourgeois" do not seem to have blended together nearly as much as had the classes themselves at their numerous points of contact in mixed marriages and "good" society. In his *The Civilizing Process* Norbert Elias has provided a way of thinking about this process of social consolidation that can explain successfully the drive for integration, but puts considerable weight on the consequences of distinctive psychic structures and cultural outlook. Elias's masterwork is an ambitious effort to understand the development of European society since the Middle Ages in terms of the evolution of codes of courtesy and politeness; the sheer magnitude of his canvas allows him to speculate on the interrelationships of social change, psychic structures, and political culture. Elias maintains that handbooks on courtesy, published more or less continuously since the Renaissance, reveal a progressive advance of the "threshhold of shame."

Readers of the earliest texts are enjoined to behave more decorously at table, to confine spitting and nose-blowing to private moments, and speak in polite formulas designed to put companions at ease.[37] Elias explains the advance of this shame threshhold as a product of enhanced "drive-control" in individuals whose social aspirations required them to adjust their behavior to the prevailing standards of "good" society. As increasing numbers of social climbers joined the highest ranks of society, the uppermost layers of the aristocracy sought to distinguish themselves from *nouveaux* elements by refining their manners to a still higher degree. By provoking in this way constantly renewed efforts at emulation by the vulgar, the cream of society served as the engine that drove the whole social organism toward a horizon of greater cultivation. The latter historical stages of this process, Elias argues, took place in court society, for which the model was the Versailles of the Sun King, who had forced a once-rebellious nobility into orbits that obeyed the laws of his own gravitational field.[38]

This state-building process represents a crucial stage in the evolution of the sentiment of shame, which, by this time, was joined in a binary opposition to honor. As I infer from Elias's account, shame was a natural human response to the persistent threat of physical violence that reigned before states gained a monopoly on the exercise of violence, humbling those without the means to defend themselves, emboldening those with recourse to arms of their own. The gradual diminution of direct threats to personal security encouraged an internalization of shame, so that violent impulses were progressively regulated and repressed by a social superego rather than exploding in bloody rituals, executions, personal combat, and the like.[39] The shame that once had been provoked by a confrontation with a physical superior or superiors, was now triggered by a "fear of social degradation or, more generally, of other people's gestures of superiority."[40] Thus, the peculiar anxiety one felt in situations of social inferiority was the internalized, psychic remnant of the fear of physical compulsion that had dominated his less civilized ancestors.

The old-fashioned flavor of this explanation—modern behavior based on "vestiges" of primitive instincts—owes much to the evolutionary psycho-Lamarckism of Freud, to which Elias is deeply indebted. But there is much merit in Elias's account of the dynamics of the shaming mechanism itself, the way it recapitulates the psychic conditions of personal threats, but makes a physical response to them utterly inappropriate. As he puts it,

> Now a major part of the tensions which were earlier discharged directly
> in combat between man and man, must be resolved as an inner tension
> in the struggle of the individual with himself. Social life ceases to be a
> danger zone in which feasting, dancing and noisy pleasure frequently
> and suddenly give way to rage, blows, and murder, and becomes a dif-

ferent kind of danger zone if the individual cannot restrain himself, if he touches sensitive spots, his own shame-frontier or the embarrassment-threshhold of others.[41]

With respect to the hierarchies of Old Regime society, the bourgeois social supplicant nearly always found himself pricked by needles of anxiety. He felt shame at his low estate when in great company, and was obliged to take special pains to align his behavior to the refined standards of those who were his superiors in honor and birth. The need for constant vigilance in a noble culture that set the ideals of taste for the rest of the civilized world prepared the French bourgeoisie for continuing "the models, the drive patterns, and the forms of conduct of the courtly phase more undeviatingly than any other bourgeois class in Europe."[42]

Elias proposes, however, that there was a separate but overlapping psychic process at work that *differentiated* bourgeois from noble. As we shall see, this process ramified in two distinctive realms: the *public* realm of work, and the *private* one of sex and reproduction, following practices characteristic of the European bourgeoisie in general.[43] As he explains it,

> The pattern of drive control that professional work necessitates is distinct in many respects from that imposed by the function of courtier and the game of courtly life. The exertion required by the maintenance of bourgeois social existence, the stability of the super-ego functions, the intensity of the drive-control and the drive-transformation demanded by bourgeois professional and commercial functions, are, in sum considerably greater, despite a certain relaxation in the sphere of social manners, than the corresponding social personality structure required by the life of a courtly aristocrat. Most obvious is the difference in the regulation of sexual relationships.[44]

As I have already suggested, for bourgeois males the private domain of sex and the public one of work required similar efforts at self-discipline and self-control if they were to attain honor and avoid shame. I will argue here that the conceptual bridge that linked together the private and the public lives of upper-class French males was the concept of honor. Honor allowed bourgeois gentlemen to plot and judge their actions in love and in work by a single set of standards, at the same time that it functioned, as it had in the Old Regime, as a spur to social advance. Though it linked the "separate" spheres together for men, honor performed an opposite ideological function for women. Since they possessed no honor *by nature,* women were relegated exclusively to the private domain, leaving the public arena a monopoly of the *sexe fort.*

To consider first the domain of work, the clearest definition of the bourgeois is still that of Bernard Groethuysen:

Neither nobleman nor poor man had had a profession as such. What
they were was more important than what they did. The nobleman had
his rank, and he had his dignity, and whether he performed a function
or not made no difference to his character, which was acquired by birth
and hallowed by God. The poor man, too, whether he worked or not,
played a specific role on earth. In this respect, great and poor were alike.
The bourgeois, on the other hand, existed primarily in relation to his
activity.[45]

Activity, boiled down, means work. This definition incorporates all
members of the bourgeoisie from financiers to master artisans, however
great their social distance. It was the need to work, and to work *successfully*
that was the "cornerstone of the edifice."[46] As we have seen, members of
the bourgeoisie did not take for granted the rank into which they were
born: "Their social status was not automatically bequeathed like capital
to the new generation; it had to be *reconquered* by means of the training
and competence demanded by social life and a professional career."[47] When
this diligence had been sustained for generations it brought honor and
standing in equal measure to the bourgeois and his profession. Consider
the wording of the dedicatory statement in the volume of documents that
had been the *vade-mecum* of the corporation of lawyers since the seventeenth century: "Do your best to preserve for our order the rank and the
honor our ancestors have acquired through their work and their merits and
pass it on to your successors."[48]

With the abolition of the legal and political privileges of the nobility
in the French Revolution, the bourgeoisie was finally able to celebrate the
honorability of work and its own honor as a class. At the outset of the
Revolution, this shift of emphasis from noble to bourgeois honor was
carried out with a singular vengeance that sought to efface all traces of a
previous inferiority. The memory lingered, however, in word and sentiment. In welcoming a wealthy merchant to the Legislative Assembly, its
president, Claude-Emmanuel Pastoret, remarked: "Monsieur, for a long
time shameful prejudices encumbered commerce. A hard-working profession must hold a unique horror for all the petty despots and absurd lackeys
who should not blush to call it their master. . . . Time and philosophy have
revealed to France the dignity of all useful things, and commerce has risen
to a rank that the services it has rendered to the fatherland have earned
it. You honor it by your talents and enrich it with your work."[49]

Thus, by the end of the eighteenth century a new spirit of independence
had penetrated the bourgeoisie. It considered itself to be a "new aristocracy" of work, competence, and wealth. It disdained marriage alliances
with the nobility, refused to connive at the acquisition of titles, and followed
an independent and liberal line in politics. As Adeline Daumard has written, "Freed of the requirement to make a career from scratch, the wealthy

bourgeois of Paris nonetheless retained the drive to succeed, a preoccupation foreign to a nobility sufficiently distinguished by its old titles. The upper bourgeoisie has become an aristocracy of money, . . . of birth, . . . of function and responsibility, but it has maintained its belief in the necessity of work and the mystique of success. . . . "[50]

The generations of effort that went into the shaping of this *mentalité* of work took place in the bourgeois family and was perpetuated there. In a certain sense the *roturier* family was itself the ground which conceived and fructified the great principles of the French Revolution—liberty and equality. These ideas, writes Emmanuel Todd, which seemed to the *philosophes* to be "natural laws and the direct products of pure reason, were in fact only an elegant transcription of a latent anthropological structure which had existed at least since the Middle Ages."[51] As Todd argues, nearly all the northern and western part of France is occupied by what he calls the "egalitarian nuclear family." The inheritance practices, as we have seen, which governed non-noble property in these regions (and largely regulated bourgeois inheritance practice everywhere) required equal distribution among all the heirs.

The apparent commitment to the *equality* of heirs implicit in starting all out in life on the same footing was yoked, however, to an equally profound belief in the *liberty* of each heir to follow their path to success. This was another way of saying that the bourgeois family trusted a portion of its legacy to the individual abilities of the heirs, who would develop it differentially according to their talents. As Daumard explains it, this practice,

> corresponded to the conviction that [the heirs] were neither identical nor interchangeable, and that only those who had the requisite capacities had the right to fully exercize their responsibilities in public and private life. To affirm that the dignity of man is more essential than any difference of milieu or origin has an egalitarian character to it, but to admit into that social equality only those of equal aptitudes reintroduces decisively the notion of hierarchy.[52]

These inheritance practices, which were made uniform throughout France during the Revolution, also set aside, as we have seen, a *quotité disponible* which could be settled on one heir in a proportion determined by the total number of legatees. In the decorous language of the lawyer François-Denis Tronchet (later one of the chief drafters of the Napoleonic Code), "How can one refuse to a father the right to express a testimony of particular affection to the child who is most distinguished by his respect and filial tenderness, who will be the most devoted to caring for his parents in old age; who, through his work, will have contributed disinterestedly to build up the common patrimony. Can the [other] sons legitimately resent that act of justice?"[53]

The question of sibling envy apart, the requirement that the heirs, and in particular the principal heir, possess the *capacity* to exercise their anticipated functions was a chief difference in the ethos of the noble and bourgeois family. This obsession with capacity placed a unique burden on bourgeois reproduction that went far beyond the quantitative question, "How many children?" to focus on the qualitative one "What will they be like?" In part this shift in emphasis was a reflection of the fact that contraceptive practices had helped diminish the size of the bourgeois family in the course of the eighteenth century. Coupled with the general decline in infant mortality, this development encouraged couples "to make a greater investment—both materially and emotionally—in their children, whose birth and survival were no longer completely the result of chance."[54] The evidence is not clear whether the higher levels of parental affection were the consequence or the cause of smaller families and more secure prospects for children, but they seem to have operated in tandem to encourage tighter emotional bonds in bourgeois families than in families of other classes.

These factors, together with the need to produce heir(s) with the talent to keep the family legacy intact, produced deep lines of cleavage in the outlook of noble and bourgeois families. As Roger Kempf and Jean-Paul Aron have argued, for the nobility, the "mythology of the hereditary line" was sufficient guarantee against the heir's "occasional misadventure or singularities of character;" "blood" alone assured succession. "The non-noble family, however, is at the mercy of its filiation, [which] may ruin it or enrich it, crown it or *dishonor* it, be an investment that will fructify— Prudhomme père et fils—or an infernal machine that will require incessant defusing."[55]

As I suggested in the introduction, Michel Foucault makes a similar contrast in his seminal history of sexuality. Whereas the aristocracy's concept of blood was rooted in "the antiquity of its ancestry and the value of its alliances, the bourgeoisie's 'blood' was its sex." He argues that from the mid-eighteenth century the bourgeoisie was bent on "creating its own sexuality and forming a specific [bourgeois] body based on it, a 'class' body with its health, hygiene, descent, and race. . . ."[56] Partly in imitation of noble caste practices, the bourgeoisie built up its own notion of caste based on "its progeny and the health of its organism."[57]

Thus, the bourgeoisie had its honor too, which it enshrined in a reproductive strategy and jealously safeguarded, just as the noblesse had once claimed for itself a set of privileges and practices that set it apart from *roturiers*. Taken in its largest sense, this reproductive strategy did far more than decide how many children should be born or how they should be spaced; it was inseparable from what Foucault has called a "technology of sex," a set of tactics for longevity, maximizing vitality, and ensuring fertility that became a "political ordering of life."[58] As has always been so, these "tactics" circulated in the form of folk beliefs on health, and as traditional moral and religious injunctions, but in the course of the nineteenth century, they were further developed and systematized by scientific "disciplines" specializing in sex and reproduction—embryology, physiology, psychiatry, and medical hygiene. The forms this largely medical discourse assumed in the nineteenth and early twentieth century will occupy us in the following chapters.

Whatever forms they took, these tactics followed a deeper strategic logic rooted in the practices of bourgeois social reproduction I have discussed previously. Their aim was to ensure the generation of healthy and competent heirs through an exclusive emphasis on *marital* fertility, and to regulate expressions of sexuality in ways that would reinforce these goals. To this end the "disciplines" mentioned earlier attempted to define what was "healthy" and "competent," to find ways to enhance marital fertility, and to valorize genital, reproductive, and marital sexual behavior over "pathological" and sterile kinds.

Foucault mentions that most popular and technical information about sex generated and consumed by the bourgeoisie in the modern era has taken the form of *scientia sexualis,* which he contrasts with the *ars erotica* of earlier times and non-western cultures.[59] Modern sexual science did not seek to abolish sexual pleasure, as the "repressive" hypothesis of "Victorian" sexuality would have it, but to yoke it to the machine of a normalized marital reproduction. The oddly schizophrenic quality of sexual knowledge in the nineteenth century—prized and yet forbidden—was a consequence of its need to bridge the domains of the private and the public. It had to meet the requirement of open and consensual discussion that information aspiring to knowledge has always had to meet, but the scene of its private application required discretion and control. Thus the "regulated and polymorphous incitement to discourse" of the nineteenth century, its dedication to "speaking [of sexuality] *ad infinitum,* while exploiting it as *the* secret."[60]

A key to understanding the nature of this modern linkage of pleasure with reproduction is that it emerged at a time when the widespread practice of contraception had first permitted the conceptual *separation* of sexual relations from fertilization. The self-conscious bending of sexual pleasure to love in marriage could only have occurred after the sensual delight in sexual relations had attained an autonomous and unmediated status in cultural life. But when a (largely bourgeois) literature celebrating conjugal love arose in the late eighteenth century, it celebrated marital pleasure in terms that reflected the long bourgeois apprenticeship to the manners of their noble superiors.

For bourgeois males, this new regime of pleasure was an aspect of the "*precieux*" customs of the "gentle" orders of society.[61] Observing French sexual mores in the first decades of the nineteenth century, the English socialist Robert Owen observed that cultivated Frenchmen practiced *coitus interruptus* as a "point of honor" to keep their women free from unnecessary childbearing.[62] Flandrin comments on the new "courtly relations" in marriage at the end of the eighteenth century, and observes that "a gallant man no longer demanded the 'conjugal due' of his wife: he made love to her when she consented, and in as restrained a manner as she demanded."[63]

As these developments suggest, western society confided to men the knowledge of sexual "technology" *and* the capacity to provide pleasure. Nineteenth-century French males were given guardianship over their women and children by both custom and law and were made personally responsible for their protection and well-being. Since the honor of bourgeois families was in the custody of the head of the household, the survival and prosperity of "his" lineage depended on his ability to fulfill honorably his duties as husband and father. The rise of an ideology of conjugal love simply added to this stewardship a responsibility to provide sexual pleasure to his wife. A man's personal honor was thus deployed more widely over a sexual terrain which he had to defend, as it were, with the same forces as before.

As I have argued, the concept of honor permeated the spheres of both public and private life in bourgeois society by the end of the Old Regime. What had begun as a noble concept narrowly attached to the public life of a warrior and court elite was adapted by an admiring yet independent bourgeoisie to ends that met its own public *and* private needs. In its new guise, honor conferred a *je ne sais quoi* of stature and prestige on middle-class work, on its marriage projects and family alliances, which legitimized the successor class to the old nobility. But, as we shall see, this ancient ideal was far more than an ideological facade for a new elite. Honor originated in a *mystique* of noble blood; though it had dissolved itself into the blood of the bourgeois body, it retained still the power to command expiation for dishonorable acts.

4

Sex Difference and the "Separate Spheres"

In the course of the years between 1789 and the end of the Napoleonic era, the values central to bourgeois social reproduction were enshrined in the nation's laws and embedded in its institutions. The bourgeois virtues of individual merit, social mobility and self-perfection were advanced with the destruction of the economically restrictive corporations, the opening of the public sector to men of wealth and learning, and the creation of a state system of centralized higher education. Equality was established through a system of courts and laws which gave no advantage to noble birth, and individual liberties were guaranteed by a doctrine of "minimum constraint," permitting citizens to do in public whatever the law did not explicitly forbid or public morality condemn.[1] This libertarian transformation of public life was balanced by a conservative codification of inheritance, family, and marriage law, in which the bourgeoisie hedged its bets against the radical aspects of its own program. As André-Jean Arnaud has written, the provisions of the *code civil* were "projections of anxiety" and "creations of fear" of a class "which has seen its individualist aspirations fulfilled, and wished to fortify itself against the risk of losing its acquired advantages."[2]

It was during this same period of time that the division of the social world into gendered public and private spheres was completed and legally sanctioned, confining women to the private realm but permitting men to roam over both. As I will discuss in this chapter, a biomedical model of male and female was constructed by medical scientists in this era that made the sexes "naturally" suited for their respective social and familial roles. The sexed bodies that emerged from this process were so constituted as to be both "opposite" and "complementary." Because the public and private spheres of the bourgeois cosmos were delineated so sharply from one another, only two wholly different beings could occupy them. But the duties of intimacy in the familial domain required that these differences be har-

47

monious, and so charged with mutual attraction that they would be fertile as well.

The particular forms assumed by this gendered world and the bodies that inhabited it were unique to the late eighteenth century, but the existence of a correlative link between bodies and the social and political order of which they are a part is as old as western culture.[3] The dialectical nature of the relation between the body and the political order has meant that political readings of human desire, the family, or the relations between the sexes are as legion in the history of biology as organic metaphors are frequent in the history of politics. But after 500 years in which monarchical metaphors had ruled over political and biological theory, new metaphors, or renewed ones, had begun to penetrate Western consciousness. When the shift to readmit democratic and republican models back into political discourse occurred in the eighteenth century, similar refigurations were taking place in biological thinking. I argue in this and succeeding chapters that the changes in these discursive domains were contingent and mutually reinforcing, operating according to a logic that validated the legal and political supremacy of bourgeois males in terms of the qualities of their sex. By concentrating on the language and theories of medical science, I hope to demonstrate the ideological function that the biology of sex and sexuality played in giving the appearance of *naturalness* to the political arrangements of post-revolutionary society.

The inseparability of politics and biology is perhaps best illustrated in the work of Jean-Jacques Rousseau, the most influential thinker of the last half of the century. Rousseau's effort to rehabilitate virtue and the classical political forms that virtue animated entangled him ineluctably in a project to outline a corollary sexual politics. For Rousseau as for most social contract theorists, theories of right were no longer subjects for theologians, but for students of society who expressed their findings in natural laws. For reasons at least partially unique to himself, Rousseau sought to ground the natural laws of politics in sexuality and the relations between the sexes. His findings on these subjects were ambiguous. The relations between the sexes were both necessary and impossible, the source of solidarity and a cause of disorder. It was sexual attraction, he pointed out in the *Second Discourse,* that set mankind on the road to civilization, but it is sexual tyranny, in the form of women's sexual power over men, that has led to the corruption and vices of modern society.

Sex difference lay at the bottom of this whole complex problem. As Joel Schwartz has pointed out, Rousseau tried in his political theory to find ways to ameliorate the negative features of this difference and exploit the positive ones. He did this by casting women out of the public realm, where men would rule by virtue of their strength and wisdom, giving them, by compensation, reign over the realm of reproduction and child-rearing, where their natural motherly tenderness might nurture new generations of fit and happy citizens.[4] For this dual sexual regime to function smoothly, women were obliged to be sexually modest. This was so because Rousseau had discovered that women's sexual capacity was considerably greater than that of men. Though they are the weaker sex, lascivious women could dominate and exhaust men by sexual manipulations, thereby reversing the "natural" relations of power. As Schwartz argues,

> Rousseau's nightmarish fantasy of sexually insatiable females suggests an alternative vision of men whose sexuality causes them to desire to be enslaved. . . . Rousseau's immediate purpose in this context is to stress not the dangers of sexuality but instead the success with which female modesty averts them: it ensures both male potency in sexual encounters and male survival despite them. In the absence of female modesty, male desire would be either too weak to suit women's desire, or too strong to suit men's ability to perform.[5]

Rousseau's notion that individual freedom and equality were (natural) rights arising in a state of nature was inseparable in his thought from his belief in the similarly natural origins of sex. He thereby problematized sex by making sexual difference a political problem and politics a biological one. By giving males, who are sexually the "weaker" sex, a monopoly of political power, he made them the custodians of a domestic regime where their authority was dependent on the consensual restraint of more sexually potent women. This unintentionally ironic account of the foundations of male political and legal dominion was incorporated into most progressive late eighteenth-century thought. We are thus reminded that the doctrine of "the separate spheres" was an ideological construct designed to conceal the weaknesses of male claims to a monopoly of power, and that it was impossible in practice to either permanently or entirely separate the public from the private sphere.[6]

If anything, this particular ideological formulation served to remind men of the fragile nature of their authority. From the male perspective sexual potency had become a crucial concept for thinking about power. Episodes of sexual impotence suffered in the privacy of the marital bed generated metaphoric connections to the public world of citizenship and work, while an experience of inferiority in the domain beyond the *foyer* recalled the tenuousness of sexual and marital supremacy at home. The intolerable tension inherent in Rousseau's scheme was partly mitigated in the discourse of contemporary biomedical science, but the primordial distinctions he established in his thought haunted all later attempts to reconcile politics, sex, and bodies in France.

Late eighteenth-century medicine realized many aspects of the Rousseauian program in the way it rethought the body as a self-contained bi-

ological entity possessed of a political capacity for self-sovereignty. A leading figure in the Montpellier vitalist tradition, Théophile Bordeu, suggested
a metaphor for the body based on a swarm of bees hanging from a branch
in which the organs of the body are linked together:

> each has its own district and action; the relations between these actions
> and the harmony that results from them constitutes health. If that har-
> mony is disturbed, whether because an individual [part] is remiss or
> because one individual is antagonistic to another, or if the actions are
> reversed or do not follow their natural order, the resulting changes would
> bring about illnesses of a proportionally serious nature.[7]

It was common for doctors and physiologists to think about the problem
of healthy systemic cooperation in terms of an equilibrium of vital forces.
These forces operated in and through the body, as Xavier Bichat demonstrated, as if the body were a kind of self-contained economy of energies
and fluids.[8] The notion of an equilibrium of vital forces broke with the old
paradigm of a hierarchy of bodily humors possessing differing degrees of
power, despite a common dependence on hydraulic metaphors. In the new
medicine no particular fluid or any individual organ enjoyed a privileged
status. The body was a holistic system in which health was a consequence
of an uniform distribution of vital forces.[9]

In this democratic holism, the brain was not the "highest" or "sovereign" element, but a particular organ with circumscribed and specialized
functions. Nor was the brain any longer the site of a dualistic soul or
universal human personality; it was materially integrated in "its" particular
body and expressed that body's uniqueness in all its functions. As such it
was subject to the same "laws" as all other organs. The *idéologue* physiologist Pierre J. -G. Cabanis put the general principle in this way in his
Rapports du physique et du moral (1802):

> Every organ has, in the natural order of things, a circumscribed and
> limited sensibility. Habitual excitation can cause the limits of this faculty
> of sensibility to alter, but always at the expense of other organs; the
> sensitive being is capable of only a certain sum of attention which ceases
> to be directed in one way as soon as it is absorbed in another.[10]

This passage should make clear that whatever other analogies the
"body" of the late eighteenth-century medical revolution shared with
triumphant liberalism, the ideal of unlimited expansion and growth was
not one of them. Indeed, in the matter of economic models, the discredited
mercantilism of the Old Regime seems far more *apropos* this "limited
energy" doctrine of vital forces.[11] This principle assumed a number of
different forms in the writings of medical scientists, but there was widespread agreement that each individual disposed of a finite quantum of
energy requiring careful management and expenditure. We may speculate

that by encouraging individuals to think of themselves as responsible for the cost-accounting of their own health, this medical doctrine also encouraged well-informed bourgeois to think of themselves as independent political monads, and to hold their own conception of health as a standard of personal identity by which to judge the bodies of "others," particularly peasants.[12]

The new medical cosmology recognized a similar gulf between the bodies of men and women. In both anatomical structure and physiological function, medicine in the late eighteenth century substituted a regime of sexual "incommensurability" for the older metaphysics of hierarchy in which women were merely lesser, unperfected versions of men.[13] The old Galenic tradition, revived and expanded in the Renaissance, had considered the bodies of men and women in terms of their respective homologies of structure and function. Sexual difference was not overlooked, but it was evaluated within a common system of relative differences in size, body heat, or metabolizing activity.[14] The female clitoris, for instance, was merely a smaller anatomical homologue to the larger male penis, among several other parallels in the reproductive systems of the two sexes. Skeletal drawings were exclusively of a universal (male) type, which implies that they were regarded as adequately representative of both sexes. It was commonly believed that women and men possessed roughly equivalent sexual appetites and capacity for enjoyment, and that orgasm in both sexes was necessary for procreation.[15]

By the late eighteenth century, however, it became popular to represent female skeletons as somehow archetypal of "their" sex. They were often presented alongside "typical" male skeletons to emphasize how gracile they were, how much smaller of cranium and wider of pelvis.[16] The organizing principle in these and other representations of sexual difference was the "discovery" that most of these differences were a consequence of women's childbearing. Women's bodies seemed perfectly designed to be the generators and carriers of children, and the more closely one looked for confirming details of this idea the more easily evidence sprang to mind. A large and influential segment of the French medical and scientific establishment devoted itself in the late eighteenth and early nineteenth centuries to working out women's unique anatomical, physiological, and moral destiny in convincing detail.

The center of a woman's body in this scheme was the uterus. This organ radiated its influence throughout her body, requiring for its labor a disproportionate amount of energy.[17] In contemporary medical writings, all female qualities followed from this aspect of their sex. Their bodies were weak and their intellectual force less than men because the vital energy needed by their sexual organs was drawn away from the other parts of their bodies, which were proportionally diminished.[18] Accordingly, in his

Système physique et moral de la femme (1775) Pierre Roussel discussed "feminine nature" as a functional whole in which a woman's sexual being determined the form and functions of her body and the nature of her mental life.[19]

Several commentators have noticed a tendency in this literature to conflate form and function, a characteristic common to much eighteenth-century writing on man's place in nature. This reflected in part the taste for holistic explanations, and in part a wish to challenge the old hierarchical teleology of creation with a secular doctrine of dynamic process. Biological thinkers assumed "function determined form," in effect that the activities of organs and life systems shaped their surrounding envelopes. These outer conformations constrained in turn the dynamic processes underway inside them, so that there was a more or less causal reciprocity between them.[20]

In a system where form and function were in such direct relation, it is easy to understand how strong ideological inclinations could shape acceptable "natural" explanations of women's place in society and their relation to men. One could argue, as did Cabanis, that habit (repetitive function) had brought about "the distinctive skeletons and musculature of the two sexes," then use this morphological difference to justify women's domestic role in the social order;[21] or one could simply characterize domesticity as the socially functional analogue of the biological function of maternity.[22] A woman's place in society could thus be identified by either of these two distinct yet mutually determining causes.

The overwhelming concern in late eighteenth-century medical writing was with women's sexuality; there was far less initial concern with the sexuality of men. When comparisons were made, it was often with the "human genre" rather than with a male sex as fully elaborated as the female.[23] Men were not invisible as sexual beings, but the stark terms in which Rousseau cast men's sexual and political dilemma made it difficult for Cabanis, Roussel, and Moreau de la Sarthe to acknowledge directly the unequal sexual capacity of the two sexes.[24] They settled instead on a strategy of portraying women as comparatively "passionless," and, as Tom Laqueur has argued, they and many of their nineteenth-century epigones vigorously denied the existence of the female orgasm.[25]

However, an equally powerful influence directing medical attention to female reproduction and fertility—a great concern of Rousseau as well—was the concern about the decline of the monarchy's population.[26] In the prevailing Old Regime tradition of *étatiste* mercantilism, a healthy and growing population was believed to be a key factor in the health and wealth of the whole society.[27] The state gathered birth and death statistics with the same avidity as figures on income and balance of payments. In their role as public hygienists, doctors were charged with the responsibility for the human sources of national fertility; in their writings on women as vessels of reproduction they helped formulate a new language for "seeing the individual body as sign—both as metaphor and source—of the health or infirmity of the larger social body."[28]

However, in the process of establishing fertility and motherhood as the nature of womankind, doctors operating under the aegis of a Rousseauian vision of society made maternity into a *mystique,* the sacralized portion of a new secular order. Without entirely detaching women's and children's bodies from a calculus of productive commodities, they nonetheless insisted that in order to flourish, women and children needed to take refuge from the conflict and exhaustion of public life in an insulating sphere of their own.[29] As we shall see, the apparent security and serenity of this hallowed domain did not rule out legal and medical intervention in the event of interior disorders; indeed, the privacy of the "private" sphere was conditional on its occupants fulfilling their social duties to the satisfaction of those who formulated state policy.

Thus, until the political upheavals of the 1790s, women's bodies held center stage. During the revolutionary era, however, the burning questions of natural and political rights made it necessary to consider who could participate in the public sphere, which in turn directed greater attention to sex as grounds for political qualification. This practical matter brought male bodies more clearly into focus, first because a clear conception of sex difference was required to justify the exclusion of women from politics, but also because only a particular kind of man could prosper amidst the terrors of revolutionary politics.

In the first flush of revolutionary enthusiasm, *monsieur* and *madame* became *citoyen* and *citoyenne,* terms that were still gendered, but whose common declension implied social and political equality. *Citoyenne,* however, as William Sewell explains, "was only an afterthought—a kind of unintentional consequence of the adoption of 'citoyen'."[30] In the parlance of the day, citizens played "active" roles in the commonwealth and citizenesses "passive" ones, a distinction which reflected and justified a male monopoly on political rights in the early stages of the Revolution. Nonetheless, by the time Jacobin radicalism had swept away both the monarchy and a moderate constitutionalism, a vigorous feminist movement had appeared and the stage seemed set for the inclusion of women in public life.[31] The politicians who strutted the stage of the new republic were not, however, the same kind of men as the ministers of the old king. They did not need the subtle skills of courtiers, who conducted their affairs in the privacy of *bureaux,* but the qualities of men whose actions were open to view. These new men embraced a public persona borrowed from stoic models of a revivified classicism, which put a premium on high moral principle and virtue.[32] Statesmen attempted to *embody* these stoic qualities by cultivating personal austerity and presenting themselves in public with an invariable reserve and dignity. As Dorinda Outram has argued, "In the pursuit of the personal authenticity so vaunted by Rousseau, and by the ideologies of solitude and intimacy . . . , they rejected the idea of putting on a mask to hide their real faces; instead they aimed to '*become* the part.' "[33]

As Outram has shown, this public "ethos of heroic dignity" was built up out of the previously established hygienic ideals of male bourgeois *physical* self-discipline and mastery of the body and its processes. These lessons in self-mastery equipped men to face the political jungle of the Terror unflinchingly. By facing death courageously a condemned man might serve as an exemplar of the high principles for which he was to die; in the same vein, a brave suicide might redeem a disgraced politics. The austere and self-abnegating manner of Robespierre was an icon for political style in this phase of the Revolution. In the insecurity of the Terror, the relatively weak solidarities of political parties were replaced by the firmer if more explosive bonds of personal loyalty directed toward notably virtuous men.[34] The rules of political allegiance that operated in these circumstances were remarkably like the honor codes that regulated the political relations of French nobles in the sixteenth century, but they were decorated during the Revolution by a discourse of antique virtue.

It was a system, in any case, which excluded women, *by their nature* from participation in politics, and which advanced the process of differentiation of the sexes. Jacobin politicians recalled the role that power-hungry aristocratic women had played in the boudoir politics of the Old Regime, how they had debauched and enfeebled a once-proud monarch to further their corrupt schemes, and turned affairs of state into *affaires de coeur.*[35] This essentially Rousseauist notion of the sexual dangers women posed to political authority in the public sphere was an important justification for their confinement in the private. As the contemporary feminist Olympe de Gouges remarked, "Women are now respected and excluded; under the old regime they were despised and powerful."[36]

This exclusion was ultimately justified along the lines of sexual difference laid out by the medical literature we have just examined. Jean-Baptiste Amar, in a speech he delivered in the debate of October 1793 denying women the vote, said "Each sex is called to a type of occupation appropriate to its nature. . . . " Men are "strong, robust, born with great energy," qualities ideal for public life, but women's tendency to act with "exaltation" in political matters must give pause to those who advocate her right to vote.[37] Giving voice to the reigning discourse of virtue, Amar expressed no doubt that he believed the *right* to govern was rooted in the personal *capacity* to do so: "To rule is to govern the public domain by laws whose confection requires extensive knowledge, an application and a devotion without limit, *a severe impassiveness and self-abnegation.* . . . "[38]

The construction of different civic roles for men and women in the early period of the Revolution was a matter, no doubt, of politics and power. But the post-revolutionary regime was rationalized and sustained by a widely shared conviction that the roles the sexes took in life were a product of *natural* difference. The challenge for the men who were responsible for legitimating a male monopoly of civil authority was to inscribe this essentially biological distinction into the laws and institutions of the new order.

The legal apotheosis of this strategy of sexual separation and inequality was the civil code of 1804, a creation of Bonaparte and his chief legal advisors during the height of his political and military power. After the revolutionary experiments with a range of new forms of civil liberties, including divorce by mutual consent and lower ages for majority, the imperial regime reconstructed more firmly than ever the Old Regime legal principle of *puissance paternelle*.[39] The code distinguished between "classes" of individuals who disposed of varying degrees of rights. Adult males made up the highest class, followed by women, minors, vagrants, the insane, and those who had committed crimes meriting "civil death." Adult women, in this hierarchy of "capacities," could not serve as guardians or legal witnesses; in the manner of perpetual minors they were subject to the authority of father, husband, or, lacking those, an officer of the court.

Though it concerns itself almost wholly with individual rights, the concept of the "family" is a crucial subtext in the civil code, inasmuch as the Napoleonic lawmaker desired to offset the libertarianism of the code with a principle of male (familial) authority. Not incidentally, this subtext also served as the basis for legalizing the main elements of pre-revolutionary bourgeois inheritance practices. In his analysis of the code, André-Jean Arnaud represents civil law as a "game" played by "players" over "stakes" they seek to retain and expand by "bets." The players in this system are adult males. A man may sit conservatively on his stakes, risking nothing, or he may engage in a wager to enlarge them by contracting a marriage alliance, having children, and passing on to them his accumulated assets, a possibility foreclosed to the conservative player. In this "chain of communications,"

> in order to avoid a rupture, one must assure the renewal of individuals of class "A" [adult males], which requires their necessary possession of the instrument of procreation: the woman who is wife and mother, and of his "fruit," until the period of its legal accession to adult life. The child, however, remains practically—in the code's conception—a property of the father until his death. In a sense, the code responds here to the *anxiety* about death by providing a "means of survival." . . . To leave something to one's descendant becomes the whole aim of life. The child allows the father to overcome his own fear of death insofar as he makes

the child his own and incorporates him into his own person as far as he
is able. . . . [40]

With respect to equality of inheritance the code adopted an intermediary position between the inflexible rigor of the revolutionary laws and
the numerous loopholes of Old Regime customary law. Most of the loopholes were closed, but a fraction of the estate could be settled on a principal
heir, varying with the number of legal heirs between one-half and one-
fourth of the total wealth. To balance this egalitarian measure, husbands
and fathers gained a monopoly of power over family decisions regarding
the marriage or occupation of children, including the "paternal correction"
of recalcitrant offspring with prison terms.

Since this principle of "masculine management" of the family was the
analogue in the private domain of male legal superiority in civil life, it
satisfied the lawmakers who wished civil law to be both logical and simple.
But male hegemony in domestic life also entailed a deeper requirement.
By giving a man absolute control over the instrument and products of his
procreation—treating both, in effect, as property (*biens*)—the code quite
literally made his legal control of his biological capital and his material
assets into aspects of the same process of self-perpetuation, making a man
put a premium on the careful management of both, especially in view of
the restrictions of partitive inheritance. As the chief player in the game of
civil life, he might lose his "stake" in one of two ways. He might distribute
his bets too widely, by having a number of children who would fractionate
the patrimony, or risk everything on a single dangerous roll of the dice.

The code protected his investments in a number of ways. It made him
the sole guardian of his children in the event of divorce. A woman's adultery
was punished more severely than a man's because she could bring a "foreign" child into the family that he might not be able to disavow. On the
other hand, though he might voluntarily settle the "disposable" portion of
his goods on his bastard, no child he conceived out of wedlock had a legal
right to the heritage, and all *recherches de la paternité* (paternity suits)
were strictly disallowed.[41] The virtual identity of family with blood was so
important that adoption was only allowed as a last, desperate measure.
Only couples without heirs over forty years old could adopt, and then only
children who had reached majority and could give assent, those whom, as
Kniebiehler says, the new parents knew were not "abandoned children,
the fruits of vice, . . . but the offspring of honorable families who have
already demonstrated their qualities."[42] A man could even control his
progeny from the grave: special testmentary provisions and a (male) guardian could oversee the upbringing of a child still in the womb at the time
of his death.[43]

It is important to understand that when the drafters of the code included a provision for divorce, partly at Bonaparte's behest, they did not regard it as a limitation on marriage or *puissance paternelle.* On the contrary, "marriage and divorce were not opposed to one another. One of them provided a warrant for the perpetuation of the different classes of players, the other a supplementary guarantee, eventual and successive, in case of the breakdown of the marriage."[44] Throughout the debates on marriage and divorce both before and during the Revolution, advocates of divorce couched their arguments as much in terms of the new procreative opportunities divorce permitted as in appeals to individual rights.[45] A love match was far more likely to produce an heir than a loveless one. Both in the Old Regime and the new, a discourse of divorce was simultaneously a *public* strategy of the "populationist" state, and a *private* matter of heirs and testamentary succession.

Divorce was overturned in 1816, leaving only legal separation to console the unhappily wed. Though abolition was the product of a long battle led by representatives of the Catholic and Monarchist right, it was a victory celebrated by arch conservatives who believed that even the flagrantly unequal rights men and women possessed in divorce proceedings infringed on the power males should exercise in the "monarchical" realm of the family. As Louis de Bonald argued, the husband's

> power will be more gentle when it is no longer disputed, when the wife has disposition over neither her person nor her goods. Peace and virtue will radiate through all households when the law of the state helps maintain the *natural* relations between husbands, wives, and children that constitute the family, and when there is no longer in either domestic society or in public life any *confusion of persons,* or displacement of power.[46]

For Bonald's generation, the concept of the indivisibility of power outweighed the benefits of personal liberty or procreative freedom; when divorce was reinstituted in 1884, the balance had reversed, but there would still be no "confusion of persons."

The new order of separate spheres and sexual segregation was not built wholly out of a discourse of incommensurability. The private realm of the family needed a compatible discursive regime that would acknowledge the difference between the sexes, but justify and reinforce the ideal of domestic happiness and unity. This task required a doctrine of complementarity which could provide a "harmony of corresponding inequalities."[47] As we have seen, the medical writings on women and reproduction of the late eighteenth and early nineteenth centuries considered men and women to be different not only in their genital structures, but in every aspect of their physical organizations.[48] The axis on which this difference turned, however, was the singular contribution each sex made to reproduction. In the act of reproduction, sexual distinctiveness was the *premise* of fertility, but the *synthesis* of a new life reconciled these otherwise antithetical principles. Indeed, it was common for medical writers to consider boys and girls sexually indifferent until puberty, when the striking physical changes that made them fertile overcame indifference in all its aspects.

Procreation finally attained from secular medical writers the privileged status it had always merited in the eyes of theologians. In this development, the attraction between the sexes gained, by extension, a new *cachet* it had never before enjoyed. Medical experts characterized the affinities on which fertility depended as an attraction of "opposite" principle. Since the view of women as "natural" wives and mothers was already well-developed by 1800 or so, doctors turned their attention to the male role in sexual arousal and fertilization, gradually elaborating a scientific discourse of procreative harmonies. Males were accordingly represented in the medical literature after this date in ways that reflected the criteria of opposition and complementarity. In the process, men gained a natural identity as sexual beings that made it increasingly difficult, despite rhetoric to the contrary, for them to be uniquely representative of the human genre "mankind," or for women to be the archetypal sexed being, the "fair sex," or, simply, the "sex."

In both popular culture and medicine, the logic of complementarity was believed to be the key to understanding human fertility. The masculinity of the male and the femininity of the female needed to be in correct proportion for the couple to have procreative success. From the standpoint of nineteenth-century medical experts, questions about "proper" complementary balance were the special province of biology, and it was their duty to interpret and apply the truths of biology to human life. The lessons of vital equilibrium were contained in two indispensable concepts that had emerged in the new "materialist" physiology of Cabanis, Bichat, Magendie, and Broussais, and which were to prove crucial to the conceptualization and representation of sexual identity and attraction throughout the nineteenth century.

The first of these concepts, described by Georges Canguilhem in his classic *Le Normal et le pathologique,* was the creation of a rule governing biological norms. The implementation of such a rule enabled medical science to establish benchmarks for distinguishing between normal and pathological vital functions. Through the gathering and analysis of proximate, quantitative measurements, medical scientists believed they could isolate the rates of certain life functions such as animal heat, respiration, circulation, and heart rate. On the basis of clinical observation, these rates could be plotted along a spectrum ranging from the lowest values consistent with life to the highest. "Normal" states were those that fell in or near the middle of the spectrum, located by a statistical average. Extreme rates of function, called "excesses" or "deficits," were much rarer and were associated with morbid states.[49] Inevitably, it happened that "to define the abnormal by the too much or the too little was to acknowledge the normative character of the state called normal. That normal physiological state was not only a disposition which was discernible and explicable as a fact, it was also the manifestation of an attachment to a certain *value*."[50]

In effect medical physiology not only declared average rates healthy, it also made them the measure of normalcy, holding departures from these norms to be pathological. As Canguilhem writes elsewhere, there is an essential ambiguity in the term "normal" that allows it to be applied both to statistical artifacts and to "an ideal, a positive principle of valuation, in the sense of a prototype or perfect form."[51] The statistical norm may be thus made into a *kind,* so that "despite the substitution in modern science of the notion of law for the notion of type, the first of these concepts may be constituted in the second, . . . [giving it] a signification as a real and immutable type. . . ."[52]

The second concept that undergirded concepts of sexual identity and attraction in nineteenth-century medicine concerned equilibria. As we saw earlier, the hydrodynamics of the old humoral medicine was converted by Bichat and other physiologists into an energy model of vital and limited forces. A proper distribution of these vital forces was regarded as essential for health. Thus various functions, internal secretions, or energies were in "harmony" within the space of the living being, or they were "inharmonious" or "disproportionally" distributed. As with rates of function, vital imbalances were believed to threaten the health of the organism, and so were considered to be pathological.[53] Concepts of normal equilibria had more analytical than empirical utility in nineteenth-century medical science, but they established the occasions for medical intervention by helping doctors judge proper organic function and the normal relations of vital systems with one another.

I would like to illustrate some of these themes by considering one of the most popular texts to celebrate the glories of marital love and fertility, *De la femme* (1825) of the pharmacist and medical publicist, J.J. Virey. This book summed up what Virey had learned in his career as a vulgarizer of the late eighteenth-century medical revolution. Despite its title, *De la femme* was essentially a book for men about the beings who are the source of "their delights and torments." Virey wrote that each sex is one half of "a complete being," whose sacred mission is the reproduction of the species. The greater the difference between them, the greater their mutual attraction, and the more certain a fertile union. The ideal couple is that

> of the most female woman and the most virile man, when a dark, hairy, dry, hot and impetuous male finds the other sex delicate, moist, smooth and white, timid and modest. The one must give and the other is constituted to receive; the first, for that reason must embody the principle

of overabundance, which aspires to pour out its forces, its generosity, its liberality; the second, on the contrary, being inversely disposed, must, through its timidity, be ready to welcome, to absorb, out of need and a feeling of deficit, the overflow of the other in order to establish equality and reach fullness.[54]

The universe of "corresponding" harmonies represented in this account of the act of love is ruled by the transformational energy of semen, a notion of humoral medicine still firmly embedded in the new physiology.[55] All the qualities of a man, his deep voice, his musculature, beard, ruddy complexion, his courage and his "generosity" are a consequence of the vital force contained in this precious liquor. "Female" characteristics are not established in women by some corresponding humor, but are the consequence of her *lack* of semen, qualities, as it were, *in absentia*. In the sex act, as this quotation describes, semen is transferred to the sexual economy of the woman, who is proportionally "virilized." Have we all not noticed, Virey asks, how much more "hardi," calm, and self-assured the married woman becomes after her timid maidenhood?[56] Courtesans, for their part, absorb more semen still, and they become progressively more "hommasses" (mannish), "transformed halfway into the other sex."[57] The equilibrium established in procreation is a natural effect of the union of opposites, but it poses dangers if carried to excess.

A man's danger is far graver because he spends more in orgasm. Women spend too, but not as much as their lovers; they are in any case reimbursed with interest for their losses. In Virey's account of the relative balance of sexual forces in men and women, Rousseau's nightmare of dominant women and exhausted males is fully delineated. Virey estimates that with respect to sexual capacity a woman is "worth" two and a half men.[58] But nature, in her wisdom, has made women naturally modest. Were this not so, men's natural ardor would provoke endless coupling and consequent male exhaustion, and "the human species would succumb by the very means designed to perpetuate it."[59] In Virey's world of reversible binaries, "Chastity is for the woman the concentrated essence of her virtue, just as valiance is for a man; her immodesty is thus a vice as vile and degrading as cowardice is for him."[60]

The fate of a man who does not cautiously manage his finite sexual economy is to be gradually demasculinized. The more frequent his debauches, especially when undertaken in extreme youth or old age, the more rapidly he will decline into an unmanly state. As befits a member of the progressive medical bourgeoisie, Virey drew his illustrations of this process from the tragedy of the Old Regime nobility. Exhausted from their greedy exploitation of "first-night" privileges, lacking genius or courage, they dress themselves in the skirts of a eunuch or in effeminate clothing in which they barely manage to creep across the ground; they tremble with fear at the very sight of weapons; they cannot think or act as men should do; they are the most scornful and vile beings in creation; their cowardice and their impotence obliges them to deal in falsehoods and duplicity, the vices of men who have simply shriveled up.[61]

As an early species of sexual self-help book, *De la femme* was at pains to tie these lessons about the dangers of sexual excess into concrete procreative advice. Virey reminds his readers that in the act of engendering a man is "dying for himself, bequeathing his life to his posterity, making out, in a certain sense, his last will and testament. To love is to die for one's own kind."[62] In view of the nature of sublime sacrifice in the male orgasm, Virey counsels men to limit their lovemaking and confine it to the years of most vigorous maturity, when the regenerative powers of the organism were at their height. The man who practices such moderation will have masculine, healthy sons; the one who has depleted himself will suffer one of three fates. In ascending order of seriousness: he will have only daughters; weakly, effeminate sons; or monsters that are "deformed and degraded, the very shame of nature, ignoble and abject abortions that are without merit or soul, where everything is confounded and annihilated."[63] The worst fate of all, and the last stage of demasculinization, was impotence, in which a man forfeited both his sexual identity and his chance for a natural heir.[64]

To sum up, the human sexual economy was believed by Virey and his contemporaries to function according to a quantitative model of energy flow in which "moderate" expenditures of (sexual) energy were most consonant with health and with reproductive fertility. Extreme expenditures of this vital force (in masturbation or coitus) were functionally pathological and led to impotence, sterility, or both. Low expenditures were *already* signs of morbidity, whether a product of inheritance or a result of previous excesses. The measure of all things in this system was the capacity to engender; all forms of sexual activity that departed from this reproductive ideal were consigned to the realm of the abnormal. Thus the medical science of this period imagined a physiological spectrum of possible rates of sexual function for each individual. If we imagine this range of possibilities laid out on a horizontal axis, the left side would register *low* rates of function (sexual indifference), moderate rates would fall in the middle (normal) range of the line, and the zone on the right would correspond to the high rates characteristic of sexual excess.

Because of their belief in the essential holism of mind and body, and the conformity of form with function, most of Virey's professional contemporaries believed they could plot other characteristics of individuals on this spectrum. By degrees a system was worked out which correlated rates of physiological activity with genital morphology, secondary sexual features, and the characteristic "moral" behavior associated with each position on the axis. The distibution of the whole population might be represented in a bell curve resting on the axis, each edge of which touched the extreme rates of function.

I also wish to emphasize that Virey's text exemplifies the various meanings of Foucault's notion that the "blood" of the bourgeoisie was its "sex." Virey articulates a system of disciplined bourgeois procreation that will replace the debauched and careless one of the nobility. When properly implemented, this system will produce vigorous offspring with distinctive sexual identities, the qualities required for both social reproduction, and the maintanance of sexual divisions in social life. Thus Foucault's dictum refers to sex in at least two senses: a hygiene of sexual relations, and a regime of sexual difference.

However, Foucault also uses "blood" in more than one way. It is of course the blood of the line of heirs, which must be kept free from taint and weakness. But blood also refers to the aristocratic principle of superiority on which the bourgeoisie also founded its claims to social and cultural hegemony. As in the old concept of noble *race*, which assumed an identity of nature and culture, this quality should have a *natural* distinction about it, yet, in order to reflect the energy and talent of each man, must be amenable to augmentation or diminution. In Virey's text, a man's sex was dependent on his sexual comportment, and vice versa. The language Virey uses to characterize that identity is essentially a language of honor transposed to the domain of sexual identity. He characterizes the chivalric liberality and generosity of the male orgasm, speaks of the courage and valiance of a male in the full flower of his manhood, regrets the shameful debauchery and self-abuse that produces effeminacy and cowardice, and abominates the abortive embryos that are the "shame" of nature. The indistinguishability of nature and culture is preserved here in the way behavior that merits honor or shame is collapsed into a biological condition described by the same binary opposition. The effects are also transgenerational in the sense that the shameful excesses of the father are visited on the offspring in the form of congenital disorders.

What was needed, once the doctrines of functional equilibria had been fully articulated, was a tableau of the anatomical monstrosities that corresponded to abnormal rates of physiological function. This task fell to Isidore Geoffroy Saint-Hilaire, the son of the man who had advocated unsuccessfully the concept of species evolution against Georges Cuvier's belief in the fixity of species. In taking up the subject of monsters, the younger Geoffroy hoped to vindicate his father's claim that the variation of individuals within species indicated that a mechanism for species change was at work in processes of embryological development, that species were not preformed *kinds* but a fluctuating population of individual types.[65] Geoffroy was also bringing to fruition a long interest in the West in the study of monsters. In the sixteenth century monsters came to be regarded as natural objects, but not part of nature.[66] For the next 200 years or so the view was perpetuated that anomalous life forms were exceptions to natural law, which presided over a regular and uniform creation. By the beginning of the nineteenth century, however, it was suspected that anatomical irregularities might be explained by the same laws that explained the "typical" forms. At roughly the time that Geoffroy coined the term *teratology* (1832) to apply to the science of anomalies, biologists were beginning to realize, as Canguilhem has written, that monsters "revealed how precarious is the stability [of forms] to which life habituates us." In his words,

> It is monstrosity and not death which is the true refutation of life. Death is the permanent and unconditional decomposition of the organism, a limitation from without, the negation of the living by the non-living. But monstrosity is the accidental and conditional threat of incompletion or distortion in the formation of the form, a limitation by the interior, the negation of the living by the non-viable.[67]

In his three-volume compendium of the anatomical anomalies of man and beast, Geoffroy wrote that an individual could only be judged abnormal when compared to other members of his group, not by some set of absolute standards. Because there is no "ideal type" in a race or species, but only a "simple average," the variation from this average is a matter of degree and may be plotted on a curve like rates of vital function in physiology.[68] The anomalies or radical monstrosities that anatomists used to classify individuals according to their deviation from (statistical) norms were the consequence of variations in the rate of an individual's embryological development. All such departures were caused by an *excess* or a *deficit* of development in the volume of an organ or organs, resulting in anomalies of size, number, or displacement. These irregularities could be classified according to a set of laws that explained the proportions and numbers of anatomical features relationally. External anomalies were the reflections of internal ones: minor variations were expressed by small abnormalities in one or a few features, while more serious internal disequilibria were represented by more extreme, multiple monstrosities.[69]

According to Saint-Hilaire's system, therefore, a single exemplary deviation was a sign that the entire organism was proportionally abnormal.

Dwarves and giants, for example, who were deviant in the matter of stature, had notably limited intellects, tired easily, were lazy, had small genitals relative to their size, and were either impotent or "quickly enervated by the pleasures of love."[70] The case of giants and dwarves demonstrates that for Saint-Hilaire sexual appetite and genital conformation were the markers par excellence of human anomaly on account of their particular sensitivity to the vitality of the internal economy.

The *pièce de résistance* of Saint-Hilaire's method was his extended analysis of human hermaphrodites. Here he showed that the "truth" of human sexual identity and capacity was revealed in "vices" of genital conformation. As with the anomalies of other organs, unusually profound abnormalities were signs of the deviation of internal dispositions. Accordingly, Saint-Hilaire believed he could identify reliably the sex of any individual by a genital examination, from which sexual appetite and other aspects of the *vita sexualis* could then be deduced.[71]

A confirmed epigenicist like his father before him, Saint-Hilaire believed that the sex of a child was not determined at conception (preformation) but by environing influences on the embryo during its development.[72] Nutrition, the relative "generational" energy in parents, and the completeness of embryological development were the essential influences on individual sexual differentiation. Saint-Hilaire ridiculed earlier physiologists who dismissed the distinguishing truth of the genitals on the grounds they performed the same *function* of reproduction in both sexes, and who thus regarded male and female genitals as "two diverse parts of the same apparatus."[73] "Analogies," he wrote, may not be reduced to "harmonies;" rather, if we consider the embryological development of the human organism to be the same for both sexes, we may then explain genital differences between them as simple variations of "mode and degree." A clitoris is an "arrested penis" and a penis a "hypertrophied clitoris," such that " . . . one is the first and the other the last degree of the evolution of a perfectly analogous ensemble of organic elements."[74]

By such reasoning Saint-Hilaire envisioned a continuous spectrum of sexual differentiation in which males were grouped on one end of a horizontal axis, and females on the other. Grouped in the middle were the hermaphroditic "anomalies," which inclined to one end or the other depending on the predominance of "male" or "female" features in their genital morphology. Individuals who fell within the range of the "normal" of their representative type experienced the usual desire for the "opposite" sex. Those located in the middle of the spectrum on account of the ambiguity of their genital structures were not, however, "bisexual"; the "law" of the balancing of organs held them to be sexually neutral because the male and female elements cancelled one another out.[75] They therefore had

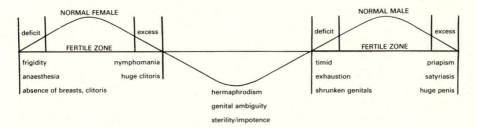

(Adapted from Isidore Geoffrey de St. Hilare. *Trade de Ieratologue*, 3 vols, 1832-37)

no sexual "penchants" whatsoever, but were monsters of sexual indifference.

All individuals were nonetheless, Saint-Hilaire emphasized, necessarily of one sex or the other, because to these "great classes belong not only different but nearly *inverse* functions in the family and in society. In that sense there are no intermediaries; our laws do not admit their existence or foresee their possibility."[76] Specialists in French legal medicine throughout the nineteenth century repeated this formula as the justification for their expertise in all civil cases arising from confusions of sexual identity in marriage, paternity, inheritance, military service, or crime, but they did so in the language of scientific and legal universals. As Gabriel Tourdes wrote in 1888, "The difference of sex establishes in all societies two categories of persons who dispose of different rights and duties; our laws do not admit the existence or even foresee the possibility of any intermediary condition. Sex determines not only civil status, but also the entire direction of life."[77]

Such statements leave little doubt that this classificational system was designed to reinforce the doctrine of separate spheres by providing an anatomical hypostatization of sex difference. It is also clear, however, that Saint-Hilaire's system was part of a contemporary medical effort to conceptualize the laws of sexual desire and square these with sexual identity, reproductive fertility, and the bourgeois ideal of moderation in all things. The new tableau thus preserved the assumption of the attraction of sexual "opposites," and declared this affinity to be the justification and basis for healthy fertility. But it warned concomitantly that such passions were only "normal" or healthy when they avoided the extremes of frenzy and indifference, both of which were inconsistent with reproductive love. In the matter of the sexual passions early nineteenth-century French medicine thus endorsed the principle of the *juste milieu,* which was not incidentally the chief bourgeois political ideal of the era. We may get some idea of the connections between political virtue and sexual harmony by considering the chart devised by J.B.F. Descuret in his influential *La Médecine des passions:*[78]

Vices or Defects	Virtues	Vices or Defects
Weakness	Force	Violence
Apathy	Calm	Anger
Fear	Courage	Temerity
Nonchalance	Activity	Turbulence
Indifference	Emulation	Envy
Avarice	Economy	Prodigality
Disgust for Study	Love of Study	Study Mania
Incredulity	Religious Faith	Fanaticism
[impotence]	[procreative love]	[satyriasis, nymphomania]

If we were to include the human sexual economy on this chart, the entry in the "virtues" column would be "procreative love." The column of "vices" of "excess" on the right would be occupied by "satyriasis" in the case of men, or "nymphomania" in the case of women. "Impotence" would be the appropriate term for both sexes in the "deficit" column on the left. My point here is to suggest that the bourgeois ideals of marital fertility and of moderation in all things shared a common conceptual situation in their adversarial relation to "others" threatening them at both flanks. The dominance of the virtues could only be maintained by vigilance against the sins of excess or deficit.

This point in turn underscores the significance of the fact that the anatomical spectrum of sex difference was equally a figurative model of physiological dynamics. Saint-Hilaire had inscribed the varieties of genital conformation upon the spectrum of normal and pathological rates of physiological function, thus creating a system of exterior signs that fluctuated with changes in the internal sexual economy. The concept of vital harmonies was as important to the life sciences of this era as the doctrine that nature abhors a vacuum was to late medieval physics. Thus, genital morphology, secondary sexual characteristics, potency, and "moral" behavior were believed to be in rough correspondence with one another.

Consider how such a system applied to the question of male sexual identity. The appearance of an atypical or non-male feature on the body or in the behavior of a man was a sign that his place on the spectrum of sexual variation was sliding toward the lower end of the male range. In that location "female" features appeared in higher proportions than in the zone of the representative male "type"; they increased in number and expressiveness as one approached the sexually ambiguous domain of hermaphrodism at the center of the spectrum. Any of the functional or physical qualities of hermaphrodites—impotence, effeminacy, untypical genitalia or body shape—were evidence of demasculinization.

A man at the other, "hypermasculine" extreme of the spectrum displayed none of these qualities. On the contrary, he was likely to be "... lean, have white, even teeth, abundant body hair, a cynical voice, manner, and expression, and unique body odor."[79] More often than not such men also wielded, "a penis of extraordinary dimensions, well-fitted for sexual pleasures, a tight scrotum and heavy and swollen testicles." They were capable of orgasm twelve times in a night, and there were records in the worst cases of men with permanent erections dying of gangrene, and unrepentant rape-murderers mounting the scaffold in a state of arousal.[80]

A sexual satyr's excessive expenditure of sexual energy threatened to exhaust him and relocate him in the lower end of the male portion of the spectrum, where feeble sexual economies were the rule.[81] It was not possible in this system for a man to actually become a woman, but from the perspective of nineteenth-century doctors he could certainly lose the characteristic qualities of male identity.

As I suggested at the outset of this chapter, male sexual potency became in the nineteenth century a way of thinking about power, both of the public and the domestic variety. As we have seen, male sexual capacity was a qualifying feature for full citizenship in the modern state, and only a man who was sexually potent could live in and through the heirs who received both his goods and the imprint of his person. In the sphere of private life, the association of potency with a scientifically sanctioned "typical" male identity meant that a man's sexual capacity figured some way or other in the calculus of power relations between himself and the "opposite" sex. By insisting so adamantly on women's "reproductive" nature, medical pundits had successfully enclosed bourgeois women in their *foyers,* but they were therefore obliged to remind men that they must make love to their wives in a gallant and "generous" fashion, *and* make them mothers.

In the Old Regime impotence had been grounds for the annulment of marriage. The medical and formal distinction between sterility and impotence was not at that time very clear—nor did it become much clearer until the twentieth century—so sterility was often subsumed into impotence to refer to reproductive incapacity in both men and women.[82] By these standards female potency could not be fully assessed, but *male* potency could at least be determined, and in the trials conducted in the ecclesiastical courts of Old Regime France a bizarre procedure was employed that placed the burden of proof on a man's ability to produce an erection or vaginal intromission under the gaze of expert witnesses and officers of the court. Ecclesiastical courts took quite literally the theological injunction that the purpose of marriage was procreation. They readily dissolved unions when one party could be shown to be infertile so that the other could fulfill their Christian mission.[83]

Marriage was made a secular matter in the Revolution, and despite the desire of the politicians of that generation to make reproduction the aim of marriage, the libertarian sentiments of the era would not tolerate the revival of the sort of clerical inquisition represented by impotence trials. The result was that impotence was not admitted as grounds for divorce, nor, after 1816, for *séparation de corps,* much to the chagrin of medical experts, who campaigned throughout the century for its rehabilitation as grounds for terminating marriage. Dr. Gabriel Tourdes argued that it would be easy to prove an "accidental" impotence sustained by injury after marriage, but he particularly impugned the honor of a man who knowingly entered an alliance suffering from a *natural* impotence on the grounds that "whoever contracts a union in conditions contrary to its end should not benefit from such a *shameful* action."[84] Indeed, in jurisprudence after the reinstitution of divorce in 1884, impotence was allowed to figure in the list of "injuries" in suits brought by wives against their husbands, particularly when the condition had been concealed before marriage, though it could still not be, in itself, a grounds for divorce.[85]

The failure to admit impotence as a cause of separation or divorce does not permit us to conclude, as Darmon does, that impotence drops from sight in the nineteenth century because of prudishness about frankly sexual subjects.[86] One might argue, on the contrary, that it had a great social and cultural resonance until the end of the nineteenth century when, as we shall see, impotence was subsumed into other disease syndromes.

We may gain a better understanding of the significance of impotence in the middle years of the nineteenth century by looking at the most important medical texts published in that period on male sexual dysfunction. These books were clearly written as medical self-help manuals. They offer diagnoses, therapies, and pharaceutical remedies for the sufferers of reproductive disorders. Their authors were well-known medical practicioners in close contact with the faculty of the Paris medical school, but though the books are heavily freighted with medical references and scholarly details, they are also larded with lascivious anecdotes and rather doubtful tales of the sexual exploits of both sexes. They appear to have been highly successful. Dr. Jean-Alexis Belliol's *Conseil aux hommes affaiblis* was first published in 1829 and was in its twelfth edition in 1877.

In general these volumes sustain Peter Gay's point that sex manuals in the nineteenth century were more in tune than we might have imagined with the "reality" of women's desire and capacity for sexual pleasure.[87] In books addressing both male and female impotence, it is women's sexuality that is taken for granted, and men's that is taken to be problematic; far more space is devoted to the sexual dysfunction of men. In a sense the assumption of women's greater sexual capacity is a *premise* of this genre of sex manual, a confirmation of Rousseau's fears about male incapacity. Thus, Dr. Rauland argues that J.J. Virey's picture of the humiliations of impotence was not dark enough. If an ardent, vital, expectant young woman marries a man who brings only "satiety, disgust and impotence" to the conjugal bed, she will be led by her unfulfilled needs to forget in adultery the "impotent who let her youth, her ardor, and her beauty wither in silence."[88]

In the male point of view presented here, the act of love was a test that was failed far more often by men than by women, not only because men were more easily exhausted by sexual activity, but also because they possessed by nature a quality or sentiment that was diminished by the failures of their flesh. Dr. Belliol called it a "sentiment of virility," which he believed was a more vital component of masculine nature than the concomitant sentiment of maternity in women. In losing his sexual function, a man lost the "intimate consciousness of his dignity." Belliol demonstrates the point I have made that impotence is a good way to think about politics by arguing that for men in general, "the anticipated loss of virile power produces a more devastating effect than the loss of worldly honors, fortune, or loved ones; the deprivation of liberty is nothing compared to that continuous interior torture."[89]

More commonly, these authors evoke the language of honor in discussing a man's response to sexual *debâcle*. Dr. Rauland tells the story of a patient who came to him complaining of two successive failures with a particular young woman. "I must find some way to regain my honor," Rauland quotes him as saying. "She is coming to Paris counting heavily on my love, and I must, no matter what, make her forget with caresses what all women regard as an insult and rarely pardon."[90] Rauland relates that he gave him some "words of courage," a little belladonna to calm his nerves, and promise of a cure. Ten days later the gentleman returned, "beaming," to announce, "I have become a man again and have completely wiped away the shame of those two terrible disasters."[91]

Dr. Belliol urges his readers to turn directly to page ninety-five of his book and choose the number between one and five that most closely corresponds to their degree of affliction. Five is "normal." Four experiences a slight weakening of "virile power." Three has considerable weakness, and a slackening of sexual thoughts and desires. Two has rare erections, is "sad," and notices the shrinking of his genitals. One has rare and "fugitive" erections, no desire, a constant sentiment of shame and disgust for life. Zero is suicidal, and "seems to have in some sense forgotten the sex to which he belongs."[92] Dr. Roubaud also writes of stages of decline, including the shrinking of the genitals, "from the simple sentiment of shame to the monomania of suicide."[93] Shame and dishonor are inseparable in all these accounts from impotence, or, rather, they mark expressively the descent into total impotence, at which point even the sentiment of shame is extinguished in the victim.[94]

The weaknesses of virile capacity were accounted for in various ways. Venereal excess, in either coitus or self-abuse, led to exhaustion and the weakening of the equilibrium of the "animal economy." Men who did not wantonly waste their semen were fortified by its retention, and generally had robust, athletic constitutions, of the sort most appealing to the members of the opposite sex.[95] Urban civilization posed certain dangers to males that rural life had never done. The genital instincts of liberal professionals could be "frozen" by "overwork" (*surménage intellectuel*), and by excessive gourmandizing, in which case the "vital force" may flee the "genital organs and take refuge wholly within the nutritive faculties."[96]

This literature fully respects the principle laid down in the teratology of comparative anatomy that the shape and size of the organ reflects the disposition of its internal forces. The discovery of smaller than normal genitalia was regarded as proof that the vital force had disappeared, either because of the general diminution of energy available to the organism, or the unusual demands of another organ. In an anecdote that underscores the interdependence of sexual identity and genital morphology, Roubaud tells us of a young medical student who came to him complaining of an inability to maintain an erection during intercourse. The student had "Lilliputian" genitals, was "effeminate," and spoke in an unusually high voice. Roubaud fitted him with an "ingeniously" designed prosthesis, which in coitus produced on him the frictions his unaided organ was too small to provoke. He recommended a regime of as much coitus as "his delicate constitution would bear," together with solid nourishment and light exercise. When he saw the patient some months later, thanks to the principle that the "organ is always in rapport with its exercise," his penis had increased perceptibly in size.[97]

As these illustrations indicate, the calculus of an attraction of opposites was an integral feature of this literature. Dr. Rauland tells what he regards as a "repugnant" story that shows how sexual difference depended on the regime of separate spheres and vice versa. A bourgeois couple owned and operated together a commercial distributorship, but were unable to conceive. Unknown to them, but not to their doctor, each was having an affair with another person. When the wife and the mistress became pregnant at the same time, Rauland concluded that their shared working environment had shaped their temperaments similarly and made them mutually unappealing, though they were not sterile with other, more dissimilar partners. Rauland "treated" the situation by advising the wife to break off *her* relationship (though the husband kept his), but to keep her spouse in the dark about the origin of the child, all of which proved to the doctor's satisfaction, "the repugnance men feel for masculine women and the scorn women have for effeminate men."[98]

Doctors could not easily give voice to the fear and contempt that impotence provoked in themselves and their readers by ridiculing at length men who were, after all, prospective patients (read customers). But they could wax indignant at the flaws in a most convenient substitute for whom no one had any sympathy: eunuchs. In the physioanatomical tableau of sexual types, eunuchs were the archetypal impotents, "the most vile class of the human species, cowardly scoundrels because they are weak, envious and cruel because they are unhappy, . . . possessing none of the expansive and generous sentiments."[99] No eunuch, averred Roubaud, "ever had an original thought," or a firm grasp on moral truth.[100] From the perspective of medical science, a man's (precious) testicles were the only thing that preserved him from eunuchism. As Laurent Martin expressed it,

> If one examines, in effect, the essential differences between men and eunuchs who have lost their [testicles], if one observes the weakness of the latter, his incomplete development, the nakedness of his skin, the timbre of his voice, the mediocrity of his intelligence, the atrophy of his sentiments and his instincts, one must conclude, with the most eminent physiologists, that between a man whose organs of generation have presided over his development, and the one who has developed without them, a huge gulf exists. And, one must insist, this gulf is being filled in, without their knowledge, perhaps, but in a sure and permanent fashion by the imprudent beings who squander the creative power residing in them at the slightest opportunity without measure or scruple.[101]

In an early eighteenth-century treatise on eunuchs, the Protestant intellectual Charles Ancillon expressed the view that eunuchs were men "without honor." The gravest insult one could offer to an "honnête homme," he wrote, was to call him a eunuch, that is, a man who was not potent, was unable to engender offspring, and who possessed the appearance and the sentiments of a woman.[102] The outlook on impotence was much the same in the mid-nineteenth century. The fear of impotence still resonated in men's minds, evoking a language of honor that encompassed all aspects of a man's moral and physical being, expressed his personal dignity, the esteem he enjoyed in the eyes of others, and that deemed him a good father and useful citizen. But thanks in part to the development of new biomedical concepts that reconfigured the world in categories of incommensurate harmonies, a man's honor was now embedded deep in the blood and bone of his sex.

5

Population, Degeneration, and Reproduction

I have now explored in detail at least one meaning of Foucault's notion that the blood of the nineteenth-century bourgeoisie was its "sex," in which were embedded the "themes" of the "caste manners" of the old nobility. This was sex in the sense of a difference between the sexual natures of men and women that consigned them to fulfill separate but complementary functions in the civil and domestic domains. As I have suggested, however, there are two other related meanings in the historical genealogy of *sex* that will occupy me in the following two chapters. In chapter 6 I will discuss abnormal sex, the constitution of nonheterosexual and nonreproductive sexualities into sexual perversions in late nineteenth-century medicine. In the present chapter I will explore the meanings attributed to sex as a science and hygiene of reproduction, wherein a body of rules governing human heredity and the evolution of sex was constructed and popularized in bourgeois culture. Both these discourses articulated the emotions that arose from the deeply intimate connection between family resources and worldly ambition in middle-class life. Because children were a form of biological capital in this outlook, one can imagine that bourgeois parents appraised their children with an ambivalent mixture of anxiety and joy, looking fearfully for traces of an ancestor's corrupting sin even as they celebrated a birthday in gratitude for excellent returns on a risky investment.

Since they constituted the major part of the political elite in post-revolutionary France, the bourgeoisie came to identify its destiny as a class with the fate of the nation. Bourgeois scientists and intellectuals extended their ruminations on reproduction to the whole population in the form of principles of heredity they believed held the key to understanding France's place in the world. In this chapter I introduce the theme that in the nineteenth and early twentieth century a discourse on sex and reproduction was inseparable from considerations on the health and well-being of the nation. This is the largest of the frames in which I attempt to show how potency was a good way for thinking about politics, in this instance the masculine qualities that were required if the status of France as a great power was to be maintained.

In the years immediately before the upheaval of 1848, the times were ripe for meditations on the fate of elites. Demands for reform of the restrictive suffrage were heard in the Chamber of Deputies and in the streets, and from below there bubbled up to bourgeois consciousness far more radical visions of social and economic reconstruction expressed by utopian and revolutionary socialists. In 1846, an article appeared in the prestigious *Annales d'hygiène publique et de médecine légale* that must have seemed premonitory to those who witnessed the end of the regime of "notables" two years later. The subject of this learned statistical investigation was the longevity of noble family lines in the Old Regime. Benoiston de Châteauneuf discovered that scarcely any of the tens of thousands of families of noble stock had maintained their bloodlines intact since the end of the sixteenth century. Many families simply died out for want of an heir; if family names did manage to survive, it was on account of contrived legal fictions involving the transfer of titles from a dying line to distant but still vital relations.[1] Robe families did not escape a similar fate. Many of the greatest families of Old Regime intellectuals—Corneille, Racine, Molière, Boileau—lasted only one or two generations before the genius of their line was extinguished. Benoiston attributed this genetic hecatomb to exhaustion brought on by overindulgence in food and alcohol and by sexual debauchery, but he also implied that the energy of this once-formidable ruling class had simply ebbed away.[2]

It would have been surprising indeed, in light of the tumultuous events of 1847–52, if the grand ideal of progress had not undergone an earnest reconsideration by contemporary thinkers. But as works such as Count Arthur de Gobineau's *Essai sur l'inégalité des races humaines* (1854–56) reveal, such pessimistic meditations often followed a biological orientation. For Gobineau, the dominant white race was doomed whether it interbred with inferior races or not. It became mongrelized in the first case, and, if it remained pure, lost its vigor and declined into a consanguineous sterility. In effect, as Daniel Pick has argued, "In the aftermath of 1848, the problems of history were displaced into the problem of inheritance."[3]

The first effort to write a compendium of the "laws" of inheritance was Dr. Prosper Lucas's *Traité de l'hérédité naturelle,* which appeared between 1847 and 1850. Lucas made it clear that he believed natural explanation took precedence over any other kind. In his words, "The vital fact always precedes the social fact . . . natural heredity becomes for us, in a word, the primordial reason and the real source of any institutional inheritance."[4] The terms in which he cast the "problem of heredity" make it obvious that he viewed human inheritance from a perspective that was sensitive to the particular requirements of the upper bourgeoisie:

In the social order, [heredity] first evokes the question of the principle and the succession of property. In the political order, . . . it raises the same question of the principle and the succession of sovereignty. In the civil order . . . it does the same for the question of the principle and succession of the ownership of art, literature, science and industry. When we return these things to their source in the natural order we find them to be no more than effects, expressions, applications, or consequences of a law, a force, and a fact . . . ; and that law, which seems to control, to produce, to spread and to multiply everything, is the law of creation, of propagation, and of life.[5]

The true inventor of the concept of degeneration was the psychiatrist Bénédict-Augustin Morel. Though he was only the director of a humble provincial insane asylum, Morel had apprenticed to the leading psychiatric practitioners of Paris and traveled widely in Europe in order to study pathologies such as cretinism that disfigured both the minds and the bodies of its victims. Morel was haunted by the misshapen and suffering humanity he found in his travels, but was disposed by his Catholic outlook to consider this misery to be the product of sinful choice.[6] In his *Traité des dégénérescences physiques, intellectuelles et morales de l'espèce humaine* (1857), Morel outlined a theory that mankind had degenerated from a pristine Adamite stock through the slow accumulation of inherited defects. These defects had taken root in populations that were exposed to environmental pathogens, suffered poor nourishment, or were addicted to vice; they ramified in complexity and seriousness until sterility terminated a breeding line.

Morel's theory came along at a time in the history of French psychiatry when many of its practitioners were seeking to reintegrate their profession into the mainstream of organic medicine by establishing the organic basis of mental illness.[7] The theory of hereditary degeneration coincided with a vigorous renewal of French experimental medicine under the leadership of the great Claude Bernard, in which an equally important emphasis was placed on the organic and material factors underlying physiological function. Under the aegis of this research tradition, a number of medically trained microscopists expanded the search for the the causes of mental disorder by examining the evidence of nerve tissue pathology. In the long run, however, degeneration theory profited far more from Bernard's belief that the health of the organism was assured by a balanced "internal milieu" of vital forces.[8] By adapting notions of equilibrium and disequilibrium to pathological mental states, psychiatrists could analyze mental illness in terms of the amount and distribution of energy in the body's nervous system, and correlate these assessments with precise observations of tissue pathology.[9] Both methods aided psychiatry's quest for scientific legitimacy and helped increase the prestige and currency of psychiatric discourse.[10]

The prevailing doctrine of species evolution in France also made use of the concept of an equilibrium of vital forces to explain the nature of intergenerational inheritance, a kind of heredity theory writ large. The chief intellectual source for these ideas was Jean-Baptiste Lamarck, an early nineteenth-century naturalist who first articulated a theory of species *transformisme* in his *Philosophie zoologique* of 1809. In Lamarck's scheme, a condition of the survival of each organism was the requirement that its internal "organic economy" be in a rough equilibrium with the external milieu in which it lived. If the milieu changed, the equilibrium between milieu and organism could only be reestablished if the organism responded to this "need" by reconfiguring its internal economy. If an organism succeeded in readapting to its environment, Lamarckian theory assumed there would be direct implications for inheritance, because the internal changes it "willed" for itself were preserved as "tendencies" that could be passed on to descendants.[11] Heredity was thus a hard-won *"force* of reproduction" but one consisting of a rather fragile balance of elements whose equilibrium—and therefore whose identity—was in constant danger of rupture.[12]

This sense of the fragility of internal balance was retained until the end of the nineteenth century, despite the fact that Lamarck's notion of willed adaptation had been replaced by a neo-Lamarckian dogma that privileged the formative power of the environment over a willing organism.[13] Thus, in his article on "Heredity" for the *Dictionnaire encyclopédique des sciences médicales* Charles Letourneau wrote that "No doubt the descendant is the image of the parents, but that image is never a portrait. . . . One quickly discovers that in fact the fixity one sees is only apparent, a kind of resumé within a slow and constant variability, having as its outcome either the perfecting or the decadence of the so-called fixed types."[14] The decadence of which Letourneau writes here is the product of an organism's successful adaptation to a environment that is ultimately dysfunctional to it; in brief, an adaptation that the organism experiences as a pathology.

Degeneration theory reached its apotheosis in the work and career of Valentin Magnan, who was chief psychiatrist at the huge Sainte-Anne asylum in Paris from 1867 until his retirement just before World War I. In revising the nosologies for the new organic psychiatry, Magnan attempted to factor into mental diagnoses every pathology that a "degenerate" individual might conceivably have inherited from ascendants or acquired in the course of his life. These criteria entailed both an elaborate search through family trees for tainted ancestors, and a careful appraisal of the "toxins" in an individual's environment and habits—alcohol, tobacco, venereal disease, or unhygienic living or working conditions. A thorough diagnosis required a correlation of these factors, and the seriousness of an individual case was expressed by degrees of degeneration, which meant, in the sense I have been discussing it, the capacity of the organism to resist the internal and external pathogens attempting to break down its equilibrium. This capacity was invariably discussed in terms of "weakness" or "strength," as we see in Magnan's definition of degeneration as,

> a pathological state of the organism which, in relation to its most immediate progenitors, is constitutionally weakened in its psychophysical resistance and only realizes in part the biological conditions of the hereditary struggle for life. That weakening, which is revealed in permanent stigmata, is essentially progressive, with only intervening regeneration; when this is lacking, it leads more or less rapidly to the extinction of the species.[15]

Thus, beginning with B.A. Morel, a whole generation of psychiatrsts assumed that the empirical foundations of psychiatry lay, as Morel's colleague Joseph Moreau de Tours expressed it, in "... the general fact of the procreation of creatures, of living creatures, and in particular human creatures."[16] This focus on procreation led psychiatrists to an unusual emphasis on what they called the "hygiene" of marriage, in reality a kind of reproductive eugenics *avant la lettre*. Convinced that "dysgenic" couplings were responsible for perpetuating and advancing degeneration, French psychiatrists formulated justifications for intervening in family affairs to promote good hygiene.

As Jacques Donzelot has written, following the publication of Morel's *Traité,* medical texts "... grew rich in imperious advice regarding indications and counterindications for matrimony. Eugenism was not far in the future. For the doctors, it was a matter of treating sexuality as the business of the state, transcending the arbitrariness of families, morality, and the Church."[17] Thus, Dr. Ulysse Trélat urged his fellow practitioners to advise "honnêtes" families on the dangers of disastrous marital alliances, and Morel himself said at a meeting of the Société médico-psychologiques in May 1868 that it was the psychiatrist's duty "... to penetrate to the bosom of families and endeavor to overcome the scruples and secrets of the pusillanimous types who seek ... to divert the doctor from the truth. ..."[18]

Wherever it spread from its French roots, degeneration theory reflected the localistic concerns of medical culture. In Italy, for instance, the problem of amalgamating the disparate and none too prosperous populations of the postunification monarchy focused most medical attention on "degenerate" criminals, who were emblematic, in a certain sense, of the backwardness of the "atavistic" south. In industrial England, on the other hand, degenerates were bred in the great urban and manufacturing centers, amidst the poverty, the drink, and disorder, and the general immorality that flourished there.[19] But while the disease spread its debilitating poisons in Italy and England principally through the veins of the most socially marginal citizens, in France degeneration was a *national* syndrome producing a *national* disease, not a "fixed identity, but a ubiquitous process." After reviewing texts from a variety of literary *genres* from Morel to Zola, Pick concludes that, for these writers,

> it was as though degeneration might be a tragic irreversible fact of the [national] body and revolution a given condition of the race. In one sense, the French Revolution had overthrown 'Heredity', (the monarchy, the aristocracy, the religious concept of original sin), but ironically in the nineteenth-century society which emerged beyond it, hereditary *dégénérescence* appeared to have become incorporated (literally embodied) as an indeterminate potentiality of the French race.[20]

It is now well known that doctors and others in the French political and intellectual elite made use of the medical idea of degeneration to conceptualize the problems the nation faced after 1848.[21] In most cases France suffered no more from social and economic dislocations than any other industrializing and urbanizing society. But there was a particular tendency in France to consider suicide and crime, alcoholism, mental illness, venereal disease, and even tuberculosis as the behavioral and organic symptoms of a degeneracy infecting the whole population. In the mode of a degenerate heredity, the drunkenness of the father became the homicidal mania of the son; a penchant for shoplifting in the mother propelled her daughter into a life of prostitution. Inasmuch as every pathology was both a symptom of the national disease *and* a cause of future hereditary decline, there was a perfect circularity in individual and collective disease metaphors, a *grande ronde* of causation.[22]

One pathology held a special status, however, because it affected so immediately all assessments of the nation's power and vitality: France's unusually low birthrate. Beginning shortly after mid-century, those who were most concerned about this problem revived the old mercantilist obsession with "depopulation" to express their fears that biological degeneration was producing not only a poorer *quality* of human being, but smaller *quantities* as well. The demographic statistics clearly reveal the source of the anxiety. After rising throughout the early eighteenth century and leveling off at about 32/1,000 per year, the French birthrate began to fall precipitously, beginning around 1825. By World War I the rate had sunk to less than 20/1,000, and continued to decline until 1939, when it stood at an all-time low of 15/1,000 per year. Other industrializing countries experienced a similarly dramatic decline as their populations became wealthier and more urbanized, but in none of them did the rate begin to nosedive until shortly before 1900.[23] Between 1872 and 1911 the French population grew from just thirty-six to thirty-nine and a half million, while in the same period Germany grew by 600,000 a year to a size 58 percent larger than in 1872. While France had grown by only 10 percent, Italy had grown 30 percent, Austria-Hungary 38 percent, Great Britain 43 percent, and European Russia 78 percent. During one five-year period (1891–95) deaths in France exceeded births by 300, as they did in several individual years—1890, 1892, 1895, 1900, 1907, 1911—before World War I.[24]

This downward trend was not a consequence of a low marriage rate— the French married at rates as high or higher than anywhere in Europe— but of a low *marital fertility*. The "average" French family had just two children in 1914, to 2.5 and three in Great Britain and Germany respectively. It is easy enough for us to imagine how all this might have been regarded by the French as a strength, not a weakness, a sign that French parents were especially concerned with the care and provisioning of their offspring and therefore superior to their improvident neighbors. Indeed, near the end of the century a vocal "neo-Malthusian" movement argued that the benefits of a higher standard of living could be disseminated more broadly in France if authorities encouraged a distribution of the technology and information on birth control.[25] However, the far stronger and virtually unopposed reaction was the opinion expressed by the influential economist Paul-Leroy Beaulieu, who, after rehearsing the apparent advantages of small families, concluded that, "The children of our families, one or two in number, surrounded with indulgent tenderness and debilitating care, are inclined to a passive and sedentary existence, and only exceptionally manifest the spirit of enterprise and adventure, endurance and persever-ance that characterized their ancient ancestors and which the sons of prolific German families possess today."[26]

The terms in which Leroy-Beaulieu cast his remarks alert us to the two related themes that dominated the discussion of the population question in modern France. First, that France was somehow not what she used to be, and second, that Germany had become a necessary dialectical element in any assessment of French power, so that, as Claude Digeon has argued, by the end of the nineteenth century, "the German menace was regarded as the sign of French decadence."[27] Historically, German and French in-tellectuals had often measured the accomplishments of their respective cultures against those of the "other," but the equation "French decline–German menace" may be traced to a particular historical event: the battle of Sadowa in 1866. This battle, in which Prussia humiliated Austria-Hungary, permitted Otto Von Bismarck to form the North German Con-federation and thereby take the first steps toward the unification of Ger-manic central Europe. It produced an immediate reorientation in French opinion toward Germany, from relative indifference to an outspoken con-cern with their own "interior regeneration."[28]

Reformers indicated a number of things requiring attention, not least a political system still hamstrung by the dictatorship of Napoleon III. But the population, its quality and its numbers, also came up for review. In a debate at the Academy of Medicine, medical experts pronounced themselves satisfied for the present, but cautioned that the fatherland "is in danger for the future, and . . . we must remain alert and act with energy and in a spirit of patriotic foresight."[29] Lucien Prevost-Paradol, perhaps the most important spokesman for liberal reform in the era, wrote in his influential *La France nouvelle* that political reformers in France could only succeed if they took into consideration the need to maintain the country's rank in the world, committing to heart the maxim: "the number of French must rise rapidly enough to maintain a certain equilibrium between our power and that of the other great nations of the world."[30] For great nations, he warned, there was no "middle ground" between "the complete maintenance of former prestige and the most complete *impotence.*"[31]

The crushing military defeat of 1870 at the hands of Prusso-German troops merely tightened these connections in the arithmetic of geopolitics. From having been the dominant military power on the Continent for a quarter of a millenium, France was on the verge, or so it seemed, of sliding into the status of a second-rate power. In the iconography and caricature that flourished during and after the war, the "German" was often represented as a brutal and physically domineering Uhlan soldier, while "France" was pictured as a provincial maid, a victim of aggression or rape.[32] The military disaster also encouraged another kind of personification, that of the nation as a wounded body. As Ernest Renan wrote in his *La Réforme intellectuelle et morale* (1871), "A country is not a simple sum of the individuals who compose it; it is a mind, a conscience, a person, a living significance."[33] The nation is an "admirably weighted and balanced machine that creates the organs of which it has need." But, he wondered:

> Have we not, in our revolutionary ardor, gone too far in our amputations, that in believing to have cut away only the unhealthy excrescences, we have nonetheless harmed some organ essential to our life, so that our persistence in not feeling well is the consequence of some terrible wound we have made in our own entrails. That is in itself good enough cause to take a number of future precautions so that this body, which is profoundly stricken, but at bottom still robust, may repair its interior wounds and return to the normal conditions of life.[34]

The emergence of an organicist discourse of national health following the defeat of 1870 simply increased the likelihood that the geopolitical situation of France would be conceptualized in terms of the health and numbers of its population. From 1871 until well after World War II the great dramas of French history were accompanied by the *basso continuo* of *dénatalité.* In the debate over the ratification of the Treaty of Versailles in 1919, Premier Georges Clemenceau reminded the Chamber of Deputies that no treaty could save France if the French persisted in having few children.[35] Philippe Pétain, when he announced an armistice with the German invader in his radio broadcast of June 1940, mourned that France had lost the war because she had "too few children, too few arms, two few allies."[36] And Charles DeGaulle, on the eve of German defeat in March 1945, began his speech to the Consultative Assembly by saying "France, alas, lacks men and we feel this terrible void not only in terms of raw numbers, but in the matter of quality as well."[37] In a telling metaphor that linked depopulation with the German threat, Alfred Sauvy, the greatest modern French demographer, explained that population density was like atmospheric pressure. Winds, he wrote, flow from areas of high to areas of low pressure. Areas that have a high density of population will have no influence, "unless there is a depression in a neighboring area, a phenomenon similar to winds, which result not from high pressures alone, but from differences of pressure."[38]

Despite the high visibility of political rhetoric on the subject of "repopulation," the political establishment showed very little enthusiasm for using state power to directly stimulate more births. Many politicians were of course themselves highly visible practicioners of Malthusianism, and may have sensed the hypocrisy of urging others to reproduce when they themselves had small families or no children at all.[39] Moreover, doctrinaire liberals, abetted by leftist neo-Malthusians, opposed any government intervention in private matters. It was not, therefore, until 1913, despite the existence of a permanent commission in the Chamber of Deputies on the population problem, that two rather timid laws were passed giving modest financial aid to families of "numerous" children, and some medical aid to pregnant mothers.[40]

Despite the bloodletting of the war, in which France lost nearly a million and a half men, the chamber did not increase these subsidies. Legislators expressed their concern more economically, by passing a law that carried heavy penalties for abortion, for the distribution or advertisement of contraceptives, and for public acts or publications (and this was very broadly construed) encouraging any form of birth control.[41] It was only in 1939, following a decade of decline in the total population and worries about a rearmed Germany, that the government finally sponsored a *code de la famille* that expanded economic aid to married couples. But even this body of new laws, which carried over into the pro-familial regime of Marshall Pétain, was as much negative as it was interventionist, taxing bachelors and childless couples in preference to an aggressive and rational pronatalism.[42]

If one looks only at the broad lines of public policy on repopulationism, one might conclude that political paralysis had made it impossible for French governments to act decisively or plan effectively for the future, or one might simply dismiss the campaign against *dénatalité* as so much inflated rhetoric. This would overlook, however, both the extent to which the state, in many other ways, contributed to a repopulationist agenda, and the myriad expressions of public concern about the problem. After 1870, a number of policy changes were made in long-standing traditions that were believed to influence natality. Legal discrimination against bastards was repealed; after 1905 they might take the name of their biological father and be cut into a share of the patrimony. After a long and bitter fight, paternity claims were facilitated, so that even unacknowledged offspring might have access to financial support (though paternity remained noto-riously difficult to prove). Marriages between close blood relations (uncle–niece, aunt–nephew) were permitted, and the official government statis-tician began tracking the rates of marriage between cousins.[43] In the debate over the reestablishment of divorce in 1884, both opponents and supporters of the bill argued that the birthrate would be improved if they were vic-torious.[44] But in view of the worsening statistics, it seems clear enough that those who argued that divorce would permit sterile marriages to be replaced by fecund ones had the lion's share of logic and political support on their side. Divorce, therefore, might well be entered in the ledger as a piece of pro-natalist policy, even if it did not have the practical effect of stimulating the rate of new births.

Though it is not often acknowledged as such, private activity in behalf of increasing the birthrate was one of the most popular kinds of civic activism in the Third Republic. In 1896 the demographer Jacques Bertillon founded the *Alliance nationale pour l'accroissement de la population fran-çaise,* which at its height in the 1920s claimed 40,000 members. This was the umbrella organization for at least eighty other local and national groups concerned in some way with supporting and encouraging families of "nu-merous births."[45] There were in addition a large number of "purity" and "moral hygiene" organizations that agitated against prostitution, alcohol-ism, public nudity, or in favor of banning all contraceptive devices and their promotion. As I have argued elsewhere, if these groups did not bluntly premise their activity on the grounds that the evils they combatted led to depopulation, they at least claimed a healthy birthrate as a worthy goal. Doctors were proportionally overrepresented in the leadership of these groups, and often articulated the movement's aims in terms of a medical model of illness and cure.[46]

As Karen Offen has pointed out, depopulation was a major concern of the feminist movement during the Third Republic. On account of this, Catholic and republican women—enemies on many other issues—allied to obtain greater governmental support for maternity, for abandoned women and children, and for hygienic and affordable housing, making France an international leader in family benefits despite an astonishing niggardliness in other kinds of welfare.[47] Feminists were by contrast rather less insistent as a group than their English or American counterparts on the need of women to obtain full legal and political equality, because they believed they were doing their part to address a matter of national concern that fell within what they regarded as their special sphere of interest. This early orientation was more or less unique in western feminist movements. Only after 1900 did the German feminist movement, in the light of a flattening of the birthrate in the German empire, begin to deemphasize their political demands in favor of greater support for maternity.[48] Though it is tempting to regard the trajectory of French feminism as a sign of the weakness of the movement, we must acknowledge the power of the flood tide of sentiment in Third Republic France in favor of a procreative "ordre familial."

I have tried in the preceding section to show how the historical origins of the population "problem" made it virtually inevitable that the low French birthrate would be regarded as a pathology and a potential disaster for the nation. I have dealt so far with public policy and with the most visible aspects of the "repopulationist" movement in order to demonstrate the remarkable degree of public consensus the issue commanded. French men and women certainly behaved privately in ways that ran against the grain of public discourse on the virtues of large families—how else to explain the constantly falling birthrate?; but there was a notable reluctance to oppose openly a movement that was loudly patriotic, was based on good "republican" principles, and which reinforced traditional moral dogma on marriage and the family.

I wish now to examine the ways in which medical and scientific writings expressed this dominant discourse during the nineteenth and early twentieth centuries. My aim here is to show how the problems studied by experts in organic reproduction and the biological evolution of sex were a reflection of the larger issue of the health and numbers of the French population. However, the language in which these experts presented their findings reveals not only their desire to reconcile their findings about the mechanisms of fertilization with the biological doctrine of sexual complementarity they had inherited from early nineteenth-century science, but also their abhorrence of the blurring of traditional gender distinctions in contemporary society and culture. On the whole, as we shall see, they were successful in reinforcing and sharpening the sexual "difference" on which the prevailing regime of "normal" familial procreation reposed.

The effort to reinforce the old doctrine of sexual difference with data and arguments from modern science was not without its problems. French men and women were changing along with the social and economic structures of the nation. New educational opportunities and political movements produced spokesmen for different if not revolutionary versions of the relations between the sexes, and fin de siècle cultural life introduced an era of unprecedented worldiness and publicity in sexual matters. It proved virtually impossible to force "modern" men and women and their families back into the molds of early nineteenth-century patriarchy; some concessions had to be made for the wave of innovations in behavior, taste, and personal freedom. Such subjects were usually treated with ironic distance in public discourse, lest they arouse a storm of outrage such as that occasioned by Léon Blum when he suggested in *Le Mariage* (1907) that women ought to sow their wild oats in the same way as their future husbands.[49]

Nonetheless, between the extremes of libertarian and Catholic conservative viewpoints, there was ample space for scientists and doctors to construct a biomedical discourse on fertility and reproduction that articulated (without resolving) the demographic anxieties of the elite and of state officials, while also acknowledging new varieties of sexual behavior. Much of the research and writing on these subjects was inspired by two related problems. The first and probably most important was that of the drastic fall in marital fertility. The second problem is less well-known today, but attracted considerable attention at the end of the nineteenth century because it was believed to be a subset of the general problem of population decline. The official demographer noted in 1872 that there had been a steady change in the *sex ratio* of live births in the course of the century, from a masculine preponderance of about 107/100 at the start of the century to less than 105/100 in 1870.[50] The fact of a preponderance of male births was well-known to all demographers and scientists, as was the explanation that it was probably a natural compensation for the higher mortality suffered by male infants over the first few years of life. The French, however, were the first to concern themselves with the changes in the sex ratio over time.

By 1900 the ratio had reached 104/100, and lower ratios still were recorded in Paris and the major urban areas in France.[51] More worrisome still was the indication that despite a similar decline in preponderance of males elsewhere, no other European power had a ratio lower than 105/100, and these seemed to have leveled off, with, if anything, augmentations in favor of male births.[52] Within France the overall female population, which had been in the majority since Napoleonic times, was increasing its advantage over French males. Thus in 1870 there had been 17,982,511 men and 18,120,410 women, a gap of about 140,000, but this had widened by 1906 to a gap of 650,000, when 19,099,721 men and 19,744,932 women were reported.[53] Contemporary readers may be amused to see these numbers referred to habitually as the "masculinity" index, as though these declines reflected somehow on the maleness of male progenitors. But that was precisely what *was* believed. There was a marked tendency for fin de siècle observers to conflate problems of population and heredity with problems of masculinity. This is not to say that the female side of the procreation equation did not receive close attention and concern, but there was, as we shall see, an underlying anxiety that the primary responsibility for the alarming population figures fell on the men of France.

Why was this so? Part of the answer lies in the assumption of the native Lamarckian tradition—updated in the second half of the century as "neo-Lamarckism"—that heredity was a *force* of reproduction based on the strength and distribution of energy in an organism's economy; likewise, in degeneration theory, insufficient energy was both a cause and a consequence of syndromes of biological decline. In contradistinction to that position, the German embryologist August Weismann was arguing by the mid–1880s that scientists should assume the existence of an unbridgeable gap between the "germ" (sexual) cells and the "soma" (body) cells, the former being the unique and independent carriers of hereditary information. This assumption was later incorporated into Mendelian and neo-Darwinian inheritance theory, which triumphed virtually everywhere after 1900 except in France.[54]

French embryologists, for their part, were inclined to resist this bifurcation of the organism between germ and soma cells in favor of explanations of epigenetic influence and concepts of vital equilibria, which had served native physiology since the mid-eighteenth century. The presence of these theories encouraged the retention of the formative role of environmental adaptation and the corollary idea of acquired characters, which were together, for French life scientists, the sources of most variation in nature. Thus, while Weismann and his heirs could speak of the "immortality" of an organism that managed to pass on its germ plasm, French scientists like Armand Sabatier problematized the continuity of the soma, which could perish in maladaptive variations or in the depletion of the energy the organism required for reproduction.[55]

Fertilization and reproduction, Sabatier held, were two separate things, or, rather, fertilization was but a moment in a reproductive *process,* which shaped the new organism from a stage well before conception until birth.[56] French embryologists continued to favor this *epigenetic* tradition well past the time it was abandoned elsewhere in favor of neo-Mendelian genetics, which held, to the contrary, that the hereditary information contained in the chromosomes of the parents could not be influenced in any way by the intrauterine environment.[57] The French persisted in exposing embryos and fertilized eggs of various animal species to different physical influences such as temperature and nutrition to see if they could influence the rate or outcome of the developmental process or the sex ratios of new organisms.[58] The results of these experiments were ambiguous and made little contribution to the scientific revolution in genetics around the turn of the century, but they decisively confirm the belief of French biologists that an organism's sexual identity pervaded its entire being, and their hope that some way might be found to perfect its forms.

With respect to the population problem, this deeply rooted scientific outlook encouraged French demographers and biologists to regard the decline in the birthrate as a matter of organic weakness or environmental pathology, in keeping with the pessimistic determinism of degeneration theory. In his review of the vast scientific literature on the problem in 1938, Joseph Spengler concluded that among the most popular of the "involuntary" causes of *dénatalité* was the assumption of an enfeeblement of the "genetic instinct" of the "race."[59] Conceived in general terms, this reproductive debility was believed to be an effect of the progress of degeneration in the whole population, affecting men and women alike, but it was also possible to focus responsibility more narrowly by studying the generational contribution of each sex in turn.

There was a well-established tradition in France for such an enterprise with deep roots in scientific and popular culture. Self-help medical books on the mysteries of human generation had became very popular in early modern Europe. They were designed to give recipes to couples who desired to improve their fertility, or to bring about the birth of a particular sex (usually male).[60] Nineteenth-century handbooks continued this tradition, advising couples to follow a moderate regime in daily life, eschew both excessive or too infrequent sexual relations, warning against conception while ill or emotionally distraught, lest the noxious effects of the disorder pass into the child. In the style of the old humoral medicine, men were hot and dry and women cold and humid, men active, women passive. The proper combination of these things could produce foreordained results. The decisive qualities were believed to be the degree of maturation of the ovum, the vigor and number of sperm, the testicle from which the sperm originated (those from the right produced boys, the left, girls), the "typicality" of each sex's secondary sexual characteristics, their age, nourishment, and general vigor. In this schema, the favorable recipes for male births were a mature egg, plentiful semen, and vigorous sperm, the right (strong) testicle, lean nourishment, men who had "masculine" physical qualities, and women who were "typically" feminine.

Books in this genre, many authored by mainstream physicians for whom human fertility was a legitimate medical specialty, remained popular in France well into the twentieth century.[61] It is perhaps more surprising that many of the same ideas and conclusions are scattered throughout the technical biological and medical literature, as if, in contrast to the usual practice in scientific vulgarization, there was a single discourse in both specialized and "vulgar" domains.[62] If one isolates the common assumptions, it emerges that males, more often than not, are the weak link in the generative equation, both with respect to the general problem of low fertility and the specific one of a deficiency of male births in the whole population.

In the absence in the late nineteenth century of any scientifically authoritative knowledge about it, the general physiological vigor of the father was usually regarded as the decisive factor in cases of infertility or stillbirth. There was a strong commitment to the notion that, in the earliest stages of embryological development, it was the male "element" that formed the "ectoderm," of the embryo where the nervous system and circulation were located, while the egg shaped the dark and passive regions of the interior.[63] Males were thus the source of the "active" parts of the embryonic economy that were analogous to electrical force fields and hydrodynamics. As the proactive agent in the reproductive process, the male's generative material could thus be held responsible for a couple's failure to produce viable offspring.[64]

Male responsibility for the *sex* of the offspring was clearer still, because of the direct relationship that was held to exist between the masculinity and vigor of the father and the production of male offspring. This assumption was often discussed in relative terms: in conception the sex of the child was determined on the basis of which sex had the greatest "hereditary power," which amounted in practice to a vague and general estimation of the sexual vitality of each individual.[65] If a woman was significantly younger or more vigorous than her spouse, it was believed her chances were excellent to produce daughters. A man in the prime of his life, on the other hand, was far more likely to father boys, irrespective of his wife's age, on the principle that, all else being equal, the "active" reproductive principle will prevail over the "passive."[66]

Some authors claimed that a father of a numerous progeny will produce first boys, and later girls, as his "*puissance*" is gradually depleted.[67] Thus, children conceived before a man had reached his sexual prime (before his twenty-first year) or very late in life (after his fortieth) were likely to be of the female sex. The underlying assumption in this reasoning is that the reproductive force of women was more "stable" than that of men, whose generative power was normally more dependent on the natural rhythms of age and sexual vigor. The unusual decline of the "masculine" sex ratio in France was not believed, however, to be a "normal" phenomenon. On the contrary, the "debility" that had caused a drying up of male births was characterized as a general "sign of the exhaustion and regression of the race, a symptom of deplorable degenerescence," an indication that the "race was wounded in its virility."[68] Both of the worrisome aspects of the population "problem" were therefore also problems of masculinity, of a deficiency of male sexual vigor that was often linked to aged fathers or "unmasculine" men, but was also observed among men of acknowledged masculine aspect.[69]

These concerns about the "strengths" and "weaknesses" in male progenitors coincided with a major reorientation in theories about sexual reproduction and the evolution of sex that also focused greater attention on the male contribution to procreation. Until 1880 or so, researchers who looked at the vast array of reproductive mechanisms employed by living forms believed that sexual reproduction was a minority phenomenon in nature, far less important than fission, budding, or asexual spore production.[70] In the late 1870s, the first careful observations were made of a sperm fertilizing an egg, and later work showed that the egg began to develop only after nuclear material from the sperm and egg had joined together.[71] It was soon apparent that sexual reproduction was more widespread in nature than previously realized, and that its "rediscovery" solved the knotty problem that had perplexed Darwin about the source of the variations within species that were the raw material of evolution. If reproduction was to be something more than the exact duplication of a parent, as was true in asexual modes, the male gamete must be the means by which variation was produced in an egg that is only the mirror image of the "mother."

When this development was considered together with the idea of organic evolution and the "perfection" of a division of labor in organisms and societies, it produced a powerful new combination. Henri Milne-Edwards had suggested much earlier in the century that there was a natural hierarchy in nature that distinguished structurally simple and undifferentiated organisms from those where specialization of function had produced more complex and thus "higher" forms.[72] Herbert Spencer later cast the division of labor in an evolutionary framework, insisting that evolutionary processes progressed from states of "homogeneity to heterogeneity," thus making complex organisms (and societies) superior *by nature* to simpler forms. As is well known, this kind of reasoning was taken up generally by evolutionary theorists in the late nineteenth century, whether of the Darwinian or neo-Lamarckian variety, where it often served as the scientific underpinning for social Darwinist, colonialist, and nationalist ideologies.

But there were implications as well in this combination of ideas for sex, and French thinkers were quick to take them up because they seemed to reaffirm beliefs of long standing. They first concluded that asexual forms of reproduction were the earliest, and therefore the most primitive kinds. Reproduction itself, they argued, had evolved from simple fission to hermaphroditic varieties of self-fertilization, concluding with sexual reproduction, where the males and the females of the species were separate beings characterized by a high degree of physical dimorphism. This was true not only phylogenetically (in terms of evolutionary development), but ontogenetically as well (in terms of the present hierarchy of species). Thus, as Armand Sabatier put it in 1886, "In the measure that one descends toward the inferior animals who constitute present-day fauna, one will see the sexual differences between individuals disappear and their reproductive elements become increasingly uniform and capable of sufficing by themselves for reproduction."[73]

In terms of French evolutionary perspectives, this meant that *ascendant* evolution was promoted by increasing differentiation because, as Alfred Fouillée wrote, "In simple fission, A's will produce A's and B's will produce B's. But without a *marriage* of letters, one would never have obtained the Iliad or the Odyssy."[74] Any organism that gradually specialized its internal functions, including those of reproduction, was able to use its energy more efficiently for purposes of adaptation, which equipped it for the "struggle for life."[75] Just as an organism's need for nourishment drove it to perfect its digestive system, the sex drive stimulated it to economic refinements of specialization in reproduction.[76]

In his authoritative review of the literature on the evolution of sex in 1893, Alfred Fouillée explained the implications of this division of reproductive labor for species. Among humans and in most other advanced species, a salutary savings in energy had been obtained by the evolution of two distinctly different kinds of gametes in each sex. The spherical and passive female ovum represents the ultimate realization of the principle of the conservation of energy, which Fouillée called the "anabolic" principle, following the usage of Patrick Geddes and J.A. Thomson.[77] The sperm, on the other hand, represents the "catabolic" principle of *expenditure* of energy, as seen by its constant motion, agility, and hardiness. Fouillée was not shy about anthropomorphizing this distinction. As he wrote, "The egg, voluminous, well-nourished, and passive, is the cellular expression of the characteristic temperament of the mother; the lesser volume, less-nourished aspect and preponderance of activity of the father sum up the masculine element."[78]

Partly because of such language, and because in most species legions of spermatozoa competed to fertilize a single egg, it became common to speak about the egg as the "conservative" element in sexual reproduction, and the sperm as the "progressive" source of variation and change, or, as Fouillée contrasted them, "tradition" and "personal innovation."[79] The anthropomorphizing of the male and female gametes was a more or less permanent feature of technical and popular scientific works in several disciplines from the 1870s through the first decade of the twentieth century, and, in various forms, is with us still.[80]

The evolutionary forces that had produced these disparate male and female gametes worked also to differentiate the bodies and minds of men and women. There were several standard arguments based on selection

mechanisms that attempted to explain aspects of male and female difference in the second half of the nineteenth century.[81] Yet, as had been true
of the "form and function" argument of the late eighteenth century, in the
end a women's reproductive function was again the principle evidentiary
basis for her "inferiority" to men. But in the new evolutionary paradigm,
it was not the simple fact of her childbearing, which had been the source
of Michelet's earlier sentimental effusions on women, but her role in the
evolution of sexual reproduction that was decisive.[82]

Charles Darwin's theory of sexual selection, which he advanced in 1871
as an appendix to his *Descent of Man,* offered one explanation for how
dimorphism drove "progressive" evolution. Within the general mechanism
of natural selection, sexual selection explained how in some species the
"fittest" males were able to pass on their hereditary material by overawing
male rivals and sexually monopolizing females.[83] On descriptive grounds
alone, this explanation was appealing to French naturalists as evidence for
the "courage" or "hardiness" of the male sex.[84] But in its focus on how
sexual selection determined *male* qualities in species already characterized
by physical dimorphism, Darwin's theory did not convincingly address the
general problem of the evolution of sexual reproduction, or the evolutionary logic behind the qualities of females.[85] Alfred Fouillée summed up
the objections of French naturalists in revealing language. Sexual selection,
he wrote,

> is an incomplete explanation. Force and agility are not simply an ulterior
> adaptation; they are a *primordial* characteristic of masculine activity. It
> is an internal not an external determinism that has produced a division
> of functions between the sexes and the 'primary' characteristics of male
> and female, for the benefit and perpetuation of life and the species.[86]

There was something too instrumental and secondary about Darwin's
evolutionary explanation of sex difference to satisfy most French naturalists. They resisted sexual selection for the same reason that they opposed
the Weismannian–neo-Mendelian notion that the determination of sex was
made by germ cells isolated from the rest of the organism. Neither provided
a sufficiently holistic account of the links between reproduction, the orientation of the sex instinct, and the sex of the organism. Darwin's theory
slighted the complementarity of sexual identities, and Weismann's "mo-
saic" theory of inheritance separated sex from other inherited characters.
After passing the whole of the literature on sexual determinism under
review in 1913, Maurice Caullery concluded that, "If sexuality is an aspect
of the entire organism, impregnated within it, so to speak, its seat is not
only in the genital glands [in the hereditary codes of the gametes, as Weismann would have it], but may be read in every one of its organs, in an
infinite number of signs distributed throughout the organism."[87] For most

French scientists and doctors who commented on this issue, individuals were literally *saturated* with their sex.

The French were not alone in having extra-scientific motives for understanding the laws of human reproduction. Class and ethnic tensions encouraged scientists and intellectuals in all industrializing countries to search for eugenical solutions to their social problems, but most of them sought to impose "dysgenic" controls on the multiplication of undesirable populations. The general demographic dilemma of the French, however, encouraged their elite to study reproduction as a way of increasing the quality and quantity of the whole population.[88] Scientific assertions about the naturalness and evolutionary superiority of sexual reproduction directed their attention toward ways of assuring its success and discouraging dysfunctional, nonreproductive behavior.

The French quest to understand reproduction yielded the finding that all of nature obeyed iron laws of sexual attraction. This is how the argument went. The origin of the impulse could be traced back through the mists of evolutionary time to an era when a division of sexual labor gave a competitive advantage to species so organized. The adaptive value of the impulse lay in its implementation of procreation; because mutual attraction promoted the survival of the species, the aim to fertilize was assumed to be inherent within it. Since physical dimorphism was the sign and the trigger for this natural drive, it seemed logical to conclude that a species which had evolved more distinctive forms of sexual dimorphism would enjoy a competitive advantage over those which were less marked because it would breed more effectively and prolifically. An excellent maxim, therefore, for a society that wished to promote a cultural politics of procreation would be: *vive la différence.*

A politics of procreation could not expect to be effective by repeating the outmoded formulas of P.-J. Proudhon and Michelet about the virtues of keeping the "weaker" sex shut up at home. Some allowance had to be made for the modern bourgeois woman who made forays outside the home, who had more input on courtship and marriage arrangements, and who might by the late 1880s have a "separate but equal" education to her husband or brothers. In order to be practical as well as *être de son temps,* a procreative discourse needed to take note of contemporary feminist concerns, but nonetheless find some way to square the new findings about the universality of sexual affinity with an updated version of the traditional doctrine of the separate spheres. A thorough review of the vast literature and iconography advocating these views between 1880 and 1914 would alone produce a book-length study; I must be content with a brief review of the principal arguments.

One of the first books to articulate the new discourse of procreation was Dr. Henri Thulié's *La Femme. Essai de sociologie physiologique*

(1885). Thulié was a well-known medical activist who served in the Paris municipal council and edited the influential public hygiene journal *Revue philanthropique*. As a militant republican anticleric, Thulié believed that the new republic could mobilize citizens to improve the birthrate more effectively than the church had ever done. By proclaiming "La République doit-être la fécondité," a chivalrous state could help liberate women from the legal constraints that forced them into unproductive, loveless marriages, eliminate the economic hardships that forced many women into a sterile prostitution, and repress the vices and "marital frauds" (contraceptive practices) that distracted them and discouraged motherhood.[89]

But if Thulié was a legal reformer, demanding equal financial and social rights for women, abolition of the dowry system, paternity searches, and state support for maternity, he was not a believer in either full political equality or in the equality of the sexes. On the contrary, it was a premise of his brand of feminism that men and women were profoundly different as sexual beings, and that their mutual attraction and fecundity depended on maintaining this difference. How, he asked, "can we confuse force with grace, will with tenderness, logic with finesse, anger with calm, a burning and vainglorious bravery with a tenacious courage free from preoccupation with glory? Man is struggle, woman is love."[90]

According to Thulié, the morality of the Second Empire had encouraged promiscuity in men, concubinage in women, and given the French an international reputation for sexual depravity.[91] Such sexual indulgence, he argued, "feminizes" men, and makes French women into coarse "viragos," thus depriving both sexes of their *honnêteté*.[92] The "shame" of France will be expunged and the honor of both sexes restored when marriage is restored to its primacy and a woman is "able to freely chose her sire [*géniteur*]."[93] The freedom of marital choice, Thulié warned, must never be confounded with either vulgar promiscuity or a utopian legal equality. Let us consider, he asks, the monstrousness of life in a world of perfect sexual equality, where a society of hermaphroditic beings can fertilize one another, and themselves, all of whom enjoy the same aspirations, pleasures, responsibilities, and aptitudes. Ordinary human lasciviousness would be doubled, sexual exhaustion would be the rule, and for any work to be done at all, we would have to castrate some of our number, like the bees, to make a worker class.[94]

Such a nightmare of sexual homogenization, sterility, and exhaustion fueled much of the serious research on human fertilization, encouraging the search for the laws of sexual attraction that governed the chain of being from microorganisms to mammals, from the sperm and egg to the sexed adult. In 1888 the French microscopist François Maupas published the results of an experiment purporting to show that single-celled ciliates could "revitalize" themselves and increase their rate of reproduction by exchanging nuclear material in a side-by-side "conjugation." This primitive form of sexual reproduction allowed them to avoid the fate of a control group of similar creatures which were kept in isolation from one another, and which eventually died out after diminishing in size and vitality.[95]

Summing up a decade of research in cytology, the experimental psychologist Alfred Binet found a host of references in French scientific *mémoires* on the love life of "sexed" single-celled organisms. As he coyly put it: "The female pursued by the male seems to be moved by two contrary desires, one to receive the male, and the other to escape him. This refusal, which is never more than temporary, and more apparent than real, has the effect of exciting the male to deploy ever greater means to charm her."[96] Armand Sabatier was moved by similar considerations to write about the sperm and the egg as "sexed" cells, driven together by their respective "active" and "passive" natures.[97] After observing sperm cells in his microscope, G. Balbiani wrote in a memoir of 1878, "I do not think, for my part, that the spermatozoa move blindly, but that they obey a sort of internal impulsion, a will that directs them to a determined end."[98] When these willful sperm reached the neighborhood of the egg, claimed Henri Beaunis, the egg bulges out in their direction, sending out tiny wands of protoplasm to make contact and ensure penetration.[99]

There thus was a general agreement among French theorists that sexual reproduction had thrived precisely because evolution selected for difference and made reproduction dependent on it. This point was made in different ways. One was to argue that evolution "develops in each sex the qualities appreciated by the other, . . . it is thus a great advantage for the conservation of the species that the sexual elements arise, not only on different individuals, but in particular on individuals who are distinguished from one another by the very characters that affirm their sexuality."[100] But, as we have seen already, these references to the "sexual elements" did not refer to the sex glands alone, but to "a sort of total polarization of the sexed individual by means of the sexual element."[101]

Another line of argument portrayed the organic drives underlying sexual dimorphism as useful collective adaptations. This view was first espoused by Alfred Espinas, whose work decisively influenced Emile Durkheim and his school of sociology. Espinas employed the popular device of treating insect societies as a stand-in for human ones. In the course of evolutionary development, he argued, agglomerations of individuals begin to interact in such a way that selection operates on them as a unit, and selects for group characteristics, of which individuals are only the exemplars. Bees, ants, termites, and human societies are the most notable examples of this kind of evolution. Highly specialized and unique reproductive mechanisms had evolved in all of them.

Espinas's idealism inclined him against the doctrine that the laws of sexual attraction were simply organic drives implanted in individuals; he preferred to think of them as social "representations" which had evolved to ensure reproduction and group survival. Thus, the collective representation shared by the two sexes instructed each to see the other as "its virtual half which propels it toward that second part by means of an organic drive. Each is drawn to the other as to the absolute condition of its specific existence, better still, as to the condition which is its complete present existence." Despite the metaphysical language he preferred, it is quite clear that Espinas's sociology also treated sex as a thing that deeply permeated individuals. Thus, male pursuit, female coquetry, the whole panoply of the symbolic discourse of love is engraved in the female's mind,

> . . . in order to determine for her, in the measure that the effects of that representation descend into the depths of her organism, the physiological modifications necessary for fertilization. Thus, the [courtship] phenomena we have just considered are symbols, but on the other hand are also biological phenomena. For what is beauty if not organization made tangible, form breathed into life![102]

However one chose to represent the attraction of the "opposite" sexes—as a sublimation of lower instinct or as the organic expression of collective ideals—the same problematic seems to have inspired all commentators on the subject. In the words of the biologist Jacques Delboeuf, "How, at the risk of zoomorphism, do individuals of healthy and robust nations marry?" If otherwise unconstrained, they go in search of mates.

> They walk together in the streets, crowd together in salons, entwine with one another at balls, but in all these contacts that chance provides, one alone succeeds in inflaming them. Why? What are sympathy and antipathy? What is it that leads this young woman to attract that young man and precipitates her toward him? . . . they are each unknowingly obeying the will of a sperm and an egg. But let us be certain about this, this is not random in either the sperm or the egg. . . . They both know what they need and what they are looking for. To that end they give their orders to their respective brains through the intermediary of the heart, and the brain obeys without knowing why. . . . *A society whose customs and laws hinder intelligent choices dictated by the sperm and the egg is doomed to depopulation and death.*[103]

In the thirty years or so before 1914, a consensus of opinion emerged in France on the relation of sex to the population problem that cut across most other ideological differences. Thus, while one might expect feminists to deplore the social and legal conventions that worked to inhibit the "natural" procreative drives in men and women, antifeminists also applauded the return of divorce, worked to further liberalize it, and demanded an end to the system of marriage and dowery contracts that constrained men and women alike in the free choice of a mate.[104] Even the bitterest opponents of female political and legal emancipation believed that allowing greater reproductive choice would promote more "variations," "associations," and "renewals," and lead to a greater number of offspring.[105]

A similar convergence marked a related debate about the merits of the scientific effort to dissect the noble sentiment of love into its component instincts, obsessions, or chemical tropisms. Catholic or neo-Kantian commentators deplored the popularity of naturalistic "physiologies of love," which reduced the noble sentiment of love to a "genital act."[106] Their materialistic opponents mocked the hypocrisy and bad faith of religious and moral teachings on love and marriage, arguing they produced misery, not happiness, and did not correspond to the passions and drives of ordinary humans.[107] However, neither camp minimized the importance of sexual attraction to love, and both were in remarkable agreement that the aim of marriage was to procreate. Thus Léon Blum, pilloried for his suggestion that women should have affairs before marriage, should be read as arguing that the traditional matrimonial system produced not only unhappy marriages, but *infertile* ones. There was, in his words, an ominous gap between "the function [of marriage] and the organ."[108] An old man exhausted by sexual adventures forced upon a young and inexperienced girl was a recipe for anger, sexual disorder, and divorce.[109] But where the attraction was mutual, a marriage between equals in age and sexual experience would be far more stable and fertile than the monstrous arranged affairs of yesteryear.[110]

All commentators, even the most progressive feminists, were worried about the malign effects on sexual dimorphism from rapid social and economic progress, which might doom the French to sterility and national suicide. Some worried about masculine women. The feminist Jean Finot hoped that the "variability" that would appear in women who entered the male work force would be countered by "the compensatory instinct of dimorphism," which alone allows the "race to survive."[111] Opponents of feminism like Rémy de Gourmont were less sanguine. He worried about the masculinizing effects of education and sport, and mused about the dangers to the "race" of destabilizing women's natural "maternal laziness" by allowing them to assume male roles in the economy. "The duty," he wrote, "of each being is to persevere in his being [*être*] and even to augment the characteristics special to him. The duty of woman is to preserve and accentuate both her esthetic and physical dimorphism."[112]

And what of men? Were there special dangers to them from a selection "against the grain"? We have seen that women were regarded as the stable and conserving influence in inheritance, while males provided the element of variability necessary for progress. With respect to the evolution of sexual dimorphism, this meant that men varied more frequently and more radically from one another, while women were believed to cleave more closely to "type." There was a risk that a greater number of "feminine" men would be produced through the normal mechanism of evolutionary advance, or because men exhausted their sexual economies through sexual excess.[113]

By rights the continued evolution of the social and sexual division of labor should assure a proportional and general differentiation between the sexes, but since an expanded capacity for reasoned behavior was also a feature of progressive evolution, it was feared this capacity would gradually crowd out instinct, including the spontaneous urge to breed. Women, of course, were mercifully spared the latter problem, being the "least developed" of the two sexes, but not so men.[114] With men, intellect could dominate instinct to the extent that their sexual "nature" could be overridden by cerebral cognition or imagination. Thus, on the whole, commentators on the identity of the sexes were a good deal less worried about aberrations or depletions of the sexual instincts of women. Dr. Edouard Toulouse, the founder and first president of the Association d'études sexologiques, wrote in 1918 that he did not fear that the homosexuality rampant in German armies would make headway in France because French women, unlike their coarse German counterparts, were so naturally feline and coquettish that, "the charm of our women will preserve us from such sentimental aberrations."[115] The notion that female coquettishness was the best prophylaxis against male homosexuality suggests something less than burning confidence in men, a theme I will develop further in the following chapter.

In his *Physiologie de l'amour moderne* (1891), Paul Bourget expressed a less sanguine opinion. A keen student of the medical theory of degeneration, Bourget was particularly concerned with the effects of this dread syndrome on men, whose greater susceptibility to sexual exhaustion he summed up in the Latin phrase, *totus homo semen est.*[116] Bourget's book purported to be the memoirs of the dying Claude Larcher, a hapless cuckold slowly drinking himself to death. One night Larcher dines with a second generation Parisian and his son, the former robust and flushed with health, the son pasty, frail, and "devirilized." Larcher muses to himself that the causes of this decline may be found in the cerebral exhaustion brought on by fast-paced modern life, and the sexual exhaustion promoted by the sex-segregated boarding school, encouraging young men in masturbation and in visits to the "beasts of prey" who crouch in wait in brothels.[117] The chief defects of men "excluded" from normal love include impotence, timidity, and effeminate qualities a woman will never tolerate in a lover. A man must therefore husband his resources for the ordeals of courtship, because a woman wants him to "spend his treasury of energy and delicacy to conquer her, . . . to triumph over her and over rivals whom he may not equal in beauty, fortune, intelligence, or audacity."[118] As Bourget sees it, the modern war between the sexes is so vicious, and modern marriage so sterile, because the sublimations of civilization have robbed men of the sheer sexual power that once enabled them to bend womankind to their will.[119]

As much of the foregoing discussion suggests, there was much wishful thinking and some ill-concealed anxiety about the depth and reliability of the masculinity displayed by French men. Most men hoped to read in nature and evolution signs of a shoring up of traditional sexual distinctions, but there were unsettling signs in some contemporary developments that nature's plan for France might be different than elsewhere. The birthrate and the "masculinity" index continued to fall despite the expressions of confidence in the "natural laws" of sexual attraction, drawing even greater attention to the shortcomings of men as progenitors. France had need of more children, especially of more boys, and it was necessary for its most masculine citizens to engender them.[120]

As the new century dawned, the honor and survival of the nation were believed by many to be at stake. Fernand Boveret, who was to be the primary leader of the repopulationist movement between the wars, wrote in *Patriotisme et paternité* (1913) that depopulation was the "dishonor" of the French.[121] In his view, much of the responsibility for regaining that honor fell to French men. They must work collectively to raise the birthrate, and, as individuals, must strive to be "complete beings," with "high intellects" and with "physical qualities at least average for their age."[122] Dr. Sicard de Plauzolles characterized the issue in similar terms: " . . . each individual must play his part," he wrote, "in the honor and glory of the acts of intelligence, goodwill, and beauty that ennoble humanity, as well as in the shame and the infamy of egoistic and cowardly acts and the crimes that dishonor it."[123] As André Cresson summed up this naturalistic ethic, "All for the species; all by the individual; nothing for the individual."[124]

In the weakened demographic and geopolitical situation of the nation, it is not surprising that when an "ideal" or "typical" male sexual identity was invoked, those features were stressed that could contribute best to the national welfare: strength, vigor, decisiveness, courage, a manly appearance and comportment, and, of course, fertility. There is no shortage of such descriptions in the scientific literature, just as there is widespread affirmation of the need to revitalize the family as the cadre within which the next generation of warriors and mothers would be nurtured.[125] Alfred Fouillée captured the spirit of this discourse of familial regeneration perfectly when he referred to the family in 1893 as the "human trinity" of man, woman, and child, and spoke of the "equivalence in the *blood tax* demanded of men for the external defense of the nation and from maternity for the conservation and education of the race."[126]

From the late 1860s until well into the twentieth century, the shock of military defeat, the fear of depopulation, and the corrosive effects of the gender revolution focused medical and scientific attention as never before on the bodies and masculine qualities of men. Just after the Franco-Prussian war, in a widely cited article on marriage in the prestigious *Dictionnaire encyclopédique des sciences médicales,* Dr. Jacques Bertillon offered advice to a father on how to choose his prospective son-in-law. If he should display "doubtful traits of virility," a high or broken voice, sparse beard, effeminate or ambiguous physique, the wise future father-in-law should escort him to a physician. If the examinations revealed no testicles, or only one which was "shrunken and flaccid," then, Bertillon urged, "...this so-called man who is soliciting a wife may be capable of erection or lasciviousness, but not of true virility or of fertile embraces. He is someone who, if he possesses even an ounce of sense and delicacy, rare virtues in these ambiguous types, should remain innocent of the matrimonial state."[127]

6

Male Sexuality and the "Perversions" in the Fin De Siècle

The third and last aspect of Foucault's notion that the "blood" of the bourgeoisie was its "sex," is one that sprang to life only in the 1870s and 1880s, coinciding with military defeat and the founding of the new republic. I refer to the "discovery" of the sexual perversions by medical experts in France, elsewhere in Europe, and in the United States. In France, as we have seen, the tradition of medical and scientific thinking in which the myriad varieties of human sexuality were analyzed was heavily disposed to a conception of sexual identity that subsumed sexuality in sex. This identity was deeply embedded in the biological structures and processes of individuals. As the physiologist Charles Robin put it in 1883, "It is in the period of embryonic development that *sex* makes its appearance and dominates all the ultimate developmental consequences that express *sexuality. . . . Sexuality,* in a word, is subordinated to *sex.*"[1]

I have also attempted to show how scientific and popular writers on heredity reflected and reinforced the bourgeois "family order" in France by vilifying nonreproductive, nonmarital forms of sexuality that threatened to disrupt the continuity of patrimony and patriarchy, if not, strictly speaking, of patrilineality itself. In this logic, the health of the family became indissociable from the health of the nation, linked together by a widely shared set of assumptions about the dangers of a degenerate inheritance. The depth of emotional intensity with which the connection nation/family was made is apparent in the following passage from Barrett Wendell's *La France d'aujourd'hui* of 1910:

> The family is an association, if you like, a corporation or a clan. It is something more than the sum of the individuals, with their human and fallible complexities, that compose it; to ensure its safety, it has a supreme and primordial right to the devotion of all its members. The individuals who participate in its life, like those . . . who belong to a nation, may fall into nothingness, but the family itself will continue in perpetuity. Thus, every being's primary duty in life is disinterested and social, not indi-

vidual. The French are profoundly devoted to that ideal of duty. If, through the generations, they had not remained so attached to it, . . . their society would not exist in the form the past has given to it and that it is now transmitting into the future.[2]

Perhaps Jesse Pitts was not so far wrong to put the French bourgeois family on a par with the German general staff, the British Commonwealth, and other similarly enduring institutions.[3] Modern France thus presents us with the paradox of being a country that was deeply devoted to the cultural ideals of family and numerous progeny, yet whose citizens had fewer children than any other industrial society. As anthropologists have shown, in societies where the desire to have children is strong, there is only slight distinction between sexuality and fertility, and the biological sex of individuals is a primary identity.[4] In France, however, the desire for children seems to have been more of a pervasive cultural ideology than a reflection of the actual intentions and commitments of would-be parents. One can speculate that the gap between avowed ideal and actual accomplishment provoked a guilty, if unconscious, unease in many French men and women, encouraging them in projections and fantasies designed to alleviate it. Sander Gilman has suggested that the creation of sexual "others" is the product of just such psychodynamic conflicts in all historical societies. He has argued that

> As we seek to project the source of our anxiety onto objects in the world, we select models from the social world in which we function. The models are thus neither "random" nor "archetypal." . . . Every social group has a set vocabulary of images for this externalized Other. These images are the product of history and of a culture that perpetuates them. . . . From the wide range of the potential models in any society, we select a model that best reflects the common presuppositions about the Other at any given moment in history.[5]

In fin de siécle France, medical professionals were deeply involved in the construction of sexual "others." French physicians were generally active in the leadership of social hygiene and "purity" campaigns, and a remarkable number pursued medical causes in the parliaments of the Third Republic.[6] For psychiatrists in particular, there is a clear sense in which their efforts to subject dangerous individuals and illnesses to medical analysis were a reflection of individual career advancement and a desire to articulate an imperialistic professional ideology.[7] However, if doctors supplied much of the vocabulary for the process of constructing sexual "others," they were aided in the invention and dissemination of these cultural representations by public officials, literary figures, and even by the individuals who were the objects of the medical gaze.

I analyze in this chapter the nature of sexual "otherness" around the turn of the century and the meaning it held in modern French culture. As I will argue, the anxiety about the health and numbers of the population, the ideology of the family, and the "crisis" of masculinity, played large roles in where the boundary between "normal" and "abnormal" male sexuality was actually drawn. My interpretation of the medical construction of sexual perversion will reveal the closeness of the fit between the dark portents embedded in the cultural discourse of national decline, and troubling new varieties of sexual degeneracy.

Indeed, I wish to advance a stronger point still: that French psychiatrists and sexologists were encouraged by the domestic environment to represent the sexual perversions, especially homosexuality, in a unique and particularly unsympathetic way. When French sexology is contrasted with sexology elsewhere in Europe, notable differences emerge that help explain why French work in this field made only a marginal contribution to modern concepts of sexual enlightenment and tolerance. As I have argued was the case with sexual identity, bourgeois ideals of masculine honor were similarly influential in shaping the nature as well as the social response to the perversions, in this instance through the projection of keenly felt masculine anxieties onto the bodies and minds of men who engaged in unconventional sexual behavior.

To begin with, the "discovery" of the perversions was really no more than the extension and elaboration of the symptoms of degenerational insanity as these related to deviations from "normal" sexual instinct. In practice this meant that all European psychiatrists, beginning in the 1870s, incorporated aspects of the *vita sexualis* that were already regarded as abnormal or dangerous into newly ramifying nosologies of degeneracy. Masturbation, for example, which had always been deplored by doctors and accorded a causal role in a variety of mental and organic illnesses, now became a symptom of hereditary degeneration prefiguring subsequent more serious disorders.[8]

The example of masturbation also illustrates how, in this era, a perversity became a perversion. Before the advent of degeneration theory, medical practicioners referred to masturbation in traditional moral terms as a "vice" and to individuals who did it as "perverse," the implication being that the practice was undertaken by free choice and therefore culpable in the eyes of God and man. Fin de siècle psychiatrists regarded themselves as more enlightened than this, distinguishing willfully perverse individuals from those in whom incipient disease took the involuntary form of self-manipulation.[9] To the horror of more conservative colleagues, many psychiatrists even espoused the belief that masturbation was never, in itself, a cause of later illness, though it might be a symptom in a degenerate nosology.[10]

The separation of symptom from cause was more rhetorical than real, however; there were so many exceptions in which masturbation portended pathology that the distinction was practically nullified. Dr. Jules Christian, for instance, who opened his celebrated essay on onanism with the shocking claim that every (man) had masturbated at one time or another, held that masturbation provoked the onset of deadly syndromes in the young, the old, and the physically debilitated because these individuals suffered from a degree of organic *weakness* unusual in healthy adult males. When men with weak constitutions masturbated, Dr. Christian asserted, it meant that their "cerebral" (imaginative) and their "spinal" (nervous) centers of excitation were no longer in a normal offsetting equilibrium, but cooperated to produce an exaggerated and excessive avidity for sexual stimulation, though one "against the grain," catastrophically depleting an already feeble sexual economy. This fact permits us, he wrote, "to understand how onanism, which is primarily a symptom of a morbid state, may become in its turn a cause of new complications. It is a vicious circle the like of which one always encounters in pathologies."[11]

In keeping with the materialistic and reductive outlook of degeneration theory, the treatment of masturbation in "progressive" medicine was more physical than the old therapeutics, consisting of exercise, surgery, or the administration of anaphrodisiacs. In previous treatments, the moral sentiments were believed to have sufficient autonomy, even in the practiced masturbator, for the doctor to appeal to them as auxiliaries in his cure. Thus Dr. P.J.C. Debreyne wrote in 1844 that one must menace masturbators "with dishonor, infamy, ignominy, and with the horrors of the most painful, degrading and shameful illnesses. . . . "[12] However, for Jules Christian, writing in 1881, the "shame" and "repulsion" felt by an adult male after masturbation was *itself* a pathology, a morbid self-contempt that appeared automatically alongside each manifestation of sexual aberration.[13] This judgment suggests that fin de siècle doctors had come to regard shame and dishonor as intrinsic, naturalized properties of the perversions they accompanied. With respect to a "progressive" medical outlook on masturbation, it would appear degeneration theory meant one step forward, two steps back.[14]

Despite a new vocabulary and therapeutics, there were still important links between the older moral discourse on deviant sexuality and the medical language of perversion. As is clear from Christian's treatment of masturbation, perversions were still discussed in terms of excess or deficit of energy, as exemplified in the physiology of the early nineteenth century. "Normal" expenditures, which were regularly recommended, were invariably associated with a moderate regime of marital, if not procreative, coitus. Judgments about the normal and the pathological were still made in terms of infinite gradations that departed from a functional or vital average; thus, despite the adoption of a new nosological semiology of apparently qualitative type, reckonings on the degree of health or morbidity continued to be made on a quantitative basis.[15] As the physiologist Eugène Gley put it in 1884, it is precisely on account of this quantitative system of measurement that science must conclude that, "every man has, in effect, some weak point in his mind or body, and there is no such thing as an *absolutely* normal condition for the one or the other."[16]

One might legitimately have expected this evaluative tolerance to have produced a correspondingly relaxed system of classifications about what was a perversion and what was not. With no "natural" line to separate the normal from the abnormal, doctors might be reluctant to conclude that a particular kind of behavior was "sick," or that a certain number of repetitions of some action was sufficient to consider its author pathological. There is indeed some evidence that an allowance for tolerance in the measurement of individual perversions permitted greater tolerance toward individuals judged to be perverts, as I hope to show momentarily; but on the whole, and certainly in French medicine, if not Europe-wide, the presence of symptoms of perversion was often taken to be adequate proof that the individual in question was a pervert, so that a *behavior* was converted into an *identity*. Michel Foucault has nicely captured this moment in the history of sexuality, when, in his words, medical specialists sought to locate sexual abnormality, the better to help contain it, but ended by giving it

> . . . an analytical, visible, and permanent reality: it was implanted in bodies, slipped in beneath modes of conduct, made into a principle of classification and intelligibility, established as a *raison d'être* and a natural order of disorder. Not the exclusion of these thousand aberrant sexualities, but the specification, the regional solidification of each one of them. The strategy behind this dissemination was to strew reality with them and incorporate them into the individual.[17]

Individuals who engaged in masochistic or sadistic behavior, performed acts of exhibitionism or necrophilia, or who evinced powerful fetishistic attractions for objects or persons of the same sex became, in the medical cosmology, and in popular culture, masochists, sadists, exhibitionists, necrophiliacs, fetishists, or inverts (homosexuals). In the course of the last decades of the nineteenth century and the first few of the twentieth, a discourse of deviant sexual identity appeared that has long since burst the bonds of the narrow medical context in which it was constructed; it thrives among us still in the form of code words that presume, as did those of medical degeneration, to sum up whole persons under the aegis of their sexuality.[18]

I wish to contend here that this process of medicalizing and pathologizing sexual identity was more widely and deeply developed in France than elsewhere in Europe in the years around the turn of the century. The model of the perversions that French doctors favored, particularly as it applied to homosexuality, differed in important respects from ones adopted elsewhere, and was considerably less generous in its judgments. I have already discussed some of the reasons why French medical scientists placed such a high value on marital, reproductive sexuality and disapproved of nonprocreative behavior. These same reasons, I will argue here, shaped the medical effort to locate and analyze the perversions near the end of the nineteenth century.

The founders of modern sexology sprang from all the European nations and America. The most influential of them wrote huge compendia of medical knowledge, like Richard Von Krafft-Ebing's *Psychopathia Sexualis* (1886), Magnus Hirschfeld's *Die Homosexualität des Mannes und des Weibes* (1914), Havelock Ellis's multivolume *Studies in the Psychology of Sex* (1897–1910), or conceptually important memoirs like Sigmund Freud's seminal *Three Essays on the Theory of Sexuality* (1905). All these writers, and many of their less famous contemporaries, were more or less consciously seeking to create a new medical specialty within psychiatry, enriched by data drawn from psychology, anthropology, history, and the arts, but whose foundations would be firmly anchored in medicine and its auxiliary sciences. Historians who have reconstructed the development of sexual science have sometimes taken at face value its claims to be a normative science built on a common body of international research and experimentation, despite their doubts about the new field's objectivity.[19]

But there are signs that the French, who produced a huge body of writing on sex and sexuality, were out of step with the mainstream of the new field. On the first page of his *Three Essays,* which appeared in 1905, Freud acknowledged the writers on whom he had most depended in his book's first section on "The Sexual Aberrations." Krafft-Ebing, Kurt Moll, Hirschfeld, and Ellis are cited, but no French work appears alongside them, this despite Freud's having spent the academic year 1885–86 in Paris at the feet of the celebrated neurologist Jean-Martin Charcot, who set the young Viennese on the track of the sexual etiology of hysteria.[20]

Arnold Davidson has argued persuasively that fin de siècle sexology employed a new style of psychiatric reasoning that invented the "modern" concept of sexuality as distinct from the older notion of an undifferentiated procreative instinct embedded in the (biological) sex of men and women.[21] The epistemological rupture represented by this distinction made it possible for enlightened doctors like Freud to break with traditional notions of aberrations as deviations from heterosexual and reproductive norms, and to regard sexual perversions tolerantly as natural variations produced in the course of childhood development.[22]

A corollary of this new departure, according to Davidson, was the replacement of an anatomical style of reasoning by a psychological one, so that the anatomical signs doctors once took to be stigmata of a hereditary degeneration were succeeded by a new symptomatology of drives, inner states, and consciousness. As a consequence, sexual variations were de-constituted as disease entities produced within a degenerational syndrome. Though they remained aberrations, it was now only in relation to a statistical, not a teratological norm, so they could be regarded thereafter as kinds of love appropriate to particular circumstances that coexist with the "normal sexual aim" and that were truly pathological only when they wholly displaced it.

The problem with this otherwise persuasive account is that it does not apply to French "sexology," if we may group French writers on sex and reproduction under that rubric. The older "style" of psychiatric reasoning persisted well into the twentieth century in the French literature, including attachments to "heterogenitality" and anatomical models. The French "anomaly" casts some doubt on Davidson's other claims, in particular the abruptness of the rupture in theoretical outlook, but on the whole, Davidson's version of the history of sexology provides a useful point of contrast with developments in France. Why, then, did British and Germanic sexologists make a conceptual breakthrough that was apparently ignored by their Gallic colleagues?

To an extraordinary extent late nineteenth-century sexology was associated closely with movements aimed at sexual reform, in particular with efforts to abolish or revise harsh laws proscribing homosexual behavior. In some cases men who were themselves homosexuals, Magnus Hirschfeld in Germany and Edward Carpenter in England, initiated these movements, combining political activity with efforts to gather and disseminate enlightened medical knowledge on homosexuality.[23] Hirschfeld's Scientific Humanitarian Committee, founded in 1897, lobbied openly for homosexual rights and issued a yearbook devoted to the study of "intermediate sexual types" (*Sexuelle Zwischenstufen*) that was a sourcebook of medical information for sexologists elsewhere. The Institute for Sexual Science, set up by Hirschfeld in Berlin in 1919, sponsored writing and research until 1933, when the Nazis burned the library, and closed it down. Hirschfeld was by far the most public figure of all the early sexologists, appearing in the celebrated Harden–Eulenberg trials as an expert medical witness, cultivating Social Democratic politicians, and agitating tirelessly for reform.[24]

More typical of the style of sexology were the technical compendia of medical authors like Krafft-Ebing and Havelock Ellis, who argued the case for the repeal of repressive legislation while presenting more or less positive accounts of "sexual inversion" or "antipathetic sexual instinct." While they did not confine their writing to homosexuality, much of their motivation to write sprang from the conviction that homosexuality was in large measure a congenital condition which deserved treatment or even benign neglect rather than penal sanction. Of the major western powers, only Germany, Austria, and England had such repressive legislation at the end of the nineteenth century. The infamous German article #175 was conceived for the new legal code of the German Empire in 1871. It forbade public or private "unnatural acts" between men, understood at the time to be anal intercourse.[25] The Austrian law was very similar in nature, and Krafft-Ebing was alarmed to note a trend in jurisprudence toward convicting individuals even for "coitus-like acts."[26]

In England there had been an antisodomite law on the books since the sixteenth century carrying the death penalty, which claimed numerous victims into the 1840s. In a law of 1861 the death penalty was reduced to a ten-year sentence, but this development was followed by the Criminal Law Amendment Act of 1885, which broadened the definition of punishable acts to include "gross indecencies," the grounds for Oscar Wilde's celebrated 1895 conviction, and yet another law followed in 1897 on homosexual solicitation.[27]

Noting that women were seldom prosecuted, Ellis and Krafft-Ebing largely confined their pleas for juridical nonresponsibility in behalf of male homosexuals.[28] They carefully established their cases for nonresponsibility in behalf of a certain kind of homosexual. Their ideal type was not led to his practices through willful depravity and did not engage in public display; he resembled other men outwardly, often married and had children, but was sexually attracted only to his own sex.[29] They both stressed that inverted sexual instinct was "abnormal," but not a disease; it was instead a variation in a range of natural possibilities.[30] Each author also sought to raise the physiological status of homosexual sexual relations to the same level as that of heterosexual relations by arguing, as Krafft-Ebing expressed it, that the homosexual *vita sexualis,* "may proceed with the same harmony and satisfying influence as in the normally disposed."[31]

Freud's *Three Essays* seems to fit well into this essentially reformist tradition. Freud does not make the direct pleas for legal change made by Hirschfeld, Ellis, and Krafft-Ebing, but he begins his book with a lengthy discussion of inversion, making many of the same arguments about the "mental masculinity" of male inverts and stressing their essentially normal anatomy.[32] He concludes his initial section by arguing, "Experience of the cases that are considered abnormal has shown us that in them the sexual instinct and the sexual object are merely soldered together—a fact we have been in danger of overlooking in consequence of the uniformity of the normal picture where the object appears to form part and parcel of the instinct."[33] My point here is that, though the writings of these early sexologists dealt with the whole range of the so-called perversions, not always, incidentally, in a complimentary way, the engines that drove them and the public movements that made use of their findings concerned the legal repression of homosexuals and pleas for a new regime of medical expertise in sexual "crimes."

It had long been standard procedure for psychiatrists and forensic specialists to advance deterministic, often highly materialistic explanations in behalf of insanity pleas or in favor of diminished legal responsibility. This had been done successfully throughout Europe and America for serious forms of mental illness in the course of the nineteenth century.[34] Essentially, this was what was being urged in behalf of sexual inverts, "urnings," and homosexuals. The task was complicated by the difficulty, which these authors overcame in different ways, of making a sound argument for psychic determinism while attempting at the same time to destigmatize homosexual behavior by minimizing the difference between "normal" and "abnormal" sexual behavior. It is therefore no accident that homosexuality, portrayed in a more or less favorable way, was a crucial feature of these early works, and that their authors were nearly altogether English, German, or Austrian.[35]

In view of the pioneering role played by French doctors in the movement toward a more humane treatment of the insane in the nineteenth century, one might have reasonably assumed they would move in a similar direction. But they did not. French doctors were conspicuous by their absence from Hirschfeld's international Scientific Humanitarian Committee.[36] There was virtually no medically-led homosexual rights agitation in France until after 1945, and then only of a tentative kind.[37]

Part of the reason for this inactivity was the very "liberality" of the Napoleonic Code on sexual crimes. The code punished only forcible rape, child molestation, and "outrage" to public decency; it laid down no penalty for sodomy or homosexual acts, indeed did not mention them by these or any other name. This silence was not one inspired by horror. In matters of sexual comportment, the code followed the same noninterventionist libertarianism that had informed the civil rights agenda of the Declaration of the Rights of Man: "All that is not expressly forbidden by the law is permitted."[38] More out of a consistent vision of the law than for any other reason, no major statutory emendations were made respecting homosexual behavior until a relatively mild law of 1941 under the Vichy regime.[39] What rights might discontented homosexuals or their medical allies claim in an atmosphere of such legal forbearance?

This is not to say that the authorities were unable to use the law against homosexual practices when they wished. Article #330 on "public outrage" was used throughout the nineteenth century against homosexual prostitution. This part of the code replaced the sodomy law that that been used as the legal pretext for arrest and conviction in the Old Regime.[40] Article #331 on child molestation might well have been designed by the framers of the code to counteract pederasty, a practice that was regarded in law and in popular culture as qualitatively distinct from sodomy at the turn of the nineteenth century.[41] Indeed, tolerance for this practice lessened in the course of the century, exemplified by the advance of the age of minority in this crime from eleven to thirteen years old in 1863.

As a general rule, however, the state seldom used the criminal law as its entering wedge into the domain of private sexuality. Unlike the regulation of sexuality in the Anglo-Saxon legal tradition, French law respected the distinction between private and public sexual behavior, for the most part confining its efforts at law enforcement to the latter domain. This had also been so in the Old Regime, when the *brigade des moeurs* conducted its sweeps through the public parks and other sites popular for homosexual encounters.[42] From what we can tell, the homosexual vice squad that was formed under the Second Empire by the police prefect F. Carlier aggressively pursued its mandate to round up homosexual prostitutes and pederasts, but did not interfere with acts unlikely to be the occasion for chance public witness.[43]

The legal and police discrimination between public and private was mirrored, perhaps shaped, in practice by a social distinction between rich and poor, between those who had the time and means to conduct their erotic relationships in private, and those whose sexual lives were more exposed to view. Thus, lower-class homosexuals were arrested routinely in vice squad raids on public urinals, but by the end of the century there is considerable evidence that upper-class homosexuals and lesbians benefited sufficiently from their relative legal invulnerability to attain a kind of tolerated status in elite life. It is nonetheless unlikely, as Eugen Weber has implied, that homosexuality and other "fashionable perversions" were simply exotic identities casually assumed by bored or esthetically inclined *poseurs* for their shock value.[44] An identity lightly worn is not necessarily one lightly chosen.

The multifaceted social and cultural life of fin de siècle Paris permitted a greater range of personal expression than had been possible at any earlier time in the capital or in contemporary provincial life, but there were definite limits on the forms these expressions might take, and these limits were not enforced by the law, but by opinion. There is reason to believe that homosexuals themselves took careful note of this fact and conducted themselves accordingly. For the discreet homosexual male, there was little need to fear direct police intervention in his private life; he had much more to fear, however, from the judgments of his fellow citizens about the *quality* of his masculinity.

It is my argument here and in later chapters that in this era assessments about a man's masculinity took on an unusual importance in social life. At least for middle and upper-class men, being anatomically "of the male sex" was necessary, but was not in itself sufficient to satisfy the ideals of masculinity articulated routinely in public discourse, a point I will illustrate by examining how contemporaries discussed sexual identities and practices that deviated from the norm of heterogenital relations. Medical language and reasoning played an important though not exclusive role in shaping this public discourse in France, as it did elsewhere in Europe and America. It is my view that the case for the distinctiveness of the French outlook on sexual deviance may be most readily demonstrated by examining this medical language and reasoning in some detail. In arguing thusly, I do not wish to be understood to be attributing to doctors or to medical discourse a sovereign power to shape the norms of society. It seems clear enough that the professional status and public mission of medical science gave its practitioners a unique leverage on the subject of sexual aberration, but my aim here is to demonstrate, as I have already suggested, that the medicalization of sexual deviance, particularly male homosexuality, took different forms in France than elsewhere in Europe and placed its emphasis on different things.

It is important to note that the late nineteenth-century medical conception of homosexuality was constructed in France without benefit of the word *homosexual*. Claude Courouve has shown that the word (*homosexualität*) was a neologism coined by a German-speaking doctor, K.M. Benkert in 1869. The term circulated in German medical circles for a number of years and did not become current in French as *homosexualité* until the late 1890s.[45] Until that time, and indeed for many years afterward, French doctors discussed male same-sex love in ways that built on older words or medical models. Before the coining of *invert* in 1882, the two favored words were *pederasty* and *sodomy*. Pederasty seems to have been regularly used to refer to the seduction of boys by adult males, and was a staple term of forensic medicine, but by the end of the century was used occasionally in connection with adult homosexuality, provoking objections from etymological purists like André Gide.[46] Sodomy had an imprecise and old-fashioned biblical quality that made it more popular in literature than in science. Once invert began to be applied to adult males, sodomy was used more exclusively to refer to bestiality.[47] The term *uranist*, or *urning*, coined by the German jurist Karl-Heinrich Ulrichs in the early 1860s never caught on in French, nor did the concept of "the third sex," which was popular among German sex reformers.[48]

Perhaps just as important as words in constructing the modern concept of male homosexuality was the traditional model of sexual types based on the spectrum I discussed in chapter 4. As we have seen, French doctors associated unmanly sentiments and effeminacy with men whose genital morphology or secondary sexual characteristics placed them near the "hermaphroditic" center of the spectrum, where male and female characters were mixed together on a single body. The German medical tradition also relied on such a spectrum, but whereas German sex reformers like Ulrichs and Hirschfeld saw a "third sex" that deserved special tolerance by both law and medicine, French doctors looking at a hermaphrodite saw an effeminate male.[49] This distinction is crucial. I have already argued that a biologically conceived notion of sexual identity was embedded in the presumptions of the French civil code about two *régimes* of rights in civil society, one male and one female, on which doctors were called to testify as expert witnesses. It was on this venerable conception of the hermaphrodite as an effeminate male (or, in the case of lesbians, a masculine female) that nineteenth-century doctors made their case for a new kind of homosexuality.

The continuing influence of the old teratological model of sexual type had two important effects on medical theorizing about sexual deviance. First, it encouraged doctors to look for physical signs and anatomical irregularities as symptoms, and to see these, in the Lamarckian manner, as both the effects of vice, *and* as expressions of sexual identity. Ambroise Tardieu, the French physician who presided over the Paris police prefecture's medical station, claimed in 1857 that the pederasts picked up from public urinals possessed penises shaped like those of dogs, while their passive partners had the rounded and soft contours of women.[50] In Tardieu's view, and in the eyes of his medical contemporaries, the "active" mode corresponded to the masculine and the "passive" to the feminine types, as was the case with heterosexuality.[51]

These ludicrous assertions were modified as psychiatrists gradually replaced the older system of anatomical classification with a psychological one.[52] However, when the dog-penis was eliminated from the nosology of pederasty so were the masculine features of the "active" partner in the pederastic act, so that by the late 1880s it was held that just engaging in such activity, "weakened the characters of the vigorous, made the most solid types effeminate, and gave rise to cowardice. It snuffs out in those who still possess them the vestiges of the noble sentiments of patriotism and family."[53] In the new system of behavioral and psychological classification, the physical signs of the sexual hermaphrodite no longer enjoyed a privileged status, but the inner dispositions and tastes of the hermaphrodite/eunuch were present still.

The second influence of the old teratological model was expressed in a continuing focus on impotence, which remained, in all later theorizing about sexual aberration, the pivot separating the normal from the pathological. Hermaphrodites, we may recall, were functionally and anatomically impotent. There was believed to be a continuum on the male side of the spectrum of sexual type that connected the most potent and "masculine" types at one end with the impotent hermaphrodites at the other. In theory, the vast majority of men fell somewhere between these two extremes, and in fact there was a mountain of clinical evidence on episodic or partial impotence to underscore the point. Clinicians also maintained that though many cases of impotence were congenital or the result of accident, the majority of them were related in some way to neurological disorders. This conviction, which was well-established early in the nineteenth century, was the basis for all psychiatric commentary on the condition.

The starting point for the psychiatric analysis of impotence was Etienne Esquirol's invention of the disease of erotomania, which he discussed in his classic *Des Maladies mentales* of 1838.[54] For Esquirol and his pupils, erotomania was a serious and invariably delusional disease that focused the attention of its male victims on a single object of erotic desire, a kind of obsessional *idée fixé*. Physicians treating impotence were not often confronted with delusional patients, but the concept of a deflected and improperly focused genital drive was a useful one that they adapted to their own ends. Dr. Félix Roubaud cited a case from his colleague Dr. Jean-Louis Alibert of a young artist who complained of impotence with women. The young man discovered an extreme sexual excitement at drawing the forms of nude men, a practice that coincided with his first symptoms of impotence. This was not, Alibert observed, a case of "vulgar" sodomy, because the bodies of living men did not move him, but was a situation in which the patient, "had so *inverted* the application of his talents that he no longer knew how to return them to their proper object."[55] Alibert treated his patient by requiring him to draw pictures of women's bodies; by degrees, "nature" triumphed over his "artificial penchants."

Roubaud, whose text we have already analyzed, concluded of this case that it was an instance of "complete perversion" successfully cured by treating the mind rather than the body, but he averred that "incomplete perversions" were much more common. In these cases the organic function and external stimulus were "normal," but the imaginative faculty was momentarily focused elsewhere, and this distraction was sufficient to produce momentary impotence.[56] As we have seen, the medical justification for calling this kind of impotence a "perversion" was the belief that it was the result of a pathological splitting of the genital drive, where the natural object of the drive was replaced by an inappropriate one. If one may use the as yet unarticulated Freudian terminology for this phenomenon, impotence was the revenge the body exacted for this deviation from the normal aim and object of the drive.

In the psychiatry of the 1870s and 1880s, a growing appreciation of the extent and influence of these kinds of perversions attracted the attention of specialists. As Michel Foucault has indicated, it was this investigation that led to the discovery of sexual fetishism. Sex, he has written, was

> referred to an instinct which, through its peculiar development and according to the objects to which it could become attached, made it possible

for perverse behavior patterns to arise and make their genesis intelligible. Thus, "sex" was defined by the interlacing of function and instinct, finality and signification; moreover, this was the form in which it was manifested, more clearly than anywhere else, in the model perversion, in that "fetishism" which, from at least as early as 1877, served as the guiding thread for analyzing all the other deviations. In it one could clearly perceive the way in which the instinct became fastened to an object in accordance with an individual's historical adherence and biological inadequacy.[57]

Foucault does not document this assertion, nor justify the year 1877 as a point of epistemological rupture, but the medical literature is generally supportive of his argument, and the date is at least an arguable approximation. At this time what later became more popularly known as the sexual perversions were usually characterized as kinds of "reasoning insanities" (*folies raisonnantes*), to distinguish them from more debilitating delusional illnesses. Doctors believed that these diseases were organic in origin, but expressed themselves only as obsessions with certain ideas or in compulsive behavior, leaving general cognition otherwise unharmed. In 1876 the forensic psychiatrist Henri Le Grand Du Saulle presented a paper to the Société Médico-Psychologique in which he discussed several cases of these "reasoning insanities." Among them was a well-educated young man of twenty years with "contemplative tendencies," who felt repulsion for women in general and found himself attracted "invincibly" to images, tableaux, and statues featuring nude men and male genitalia. He was arrested one day in a public urinal in the Place de la Bourse in reciprocal genital exhibition with an elderly man.[58] Le Grand Du Saulle seemed confused about how exactly to diagnose this individual, other than to suggest he suffered from a "genital perversion"; but the similarity to the case cited by Roubaud is striking.[59]

The model, if not the term for the fetishistic nature of sexual perversions was provided a few years later by the classic paper of Jean-Martin Charcot and Valentin Magnan entitled, "Inversion du sens génitale." A second section published shortly thereafter added the words, "and other sexual perversions."[60] In this paper, Charcot and Magnan argue that in order to prove that, "the form taken by these obsessions modifies in no way the basis of the illness, we are going to present some observations of genital perversions different from the inversion of the genital sense." Although they might appear to be different illnesses, "they are simply some of the semiological variations that degeneracy presents to us."[61] These "different" perversions are what we have since come to know as classic sexual fetishes: obsessions with night bonnets, aprons, shoes, and shoe nails.

It is clear that for Charcot and Magnan, "inversion," a term they coin here, is simply a genital perversion in which the genital appetite has fixed itself on a person of the same sex, a point not heretofore appreciated in the history of homosexuality.[62] The authors reveal their debt to the medical tradition by explaining these perversions to be consequences of masturbation or sexual exhaustion, which have "weakened" the "natural" instincts and opened the door to obsessive ideas.[63] All the victims of these perversions are impotent except in the presence of the object of their desire; even so their orgasms are weak and are usually accomplished without genital manipulation. Commentators elsewhere who made use of Charcot and Magnan's findings made the same connections between these sorts of perversion and functional impotence.[64]

It is a striking fact that Charcot and Magnan felt obliged to view these (fetishistic) perversions as, "the degrading consequences of a weakening of morals in a profoundly vitiated society."[65] This argument, which would be amplified in subsequent medical discussions of these same phenomena, testifies to the unease medical specialists felt about identifying and analyzing forms of behavior that recalled the excesses and sexual peculiarities of Imperial Rome, and which seemed to be analogous, in their manifestations of impotence, to the cultural and political exhaustion of ancient society.[66]

It was not until 1887 that Charcot's student Alfred Binet finally gave a name to these strange perversions. Binet published "Fetishism in Love" in the prestigious *Revue philosophique,* thereby ensuring a wide audience for his synthesis of the technical literature. As had Charcot and Magnan before him, Binet set the whole problem of fetishism against the background of cultural crisis and biological exhaustion. The very appearance of these multiple erotic attachments, he wrote, is the consequence of the unique need, "so frequent in our epoch, to augment the causes of excitation and pleasure. Both history and physiology teach us that these are the marks of enfeeblement and decadence. The individual does not look for strong excitations with such avidity save when his power of reaction is already in a weakened state."[67]

Binet admitted that all love was to a certain extent fetishistic. How else, he asked, could we account for the odd pairings we see between ugly and beautiful individuals? But in some predisposed beings a "hypertrophy" in the normal level of genital excitement occurs, and, often by accident, the full attention of the erotic impulses is focused on a single feature or object, a true perversion of the genital instinct.[68] Eventually, the obsessive attention that fetishists paid to a particular feature of the loved one, an article of clothing, or, worse still, an inanimate object led to a "psychic impotence" culminating in degeneracy and sterility. Though Binet agreed with Charcot and Magnan that a "perverse predisposition" was the "characteristic fact" of fetishism, he insisted that heredity alone could not explain the particular attachment each fetishist displayed, because the origins of an individual fetish harkened back to some accident in the victim's psychic past.[69] In the minds of these French pioneers, therefore, the only difference between an invert and a boot fetishist was a variation in life experience.[70]

Binet was scornful of the modern penchant for cosmetics, which he regarded as an unhealthy incentive to fetishistic attachments, where the lover fixes his attention on the artificial rather than the real, on the actress rather than the woman hidden behind the mask.[71] True love, he argued, was a kind of symphony, an emotional "polytheism" which celebrated all the glories of the beloved, not an impoverished "monotheism," which focused impotently on a single unworthy object. "Normal love," he wrote, "leads always to the deification of the whole individual, a natural enough consideration *given its aim of reproduction.*"[72]

In view of psychiatrists' willingness to acknowledge the role that fetishes played in normal love, it is interesting to consider where in practice they drew the line between normal and pathological manifestations of these attachments. In theory fetishism concerned an overvaluation of an object that normally came in for a more modest share of erotic attention. Thus, the degree of exaggeration of the attachment—a wholly quantitative evaluation—might have formed the basis of such judgments, but in practice the appropriateness of the object and the aim weighed heavily in the balance. Necrophilia, bestiality, masochism, sadism, and exhibitionism were in one sense exaggerations of affections and experiences most persons normally experienced, but the psychiatrists who analyzed these acts as fetishistic phenomena regarded even the faintest gesture in their direction to be deeply pathological.[73]

Other cases were harder to decide, but Dr. Emile Laurent had no difficulty concluding that a young student from an excellent family who fell passionately in love with a barmaid was manifestly ill, since "it is shameful to love someone whom one does not wish to marry."[74] The sociologist Gabriel Tarde also concluded that "morbid love" was a matter of "nature" as well as degree, and this latter category was violated when the reproductive "ends of nature are not served."[75] In general, psychiatric observers agreed, there had been an explosion in the fin de siècle in the number of sexual fetishes, and in the ardor with which they were pursued. Both things were symptoms of a grave disorder. As Charles Féré put it, "The sexual preoccupations [of individuals] are often in inverse ratio to their sexual powers. Nations that perish through sterility are remarkable for licentiousness."[76]

The stern tone taken by medical commentators was generally mitigated, however, when the subject was confined to the erotics of "normal" heterosexuality. Some doctors held, for instance, that even where a man's love for a woman was not medically suspect, there was invariably a fetishistic element underlying it that was the "keystone" to the structure of the sentiment. Just as a clever women knew how to employ her lover's fetish to keep his love alive, a doctor might make a man's fetish the therapeutic key to his sexual dysfunction.[77] Dr. Emile Laurent underscored this point when he asked,

> Have you ever contemplated at the National Museum of Naples the Venus Callipyge, that divine piece of marble which throws off sparks of life, grace and love? Is it not the most beautiful, the most life-like, the most voluptuous, the most desirable of antique Venuses? In the presence of that incomparable spectacle the fetishism of buttocks is self-explanatory, for it is highly unlikely that all the admirers of the Venus Callipyge are sick.[78]

As this quotation suggests, in all the medical literature on sexual fetishism, the fetish was an aspect of the male gaze. Males alone were believed capable of a *subjective* orientation toward sexuality; women, though they were regarded as eminently capable of *subjectivity,* were simply the objects of this gaze. This supremely male outlook was reinforced by the belief that fetishistic perversions arose when the sexual drive was depleted through overuse or was congenitally weak. The "normal" reproductive aim inherent in the enfeebled drive could be overridden, wherein the mind assumed, by default as it were, the power to deflect the instinct in abnormal directions.[79] The supreme irony of this development is that it affected men more readily than women, because, as we will recall, men were believed to be more evolutionarily advanced than women. The male's superior intellect and capacity to reason, strengths in the struggle for survival, were liabilities in love. In the words of Dr. Julien Chevalier, women are more instinctive, and so "resemble one another in love, while men, more conscious, more cerebral, love in a particular and personal fashion. This is, in the end, one of the reasons that the instinct is more fragile in men, insofar as complexity is synonymous with instability."[80]

In keeping with this conviction, the invert in the medical literature was nearly always a male; whether innate or acquired, sexual inversion was part of the larger family of fetishes. Paul Garnier wrote of a "homosexual fetishism," and Georges Saint-Paul referred to inversion as an exaggeration of male friendship in a morbid guise.[81] The direct consequence of the adoption of the model of the fetish by French psychiatry is that homosexual desire was invariably characterized as a weakly pallid version of "normal" love, not a simple inversion of heterosexual love grafted onto sexual instincts of normal power, as the term *invert* might suggest. French medicine was reluctant to attribute to a male homosexual an *innate* attraction for his own sex. Doctors preferred to believe that the invert's weakened vital force and tepid genital instincts left him in a state of relative sexual indifference, and therefore prey, as we have seen, to "cerebral passions" that might produce "monstrous attachments." We hear clearly in this characterization the echo of the old teratological formula for hermaphrodites and eunuchs. For Paul Garnier the man attracted to other men was an effeminate and impotent hermaphrodite. Even the "most reasonable" of these so-called men was, "wounded in his pride, degraded in his intelligence, deviant in his moral life, afflicted with genital perversions of the most hideous kind, and marked by genital anomalies."[82]

The inability of inverts to engage effectively in heterosexual reproductive relations was a sign in this medical system of their sexual inferiority. Doctors denied to all inverts and fetishists the capacity for true potency, because their orgasms were dependent on abnormal sexual stratagems or objects. Even the interest of such beings in sex was considerably under the average, notwithstanding their occasional bouts of obsessiveness; their orgasms, when they had them at all were troubled by hyperesthesia or "irritable weakness" (premature ejaculation).[83] Because of the unusual demands it made on their sexual economies, coitus with a woman caused inverts to suffer a profound exhaustion that often endured for several weeks.[84] Finally, in the most extreme cases, or as a consequence of galloping degeneration, the invert assumed a wholly passive or oral position in sexual encounters, experienced little pleasure, and enjoyed no orgasm.[85] Thus homosexual love was practically a contradiction in terms; when it could be sustained at all, it was often "platonic," or consisted of mutual caresses leading nowhere in particular.[86]

As I have already noted, inverts, with their weak genital drives, were presumed in advance to be effeminate in appearance, in manner, and in tastes, so that the appearance of any of these "symptoms" was set down as clinical evidence for the condition. Many doctors acknowledged that episodes of homosexual behavior in youthful sex-segregated situations did not automatically provoke effeminization in its participants.[87] But the appearance of feminine qualities in adult males was a universally recognized sign of a congenital or acquired sexual disorder, of which inversion was the most common type.

Doctors who praised the "feminine" qualities of sensitivity, tenderness, and steadfastness in women, presented these same features in men in the most negative way imaginable. Effeminate men were held to be "timid,"[88] "wicked and pusillanimous,"[89] or to be "fearful, and lacking in the grandeur of mind and spirit that undertakes vast enterprises or spontaneously expresses courage and devotion."[90] Louis Thoinot deplored their vanity, their tendency to gossip and commit "indiscretions." Julien Chevalier found inverts to be "capricious, envious, and vindictive," given to lying, men for whom, "writing an anonymous letter is the most exact expression of their courage."[91] Emile Laurent characterized inverts as "incomplete men and failed women" (*homme incomplet, femme manqué*), a sentiment echoed by Louis Reuss in his description of the invert as, "capricious, vain, cowardly, envious, vindictive, susceptible, uniting all the flaws of a woman without balancing them off by any of the qualities of a man; thus he will be detested equally by both sexes."[92]

In Georges Saint-Paul's account, homosexuals were either "born inverts" (incurable) or "feminoform," a condition which, depending on the degree of hereditary predisposition, was potentially reversible. In his scheme, the degree of pathology corresponded directly to the degree of feminized behavior, so that by definition, the "male" character in a typical homosexual union was of the "accidental" or "occasional" type.[93] Saint-Paul questioned the "courage" of men who engaged in homosexual relations because they typically sought out domestics, soldiers, and other men whom they were likely never to see again. This, he alleged, was also characteristic of the "timidity" of men who seek the company of *grisettes* or prostitutes; thus, "it is out of *timidity* that men become homosexuals, since they cannot summon with women that *familiarity* that authorizes love."[94]

In their persistent efforts to present the relations between the sexes as complementary and harmonious, doctors generally fashioned their analyses of women to present their feminine qualities in a positive manner, not as the inverted "other" of a positive masculinity. But they were under no such constraints in discussing these feminine qualities in men, where their mask of solicitude for the "weaker" sex could be temporarily and revealingly set aside. In short, when reading the medical discourse on inversion in this era, one cannot be certain whether one is reading the fear and contempt doctors felt for effeminate males, or the ferocious misogyny that undergirded their whole outlook on sex and sexuality. In all likelihood both factors operated together to produce this virulent and unsympathetic perspective.[95]

I will consider three final medical themes that suggest the uniqueness of the French conception of the homosexual, and carry the consideration of homosexuality into the 1920s and 1930s. First is the persistent reluctance of French medicine to distinguish between "sexuality" and "sex." Arnold Davidson uses the Oxford English Dictionary to date the first appearance of the word *sexuality* in English, a usage which first appears in 1879 in a British gynecological textbook.[96] The word *sexuality* was employed in the course of an observation by the doctor that removing a woman's ovaries did not destroy her sexuality, thereby appearing to confirm Davidson's argument that it was now possible to conceive of sexuality as a force or drive independent of the sex organs and the sex of the individual in question.

However, if one takes a look at French etymological dictionaries, one finds something rather different. The Dictionary of the French Academy (1878 ed.) has no *sexuality* entry. A recent *Grand Robert* notes an appearance in 1838, as does the Littré of 1882, but the definition in each is "that which forms the sex," followed by references to genitalia and the "typical" physical features pertaining to each sex.[97] The first use of *sexuality* in the "modern" sense in French is identified in *Le Grand Robert* and the *Grand Larousse* as 1924, both in reference to Freud's *Three Essays,* which first appeared in French the year before.[98]

Second, one might well have expected the growth of a French psychoanalytic movement to have popularized Freud's new conception of sexuality, but even here the story before 1945 suggests more continuity with the older views than conversion to the new. The reception of psychoanalysis in France bears some comparison with the reception fifty years earlier of Darwinism. In both cases certain adaptive variations were introduced that hybridized the foreign cutting and the native stock. In one of the first psychiatric texts to incorporate Freudian theory, Emmanuel Regis's popular *Précis de psychiatrie,* the author warned against the "snobbism" that regards only foreign research to be of interest, and vowed he had made his book "a specimen of French psychiatry," which seems amply borne out by his treatment of inversion and the other perversions as aspects of degeneration.[99] The first French treatise to bear the title *sexology* was published in 1933 by a founder of the Psychoanalytic Society of Paris, Dr. Angelo Hesnard, one of the more doctrinally wayward of this generally wayward group.[100] In his vast survey of more than 700 pages, Hesnard warned that he was going to treat sex as "a branch of biology," and distinguished this orientation from a pure psychological Freudianism.[101] Despite some material adapted directly from Freud, including an account of the stages of childhood sexuality, Hesnard is committed to the standard French positions on sex. He finds, for, instance, much evidence for the influence of "sexomorphology," a system of correlations between sexual capacity and behavior with genitalia and secondary sexual features, which are sharply differentiated with respect to the two sexes.[102]

Hesnard ranks the "erotic objects" of men and women in a descending order from the most "normal" to the most "pathological." The male list is headed by "young adult female," and descends through women of middle age to little girls, old women, boys, men, and, finally, old men.[103] But in accounting for the underlying pathology in cases of attraction to the lower ranks, Hesnard does not "unsolder" object and aim as Freud had done, but treats each instance as a case of "genital impotence" which is "masked" by an "imaginative function" linked to a "short-circuit in the spinal column." Thus a "general degradation" of libido is in step with the "degradation" of the erotic object corresponding to its rank order. This in turn prevents, Hesnard insists, "the rich synthesis of impressions and actions which characterizes the natural sexual union. Thus the extreme fatigue after the [abnormal] act, the repeated feelings of inferiority, and, in everyday life, a generally unvirile comportment."[104] "Complete sexual satisfaction," he averred, may only be obtained by a "moderate and normal genital function in the service of sentimental satisfactions assured by a regular life *en couple* and the joy of procreation."[105]

Third, let us consider homosexuality in Greek antiquity as a touchstone for European sexologists. Freud observes in an important note in the *Three Essays* that, thanks to Iwan Bloch, the "anthropological" approach to the study of inversion, including the civilizations of antiquity, is replacing the "pathological" model.[106] Freud clearly embraces here a perspective of cultural relativism, and this allows him to consider Greek homosexuality in a tolerant spirit, and even contrast favorably Greek glorification of the sexual instinct (as apart from its object) with the modern penchant which can "find excuses for it only in the merits of the object."[107]

In England the outlook was much the same. John Addington Symonds wrote a brilliant essay in 1883 entitled *Studies in Sexual Inversion* in which he praised Greek homosexuality and subjected modern medical accounts of ancient pederasty to withering criticism. He emphasized the high idealism and spirituality of this "powerful and masculine emotion in which effeminacy played no part, and which by no means excluded the ordinary sexual feelings."[108] Symonds endorsed a congenital theory of homosexuality, but was careful to consider the formative influence of the environment on its social role and expression.[109] Havelock Ellis endorsed this view on the whole, writing of homosexuality in ancient Greece as a "fashion" which led men whose "mental and physical constitution was perfectly normal" to adopt a custom that was "regarded as respectable and sometimes as even especially honorable."[110]

French medical commentators could not bring themselves to adopt a relativistic perspective, despite a French tradition of admiration of antiquity in no wise inferior to other European countries. Thus, they referred to the "turpitudes" and "vices" of the Greeks, warned against the unisexual garb of the ancients, or urged censors to "ban Plato as he banned Homer."[111] For the French Freudian, Angelo Hesnard, what was acceptable to the Greeks could not be so for us, because, as he patiently explained,

> While the Greek, who was a homosexual by education and culture, could harmonize his cult of masculine beauty with his sexual potency simply by allowing a considerable latitude in the choice of erotic object, our homosexual, who is endowed with a sexual constitution in discordance with the social milieu, suffers most frequently from a weakening of his procreative sexual power; which justifies in turn his classification among the neuropaths and abnormals.[112]

In France the power of this highly tendentious, biomedical discourse of the effeminate invert was so great that it directly influenced or subverted most literary treatments of the subject. Of course, literary portrayals of homosexuality at the turn of the century were only part of the spectrum of literary representations that considered the effects social and economic change produced on sex roles and sexual identity. As several scholars have noted, the writers and painters of this era, men and women alike, were fond of themes that tested the male response to the new female assertiveness in public life and to the "eroticization" of bourgeois marriage.[113] The binary term strong women/weak men—and its sexual analogue, fatal women/impotent men—was popular both with authors who feared the effects of female emancipation, and with those who supported it.[114] As Annelise Mauge has written about these characterizations, "With the [anticipated] emancipation of women, something has been refused males which seemed so much constitutive of their identity that they felt themselves totally rejected as men."[115]

As was the case in the medical literature, these themes were closely related, if not inseparable from literary explorations of homosexuality, implying in particular the notion that the appearance of new male and female types announced the eventual disappearance of the traditional sexual order. Although the domestic family-loving wife by no means vanished, the lesbian and the "androgyne" appeared alongside her, while the strong male, the "mari-pédagogue," and the oversexed male were joined by less virile types.[116] Marcel Prévost, Victor and Paul Margueritte, Adolphe Belot, Colette Yver, Catulle Mendès, and many other authors whose names have faded from memory peopled their novels and plays with the same sexually ambiguous characters as more famous authors: Emile Zola, Joris-Karl Huymans, Marcel Proust, André Gide, Rémy de Gourmont, Joséphin Péladan, Pierre Louys, Rachilde, and Jean Lorrain.[117]

Despite the zeal that the authors of this era exhibited for representations of homosexuality and sexual perversion, openly sympathetic homosexual novels were rare indeed.[118] More typical of the "decadent" novel was the assumption of a gravely ironic or a comic perspective on unusual couplings or peculiar desires. The *ur*-text for many of these novels was perhaps the most famous of them all: Joris-Karl Huysmans's *A Rebours* ("Against the Grain"), which appeared in 1884. Huysmans, whose explorations of the underworld of human perversion tipped him eventually into a mystical Catholicism, presented in the person of his hero, Des Esseintes, the perfect type of exhausted and degenerate aristocrat, a last anemic shoot from a once-vigorous warrior stock. Des Esseintes can arouse his feeble energies only by employing parapraxes or elaborate subterfuges that are, without actually taking the name, fetishes. Three episodes of recollection in chapter 9 chronicle his progressive sexual collapse in a style that is virtually interchangeable with the psychiatrist's case study.

The first of these episodes involves the American acrobat Miss Urania, she of the "supple body, sinewy legs, muscles of steel, and arms of iron."[119] The fragile Des Esseintes imagines a kind of "change of sex" in which she would take the man's role in their relationship, because he was himself "becoming increasingly feminized."[120] He is bitterly disappointed, however, because her sexual comportment is in fact conventionally coy and passive, aggravating his already "premature impotence." His second mistress was a café-concert ventriloquist, a dark and boyish woman who captivated Des Esseintes by her consummate ability to project exotic literary dialogue into statues of the Chimaera and the Sphinx.[121] Inevitably, however, "his [sexual] weakness became more pronounced; the effervescence of his brain could no longer melt his frozen body: the nerves no longer obeyed his will; the mad passions of old men overtook him. Feeling himself grow more and more sexually indecisive, he had recourse to the most effective stimulant of old voluptuaries, fear":

> While he held her clasped in his arms, a husky voice burst out from behind the door: "Let me in, I know you have a lover with you, just wait, you trollope." Suddenly, like the libertines excited by the terror of being taken *en flagrant délit* outdoors . . . , he would temporarily recover his powers and throw himself upon the ventriloquist, who continued to hurl her shouts from beyond the door. . . . [122]

Rejected finally by this woman, who preferred a man with "less complicated requirements and a sturdier back," Des Esseintes embarked on a homosexual affair with an effeminate, young Parisian *gavroche,* the last stage, so to speak, of his sexual decline: "never had he experienced a more alluring and imperious liaison; never had he tasted such perils nor felt himself so painfully fulfilled."[123]

Characterizations such as this of homosexuals and of homosexual love reiterated the standard medical portrait of the invert as an unmanned degenerate, condemned to a kind of love in keeping with his reduced biological condition. Though, as we have seen, it was possible elsewhere to write and speak about a different, more masculine kind of homosexual, in France the concept of the effeminate invert invariably subverted all other varieties. When André Raffalovitch, a francophone propagandist for homosexual rights, tried to make a case in French medical journals for the existence of a type of homosexual who was manly, married, and head of a household, he did so while heaping abuse on "effeminate" inverts, arguing that their moral worth was in inverse relation to their degree of effeminacy.[124]

Emile Zola, Dreyfusard and noble crusader for unpopular causes, pleaded the cause of inverts in his preface to Georges Saint-Paul's book on sexual perversions. He observed that one does not condemn a hunchback for having been born that way, so why scorn a man for acting like a woman when he has been born half woman? But Zola follows his half-hearted plea for understanding with a piece of bald familialist propaganda: "And in the end everything which touches on sex touches social life itself. An invert is a disorganizer of the family, of the nation, of humanity. Man and woman exist to make children, and they will kill life itself on the day they decide to make no more of them."[125]

André Gide, himself a homosexual, attempted to refute such arguments in the dialogue, *Corydon*, his celebrated defense of homosexuality, begun in 1907 and privately printed in 1911. Gide had Corydon complain, "The only serious books I know on the subject are certain medical works which reek of the clinic from the very first pages."[126] Gide explicitly acknowledges the force of such texts, however, by taking pains to distinguish between "normal homosexuals" and "inverts," whom he admitted were effeminate and perhaps even "degenerates."[127] Seeking to show the compatibility of tolerance for homosexuality and martial values, Gide drew upon the "heroes" of ancient Greece as exemplars of this point, concluding, "I can think of no opinion more false, and yet more widely held, than that which considers homosexual conduct and pederasty as the pathetic lot of effeminate races."[128] Gide also revealed that his nation's fear of "depopulation" was not far from his mind by having Corydon throw the blame for the low birthrate on "the shameless stimulation of our popular imagery, theaters, music halls, and a host of publications [which] serves only to lure woman away from her duties; to make her into a perpetual mistress, who no longer consents to maternity."[129]

Gide based his own ideal of pederasty on the ancients, and contested the modern medical use of the term. In a note he added to the 1922 edition of *Corydon*, he contrasted that manly relationship to the cases of "inversion, of effeminacy, of sodomy," which Marcel Proust had, alas, discussed at such length in *Sodome et Gomorrhe*.[130] Gide's fear of being associated with inversion may have been reinforced by his direct contact with medical authority. In his early manhood he consulted the renowned Dr. Paul Brouardel about his homosexual interest. Encouraged by Gide's testimony that he was "virile," that is, potent with women, Brouardel dispensed the standard medical advice that the condition was temporary and would disappear after marriage.[131]

In a much more complicated, but no less troubling way than Gide, Marcel Proust also assessed the variety of homosexualities in his great novel cycle, *A la recherche du temps perdu*. As several critics have pointed out, he was aided in this effort by his familiarity with the medical and biological literature of the era, particularly that of mental pathology. The most remarkable of these commentators, J.E. Rivers, argues that Proust's apparently detached account of life in Sodom and Gomorrah was heavily influenced, and ultimately enriched, by his internalization of the social prejudices against the homosexual impulses in himself. The unflattering accounts of inverts in his novel were the result, Rivers argues, of a homosexual self-hatred that moved Proust to deny his own nature and yet express his unhappiness in portraits that were alternately scornful and pitying.[132]

In the brilliant opening passages of *Sodome et Gomorrhe,* Proust reveals to his readers that, in an unguarded moment, a certain gentleness and spirituality could be seen in the face of the formidably imperious Baron de Charlus, "who prided himself so upon his virility, to whom all other men seemed odiously effeminate, what he made one suddenly think of, so far had he momentarily assumed her features, expression, smile, was a woman."[133] Charlus is suddenly transformed in the narrator's eyes into a "new person" whose whole being becomes more "intelligible" in light of this discovery. The narrator then speculates that Charlus belongs to "that race of beings, less paradoxical than they appear, whose ideal is manly simply because their temperament is feminine and who in their life resemble in appearance only the rest of men."[134] Charlus, of course, is an invert with an "incurable malady" of a degenerate kind, the chief symptom of which, as Proust reveals in later volumes, is a diminished capacity to conceal his progressive effeminization.[135] Proust admits of a kind of love between inverts, but only where the gap between the more masculine and feminine among them resembles the "normal" dimorphic attraction of men and women, as in the case of Charlus and Jupien. The tragic aspect of inverts' search for sexual complementarity is that they often "fall in love with precisely that type of man who has nothing feminine about him, who is not an invert and consequently cannot love them in return."[136] The close kinship of the "hermaphroditic" invert to women ensures their "sterile" relations, and leads Proust to speculate that it is the kind of self-fertilization that typifies hermaphrodites that ends by producing inverts' "degeneracy and sterility," though in the strictly moral sense, one invert may fertilize another with his "music, or his fragrance, or his flame."[137]

Though Proust occasionally endows the inverts in his novel with wholly masculine qualities, as in Saint-Loup's personal bravery and energetic patriotism, he more frequently represents them in the unforgiving discourse of inversion: as sterile, repellently effeminate, and mentally unstable beings.[138] The prejudices that the socially ambitious Proust feared the most were exactly those of the medical stereotype he constructed in his novel. We know that the youthful Proust chose his male friends from among those who were "physically well made, sportive, at once aristocratic and liberal."[139] We also know that Proust fought a duel in 1897 with the novelist Jean Lorrain over Lorrain's insinuations Proust had a homosexual relationship, and nearly provoked another a decade later when one of his friends did not deny strenuously enough the suggestion by a third party that Proust was a homosexual.[140] In yet another incident, when Proust was forty-nine years old, he scolded Paul Souday for attributing to him a "feminine" sensibility, in terms that leave little doubt about the precise nature of his fears:

> At a time when *Sodome et Gomorrhe* is about to appear—a time when, since I will be talking about Sodom, no one will have the courage to come to my defense—you are blazing the trail (without malice I am sure) for those who *are* malicious by treating me as being "feminine." From "feminine" to "effeminate" is one short step. Those who served me as seconds in my duel will tell you whether I have the softness of effeminates.[141]

Proust's attempt to counter suspicions about his (effeminate) homosexuality by emphasizing his willingness to duel reveals how a man's sexual identity was a public matter fully entangled in the honor codes regulating male sociability. Proust was not alone in having recourse to the duel to defend his sexual honor. Jean Lorrain, Proust's opponent in 1897, was widely rumored to consort with male prostitutes, but though his reputation as a literary observer of the *bas-fonds* of society profited from this gossip, he was nonetheless careful to present himself as a man of courage willing to risk all for his "honor."

When the papers covering Oscar Wilde's libel trial against the Marquis of Queensbury in the spring of 1895 reported the details of Wilde's homosexual love life, it created quite a stir among his French literary friends. Jules Huret, a literary critic at *Le Figaro,* provocatively published the names of some of the writers Wilde had sought out on his triumphant Paris trip of 1892, singling out "Jean Lorrain, Catulle Mendès, Marcel Schwob and other subtle writers." Huret assured his readers that he wished to do no more than inform his readers on Wilde's "purely literary relationships," although, he added disingenuously, this "might only imperfectly satisfy their curiosity."[142]

Mendès replied to this impertinence with one of his own, replying to Huret that "if you meant that as a witticism, you are all the more an imbecile," to which Huret replied in turn, "Since it pleases you to interpret my remarks in their larger sense, I can only reply that I would never dare oppose the opinion of someone who is better placed than myself to judge the truth of the matter."[143] Schwob and Mendès responded to this last sally by sending their seconds to Huret, who chose to fight Mendès, wounding him in the process.[144] Lorrain, for his part, took a somewhat less direct course to clear himself of the taint of having consorted with Wilde. He wrote to Huret assuring him that, far from being an intimate of Wilde, he scarcely knew him at all, and that Wilde had, moreover, met with other (obviously heterosexual) authors such as Anatole France, Maurice Barrès, and Henry Bauer (a notorious dueler). Moreover, Lorrain intimated, Wilde had gone to some lengths to avoid him, "considering me a terrible and dangerous man, which I had some difficulty taking as a flattery."[145]

All these strenuous efforts to avoid association with the prevailing conception of the homosexual made use of ritual conventions or rhetorical postures that asserted the possession of masculine honor and the willingness to defend it by force. The need to resort to such stratagems suggests that the conceptual link forged in medicine and literature between perversion and dishonor was often respected in social practice. The particular emphasis on displays of courage also suggests that the most fearsome aspects in the stereotype of (homosexual) perversion were the imputations of weakness, of femininity, or of cowardice that were believed to be the moral expressions of "genital" impotence or sexual aberration.

As I indicated was the case in the older clinical literature on impotence, I have tried to argue here that the fin de siècle medical outlook on perversion presumed dishonor to be a natural consequence of sexual disorder in adult males. Benjamin Ball wrote of an exhibitionist who, "in order to give himself a ridiculous pleasure, sacrificed his reputation, his honor, and his interests in the most ridiculous way."[146] Other specialists wrote of the "dishonorable" end such conditions brought to marriages, or spoke of the "cowardly" and "pusillanimous" way that men afflicted with some "shameful madness" treated their wives.[147] Psychiatrists were particularly conscious that when diagnosing the seriousness of a man's sexual perversion they were simultaneously passing judgment on his honor.[148]

This responsibility was felt with special immediacy when a doctor was called as an expert medical witness in a trial involving accusations of sexually abnormal behavior. In this situation a man's sexual honor was directly on view and thus explicitly linked with his public reputation. We obtain in such cases a clear view of the power of *social* as opposed to mere *legal* judgments, and how it was that a man's honor seemed to inhere in his person rather than in a verdict of guilt or innocence. This point is clearly illustrated by the following case, written up in 1880 by one of the leading forensic specialists of the era, Alfred Fournier. The doctor, testifying in a preliminary inquiry, was convinced that a respectable man was being blackmailed by an unscrupulous family claiming that he had sexually attacked their eight-year-old daughter. This man faced a trial in which he would be *"surely dishonored, and possibly convicted."*

> An outstanding and upright man, head of a family, highly esteemed and absolutely incapable of any dishonorable act (I will gladly vouch for this), allowed himself to get caught in a trap of this kind. All the evidence, both material and moral, spoke in his favor. . . . Moreover, the child's family was publicly disdained for a deplorable lineage. Well, in spite of that . . . , the man preferred to pay the ransom . . . rather than face a battle from which his innocence would certainly have emerged unharmed. "Yes,

surely," he told me, "I would win the case, and I would confound those imposters; but I would lose more by insisting on a trial than I would gain. Something of the calumny always remains, as Bazile showed. An acquittal is not a badge of innocence; an acquittal leaves behind a suspicion of guilt that could not be proven, and I owe it to my family, to my children, to the honor of my name, that such a suspicion not even be allowed to touch me. . . .[149]

The fear of effeminacy, sexual perversions, and homosexuality was common throughout western Europe in the decades prior to 1914. This widespread public concern was certainly stimulated by growing military tensions, a number of prominent homosexual scandals, and the multiple strains put on sex roles by the social and political emancipation of women. These influences produced in Germany and England the same kind of antihomosexual animus that existed in France, blunting the impetus of fledgling homosexual rights movements, and encouraging defensive denials by homosexuals and their defenders that homosexuality was incompatible with manliness or constituted a threat to national security.[150]

Carroll Smith-Rosenberg has written that women have historically been able to make a positive virtue of the dominant medical discourse on "lesbian" androgyny by exploiting this identity in new social and economic roles.[151] But male homosexuals and their defenders could not do the same with the image of effeminacy fashioned for them without gravely threatening the relatively more tenuous foundation on which male identity was believed to rest. This was nowhere more true than in France, where the developments I have discussed in foregoing chapters encouraged an unusual stress on the connections between normal sexuality, family life, and national survival, and which lent to medical discourse an authority it would not otherwise have possessed. As Dr. Georges Saint-Paul intoned: "Entirely normal love is very rare, I must confess, at least in that state of perfect normality in which not only the vital ends of generation and the purity of race, but also the social aims of patriotic grandeur, the conservation of the family and the purity of morals are all bound together."[152]

When the politician Ernest Charles proclaimed in 1910 that "if there is one vice or sickness especially repugnant to French mentality, to French morality, to French health, it is—to call things by their name—pederasty," he was tapping into this medical discourse and acknowledging the existence of a system of masculine identity for which sexuality had become the sign.[153] As Pierre Hahn has written in his study of the invention of homosexuality, "By the end of the century, no man could call himself sane or normal if he could not affirm his sexual identity from head to toe."[154]

There remains the irony of this apparently sexually permissive society embracing a rigid familialist ideology. The letters of the young Sigmund Freud to his fiancé, written during his Paris sabbatical year of 1885–86, are full of wonder at the worldliness of French doctors, the public obsession with nudity, and the cynical separation of sex from conjugal life. Yet it was Freud who transformed the lessons of Charcot's clinic into the most powerful sexual science of our times, while French sexology was shunted into a siding with no outlet into the wider literature. Perhaps, as Elizabeth Roudinesco has suggested, it was precisely on account of their actual *practice* in separating sexuality from conjugal sex that made the French anxious to keep it united in *theory:*

> The bourgeois generated his offspring in the heat of the marital bed, but he gave free reign to his instincts only with prostitutes. He mixed together hygiene with the defense of the race, loved pleasure, but dreaded its maladies; syphilis and hysteria struck at the very heart of his expectations of progress, his traditions, his hereditary patrimony, as if the brothels he frequented were injecting their poisons into the loins of his conjugal values. Thus the effort to analyze sex, to cure it, to pass it through the sieve of a medical discourse.[155]

7

Bourgeois Sociability and the
Point d'Honneur: 1800–1860

In this chapter I begin to consider more of the public expressions of masculine honor that will occupy the next three chapters. To this point I have attempted to show how conclusions about a man's honor and honorability could be drawn from his sexual comportment and personal appearance—areas usually regarded as part of the silent if not inscrutable "private" domain. I have also maintained, however, that for bourgeois men there was a far less dramatic rupture between public and private life than was the case for women; a single code regulated both domains of a man's life, permitting him to cross his threshold without feeling he had passed into a wholly different world.

This does not mean there were no differences between public and private; in the secrecy of his *foyer,* a man could dissimulate aspects of his sexuality, even to himself, and avoid the censure of opinion or the law. But in public life the authority and scope of codes of honor were more exigent. A man with social aspirations could not hope to escape the ubiquity of judgments about his worthiness as a man of honor and courage because these were the very qualities he required for his worldly prosperity. We shall learn even more forcefully in the following chapters the extent to which men believed their personal lives to be playthings of a higher power. As an early twentieth-century writer on honor expressed it, the effort of individuals to act honorably is only *apparently* egoistic; in fact personal distinction is only one "indispensable condition" for realizing the ideal which demands that men "pay tribute to the divine idol of which we are all servants and priests."[1]

Inasmuch as it is only possible to fully *explain* the social *by* the social, I hope to show here how the values of male honor were generated and maintained in various contexts of male sociability. I shall contend that considerations of honor were embedded in the *ensemble* of the formal and informal codes that regulated the relations between bourgeois men, from the most humble elements of *politesse* to the rules governing personal combat. I therefore intend to treat social etiquette and the code of the duel equally as aspects of a rule-ordered continuum that regulated male conduct in both prosaic and life-threatening matters.

The origins of male bourgeois sociability are coeval with the development of freemasonry in the eighteenth century. The earliest masonic lodges were a microcosm of the social amalgamation of noble and bourgeois taking place throughout French society. Although the social hierarchy was acknowledged in some lodges by a distinction of the grades of masons (*frères à talents, frères servants*), there was in general a scrupulous recognition of the equality of all members and considerable efforts were made to stress the ideal of harmony between "brothers."[2] The commitment to the principle of egalitarianism in the lodges may well have stimulated the growth of a democratic sensibility in late eighteenth-century Europe, but the driving force in masonry was the desire for a venue where men could meet on an equal footing in pleasant society and fellowship.[3] From their governing statutes and correspondence, we learn that the lodges did not simply take their internal harmony for granted; they proscribed disputation or harsh words between brothers and recalled to members their vows of friendship and mutual respect.[4]

The enforcement of polite relations was also a dominant preoccupation for the *cercles* that later sprang up throughout France in the decades after the Revolution. Lying somewhere between the aristocratic salon and the popular club and café, the circle was a uniquely bourgeois institution, selective but egalitarian.[5] By 1840, 2,000 circles or *sociétés à plaisance* with 120,000 members were spread throughout France, having no other mission but recreation and sociability.

Edmond Goblot has pointed out in his classic study of the French bourgeoisie that it was by insisting on an equality of relations within their class that groups such as the circles guaranteed "the condition of [the bourgeoisie's] superiority *as* a class."[6] Once they had been admitted, through their own merit, beyond the escarpment of class, those on the "plain" behind were obliged to treat one another as brethren on pain of banishment. A parallel process operated in the domain of liberal politics throughout the first half of the nineteenth century. The governing elite of notables evaluated an elector's "political capacity" as though it were a "faculty" that was "at once personal and impersonal," something that distinguished him by nature from *non-capacitaires,* but which he could not pretend to possess in permanence or imagine to be unattainable by others.[7] Apalled as they were by the *idea* of democracy, the meritocratic values of the bourgeois elite nonetheless encouraged them to practice a democratic civility amongst themselves that prefigured the later rise of full political democracy.

This egalitarian civility is expressed eloquently in the manuals of etiquette and politeness that were printed and reprinted in the first half of the nineteenth century. These manuals replaced the courtesy books that had guided young nobles and rich bourgeois into virtuous adulthood in the Old Regime. They were not aimed so much at moral perfection as at smoothing the path of sociability for guests and hosts in various social situations.[8] But etiquette books were not, for all their concern with the mechanics of politeness, devoid of moral implications. They explicitly recognized that the citizens of a new political order needed an egalitarian *politesse* to suit the times. In the words of Louis-Damien Emeric, "All men should be equal before *la politesse* as they are before the law."[9]

There were, however, no neo-Rousseauist musings in the manuals about a primordial, "natural" sociability. On the contrary, as Edouard Alletz put it, "*La politesse* is the simulacrum of love for one's neighbor; it is a tacit truce between men consumed by self-love, the silence of egotism, an involuntary respect for human dignity. It has been invented to re-establish in this world the *appearance* of equality."[10] The gestures and verbal formulas one employed in good society may only be "exterior signs," but the socially polished man presented to the world a self-creation whose good sense and moderation was indispensable to the civilization of the "juste milieu." If a man is "polite without being opportunistic, gallant without tastelessness, disposed to an even-handed kindness and to appropriate expressions of intellectuality, discreet, indulgent, generous, he will discover that he exercises a certain moral authority."[11]

The cautious, almost defensive quality of this "moral authority" alerts us to its fundamental weakness as a reliable basis for social action. Bourgeois *politesse* was designed neither to win accolades or admiration, but to avoid giving offense. If there were a few conventional ways to please, there were myriad ways to offend, and the manuals reflected this balance in their advice to "not give offense, nor humiliate, nor importune, nor intimidate; if one must give pleasure to others, flatter, but with a flattery which never appears to be either excessive or self-interested."[12] Horace Raisson stressed the thin line that separated "civility from affectation, familiarity from kindness, a pleasantry from an epigram, a dignified bearing from stiffness, a natural manner from a rude one, gaiety from abandon. . . . The great art is to know what to avoid."[13]

A boasting manner, an ill-considered pleasantry, a salutation not returned, or a stare fixed too long on the face of a young lady could provoke rude disputation and give rise to a duel. Commentators deplored this extremity, but acknowledge it often served as an inhibition to gross incivility; some advised their readers to acquire familiarity with sword or pistol and to know the "rules of the true code of honor."[14] The duel, in this system, was continuous with *la politesse,* serving as a court of last resort when delicacy failed in the breech.

Edmond Goblot, the keenest modern observer and critic of bourgeois society, accounted its manners less superficial than one might think; it supported a moral point of view, "which, without being sufficient, is yet far from scornful since our bourgeoisie has been and remains a society of honorable individuals [*honnêtes gens*]."[15] Delicacy alone, Goblot wrote, will take a man only so far; if he falls in the water, it will not be a man of delicacy who rescues him, but a more rough and ready type. Ruse, which is a permanent ingredient in the artifice of social life, is linked necessarily at some level with violence. The analogy of manners with the duel is thus entirely appropriate:

> In the duel, where two adversaries confront one another in the presence of witnesses and according to forms assuring a loyalty of combat, sword thrusts are justly called "feints": the whole art of attack, in fencing technique, is to menace one's adversary in one direction in order to strike him in another, without revealing the maneuver by the expression on one's face. The noble skill of swordsmanship is thus an art of dissimulation.[16]

However, Goblot observes, though bourgeois life is a "tissue of lies," the honorable man, like the dueler, confines his lies to the little things; he teaches his children the worth of "frankness and sincerity" just as he observes the rules of loyalty in the duel. How, he asks, could the bourgeoisie have survived so long as an elite without this deep structure of moral belief and a willingness to sustain it with action?[17]

Understandably, the earliest nineteenth-century circles and societies of men hoped that differences between members would stop far short of personal conflict, not simply because the harmony of internal relations was in a certain sense the *raison d'être* of group life but because it was also the basis of the group's reputation in the community. To ensure this harmony, bourgeois circles of all variety explicitly required new members to have lived "honorable lives," and possess good reputations and morality.[18] The *société à plaisance* in Saumur stated that the aims of its organization were to observe the rules of "honor, the respect for self and others, and all the social virtues that provide the foundation and bonds of this society."[19]

Despite their oft-affirmed hymns to friendship and brotherly love, few circles trusted members to police their own manners. Most spelled out undesirable behavior and appointed committees to levy appropriate fines or, in especially serious cases, to expel incorrigibles. The literary circle of Parthenay forbade "any injurious remarks, vulgar language, oaths, or indecent gestures; in addition any conversation having the object of wounding the self-esteem or reputation of fellow members. . . ."[20] Jean-Luc Marais cites numerous examples of societies in small-town western France proscribing "epithets," verbal "injuries," "menace," or rude gestures. Physical aggression of any kind required automatic exclusion, as did any behavior that sullied "the honor of the society or one of its members . . . ," since "honorability is necessary to be admitted to the society, and respectability to remain a member of it."[21] It may have been that violence was less a problem by the end of the century than it was at the beginning. Marais notes an appreciable fall by the 1890s in the percentage of societies mentioning physical aggression, but no society or circle, even Parisian groups composed of the cream of the Parisian elite, believed they could dispense altogether with punishments for "grave infractions of the laws of honor or proper decorum."[22]

We may catch a glimpse of the stuff of bourgeois honorability in small-town France from Marais's excellent study of the bowling and recreational societies in the west. Fines were levied for "speaking badly" of those not present or for purveying malicious gossip about members beyond the confines of the group, whether or not it was true.[23] Solidarity was required even in death; members *and their wives* were obliged to attend the funerals of deceased *sociétaires* on pain of expulsion. Significantly, it is clear that women were both a threat to the treasured intimacy of male society, but an acknowledged part, nonetheless, of each man's sphere of personal honor, for which he bore responsibility to the group. If a man's wife made bold to seek out her husband on the sacred *terrain de jeu* and spoke sharply to another member, her husband was assessed a fine. Since, however, there were occasionally "legitimate" reasons for such intrusions, an untoward remark by an intolerant bowler was equally subject to penalty, all this by way of short-circuiting the escalation of such incidents into full-blown affairs of honor.[24]

Though particular women were excluded from the circles, the woman was ever-present in the frankly misogynistic discourse that passed then, and passes still, as a staple of male *camaraderie*.[25] The circle was "a pseudonym for divorce, like the cigar," where men were encouraged to use "just the right word, be it picturesque or strong or even vulgar, if that is what one means to say."[26] Jules Claretie likened the repartee traded at Parisian dining clubs to a fencing match, " . . . something like an electrification of talent, a digging of spurs of comrade into comrade, a kind of fencing where the fencing hall is the table and your neighbor is the padded shirt [*plastron*] your foil seeks to touch."[27]

The informal dining clubs, such as the *dîner* Bixio, the *dîner* Magny, or the *dîner* de la Marmite, had none of the disciplinary apparatus of the permanent *cercles,* so when Claretie assures us that there were only "smiles," no "storms," or "wounding or offensive" talk, we may be sure that the honor code of gentlemanly conduct was being scrupulously observed. Devoted as these dinner companions were to their pleasure, the tensions that arose between men who were drinking, gambling, and speaking frankly sometimes spilled over into personal combat. The *politesse* of good society and the *politesse* of the dueling ground were, as we shall see, cut out of the same cloth.

Owing to its private nature, we do not know much more about dueling in the period after the Revolution than in the Old Regime. Bonaparte formally dispproved of the practice between officers, preferring them to shed their blood for him, but it is clear that affairs of honor were frequent in French armies of the era. Duels occurred between regimental "champions" and between officers of widely different rank; even collective duels in the spirit of the Old Regime were not unknown.[28] The civilian duel may well have reached a nadir at this time; few able-bodied men remained out of uniform, after all, and for those who did the pejorative "Pékin" (in mufti) had been newly minted.[29] The socially mixed nature of the Imperial officer corps guaranteed a further erosion of the noble monopoly on dueling, and with it, apparently, a certain relaxation of the traditional rules governing the *point d'honneur* and who might participate in it.

For military men, the display of courage in a personal affair of honor was indistinguishable from courage displayed on the battlefield. As in the armies of the monarchy, Napoleonic chieftans continued to punish officers who refused to respond to legitimate challenges, thinking thereby to cultivate both valor and a certain *bon ton* among officers. By 1815 this custom had achieved the force of an unwritten law and was jealously maintained throughout the nineteenth century. From time to time, efforts were made to abolish the practice or to institute automatic mediation in special honor tribunals, but in fact regimental commanders were successful in retaining the power to cashier an officer for turning the other cheek.[30] In any event, the segregated venues of military duels and the desire of commanders to protect duelers from the claims of civilian prosecutors (there was no independent military law governing the duel) meant that few military duels achieved the publicity accorded to civilian ones.

During the twenty-five years from 1790 to 1815, practically endless warfare kept European armies huge and nourished the spread of the military virtues throughout civil society. It stands to reason, as commentators have argued, that the duel in this era owed most of its momentum to this experience of permanent mobilization and the high prestige of military elites.[31] There was a notable revival of the practice in England, central Europe and France, a high proportion of which were wholly intramilitary or involved one combattant in active service.[32]

Where the military ethos remained strong after 1815, as in Prussia, the duel continued to be regarded as a ritual of military type strongly associated with Junker caste values, even when the antagonists were bourgeois civilians.[33] From the 1830s onward a typically legalistic formulation of the duel emerged in Germany articulated by bourgeois lawyers and academics that made the duel a requirement of all men who aspired to honor, but all "serious" duels in Prussia in the nineteenth century were fought nonetheless with pistols, the weapon of choice of officers, and followed essentially the lines of the military ritual.[34] In England, despite the long tradition of a militia army, a remarkable proportion of duelers (seldom below 30 percent in any year) were officers through the 1830s.[35] Despite the military flavor of English and central European duels, it is clear that the Napoleonic wars helped to loosen the aristocratic monopoly on the duel by requiring the wholesale commissioning of men from the bourgeoisie.[36]

The *embourgeoisement* of the duel in France was, as I have already noted, underway well before the end of the Old Regime, and this process was certainly accelerated by the wars of the Revolution and Empire. But military influences on the French duel were far less than has been claimed by some commentators, nothwithstanding the huge influence of warfare on a whole generation of Frenchmen.[37] France was the society par excellence of the civil duel. The English duel, had it survived past the 1840s, might have evolved in a similar direction, but eliminating the pensions to the widows of officers killed in duels could not have given the *coup de grâce* to the duel in France the way it did in Britain.[38] In German-speaking lands the duel became increasingly an affair of the civil and individual honor of bourgeois men, but seems to have remained suspended in form and participation somewhere between aristocratic and bourgeois notions of honor.[39] In France, dueling was firmly entrenched in upper-class (largely urban) life by 1815 and would flourish there for the subsequent 100 years.

In Europe generally, even where dueling or the issuing of challenges was forbidden by statutory law or in jurisprudence, judicial statistics are of only marginal utility. Only fatal duels, or affairs involving serious injury, were liable to be prosecuted, and then only when there was some reason to suspect in advance that the "laws" of the dueling code had been contravened.[40] In England there were statutory laws and a tradition of jurisprudence equating "deliberate" dueling with attempted murder and punishing dueling homicide (after 1803) with the death penalty. Prussian law and the later criminal code of the Second Reich made the duel the subject of special laws, setting down six months in prison for the issuing or accepting of challenges, three months to five years for dueling, and two to fifteen years for homicide.[41] In neither Germany, where the law threatened moderate punishment, nor Britain, which decreed the ultimate penalty, did the law either deter dueling or leave a reliable statistical record for historians, apart from an overwhelming preponderance of acquittals where duels were tried by juries.[42]

France differed from all other western European nations in not making the duel the object of special legislation. A bit of apocrypha that circulated amongst partisans of abolition during the nineteenth century had it that the framers of the Napoleonic Code did not wish to honor the duel by naming it, but if such sentiments were indeed expressed, it was surely done in private.[43] Though efforts were made at regular intervals—1819, 1829, 1848, 1851, 1877, 1883, 1888, 1892, 1895, 1921—to abolish or regulate dueling through legislation, in each case abolitionists suffered overwhelming defeat. The visibility of parliamentary life, where a man's style was as important to his political fortunes as his convictions and his allies, made it unlikely that repression of the duel would originate in French legislative assemblies.

Disapproving jurists, on the other hand, made fairly strenuous efforts to repress dueling through jurisprudence, by establishing a body of precedent on aspects of the duel mandating punishment for offenders. Nothing much was achieved in this respect until 1837. Indeed, an 1819 ruling of the Court of Cassation, France's highest court of appeal, held that "A homicide or wounds incurred, without disloyalty [*déloyauté*], in the course of a duel agreed to by both parties is neither a crime nor a felony."[44] A ruling of 1827, however, while acknowledging the noncriminal nature of the duel, did open the way for civil awards to the survivors of a dueling victim, even where no suspicion of disloyalty was alleged.[45] Other rulings in the Restoration attempted to repress duels requiring unusual or murderous conditions.

In July of 1836, Louis Philippe's chief prosecutor, André-Marie Dupin announced that his office would treat the duel in the future as a species of attempted murder. Prosecutors must consider, he wrote, the motives, seriousness, and conditions of the duel, and whether one man provoked another or was vastly more experienced in weaponry. Punishments might vary anywhere between acquittal and the death penalty, depending on the assessment of responsibility involved. Dupin had, in effect, declared war on the duel by attempting to assimilate it to crimes of personal violence.[46]

Dupin's hopes were quickly realized. A duel between Mssrs. Baron and Pessen following an altercation at a ball ended in the death of M. Baron, who had provoked the duel by slapping his antagonist. The assizes court nonetheless held Pessen responsible for willful manslaughter because he ignored a last-minute appeal by Baron's second admitting his client's wrongful behavior.[47] The Court of Cassation upheld this decision on 15 December 1837, opening the way for a string of later rulings fixing blame on duelers or their seconds when the motives that gave rise to the duel, or the circumstances under which it was fought, departed from established convention.[48]

The will to prosecute the duel in this way was sustained throughout the July monarchy and well into the Second Empire. However, though Dupin and his successors may have won the high legal ground in their battle against the duel, they by no means won the war. Some concrete gains were made. A report of the Ministry of Justice in 1846 did indicate a dramatic reduction of dueling mortalities after the 1837 decision. Twenty-nine deaths were reported in 1828, and in 1833, thirty-two men died on the dueling grounds, while in 1839, 1840, and 1841, only six, three, and six died, respectively.[49] These lower numbers were seldom exceeded throughout the remainder of the century. But Dupin's efforts to eliminate the duel altogether merely succeeded in encouraging its less murderous forms: swords began to replace firearms, and pistol duels were fought at a greater (and safer) distance.

In any case convictions for death or serious injury in duels were not forthcoming. A pro-dueling article noted smugly in 1845 that between 1837 and 1842 the assizes courts heard cases involving thirty-four duels and their juries acquitted all thirty-four.[50] Before long prosecutors began to indict on the lesser charges of involuntary homicide or simple assault and try cases in the correctional courts in the presence of magistrates, but there is little proof that even this strategy achieved higher conviction rates. Duelers who followed the prescribed forms of the dueling ritual appear to have been more or less safe from serious punishment.

It was between 1815 and 1848 that the modern French civil duel put down roots and assumed the forms it would retain until after World War I, even as the two countries of the Atlantic community which France most resembled politically and socially—the United States and Great Britain—were eliminating this feudal vestige from public life. As we shall see, the passion for dueling increased in France after 1850 while the nation made democratic and libertarian advances that far outpaced other continental countries that conserved the duel. These developments pose particular questions of fact and interpretation for the historian that I intend to address in the remainder of this study. How many duels were there? How did the duel assume its modern form of duel *au première sang* (first blood)? Who dueled and why did they resort to this archaic method of resolving differences? Finally, how were the duel and its rituals related to the aspects of manhood, masculinity, and male sociability we have already considered? As I argued at the outset of this study, anachronisms must be explained as conscientiously as historical novelties. The historian cannot simply invoke tradition to account for the persistence of earlier practices or beliefs; even the most "vestigial" social and cultural practices serve some useful purpose and convey meaning to contemporaries.

The first and perhaps most vexing question is, how many duels were there? These figures are difficult to know even for European societies where the duel was the subject of special laws. Duels were often very private affairs, and, like infanticide or suicide, fatalities were either not reported or were represented to be a consequence of natural causes. In France, short of a search of the manuscript judicial records, court statistics are of little help at all. If it did reach the courts, a dueling incident was entered in the records as a homicide (*assassinat*), manslaughter (*meurtre*), or simple aggression. Historians must make use of rare local studies, the odd bibliography or repertory compiled by dueling enthusiasts, and, above all, the newspapers. Since the *faits divers* section of newspapers—where events like the duel were reported—began to appear only in the 1860s, even the newspaper is not of much help until well into the Second Empire. By the time of the Third Republic, however, because of the recently accepted convention of a written account (*procès-verbal*) agreed upon by all four seconds, newspapers could provide not only a timely version of affairs of honor, but one that, however brief, was also likely to be free from one-sided exaggeration. Even in this later period, we are still left with a mysterious set of "black" or unknown figures. These might be secret duels between men with reason to be fearful of prosecution, duels unreported to the papers because of an unexpected or serious outcome, or, above all, a duel fought over a "private" matter in which both champions preferred to avoid publicity, usually involving a wife, daughter, or mistress. The latter kind may have been a particularly large category.

Some of these themes are reflected in two of the rare local studies of the nineteenth-century French duel. In his study of duels in Poitiers and the Department of the Vienne between 1814–50, Raymond Duplantier supplemented local assizes records with police reports and newspapers. He found evidence of thirty duels, six of which produced a fatality. In only one instance was the survivor brought to trial.[51] Using the same kinds of sources, Yves Baron's study of the duel in the Calvados department claims fifty-nine duels there over the whole century, which produced four deaths and thirty-four serious wounds.[52] Baron's study is unfortunately marred by his taking the local police official's conception of a "duel" at face value in his heavily rural sample. He included any encounter in which a challenge to fight followed a provocation of any sort, even though in at least four out of every five of these encounters the combatants engaged in their fights more or less immediately after the decisive affront and with weapons that came to hand, or, lacking these, with fists. These common disputes (rixes), undertaken without seconds or the obligatory waiting period, would never have passed muster with more urbane men of honor. Another suspect bit of evidence in Baron's study was the preference for weapons. The saber was used in 38 percent of the duels and 15 percent employed pistols, but the rest of his sample went at it with bare hands or sticks. Hardly any of his antagonists chose the épée, which figured in half of the encounters (the other half being pistols) in Duplantier's more gentlemenly contingent in Poitiers.[53]

More usefully, both studies found a number of examples in the first half of the century of collective duels with more than one person on each side, a clear vestige of Old Regime practices, and neither found that women figured significantly as a dueling motive, suggesting, as I mentioned earlier, that encounters of that nature were conducted in great secrecy. Perhaps their most interesting correlation was the finding that in both provinces the duel had become a democratic phenomenon in the nineteenth century; the overwhelming majority of legitimate duelers in both cases were soldiers, students, or members of the small-town bourgeoisie.[54] The motives for the vast majority of these duels were not "serious," but seem to have been fought for slights or imputations of unworthiness ("ne merite pas ses galons").

In the first half of the century the seriousness of the disputes between men may not have been as important a factor in dueling fatalities as the relatively unregulated and dangerous way in which duels were fought.[55] Pistols at ten to twenty paces, or saber duels where duelists could both slash with the cutting blade and stab with the point carried great risks. There was much confusion as well about the proper role that seconds (*témoins*) should play in the duel. Were the "seconds," as in the Old Regime, free to enlist their weapons against their man's opponent or his entourage, or was their role more in the spirit of their modern title, that of semi-juridical witnesses to the proceedings and guarantors of fair play? In the circumstances, Jean-Claude Chesnais's cautious estimate of 100 French duels per year in the period 1815–48, when correlated with the 1846 figures on fatalities, suggests that as many as one-third of armed duels (épée, saber, pistol) might have ended in the death of one of the combatants.[56] There were very likely more than 100 serious duels per year, civilian and military combined, but we must be content with that figure, lacking as we do the documentation of the later period.

As we have seen, the dueling mortality rate appears to have fallen in the late 1830s despite no apparent reduction in the number of duels. Though we cannot overlook the possible influence of the general prosecutor's zealous repression, a more likely explanation is the widespread acceptance of a new dueling code published in 1836, the first of its kind since the seventeenth century. This code was authored by the Comte de Chatauvillard and countersigned by men representing France's most illustrious families, including eleven peers of France and the cream of the military elite.[57] Chatauvillard claimed he was publishing this code because he regarded it as his humanitarian duty to modernize and regularize a practice that was a necessary and inevitable feature of civilized life. In the absence of any clear statutory guidelines, it was advisable, he wrote, to have a dueling code that could attain the force of "law," a term "we ought not to hesitate to give to the rules imposed by honor, because honor is no less sacred than governmental laws."[58]

Chatauvillard's *Essai* appeared in the wake of several very public and tragic duels and at the moment that Dupin's anti-dueling campaign was moving into high gear. In the sporadic national debate on the duel that had recently flared anew, Chatauvillard hoped to give support to the "men of heart" who favored retention by making such encounters rarer, less dangerous, and more fully subject to lawful norms supervised by the "best" sort of men. Inasmuch as the duel was clearly establishing itself in more popular *milieux,* Chatauvillard and his peers were determined to exclude irregularities that smacked of an impassioned vulgarity or that lowered the gentlemanly tone of the ritual. However, despite the preponderance of aristocratic signatories to this document, there was no question here of returning the duel to some edenic form purged of modern excrescences, but of acknowledging and strengthening those aspects of the ritual most compatible with bourgeois civilization.

Some recent duels had provided dramatic evidence that even well-bred men did not always behave reliably when they believed their honor to be at stake. A discussion in the winter of 1834 in the Chamber of Deputies on military policy precipitated a brief exchange between Louis-Philippe's war minister General Thomas-Robert Bugeaud and Dulong, a liberal deputy who challenged the minister's rigid conception of military command authority. To Bugeaud's insistence that "One must above all obey given orders," Dulong apostrophized, "Must one do so to the point of making oneself a prisoner, to the point of ignominy?" The *Journal des Débats,* the "official" press organ of the July Monarchy, fanned the flames of the controversy by referring to Dulong's "outrageous expression" and hinting that Bugeaud had demanded explanations.[59]

Following three days of negotiations between the seconds, a cautiously worded apology was delivered to Bugeaud, who, impatient to have it printed, provided a copy to the *Bulletin du Soir.* Dulong, believing Bugeaud had violated the spirit of the agreement, withdrew the letter, but though great efforts were made to stop its publication, a few copies were printed in a provincial newspaper.[60] A confrontation might still have been prevented, but one of Dulong's seconds declared himself satisfied with the original statement and yielded his position to a more bellicose associate, and Bugeaud's chief second, his colleague General Marie-Théodore Rumigny, apparently advised him against further conciliation. A comparatively dangerous form of pistol duel was selected, Dulong received a ball in the forehead, and died instantly.[61]

The anti-government press both left and right erupted in indignation at what they regarded as an unwarranted intrusion of personal honor into the public domain of free and open debate, producing the first parliamentary duel in eighteen years. The legitimist *Gazette de France* spread the blame widely, including seconds and official press, and indicated, for good measure, the absurdity of a dishonored regime professing sensitivity to the *point d'honneur.*[62] On the left, Dulong's colleague Armand Carrel spoke eloquently in the chamber and in his paper *Le National* against the "doubtful" nature of the outrage, and of General Rumigny's inflammatory behavior, opining that the "miserable" point of honor had no place in public life.[63]

Two years later, in an ironic illustration of the power of the ritual he had deplored, Carrel found himself staring down the gun barrel of the press magnate Emile de Girardin for a motive more futile still than the "outrage" that killed Dulong. One of Carrel's editors had editorialized on a dispute between Girardin's "mass" paper, *La Presse,* and the old format *Bon Sens,* doubting the wisdom of Girardin's use of defamation laws to muzzle *Bon Sens*'s criticism of his new venture.[64] Reviewing his options, Girardin believed he could either start a new suit against *Le National,* reveal the identity of the "calumniator" who wrote the unsigned editorials, or duel with the paper's director.[65] He chose the last alternative, sent his seconds, and killed Carrel in the subsequent "barrier" duel, pausing to aim carefully after Carrel's ball buried itself in his thigh.[66] As had the Bugeaud-Dulong duel, this duel also raised questions about the location of the boundary between public and private life.[67] Girardin, who later printed *éloges* from other papers justifying his action, argued that the offense to him consisted of the implication that he was using his personal fortune to drive his political opponents out of the marketplace.[68]

Though there were important issues raised about the propriety of both these duels, no one thought to bring the survivors to trial since their own behavior had been, from the broad latitude of the prevailing dueling code, irreproachable. This was not the case with another celebrated contemporary duel, where a string of irregularities landed the survivor of a fatal duel in the assizes court on charges of willful homicide. By August 1836, when the trial of Aimé Sirey took place in Paris, the Orleanist regime was determined to stamp out the duel once and for all. In his summation the prosecutor made clear that the duel itself was on trial, and he urged the jurors to hasten the end of the "disgraceful practice" and thereby win for justice the plaudits of "genuine honor and of civilization itself."[69] As we shall see, there was a defect in the logic of the prosecution's case that not only damaged his brief against the duel as an institution, but in fact helped legitimate it as a kind of private law for settling personal differences between gentlemen.

The case arose from a dispute between two cousins over the financial administration by Sirey *père,* a celebrated jurist and editor of legal reference works, of the Souillant family estate, of which Durand Durepaire, his nephew, was a member. Durepaire, an otherwise unambitious *rentier* in his thirties, had long been dissatisfied with the portion of his income from the estate trust, and became convinced that old Sirey was cheating him of his just share. He began speaking openly about filing a civil suit against the venerable lawyer, and gave voice publicly to his opinion that the Sireys were "thieves" and a family of *canaille* (scum).[70]

When Sirey *fils* was given an account of this slander, a matter that had until then festered within the bounds of the family exploded into public view. Sirey drafted a letter to his cousin demanding that he foreswear any "hostile project against his father or himself" or, he warned, "this world will be too small for both of us." He confided this document to two seconds, who carried it to Durepaire. Just as the negotiations were taking place between Sirey's seconds and Durepaire, Sirey strode into the premises and roughly slapped his adversary in the face, making a duel inevitable, and compelling Durepaire to engage two seconds of his own. But when Sirey then claimed the right as the offended one to the choice of weapons, in contravention of the usual rule that gave first choice to the man who was struck, and both men talked wildly of a "duel to the death," all four seconds chose to abandon their responsibilities.[71]

As happened so often in these matters, four fresh and more pliable seconds were found to carry on the affair to its lamentable conclusion. Though Sirey persisted in claiming first choice of weapons, Durepaire's new colleagues countered by demanding a saber duel, in the conviction that Sirey was practiced in épée and pistol and their man, who was presumably innocent of arms, would stand a better chance with a weapon Sirey had never handled. In the end, this standoff produced a drawing of lots in which the saber was selected. The combat, which took place on 27 November 1835, was brief but filled with incident. Sirey was passionate and furious, Durepaire calm and self-contained. Though the second's official *procès-verbal* contained no reference to it, the *directeur du combat,* Comte de Cailleux, testified that he had been obliged to intervene when Durepaire attempted to strike Sirey after the latter had stumbled to the ground.[72] The duel ended with what a doctor later testified was a "loyal," though fatal, blow struck by the vengeful son.

The prosecution gutted its case against the duel from the outset by conceding that "in this world" the "powerlessness" of the law sometimes compelled a man to have recourse to force to redress grievances. But the duel, argued the prosecutor, runs against the grain of morality when it is used "as a pretext for assassination," as in the present case where Aimé Sirey provoked a duel to forestall a potentially expensive and embarassing suit against his father. Not only did Sirey dishonor himself by fighting for money, said the prosecutor, warming to his theme, but he "conducted himself unchivalrously" by slapping a man he knew to be weaker than himself in arms and then demanding the choice of weapons in the bargain, a clear case of "premeditated ambush," which had the effect of driving away the first set of seconds.[73] The prosecutor, M. de Chaix-d'est, even found words of praise for the unfortunate victim, who had not refused to duel even in these unpromising circumstances, and who "had, as you know, behaved courageously."[74]

Sirey's defense was conducted by the young radical lawyer Adolphe Cremieux, who would serve later as justice minister in both Second and Third Republic governments.[75] Cremieux knew well enough to take his cue from the prosecutor's ill-conceived attack on Sirey's lack of chivalrousness. It was his intention, he began, to show that, in avenging the honor of his aged father, his client was not guilty of "disloyalty, perfidy or untruth."[76] He took pains to align himself with the prosecutor's own ambivalence about affairs of honor, observing that "unhappily, at the bottom of our souls as Frenchmen, there is a certain sentiment that oppresses and devours us, compelling us to a deplorable vengeance when we have received an outrage." It is a "terrible evil, but nonetheless a leprosy that we, as imperfect beings, must endure." Cremieux readily agreed that a duel, under certain conditions, might become a cold-blooded murder. Citing Chatauvillard, whose book had just appeared, he reminded the jury that the duel has its "rules" and its "code," and if they are openly violated, the offender should get the death penalty, "not because he has engaged in a duel, but because he has violated the laws of honor on the very terrain where he had sworn to defend them."[77]

Cremieux recalled to the "men of the world" in the jury box the recent Carrel–Girardin duel, in which no charges had been filed, and asked them to regard Sirey's actions as no less loyal than Girardin's. How, he queried, could a man of honor ignore public insults of the sort tendered by Durepaire, and what sense did it make to accuse young Sirey of fighting for mere financial gain when he was clearly prepared to risk his life in a duel to the death? One does not behave thusly, he reflected, "when only money is at stake; but for honor, honor, honor, as you have heard here, it was either retraction or vengeance, indeed a blind vengeance." Cremieux closed his case by recalling earlier testimony about Durepaire's seconds shaking hands with Sirey only moments after he delivered his fatal blow, by then reading into the record a letter from Sirey's sister begging him to avenge their father's honor, and finally by asserting that Durepaire had been a crack pistol shot, far from the hapless victim pictured by the prosecution.

The jury took twenty minutes to acquit Sirey of murder, and another forty-five to require him to pay 10,000 francs in civil damages to Durepaire's widow. By deciding thusly, this assizes jury helped anchor a judicial precedent that would endure throughout the century. After 1836, the "law" that regulated all affairs of honor, from the moment of insult to the "washing" of dishonor in blood, was the private law of the dueling code, for which Chatauvillard's book served as a semi-official reference work, and whose "expert" witnesses were fencing instructors and masters of arms. The generous civil award, which occasionally accompanied duels that came to trial, frankly acknowledged that the only victims in a loyally conducted affair of honor were the dependents of the deceased.

Chatauvillard's book achieved its quasi-juridical status by disapproving of the more dangerous forms of the duel, recommending a *régime* of more responsible intervention by seconds, and by attempting to define genuine affairs of honor to minimize the kinds of motive that complicated the duels we have just considered. For this Solon of the modern duel, it was crucial that these codes of honor become a "common law" known to all "men of heart" and taught as a bill of rights to the young.[78]

To begin with, Chatauvillard was outspokenly opposed to any "exceptional" duel, because "honor might require us to risk our lives, but not to play with them."[79] The situation of two men fighting with only one loaded pistol was absurd not only on account of its bloody nature but because it risked pitting a "man of good faith" against a "scoundrel" if the latter found himself in a situation to dictate a brutal duel, "recalling the horrible heritage of our barbaric past."[80] Chatauvillard included in this category pistol duels at unusually short range, duels which mandated a great number of shots, or duels with rifled, rather than less deadly smooth-bore weapons. He did not so much disapprove of the barrier duel, which still remained acceptable, as strongly endorse its less dangerous alternative, the signal duel, to which he devoted pages of procedural detail.[81]

By disallowing or strictly regulating pistol encounters, Chatauvillard appears to have shared in a general evolution of sentiment in favor of "first blood" duels. As he put it in the *Essai*, "in the present state of our manners, an ordinary duel (*à première sang*) suffices the noble need to expunge an offense."[82] The most renowned master of arms of the era, Augustin Grisier, had long counseled such a development because, as he wrote in 1828, duels to the death were absurdly out of proportion to the relatively trivial offenses that often inspired them. Should not the French, whose nature is "more ardent, more easily irritated, who are quicker to have recourse to the point of honor to prove that we are second to none in the matter of bravery," practice a form of the duel that is less dangerous?[83]

Duels *à première sang* were necessarily sword duels of some type. Whereas pistol duels could only be concluded by death or by the exchange of the agreed-upon number of shots, épée or saber duels could be halted when a wound produced a flow of blood or when one combatant, bloodied or not, was in a condition of notable inferiority. Of the two side arms the épée was much preferred. Chatauvillard weighed in against the pointed saber (*sabre à point*), restricting saber duels to a weapon with a single cutting edge and blunted tip, and confining such combats to the military officers who carried that weapon and were practiced in its use.[84]

The tradition was invented in this era that the French were a race of the sword, naturally inclined to the energetic but disciplined gymnastic of fencing with the tapered, triangular épée favored by good king Louis's musketeers. As Augustin Grisier, the principal champion of this weapon put it, honor itself depended on the "noble and chivalrous" épée as against the pistol, "which has nothing generous, nothing truly French about it." In the pistol duel, "courage and vigor cannot lend their support to skill [*adresse*]; one is obliged to kill one's adversary, who waits, immobile, the shot that will strike him, as the other awaits, in turn, the murderous fire of his enemy."[85] As a general thesis, Grisier argued,

> The sword is the arm of the brave and the gentleman, the most precious relic that history has preserved for us and for the great men who have been the glory of the fatherland: one speaks of the sword of Charlemagne, the sword of Bayard or of Napoleon; who has ever spoken of their pistol? It is a pistol to the throat that makes us sign false letters of credit; a pistol in the hand with which one stops a carriage in the shadows of the woods; it is with a pistol that the bankrupt blows his brains out. Fie on the pistol! The sword is a man's best friend and confidant; it guards his honor or avenges it.[86]

How responsible this or similar rhetoric was for converting later generations of duelers to the épée is not clear. Whether historical conceit, discretionary strategy, or a bit of both, the épée, which was probably the least favored of the three sanctioned weapons in the period before 1848, became the overwhelming favorite of duelers in the fin de siècle. There is no doubting the historically informed self-consciousness of such a development. It is a peculiarity of national dueling traditions that they are proud of the uniqueness of their own rituals and dismissive of those of others. German gentlemen had their lethal pistol barrier duel and German students the sabers and padding that produced facial scars. Austro-Hungarians fought ordinarily with sabers, extraordinarily with pistols, and the Italians were overwhelmingly disposed in favor of the saber.[87]

In addition to nudging the French duel toward less dangerous forms, Chatauvillard invested the seconds with quasi-judicial powers and entrusted them with safeguarding the honor of their champion, and, by extension, their own. The *témoins,* he insisted, must be chosen for their known bravery, experience, and moral rectitude, but also for their integrity and discretion. They fulfilled the role of lawyers in the negotiations in which weapons and conditions of combat are selected, but must become judges during the combat and when they sit down afterward with their opposite numbers to draft the official *procès-verbal,* which had a fully legal status.[88]

They must be the confessors of their client and the guardians of his secrets, but, in protecting his interests, they must see clearly enough to know when they are putting him in danger and that there is no shame in urging him to make his excuses to an adversary whom he has wronged.[89] They must have the "delicacy," above all else, to obey the *point d'honneur* in all matters, looking into their hearts to do for their champions "what they would do for themselves." For Chatauvillard the most reliable assurance of this conduct lay in choosing the best class of men, "because it is well understood among all of us that justice, equity, and good manners [*politesse*] are the foundations on which the seconds must rely to regulate the conditions of the combat."[90]

Finally, Chatauvillard assumed that this same mastery of the conventions of upper-class *politesse* ensured that seconds would understand the hierarchy of possible offenses men could commit, so they could fairly assess the rights each man merited in the code of the duel. The cardinal rule and starting point for any discussion of honor was that no one could claim the rights of the offended party "where the conventions of good taste *savoir-vivre* and politeness [*politesse*] have been followed to the letter."[91] In the text of good manners, there were three degrees of offense, each of which carried a proportionate disposition in the combat. An "impoliteness," serenely undefined in Chatauvillard's text, gave a slight negotiating advantage to the seconds of the offended man, allowing them to press for choice of weapon and, perhaps, certain other conditions. More serious was an "injury," where the gravity and personal nature of the words uttered, or gesture threatened, gave a considerable advantage to the seconds of a man so offended, allowing them more leverage for setting the conditions that would permit their champion to obtain satisfaction. Duels of this kind were by nature more dangerous, and ordained a combat likely to produce more serious results. No one could object if the seconds of an injured man chose a weapon in which he was particularly adept.[92]

The last degree of seriousness was reserved for an offense involving a blow, touch, or slap (*soufflet, voie de fait*). If a man lost his temper in this way, the seconds of the offended man could virtually dictate terms even if, as in the Sirey case, it was delivered in response to a preceding injury. The seconds of the offender in such cases were not entirely without resources; they could negotiate to mitigate particularly harsh conditions, or appeal to a respected dueling expert who would decide the propriety of conditions. But in the code of the duel, as in polite society in general, the man who had the better command of his emotions, who could cooly adapt his word and actions to whatever the circumstances required, enjoyed a certain edge over a man who readily lost his temper. This quality, which the French express as sangfroid, was highly prized by upper-class gentlemen in the nineteenth century. It not only promoted social mobility, but conferred, it would appear, a selective advantage on the men who possessed it in the highest degree.

The effort to eliminate the duel from French society in the first half of the nineteenth century failed miserably, despite the fact that important gains in this era of bourgeois philanthropy were made in prison reform, education, and public health. There are several reasons for this failure. First, eminent supporters of the duel sought to contain its most unpredictable excesses by popularizing a new dueling code that frowned upon irregular or risky encounters and that, in the spirit of bourgeois penal reform, made the danger of the duel proportional to the level of the offense. Second, the friends of the duel were aided, perhaps inadvertently, in this endeavor by their adversaries, who, despairing of outright legislative abolition, admitted the code of the duel into official jurisprudence as a private and quasi-legal basis for assessing equity.

Finally, and of greatest importance, the duel survived in the early industrial era because the conventions of honor upon which it depended were embraced by the bourgeoisie, a process that had begun much earlier in the Old Regime. It was during the first decades of the century that the social and political amalgamation of the old nobility and bourgeoisie was cemented. Addressing the bourgeois *notables* and aristocrats in the Chamber of Deputies, the Duc de la Rochefoucauld-Doudeauville protested the putative differences between them, saying that for his part, "I see only nobles before me, only men of honor. That is the true nobility."[93]

The real secret of the duel's success, however, was the penetration of the usages and presumptions of honor into deeper layers of the urban bourgeoisie, where they blended with the egalitarianism and nationalism that flourished in those milieux. Whether or not professionals, businessmen, or *rentiers* themselves made use of the duel, they apparently regarded its existence as both a buttress of their political identity and a distinctive aspect of the national patrimony.

During his campaign to eliminate the duel, Louis-Philippe's prosecutor general repeatedly assured the public that only the rule of law could keep the discredited social distinctions of the Old Regime system of honor at bay, "putting all citizens on the same level." "The law," he argued, "is the same for all; it has one aim, namely to punish all those equally who fight and kill with any kind of weapon whatsoever."[94] In a later verdict of the Court of Cassation, which reversed the acquittal of a dueler by an assizes jury in Orléans, the court adopted Dupin's position in language that updated but eerily echoed the similarly fruitless antidueling edicts of Louis XIII. In failing to punish even equal combat, the court argued, "We would be acknowledging the right of each man to make his own justice, when it is a fundamental axiom of our public law that justice is a debt assumed by the entire country, and comes from the king alone, in whose name is it rendered."[95]

The right to make justice for oneself was, however, precisely the right most coveted by much of the urban bourgeoisie. The nation was governed by a narrow elite of electors and legislators, whose ranks also supplied the prefectoral corps and the highest levels of the administration and magistracy. For the bourgeois not lucky enough to be of this happy few, the duel provided a measure of personal satisfaction. If he qualified as a man of honor, he shared with the great and near great of his nation access to a ritual once reserved to an aristocracy of blood. The duel, wrote one of its most effective publicists, "equalized ranks and fortunes without pity."[96]

The radically individualistic ideal of justice this view endorsed damns, by implication, the cronyism and the self-interestedness of "official" law, giving the lie to its lip service about equality. It made of the dueling code a system of alternative law that rendered swift and certain justice, and put its faith in qualities all men of honor were presumed to possess in equal measure: manliness and personal courage. Men who dueled were not, for all that, engaged in a barbaric practice that diminished them and, by implication, the society of which they were a part. As Anatole France later wrote, the sword is "the first tool of civilization, the only means man has found to reconcile his brutal instincts and his ideal of justice."[97] Jules Janin, the foremost literary critic of the 1830s and 1840s put the case more strongly still:

> I would not want to live 24 hours in a society constituted without the duel. The duel makes of each of us a strong and independent power; it makes of each life the life of the whole of society; it takes up the cause of justice the moment the law abandons it; alone it punishes what the laws are unable to punish, scorn and insult. Those who have spoken against the duel are either poltroons or imbeciles; he who has spoken both for and against it lies out of both sides of his mouth. We are still a civilized people today because we have conserved the duel.[98]

Men more highly placed than Janin echoed similar sentiments. François Guizot, prime minister and chief ideological supporter of the July Monarchy, begged to differ with his own government's prosecutor general, stating at various times in Parliament his belief in the progressive, civilized, and essentially French nature of the duel.[99] The Frenchness of the duel was invariably connected to those virtues promoting progress and equality. As Alphonse Signol wrote, the nation's greatest strength and weakness was her pride, but out of that quality has come "that loyalty, that courage, that patriotism, . . . which has made such rapid progress in our constitutional order."[100]

It seems indisputably true that the men who favored retaining this ancient ritual were by no means either unregenerate Old Regime nobles or political reactionaries. They were solid, respectable bourgeois whose progressivism was joined to patriotism in the manner of the buoyant liberalism of the era. By engaging in affairs of honor as principals or seconds, or by merely speaking in public in favor of this manner of resolving differences, men could express simultaneously their patriotism, their right to membership in a democratic civil order, and their manliness.

8

The Culture of the Sword: Manliness and Fencing in the Third Republic

Perhaps the most popular novel of the early Third Republic was Georges Ohnet's *Le Maître des forges* (The Ironmaster), first published in 1882, and in its 181st edition in 1884. Though not a writer of the first rank, Ohnet achieved a considerable following for his works by treating subjects of contemporary interest and employing the formulas for literary success of his day. His melodramatic play of the same title was a *succès fou* in 1883, earning the plaudits "moving" and "true" from the fashionable critic Francisque Sarcey.[1] Ohnet's novel is interesting to me because it displays the social and cultural implications of male honor more fully than any literary production in the era of the fledgling republic, in terms that spoke directly to the immediate concerns of its readers.

The hero of Ohnet's story is Philippe Derblay, a bourgeois of early middle age who has accumulated a fortune by reviving the failed ironworks he inherited from his father. Educated as an engineer at the prestigious Ecole Polytechnique, Derblay was a hero in the war of 1870, "dark and male" with great personal courage and a distinctly unbourgeois taste for hunting and firearms.[2] All that is lacking in his worthy and productive world is a wife.

Philippe falls in love with a young aristocratic lady of the neighborhood, Claire de Branlieu, whose mother sees in Derblay the kind of match that noble families with good names but scarce resources made frequently in the nineteenth century. Claire's brother, Octave, regards Derblay as the wave of the future and hopes that the alliance of their families will make an "aristocracy" in the "new democracy," uniting those qualities that make a nation great: "past glories and progress in the present."[3] Alas, Claire is still pining for her childhood companion the callous Duke de Bligny, a diplomat whose dissolute ways and gambling have "marked and hardened" him, making him an unsuitable match.

Ohnet makes much of the physical contrast between Philippe and Bligny. The latter is blond and "slender" with an elegant manner and "spiritual" mouth, a "finished model of the delicate grace and weakness of the nobility." Bligny plays the golden-corseleted "wasp" to Philippe's industrious but less glamorous "honeybee," but the nobleman still possesses a sting in the courage and dueling skills that are the heritage of his "race."[4] Up to no good, the idle duke, now married to a woman of his own ilk, moves into the neighborhood.

Claire meanwhile, is inconsolable and distant, her marriage to Philippe unconsummated. Crushed by her disdain, the saintly Derblay treats her with tenderness and consideration, but is too gallant to demand his marital rights. By degrees, his generosity, self-control, and moral superiority win her grudging admiration, if not her love. She recognizes that men like him are the "dominant force of the century," becomes his helpmeet in the business, and begins to regret her pride.

At this point the duke and his new wife make an appearance at a reception *chez* Derblay. Finding Claire alone, the duke attempts to reawaken her love for him by disparaging Derblay's *roturier* origins, at the very moment that Claire catches sight of the duke's wife flirting with Philippe in the garden. She flies to her husband, and, in the presence of the guests, demands the duke escort his wife away. An occasion for an affair of honor has presented itself, and the women become suddenly invisible.[5] The duke asks Philippe if he will make his excuses, and the latter raises himself up in his "male vigor" to declare that all Claire does is "well done" in his eyes. Turning away, Bligny declares to a crony that Philippe is a "dead man," as Philippe assures his wife that "in defending you it was my honor that I was defending."[6]

As the offended party, the duke chooses pistols and dangerous conditions for the duel. Claire spends an agonized night in fear she has caused her husband-champion's death, while Philippe, serenely untroubled, makes out his will, regretting only not having tasted the joys of love. The following morning, in a caricature of such occasions, Claire begs Philippe not to go, but he is in fine manly spirits and can speak only of the perfect weather and of "duty and honor." At the scene of the duel, however, there is a surprise ending. Claire rushes between them at the last instant, receives a wound in the hand, and is carried, bleeding, back to the house. The affair of honor is concluded amicably, both men having displayed their courage, and Philippe returns home to exchange with Claire their "first kiss of love."[7]

Save for Claire's dramatic intrusion, Ohnet's chivalric representation of the French affair of honor reproduces in all important respects the late nineteenth-century conventions of the ritual. His close association of the concept of personal honor with the themes of class integration, patriotism, and national revival also expressed sentiments common in France in the decades after the humiliating Prussian victory in 1870 and the ensuing terrors of civil war, as if the organic spirit and knightly virtues of the Middle

Ages might help regenerate modern French society. However, outbursts of enthusiastic medievalism were by no means restricted to France in the nineteenth century. Mark Girouard has chronicled the astonishing rebirth of chivalric ideals in British upper-class culture, which he connects with the search for a gentlemanly code that might ease the progressive intermixture of old and new elites.[8] In England, Germany, and elsewhere, the most fantastic expression of this obsession with chivalry and its values was the effort to stage authentic medieval tournaments, complete with armored warriors, costumes, and knightly insignia.[9] More effective and lasting gains in this cultural movement were registered in the decorative arts, painting, architecture, and literature, but behind all these activities lay a hunger for an integrated and spiritual society that might redeem the strife and class warfare of the contemporary industrial order.

In France, paradoxically, the glorification of chivalry was to a remarkable extent the work of liberal and progressive thinkers. In the hands of an early nineteenth-century liberal intellectual like the historian-politician François Guizot, the rediscovery of the "moral" component in medieval life had both a political and a patriotic significance. First, it allowed bourgeois thinkers of the post-revolutionary era to praise the parts of France's royalist past that had shaped French civilization but that transcended the monarchy itself, in order to prove, as Stanley Mellon has said, that "France of the Revolution need not be ashamed of the Old Regime and that the Revolution had been wrong to despise the French past."[10] By employing a discourse of chivalry, liberals could celebrate a richer and deeper moral heritage than could be derived from the egoistic doctrines of liberal economics and legal individualism, but they could also present themselves and their politics of the *juste milieu* as lying somewhere between the extremes of royalist tyranny and revolutionary anarchy.

Second, by identifying with chivalry, which Guizot (after the example of Tacitus) believed had descended from the military rites of the ancient Germanic tribes, liberals were able to appropriate for themselves the quality of courage in the warrior ethic that was the irreducible core of the French patriotic tradition. As Léon Gautier, the foremost nineteenth-century historian of chivalry, expressed it in 1884, we are fortunate that the "French race . . . still loves the fatherland," since there are still many Frenchmen who "know and practice all the delicacies of honor and prefer death to the felony of a single lie."[11]

In his "History of Civilization in France," which he first presented in his Sorbonne lectures of 1828–30, Guizot disparaged the social heritage of feudal chivalry, but praised its moral nature, which made medieval life "appear beautiful and pure amidst the licentiousness and grossness of actions."[12] In Guizot's account, the efflorescence of chivalry in the early Middle Ages made *seigneurs* both valorous and courteous in dealings with their fellow nobles and civilized relations between husband and wife within the castle walls. In his words, "There is no one but knows that the domestic life, the spirit of family, and particularly the condition of women, were developed in modern Europe much more completely than elsewhere."[13]

In his description of France's chivalric past, Guizot articulated a body of interlocking ideals that remained central to the value system of the French bourgeoisie for the remainder of the century. It is tempting to contrast this bookish syncretism unfavorably with the genuine aristocratizing activity of the Old Regime bourgeoisie, but this would risk overlooking how successfully chivalric ideals expressed the practical aims of the French bourgeoisie at virtually each moment of its development. Chivalry was by no means inconsistent with the middle-class work ethic or with political and civic egalitarianism; a rhetoric of knightly honor also permitted bourgeois males the luxury of thinking themselves to be men of courage and the protectors of women and the weak.

The prestige of chivalric values may have ebbed for a few years after the democratic upheavals of 1848–49 and the onset of the new Napoleonic dictatorship, but a discourse of honor emerged in the last half of the century that articulated the ideal of a reinvigorated republican manhood and the social and political values of a new democratic order. It may seem paradoxical that a cultural discourse born in a world of warring, unlettered nobles could retain its meaning in a democratic, industrial society, but as Norbert Elias indicated in *The History of Manners,* linguistic terms may fall into a state of sleep at certain times, but may "acquire a new existential value from a new social situation. They are recalled because something in the present state of society finds expression in the crystalization of the past embodied in the words."[14]

The material conditions that supported a bourgeois discourse of honor also encouraged a cautious but inexorable strategy of class integration. From the Second Empire through the end of the century, the route for bourgeois social advance was much the same as it had been in the first half of the century. Industrialization and the modernization of the agricultural sector of the economy did not proceed fast enough to either sweep away traditional social and economic elites or guarantee the hegemony of the new productive classes. Even in the periods of most rapid industrial advance, archaic sectors of the economy were able to survive more or less intact, giving the French economy a mixed aspect.[15] The political alliance of "wheat" and "iron" that arose in the last decades of the century was a tacit acknowledgement that this "dualistic" economy could not compete in the international economy; in the 1890s protective tariffs for industrial and agricultural products alike further assured the survival of "stagnant" economic backwaters.[16]

There was no rapidly rising economic escalator in nineteenth-century

France to whisk new men into social and political prominence. Social advance proceeded in the time-honored fashion by slow accumulations of social and educational capital, "synthesized" and "conditioned" by astute marital alliances.[17] Prejudices against marriages between individuals in the upper social ranks were rapidly crumbling. A popular etiquette book of the 1850s and 1860s advised both old and new elites to acknowledge the fact that, "since power these days is scattered throughout society, constituted in blood, in fortunes, and in rank, each may lay claim for himself the respect and the consideration he accords his neighbor."[18] Thus, social and marital relations with nobles continued to be valued by ambitious bourgeois, less perhaps for the economic or political power they wielded than for the *cultural* capital they possessed. As Pierre Bourdieu has pointed out:

> The embodied cultural capital of the previous generations functions as a sort of advance (both a head-start and a credit which . . . enables the newcomer [and his or her heirs] to start acquiring the basic elements of the legitimate culture from the beginning, that is, in the most unconscious and impalpable way. . . . Legitimate manners owe their value to the fact that they manifest the rarest conditions of acquisition, that is, a social power over time which is tacitly recognized as supreme excellence. . . .[19]

Although the "innateness" of the old nobility's "natural" taste was much admired, and emulated by the boldest of social climbers, bourgeois resentment of aristocratic snobbishness was still keenly felt. The inherent ambivalence of this relationship was played out, so to speak, in late nineteenth-century Parisian theater, which examined the tensions in the upper classes from every conceivable angle. Emile Augier, whose plays dominated the popular stage in the last half of the century, specialized in this theme. Despite his sympathy with the values and political goals of the liberal bourgeoisie, for Augier the distinctions of wealth meant little in the struggle for social supremacy. Manners and grandeur of outlook were everything; in this the middle classes had much to learn from their class rivals. Augier could not bring himself to make the following words, uttered by a noble personage in his *Les Effrontés* (1881), appear ridiculous: "Our orientation has a certain grandeur, our impertinance a certain grace. We have other convictions than our interest; in the end we are obliged to pay only one tax, which you others never pay, the blood tax."[20]

The most complete expression of the modern discourse of honor appeared in 1868 in *La France Nouvelle,* a book by Lucien Prevost-Paradol, a foremost liberal critic of the Second Empire. Prevost-Paradol's work was inspired by Bismarck's creation of the North German Confederation the previous year and by his fear that Napoleon III's corrupt and politically bankrupt regime no longer commanded enough popular support to resist this formidable new power. Despite Claude Digeon's characterization of him as a "realist" (on account of his demographic anxieties), Prevost-Paradol argued passionately for a spiritual renewal in his countrymen.[21] He suggested a republic might replace an imperial order that had coupled a materialistic "cult of success" with political repression. "Self-interest and force," he wrote, must be replaced by the free exercize of "honor, or better still, the point of honor, the last powerful rampart of aging societies, and particularly that of France."[22] Our fatherland, he wrote, "is the unique example in the world of a society in which the point of honor has become the principle guarantee of good order and which enjoins the duties and the sacrifices that religion and patriotism have lost the power to inspire. If our laws . . . are generally obeyed, if the young soldier willingly follows the flag and remains faithful to it, if the bureaucrat respects the integrity of the public coffers, if Frenchmen perform in a timely fashion most of their obligations to the state and their fellow citizens, it is to the point of honor that we are especially indebted."[23] The point of honor also teaches us "to draw our swords if we would not lose our rank, lest our weapons remain in their scabbards out of a misguided conviction that they no longer play a role in regulating human affairs."[24] This same regime of honor, he hoped, would ameliorate the "perversion of the moral sense" that was causing the French birthrate to fall below that of neighboring states, particularly Germany. We must reproduce ourselves rapidly enough, he wrote, "to maintain a certain equilibrium between our power and that of the other great nations of the world."[25]

Events revealed Prevost-Paradol to be both a prophet and a man of his word. The "liberalization" of the empire that took place between the appearance of his book and 1870 seduced him into accepting Louis Napoleon's offer of the ambassadorship to the United States. But on hearing the news of the French military catastrophe at Sedan, he felt shame at this collaboration. "My friends," he wrote, "will believe that I knew in advance of the Emperor's bellicose intentions and will accuse me of bad faith." Moved by his "overriding sense of honor," he committed suicide at the very moment of the emperor's abdication.[26]

It was France's crushing defeat in the 1870 war that raised a discourse of chivalry to higher levels of visibility. In its new year's day issue of 1871, the popular parisian newspaper, *Le Petit journal,* expressed the conviction that though French soldiers had been badly led, even betrayed by their commanders, the "honor of the ordinary fighting man emerged unblemished, as did his native, "sense of justice, frankness and generosity," and his "chivalric loyalty."[27] In the same year, but in a more pessimistic vein, Ernst Renan ruminated in his *La Réforme intellectuelle et morale* that France's predominantly *roturier* social order had somehow weakened her will to fight. Struggling to find a formula that would help encourage a national revival, Renan contrasted favorably France's essentially "democratic" honor with the class-bound honor of Prussia, but he hoped that his nation's egalitarian national identity could be reinfused with the positive qualities in the aristocratic and military spirit: the spirit of the *honnête homme* must be married to that of the *galant homme*.[28]

Though Renan was no friend of the republic, it became clear in the years after 1871 that a monarchical restoration was impossible; a republic would be the form of government that would divide France least and permit the country to regain its equilibrium. The political events that led to this eventuality are well-known, as is the story of the emergence into the political arena of the "new social strata" to which Gambetta and the radical republicans pitched their appeal. However, apart from a brief ministry before Gambetta's death in December 1882, the radicals initially had little chance to shape the policies of the new regime. Instead, power was exercised after 1878 by the so-called left-center republicans, the immediate forerunners of the "opportunists," who dominated the politics of the 1880s and early 1890s. This faction based its program on a cautious balancing between the radical implications of democratic sovereignty and the profound social and economic conservatism that united both old notables and peasant proprieters. As Daniel Halévy tells the story, this policy received its baptism at the end of 1876 in the remarks with which the center-left republican Jules Simon inaugurated his new ministry. To the Chamber of Deputies he announced, "I am *profoundly republican* and profoundly conservative," changing his inflection in the more conservatively elected Senate to, "I am profoundly republican and *profoundly conservative*."[29] The ambiguous nuance of Simon's formula was the strength of his pragmatic politics, but it inflamed his ideological opponents, as in an outburst by the then-Bonapartist, Ernest Lavisse: "We are engulfed by sterility. Opportunism is an excuse for impotence. . . . The center-left has no sex [*n'a pas de sexe*]."[30]

Despite characterizations of this kind, the radicals, though at odds with the opportunists on the pace, and sometimes the aim of political reforms, were largely in agreement with them on the matter of the kind of man who would be the ideal citizen of the new Third Republic. This new republican man must embody in himself the qualities of citizen, worker, and father that his sworn enemy, the priest, could not attain. As Katherine Auspitz has written in her review of the radical literature of the 1850s and 1860s, French radicals did not, as is often assumed, trust to the sole efficacy of political reform. A republic must, they believed, be grounded in shared assumptions about each man's personal dignity, that is, on his personal and civic identity. Republicans wanted to "reunite in one personality the masculine roles dispersed by the old regime among the three estates and to dignify the tasks degraded by it."[31]

The new man, "pur et dur" (pure and hard), would be shaped to a certain extent by a new secular education that would not simply teach him skills or a profession, but enable him "to be a man worthy of the name man."[32] As the Minister of Education Eugène Spuller put it in a prize-day speech in 1887, "Character in our troubled times is worth far more than talent."[33] Masculine character was also to be cultivated in militant reform organizations like the crusading *Ligue de l'enseignement,* and in the egalitarian culture of all-male voluntary societies, clubs, and Masonic temples.[34] Jean Macé, the founder of the *Ligue,* had written his own courtesy book, *Les Vertus du républicain* (1848), as a basis for the collective relations of such groups because, "positive law is never exhaustive and *politesse* must make up for the gaps in the code . . . [supplying] fraternal love . . . , reciprocal egalitarianism . . . , universal suffrage."[35] The need to develop "respect for persons in myself and others," Macé believed, was the ideal "civic apprenticeship" for new cadres of republican activists.[36] Though he thought himself the founder of a new republican ethic, Macé was giving voice to principles that had guided bourgeois male sociability more or less continuously since the eighteenth century.

Thus, despite the social and political differences that separated them, the principle factions of progressive bourgeois opinion in the second half of the century shared a nexus of common values—social integration (solidarity), patriotism, patriarchy—expressed in a discourse of masculine honor. One of the most popular spokemen for this set of themes was the *académicien* and playwright, Ernest LeGouvé. Though of an advanced age by the 1870s, LeGouvé continued to be an avid fencer; he encouraged the art, he wrote in 1872, because, "I would like our democracy to remain aristocratic in its manners and its sentiments, and nothing can achieve that end more effectively than familiarity with the sword."[37] This cultural amalgamation would have the happy effect, LeGouvé believed, of both harmonizing the classes in the new regime, and of improving the status of women.

He explains this relation in his essay "Aristocratic and Democratic Politeness." In a dialogue about manners between a marquis and his bourgeois lawyer, the marquis observes that the lawyer's son had spoken abruptly to his father and seemed unable to speak courteously and naturally to the young woman seated next to him at dinner, and, on a subject the marquis knew quite well, the boy had spoken bluntly to him "as though to an equal."[38] The lawyer defends his son, contrasting the contrived dissimulation of old-fashioned courtesy with the "sincerity" and "love of truth" of democratic manners. He reminds the marquis that one may no longer insult one's social inferiors with impunity: "You say monsieur to a peasant who calls you monsieur," and you risk having an altercation with a coachman if your requests to him are delivered in a threatening manner.[39] The lawyer admits his "principled" politeness lacks a certain grace, but maintains that in a democratic society this quality eliminates the "impertinences" of the old hierarchical order.

In response, the marquis points out that impertinence is an "art" enabling a man to respond in proper measure to the offenses he must occasionally suffer in society, so as to avoid having to resort to a vulgar and undifferentiated insolence. This same skill at verbal distinctions, he continued, may also be used to speak with respect and delicacy to women and to acknowledge and confirm the differences in age and sex within the family.[40] In the end the marquis and the lawyer agree that "to make a perfectly polite man, one needs the principles of today and the manners of yesteryear," and that in all matters pertaining to politeness, "women are the sole authority for us both."[41]

LeGouvé's particular brand of feminism—"difference in equality"—won widespread approval, as we have already seen, from male and female feminists alike, as well as financial and moral support from the republican parliamentary establishment. The widespread concern about "depopulation" also clearly helped influence the forging of this discourse of chivalric concern for the "weak." As Offen and others have argued, however, the new regime's support for legal and social benefits for mothers and abandoned women was obtained in exchange for maintaining the status quo on political rights and access to elite occupations.[42]

But the obligations of this feminist chivalry cut more than one way. If women personified "the graces, beauty, and love" and were "sublime in their maternity," men, "ennobled in nature through their initiative," were required to embody the opposing principles of "force, resolution, and work."[43] Some excellent scholarship has been done on the textbooks and educational practices of the republican regime that show the ways that sex roles and occupations were indoctrinated.[44] Republican educational theorists did not wish to keep women in the new order ignorant and prey to superstition; only a literate and intelligent woman was a fit companion for the new republican man.[45] Though women learned from a restricted syllabus that prepared them for family life, not the *baccalauréat,* the Sée law of 1880 established a parallel network of state secondary schools reserved for them. Republican educators made it clear that the new educational regime was not an endorsement of occupational gender integration. In a speech defending the Sée law, the minister of education, Paul Bert, told his male audience, "Don't worry, women will only compete with men in jobs that men have wrongly filled by virtue of their superior force. But equality is not identity; if men have stepped outside their natural roles, they deserve this fate, and will perhaps return to their rightful place. Indeed, in a society where men have made themselves into dressmakers and designers, it is patently bizarre to hear them complain of female competition."[46]

In the writing of Ernest Le Gouvé, the symbol of the sword and of chivalry toward women were indissolubly linked concepts, recalling ancient images of ladies won or defended by the noble steel of knights-errant. Such a coupling was not unique to LeGouvé; other scholars and popularizers of chivalry in this era took special care to underline the historic connection between honorable deeds and love.[47] Of course, the sword was also used in this era, as it is today, as a general metaphor for military action, and the manly qualities that sustained it.[48] Thus, the device of Jean Macé's *Ligue de l'enseignement* was "Pour la patrie, par le livre et par l'épée." As we have already seen, however, there were at least two additional and contingent meanings attached to the image of the sword that were more particular and more particularly French, which also resonated in the minds of contemporaries. I refer to the notions of the sword as the weapon par excellence of past French military glory, and as the weapon of choice in French affairs of honor. LeGouvé himself used "sword" to evoke both these meanings, but, whether he knew it or not, he was engaged in a task of myth-making, combining powerful images from the past with the passions of the present (See Figs. 1 and 2).

In the seventeenth century, gentlemen would have understood intuitively the equation of "sword" with vengeance and justice; in the 1870s, this relation needed some cultural and social reinforcement. There was no question here of "inventing" a new tradition; the tradition existed already. It was more like adapting a historic memory to new social and political circumstances, while preserving the romantic associations evoked by this memory in the novels and plays of Alexandre Dumas and other authors of Old Regime nostalgia. It was certainly the distilled essence of this memory that provoked Henri de Pène to write with disarming disingenuousness the following lines in his preface to a modern edition of Brantôme's *Discours sur les duels* (1887): "The duel, happily, has changed considerably from the days when our writer related these anecdotes from the French courts of Henri II, François II, Henri III and Henri IV. Our contemporary duelist, however, often resembles his ancestor trait for trait."[49]

The distillation of a culture of the sword in late nineteenth-century France is the focus of the remainder of this chapter. By analyzing the revival of interest in fencing and the duel, we may better understand how the masculine ideals of the upper levels of French society were constructed and maintained in this era. This interest was cultivated in a context of male club sociability, where it advanced individual careers and promoted social integration, and in the political sphere, where it served as an important part of the rhetorical arsenal of republicanism.

Throughout their history, fencing and the duel have been tied inextricably together. From the late sixteenth through the seventeenth centu-

Figure 1. "The Past. In the good old days of the church and barbarism, it called itself the judgment of God."

ries, any good-sized town had a fencing hall owned and staffed by a master of arms and his apprentices. The master was subject to the rules of the Royal Academy of Arms, which governed the activities of the halls in the manner of all guilds. The academy was abolished with all other corporate

Figure 2. "The Present. Today it takes place, in general, in a popular duelodrome with all the comforts of hygiene and progress. It is a spectacle for the elegant."

monopolies in 1790, and by 1840 the number of halls in France had shrunk to about ten.[50] The art was kept alive during this period, for the most part, by retired regimental *prevôts* whose students were themselves ex-officers or bored gentlemen-about-town.

Near the end of the Second Empire, to the delight of *amateurs* of the art, demand grew sufficiently to allow a modest increase in the number of masters to perhaps 35 "professors." A phenomenal expansion took place a few years after the Franco-Prussian war. By 1890 there were more than 100 masters-at-arms in Paris alone, and *salles d'armes* had sprouted in virtually every provincial city. Bordeaux's halls attracted 250 fencers, and Lyon and Marseille were not far behind. Nancy, Bourges, Clermont-Ferrand, Toulouse, and other towns of their size had at least two fencing venues.[51] In 1882 a *Société de l'encouragement de l'escrime* was founded for serious Parisian amateurs; by 1889 it had well over 400 dues-paying members, an office, and an official publication.[52]

In 1886 a group of Parisian masters reconstituted the Academy of Arms. They hoped to raise the standards of the art, but also, it was alleged, to limit competition for students in the capital by excluding newcomers to the trade. The academy also functioned as a mutual aid society for aged members. From 1878 the Parisian masters held an annual assault to replenish their retirement fund.[53] This event was a grand *succès d'estime* because it attracted an "elegant and *mondaine* crowd, clubmen, and noted fencers," and because it was the only assault at which most Parisian masters went head-to-head, watched eagerly by their *prevôts* and students.[54]

Many of the new department stores and a score of Parisian newspapers, such as *Le Figaro, Le Gaulois,* and *La France* maintained fencing halls and masters to keep their male personnel in working and fighting trim.[55] Beginning in 1882 the *Société de l'encouragement* sponsored an annual fencing assault in the lobby of the Grand Hotel in Paris, featuring some of the best masters and socially prominent amateurs of the capital. This assault, like that of the Academy of Arms, was held in the midst of the Paris winter social season, attracting men and women in evening dress who were, by one account, the "flower of the fencing world, of sport, of Parisian elegance."[56]

The republican nature of the art was emphasized by regular Sunday morning assaults originally organized at the Elysée palace by President Grévy's son-in-law, Daniel Wilson. These assaults, which continued through the term of Félix Faure, who was an enthusiastic amateur, were timed to coincide with the traditional hour of the Sunday mass and to attract the cream of the republic's judicial and administrative elite.[57] The private assaults of banquet societies such as the *Société du Contre* de *Quarte* were more exclusive, giving themselves the "luxury of capriciously blackballing new applicants like the most chic *cercles.*"[58] The fencing press carried reviews of all these affairs in copious detail. In short, as one commentator put it in 1886, fencing is now the "official mode" of the "cultivated" set.[59]

A typical assault of the 1880s entailed consecutive single combats between men of roughly equal skill. Dress was optional, but most men wore standard fencing hall gear and were fitted with a padded vest (*plastron*) and fencing gloves. The sharp tips of the foils were padded (*mouchetés*). The names of fencers were announced by a "herald-at arms," and organizers built drama into the proceedings by arranging the last few matches between well-known professionals or between two men known to dislike one another, not a difficult matter in these competitive and prickly milieux. Before every match, each man would bow elaborately to his opponent, sweeping his sword laterally in imitation of the flourish of a courtier's plumed hat. More gallant still, the professional Lucien Merignac invented an opening gesture in which he lunged toward his opponent in the classic attack position, but inclined the point of his foil backward along his arm and shoulder, symbolizing his wish to engage in combat but do no harm. The presence of women at these affairs presented further opportunities for ritual acts of courtesy. At an assault at the Ecole de Guerre in 1889, young ladies were each presented a flower by the officers participating in the match.[60]

In keeping with the archaic spirit of the occasion, observers commonly described the action in terms evocative of knightly combat. Ernest Le-Gouvé, who probably set the style for such description, portrayed the first public assault following the 1870 war as a "tournement" whose champions conducted themselves "chivalrously," with "frankness" and "loyalty."[61] The participants in these combats were believed to reveal their individual temperaments in their fencing styles. Thus, Féry D'Esclands, counsellor of state, was "impassable," "never breaks" (retreats), and "executes you with his touch." Another fencer was a (clever) "tireur de tête," a virtual "Talleyrand of fencing"; another still a man of "brio," impetuous in the attack. And Prince Georges Bibesco, winner of the 1872 international pistol-shoot, and a French hero of the war of 1870, was a picture of "taste, grace, and ardor, mixed with elegance, . . . a Prince combatant of knightly manner."[62]

Individual matches were not judged or refereed in any formal way. If a man was touched by the tip of his opponent's sword on his chest, he was obliged to call out "touché" in a firm voice. Winners and losers were not declared in assaults; the emphasis was on a demonstration of "correct" style and virtuoso technique. Thus, it was not good form to add up touches and declare a winner, though the writers in the fencing press found it hard in practice to resist the temptation to do so. More importantly, a man was universally condemned for refusing to acknowledge a touch. This was much more than a mere sporting venality; it was a stain on a man's integrity, an act of "disloyalty" or of "bad faith."[63] A man who could lie in a fencing assault to gain an advantage over another was capable of far greater moral enormities in life itself, where, unlike the public assault, most of his actions went unobserved (see Fig. 3).

Figure 3. "Honor is like an old pair of shoes. It may be mended, and here is the needle."

This judgment underlines the point that fencing was believed to be a school for character, just as the individual fencer was believed to display his character in his style. As Ernest LeGouvé was fond of saying, a man could find out far more about his future son-in-law in one hour of fencing than in six months of investigations.[64] Only when they are under arms, wrote the fencing master Arsène Vigeant, can we gauge clearly the "character and moral worth" of men; squaring off with another man in single combat, weapon in hand, was the closest approximation of life lived *in extremis* that could be mustered in civilization.[65] The art developed both self-respect and respect for others by teaching men "how to keep their proper distance from one another, and to judge the practical matters of life down to a centimeter."[66]

There were three different arguments advanced by proponents of fencing that they believed illustrated the moral and character-building qualities of their art. Individual character formation was likely the most important of these, but fencing was also believed to breed courageous warriors for the fatherland and, in addition, to refine and socially perfect its devotees. Since fencing was a skill that harmonized a complex "technique" with force, it required a unique blend of mental powers, physical conditioning, and disciplined training, representing, wrote Féry d'Esclands, "the triumph of thought over matter, of the spirit over the body."[67] This feature of the art cultivated the faculty of judgment to a high degree. A fencer needed to assess an opponent's skill, anticipating his *jeu* (tactic), while simultaneously choosing a *jeu* for himself that reflected his own level of skill and promised some measure of success. A fencer who performed this operation well possessed *l'à-propos* (aptness), and if he had the physical resources to carry it out, he was held to have *l'adresse* (skill, adroitness).[68]

Fencers were never praised for their strength. Speed, dexterity, quick reflexes, and endurance more than compensated for deficiencies of physical force. Great strength was, on the contrary, a liability, encouraging its possessor in ill-advised attacks that opened him up to dangerous *ripostes*.[69] Most importantly, fencing developed in men the "virile" qualities of self-mastery, of calm under pressure (sangfroid), and of "confidence in one's own force."[70] Taken together, these characteristics made a man "brave," but never arrogant; a man with experience in the fencing halls quickly learned that sublime skills were often hidden beneath the most unprepossessing exteriors. Thus, as Hebrard de Villeneuve wrote, a disciplined fencer "will count only on himself, and will neither provoke nor incite envy in others."[71] It was precisely this "air of nobly reserved assurance," that developed in fencers the "sentiments of true honor."[72]

These personal qualities were also useful to the nation. Indeed, though it preceded the defeat of 1870 by a few years, the modern revival of fencing was virtually coeval with the determination of patriots to rebuild the strength of France and prepare for revenge. Within the republican camp in particular, the 1870s and 1880s were years when sport and fitness were yoked to patriotism.[73] The rapid growth of gymnastic societies, shooting societies, and the popular paramilitary "batallions scolaires" of secondary school students reflected a widespread conviction that if France were one day to regain the lost provinces of Alsace and Lorraine, Frenchmen needed to acquire, or, more exactly, reacquire the military qualities of the "race."[74]

Fencing advocates were second to none in the claims they made for their art. Ernest LeGouvé begged mothers to make their sons learn to fence and acquaint them with the "friendships of companions in arms," for France has need of "virile hearts and bodies."[75] Fencing was portrayed as a natural continuation of the tradition of French skill in *armes blanches* (steel weapons), a "national glory" that nourished courage and resilience.[76] In a speech to the revived Academy of Arms, Duc Féry d'Esclands argued that a child trained in the art would achieve a kind of moral equilibrium and self-control that would preserve him from "either ridiculing a defeated opponent or envying a more fortunate one." He would learn that success was dependent on "an acquired superiority maintained by painful and patient effort in which a defeat will provoke the effort required for revenge."[77]

Fencing experts often likened the confrontation between two swordsmen in combat to a duel between nations. One wrote, "The battlefield is like the dueling ground, war like the duel, in the sense that all the courage in the world will shatter against the ramparts built on twenty solid years in a fencing hall."[78] A soldier trained in *armes blanches,* wrote another, would spill his blood more willingly since he likely believed himself to be defending not only the honor of the fatherland, but "his personal honor and dignity" as well.[79] It undoubtedly heightened the convictions of those who subscribed to a French honor forged in steel to contrast the native tradition with foreign varieties. Thus, a member of the fencing press decided that, unlike the "disinterested" nature of French devotion and courage, the British kind is rooted in money and gain. No Briton regarded himself as dishonored, therefore, providing he gained some profit from his actions, while a Frenchman cared nothing for such calculations. The blood sports and pugilism popular in Britain shaped a brutal citizenry, while the national pastime of France formed "courteous" and chivalrous men.[80]

The final way that fencing was held to shape moral character lay in the claim that the *salle d'armes* was a school for politeness which civilized men and harmonized the classes. Far from provoking tension, the fencing hall was praised as a realm of "unity and perpetual peace."[81] Men who crossed swords, it was argued, shared a kind of "freemasonry" of mutual regard, by observing a "cordiality which smoothed over the most irritating issues."[82] Thus, an excellent fencer might know a thousand ways to offend another man, but would also have learned "all the ways he could avoid conflict without loss of honor or dignity."[83] Indeed, the better the fencer, the more confident he would be in his own prowess and the more likely he would possess a natural "chivalric generosity." In the prevailing discourse, the few "quarrellers" one found in a fencing hall were invariably the weakest swordsmen.[84]

Recalling the atmosphere of the *salles d'armes* in his youth, Pierre d'Hughes relates that, "In those days the fencing hall was something more than a gymnasium. It cultivated in fencers the sentiment of honor and comradeship to the extent there was no need to have resort to juries of honor [in the event of a disagreement]. There was a better way: one was in the company of *connoisseurs,* and this intimate public mediated these affairs."[85] In fact all fencing halls posted a set of rules that varied little in their particulars and which were enforced by common consent. Drinking, swearing, and smoking were banned, and fencers were warned against raising their voices above a conversational tone. Members were enjoined to pay their fees on schedule; if a visitor appeared at the door, one offered him a foil; if he broke it, one paid for its replacement. Fencers were warned to be polite to onlookers, not to distract men *en garde,* and not "to joke with anyone about the quality of their skills, because there might be unpleasant consequences."[86]

Though men who fenced together for years often became good friends, they were careful not to *tutoyer* (the diminutive form of address) one another on the premises. Excessive familiarity or a jocular manner were frowned upon in the interests of maintaining formal relations and *bon ton.*[87] To this end the comportment and authority of the fencing master were important ingredients. Masters-at-arms, as they continued to be called, were invariably of lower-class origins; most of them had learned to fence in their regiments and had set up their fencing halls on modest budgets. To attract the upper-class clientele that ensured their prosperity, masters were obliged to cultivate good manners and a refined decorum, which many did with notable success. Their authority in the hall depended as much on their elegance and *bienséance* as on their skill with the foil. Indeed, because fencers regarded the fine manners of their masters as the best proof that the usages of the art ennobled its practitioners, the fencing press took proud note when a master attended the opera, seasoned at Deauville, or celebrated a fashionable marriage at the Madeleine.[88]

To the dismay of traditionalists, the independent status of fencing masters and their halls was gradually eroded in the course of the 1890s. Beginning in Paris, the most prominent of these utilitarian, often unhygienic old halls were converted into tastefully outfitted social *cercles.* Members bought out the master's interest and then rehired him and his staff as salaried employees. The remodeled or relocated halls were, by all accounts, elegant and spacious. Many had showers and massage rooms and decorated salons where members could read or chat.[89] This transformation of the *salles* into private fencing clubs gave the members rather than the masters control over new memberships, and eventually diminished their status and their authority in the hall.[90]

Though some of the fencing halls and clubs were primarily either aristocratic or bourgeois in their clientele, class diversity was the general rule.

A largely aristocratic *cercle* like the one in the Rue des Pyramides had a sprinkling of bourgeois, and aristocrats could be found crossing swords with the predominantly bourgeois membership of the Salle Ruzé, near the Saint-Augustin church. On the whole, *salles* tended to reflect the class or occupational composition of their neighborhoods. The Cercle St. Simon on the Boulevard St Germain was frequented by middle-class professors, the Cercle de L'Union Artistique by right-bank esthetes like the painter Carolus Duran.[91]

It is certainly the case that the professional men, bureaucrats, and intellectuals who joined these circles were engaged in an exercise of upward mobility. A genial fencing session with a wealthy or aristocratic opponent might lead to useful future business or social connections. So, while there is reason to consider the much-vaunted comradeship of fellow fencers to be an exaggeration, it seems likely that men who joined these groups to make useful contacts with other members were not disappointed.[92] Moreover, it was a deeply rooted conviction among fencing enthusiasts that skill with the foil and natural grace could compensate for lack of social distinction. Hughes LeRoux tells the story of an awkward-looking boilermaker who stopped in at a Parisian *salle* on his way home and asked to take a turn. Sword in hand and outfitted, the worker was "transfigured." He "fenced with as much precision as grace. Once he took his guard, his lopsided posture disappeared and he moved as academically and elegantly as any gentleman in France."[93]

Despite the distinctly aristocratic tone of the fencing halls, the work ethic was strictly bourgeois. An invidious comparison was drawn regularly between the indolent "clubmen" of the Jockey club variety—men unfamiliar with arms or physical exertion—and the fencers who came to exercise each evening after a day of labor. It was this devotion to discipline, wrote Daniel Cloutier, that makes "our bourgeois *fin-de-siècle* cede nothing to old regime nobles in courtesy, correction, and probity."[94] The egalitarianism of work was a popular theme in the early Third Republic; it reminds us that if bourgeois men sought to move into *société,* they did not abandon the work ethic as they did so, but attempted to amalgamate it with the manners and usages of their social superiors.

There is a political reading that may be made of this archetypal bourgeois social strategy. The social integration, character formation, and refinement that were believed to take place in the *salles d'armes* were linked directly to the republican and democratic ideology that was sweeping simultaneously through France. Echoing the sentiments of Ernest LeGouvé, the *doyen* of the art, Hebrard de Villeneuve wrote in 1888: "A daughter of the feudal era, fencing still cuts a proud figure in our era of equality. It can and should remain in honor in a democracy; why can we not conceive and found a chivalrous democracy?"[95] Aurelian Scholl laid a slightly different stress on the argument, asserting that, "Fencing has for some time now been an important part of our education. It confirms the Declaration of the Rights of Man; and, if anything, has done more than [the Declaration] to advance the cause of equality."[96] These views were, as we have seen, part of the larger republican effort to shape a new generation of proud and vigorous men whose training in arms would make them both good patriots and democratic citizens. As Paul Bert argued in 1882, such training, "does not develop servile tendencies, but the qualities of a truly free man whose liberty is not constrained by rule and law, but assured and consecrated by them."[97]

Fencing and the duel served to dramatize and symbolically represent the principal ideological components of republican ideology—individual liberty and equality—and therefore helped universalize and popularize the civic value system of the Third Republic. In principle, any man, no matter what his origins, could cultivate the art of fencing and engage in duels because the new regime recognized all men as free agents responsible for their actions. On the other hand, fencing and the duel helped promote equality because no man could refuse to cross swords with a legitimate opponent at the risk of personal shame and public ridicule. A world that recognized, at least in theory, no social boundaries in an activity once reserved for a narrow elite was a male social universe of perfect individualism and equality. Male societies governed by honor codes have always possessed this egalitarian potential. It was the medieval historian Johan Huizinga who wrote, "The idea of chivalry implied, after all, two ideas . . . the ideas, namely, that true nobility is based on virtue and that all men are equal."[98]

In all important respects the fencing halls shared a common ethos with the duel. They were the sites where duelers sharpened their skills, discussed the etiquette of the duel, and exchanged the latest gossip about affairs of honor. Despite the oft-repeated dictum that serious incidents seldom arose in the fraternal domain of fencing, duels were not uncommon between members of the same *cercle,* and, whether deliberately or not, masters-at-arms often drew attention to the close relationship between their art and affairs of honor by engaging in notorious duels with one another. Albert Thomeguex, who was a bully and the most persistent dueler of the era, was sitting one afternoon in the fencing hall at the newspaper *Le Figaro* when someone accidentally trod on his foot. As was his manner, Thomeguex leaped to his feet and pulled his calling card out of his coat pocket (he thought it made him look indecisive if he had to fumble for his card in his wallet). His offender was none other than the Italian fencing-master, Pini, regarded as one of the great technicians of the art, a discovery that would have made a saner man than Thomeguex seek conciliation.[99]

Duels also arose occasionally from incidents in assaults. In 1880, when the more flamboyant style of the Italian fencers was still hardly known and little tolerated by the more restrained French school, the French master Pons reproved the Neapolitan master Athos de San Malato in the midst of their assault for his habit of shouting exuberantly while on attack. San Malato lowered his sword, raised his mask and said in perfect French: "M. le professeur, if you have further observations to make, I may be found at 22, rue de la Pépinière." He then lowered his mask and the assault was concluded. Their subsequent highly publicized duel ended when Pons wounded San Malato, following which the two men embraced with evident relief.[100] Pini and the brilliant left-hander Kirchhoffer once dueled after a particularly heated assault (*gauchers* were regarded as extremely temperamental), and Arsène Vigeant crossed swords with fellow masters Rue and Merignac as a result of differences of opinion in assault pairings and judgments.[101]

After 1880 or so, the line dividing the *jeu de salle* (fencing-hall technique) and the *jeu de terrain* (duelling-ground technique) eroded further still. Until then, only the foil was permitted in the fencing venues or at assaults. The triangular-bladed military épée, which had become the conventional weapon of the French duel, was relatively heavier and longer than the lighter, four-sided *fleuret,* and was regarded by traditionalists as too cumbersome for the intricate movements and speed required in classical fencing technique. The aim of the *jeu de fleuret* was the *coup de bouton* square on the chest—nothing else counted as a score.

In the *jeu d'épée* combatants sought a touch anywhere on the opponent's body, since the object was to bring a flow of blood. This strategy made the swordhand, forearm, head and face, even the leading foot, the likely targets. Epée combat tended, therefore, to be at once more tentative and less schooled than the brilliant and athletic skirmishes of *fleurettistes,* who scornfully dismissed the *jeu d'épée* as "utilitarian." However, the rough and ready style of épée battles were believed by everyone to equalize differences in fencing skill. What counted most in the *jeu de terrain* were the qualities of the individual man: sangfroid, aplomb, courage.[102]

Masters-at-arms usually knew enough épée technique to give emergency lessons to those of their charges who found themselves embroiled in an affair of honor. Typically, such sessions consisted of teaching some elementary thrusts and *ripostes* and giving a man the feel for the heavier weapon. In the late 1870s, however, with the popularity of duelling on the rise, some enterprising masters worked up a more elaborate *jeu d'épée* to teach on a regular basis. In the early 1880s, would-be duelers sought out Jules Jacob, master-at-arms at the prestigious Ecole d'Escrime Française; indeed, his students were so seldom bested that word circulated among duelers—by no means a bad thing for business—that he knew certain secret thrusts (*bottes*) that never failed to find their mark (see Fig. 4).[103]

Figure 4. "A Brave Man." "Master, I must duel tomorrow, but have never fenced. Teach me a secret thrust."

In time, most *salles* came to offer training in preparation for duels, and, inevitably, the épée was seen occasionally in assaults as more men became schooled in its use. Traditionalists and older masters scorned these innovations, but there is little doubt that "grafting" the épée onto the extant technique of the art promoted the cause of fencing and prepared a larger number of men practically and psychologically to engage in affairs of honor.[104] Most fencers did not regret these developments; their art had never been so popular. Public assaults, national, and even international competitions became a regular part of the sporting scene in the 1890s. But the true foundation of appeal for fencing in the fin de siècle lay in the rich associations it evoked of chivalry, a manly independence, and the defense of personal honor. Thus, the motto of the *Société pour l'Encouragement de l'Escrime* did not celebrate fencing, but the duel: "Ne tire pas l'épée sans raison, ne la rentre pas sans honneur [Do not draw your sword without reason, nor resheathe it without obtaining honor]."

No doubt men took up fencing as exercise; fencers were reputed to be long-lived and to retain their faculties to an advanced age. The social *cachet* attracted others. There was a *mondain* atmosphere in the salons and changing rooms of the very best fencing circles; one could encounter a duke, a general of the army, or a society painter in an exclusively masculine ambience which lent their relations a certain intimacy and confidence. A few men, indeed, may have taken up the practice of *armes blanches* because they wished to participate in some vague way in the fatherland's military rebirth, to be ready in body and in mind for some future war of revenge against the Germans.

For most men, however, the primary motive for taking up the art of fencing was probably the opportunity it offered to gain experience in the use of arms. The benefit here was twofold. First, fencers in fact made better duelers. It was well-known that a good preparation in foil also provided an excellent foundation for the deployment of defensive tactics in épée as well, so that a man could, at the least, defend himself against both a skilled or an unskilled (and therefore perhaps more dangerous) foe. The second advantage is less tangible but perhaps just as important. It seems likely that many men took seriously the rhetorical claims of fencing *habitués* that learning to handle a sword in close combat steeled one's nerves, gave one courage, and taught judgment under fire. But whether or not a man thought he already possessed these qualities, or could acquire them through practice, he certainly knew that learning to fence would give him the reputation of having them, and, from a certain point of view, that was all that mattered.[105]

In his astute little novel *Six heures; la salle d'armes*, Georges Ohnet canvasses all the foregoing motives for dueling, but settles in the end on the gains it brought one's reputation. A fat baron has become one of the hall's chief patrons, arriving earlier and leaving later than anyone. The baron has a pretty and flirtatious young wife, who, even as he sweats and puffs under his fencing gear, is placing his reputation in doubt by having tea with some stylish gentleman. But, as Ohnet tells it, the baron does not feel jealousy so much as he fears ridicule. And it is precisely a reputation as a fencer that will allow him to "aspire to the moment when it will be said of him: 'Take care! If the baron had the least suspicion . . . , you would be a dead man.' "[106]

If a man's reputation did not prove an adequate prophylactic, sterner measures must be taken. As Carle des Perrières advised the readers of *L'Escrime* in 1881, a man who seeks to avoid "ridicule" is ill-advised to commence adultery proceedings against his wife because, "although he might continue to be regarded as an *honnête homme*, his situation in the world will always have something of the grotesque about it." He should instead provoke the lover to a duel. Even if the worst should happen, and he is so badly wounded that he is in bed for three months, "on his return to the world, will he encounter a single individual who greets him with a smirk on his face? I think not."[107] There was something in the air, wrote Jules Claretie in 1884, that makes men nowadays put all their efforts into avoiding any extreme or eccentric act, "from the grandest act of lunacy to the slightest incorrection. The whole moral outlook of this school of thought is to avoid ridicule at all cost."[108]

9

Honor and the Duel in the Third Republic: 1860–1914

When they set a new republic on its constitutional foundations in 1875, the French could rightly claim to be living in Europe's most democratic society. That the triumph of the Third Republic also invigorated the ancient ideal of honor and its ritual combats does not signal the existence of a contradiction at the heart of the new regime. On the contrary, the extraordinary currency of honor in late nineteenth-century France owed much to the fact that the republican political credo put honor, in principle, within the reach of most men. Honor was no longer the fetish of a tiny elite, but a quality of any Frenchman who was conscious of his civil dignity, jealous of his personal rights, who loved his fatherland and dreamed of revenge against its enemies. The hegemony of honor was such that a larger number of men than ever before felt themselves obliged to lay claim to these goals, whether or not they shared the more narrow political ideals of the republican program. Many of the conflicts between them, whether political, esthetic, or personal in nature, were fought within a discourse of honor whose last resort and ultimate guarantee was the *point d'honneur* that regulated the duel.

Proponents of the duel argued that neither religion, philosophy, nor the law were able to resolve such conflicts equitably and could not "erase the stain of infamy from the forehead of a man who has failed to respond to a brutal insult by having recourse to arms to defend his reputation or avenge his honor."[1] There was much truth in this claim. Though dueling was expressly forbidden by the church, even sincere Catholics found their belief an inadequate barrier to a direct assault on their honor; when their antagonists were impudent anticlerics there might even be a positive incentive to present oneself as a champion of the faith. But as critics of the papal injunction attempted to argue, Catholic men who engaged in duels were not arrogating to themselves the right to dispense divine justice, they were protecting a natural quality of their persons in the name of legitimate self-defense.[2]

Deeply felt philosophical objections to the duel were no better refuge (see Fig. 5). Gabriel Tarde noted that, having refused on principle the challenge of Félix Pyat in 1849, the otherwise iconoclastic Pierre-Joseph Proudhon thought the better of it and chose his seconds, because he "did not think himself of a stature to brave public opinion on this particular point."[3] In the same vein, Jean Jaurès, whose socialist ideals made him an inveterate enemy of violence against the poor and colonial peoples and an opponent of the legal vengeance of capital punishment, could not invoke these principles as a shield against personal insult. In December of 1904, *à propos* Jaurès's defense of a Sorbonne professor's alleged slander of Joan of Arc, Paul Déroulède sent Jaurès a deliberately provocative telegram from his political exile in Spain. Joan, he wrote, was "the most sublime heroine in our heroic history," which made Jaurès, "the most odious perverter of consciences who has ever served foreign interests in our country."[4] In his widely published response, Jaurès rebuked Déroulède for returning an "insult" for his own "pleasantry." "The Socialist party of which I am a member," he wrote, "condemns with good reason this inept and barbarous way of resolving conflicts of ideas. My excuse for departing from these principles is that I have not engaged in this matter in provocation, but have instead myself been the object of the most direct, evident and unjustified provocation."[5]

Thus acknowledging the inevitable, Jaurès made his way to the frontier with his seconds, where he found that Spanish authorities had detained Déroulède in order to prevent the encounter on their soil. Since he feared ridicule by acquiescing too readily to this obstacle, Jaurès wired Premier Emile Combes for a temporary suspension of his opponent's exile, which Combes quickly granted (after all, Jaurès was defending the regime). On December 6, two shots were exchanged at twenty-five paces, without effect, in a crowded cow pasture on the French side of the frontier, after which, in the manner of medieval cavaliers, both Déroulède and Jaurès distributed alms.[6]

Dueling and the Law

The law, far from providing much disincentive to would-be duelers, much less protection for the prudent, had in fact made the duel more inevitable than ever before. During the Second Empire, providing they were apprehended, duelers and their seconds were brought before the correctional courts and meted out mild punishments. In a typical case from 1869, the correctional magistrate gave the journalist Carle des Perrières only a month in jail for a duel in which he seriously wounded his opponent.[7] After 1880 or so, such prosecutions were exceptional; duelers no longer felt

Figure 5. "Fine words." "In a Republic, monsieur, a socialist is as good as a prince, and when a prince acts like a scoundrel, the socialist is permitted to honor him with a sword thrust."

obliged to cross into Belgium or Switzerland to conduct their affairs of honor.

Fatal duels, in accord with Dupin's jurisprudence of 1837, were tried in assizes courts as homicides, but acquittals were invariably brought in by juries where the "law" of the duel had been observed. Frustrated assizes judges had to content themselves with awarding generous civil settlements to dependents and making speeches that dueling was contrary to "religion, morals, and public peace," and an affront to the "power of the sovereign."[8] After 1870 there was no longer any sovereign to affront, and, by the end of the decade, police surveillance and legal punishment had become infrequent. If a duel occurred on his beat in one of the wooded areas favored by duelists, a gendarme might pause to watch, or even obligingly shepherd other onlookers out of harm's way.

Nor did the law effectively protect men against the most typical cause of wounded honor: spoken or written slander. An original criminal law of 1819 punished slander against public officials attacked in their public function; slander against private individuals was regulated by jurisprudence that grew over the century to include every imaginable occasion for the offense, stooping to exclude, for instance, a case in which someone had given his dog the name of a business rival.[9] But penalties were mild, especially when compared with Anglo-American slander statutes. Moreover, in the worthy cause of censorship, so much special legislation regulating the press had been promulgated in the course of the century that by 1880 the distinction between private and public affronts had become, at the very least, unclear.[10]

To unshackle the press and promote free public discussion, the new republican majority passed a press law in 1881 that superceded all previous statutes. The wording followed the traditional formula, punishing "Any allegation or imputation of a fact striking a blow at [*porte atteinte à*] the honor or the consideration of a person or a body [*corps*] to whom that fact is imputed." The law distinguished between levels of offense (*diffamation-injure*) and between public functionaries and private citizens. While defaming a man in his public capacity drew up to one year imprisonment and a 3,000 franc fine, injuring a private citizen might cost as little as 18 francs or six days in jail.[11]

The rather mild punishment for slander contained in the law was made weaker still by the exemption from punishment of any statement made in parliament, judicial tribunals, or, by implication, administrative councils. A public official, in other words, could not be legally construed to have slandered a colleague, no matter how personal the nature of his affront. With the best of intentions, legislators had hoped to provide some measure of protection for public officials by requiring that the courts determine the truth of slanderous accusations against them, but this provision overlooked the sinister variety too vague to prove (or disprove) or which touched on hidden matters such as motive or intention. By the same token, legislators hoped to shield private individuals from embarrassing courtroom revelations by instructing magistrates to assess only the degree of offense contained in the slander, *forbidding* investigation into the truth of the charges.[12] Their laudable intention was to secure personal privacy and to permit the civil rehabilitation of every poor wretch earnestly trying to right some past failing in his life.[13]

The effect of the new law, as some politicians forsaw, was to encourage more personal innuendo, half-truths, and vague allegations than ever before.[14] "Pornography and slander," wrote Gabriel Tarde, "have become the life-blood of the newspaper."[15] With the sudden expansion of the mass press in the last decades of the nineteenth century, there was a simultaneous growth in attacks on personal honor.[16] Each daily had its columns of "faits divers" and "echos," dealing in rumor, speculation, and, occasionally, character assassination.[17] Guy de Maupassant, who wrote up such material for *Le Figaro, Le Gaulois,* and *Gil Blas* described the techniques of this practice in his 1885 novel, *Bel-Ami:*

> You have to hint at what you say, issue a denial in terms which confirm a rumor or state something in such a way that no one believes your words. In such a column, everybody must be able to find one line at least that interests him every day, so that everyone reads it. You have to think of everything and everybody, every section of society and every profession, Paris and the provinces, the army, the arts, the clergy, the university, the law, and the *demi-monde.*[18]

This combination of untrammeled publicity, risible punishments, and inconclusive trials simply encouraged a man who had received a public insult to send two friends to his antagonist without delay. If a duel ensued, providing he was not spitted on the sword of "his man," he gained immediate public satisfaction, a reputation for courage, and, if he was the vengeful sort, a chance to wound a man who had wounded him. In a letter to *Le Temps* in 1887, M. F. Boissy d'Anglas demanded rectification of "calumnious" allegations printed about him the day before. He was obligated to act directly, he explained, "because of the frivolous way that French justice deals with the honor of French citizens. . . ."[19]

Indeed, both defenders and opponents of the duel agreed that a man who took his case to the courts would be perceived as a "coward" whose sense of "independence" was so feeble that he was willing to entrust a decision about his personal honor to complete strangers.[20] Worse, even if a judgment was brought against the *fact* of the slander, the slander itself was not refuted; a man was obliged to drag it around with him thereafter like a ball and chain.[21]

Of course a duel could not establish the truth of an insult or slander either (unless the charge was that a man was a coward), but it did indicate for all to see that the offended party preferred to risk death or disfigurement to refute the charge against him than content himself with a legal judgment that fined his antagonist "the price of a lunch at the Café Riche." By the same token, the author of the insult was unlikely to seek a legal resolution once his victim's seconds had paid him a call, because that would imply he was satisfied to escape with the *cost* of a lunch at the Café Riche, and therefore not the equal in courage of the man to whom he had given offense.

The act of sending seconds did not mean a man was denying the truth of some remark about him; he was saying to the author of the remark, "You have lied about me," responding, as it were, *ad hominum* to another's attack on his own person. The modern duel thus repeated the forms of the duel of the Old Regime: an insult refuted with a charge of lying (*démenti*). To have been called a liar was a serious charge; unless the offense that provoked it was unusually grave, it earned the original offender certain rights in the forthcoming duel.

If a man of honor sought to avoid the courts and adjudicate all matters pertaining to his personal honor through "private" justice, he nonetheless occasionally found himself in the dock for some other kind of crime. When he did, he often found it convenient to justify his actions by appealing to the code of private justice. In her remarkable study of crimes of passion in the fin de siècle, Ruth Harris has found that the courts regularly affirmed the defense that a man had been moved by outraged honor to avenge himself on a wife, mistress, or her lover. In a typical crime of passion, "as with the duel, the murderer asserted that honor underpinned his action, admitted premeditation, and took pains to have his deed publically known."[22]

The "honor" defense was most effective, Harris points out, when it was combined with a plea of temporary emotional disturbance—another of the traditional justifications for juridical nonresponsibility—though it was usually enough for a man to indicate he had found love letters or, better still, to show that her affair had become public knowledge, requiring his own public intervention.[23] When Charles du Bourg found his wife Denise in bed with a certain M. de Précorbin, he killed her, and later explained to the court, "I was like a savage beast; when someone attacks my honor, I am the sort of man who is able to defend himself."[24] Du Bourg was acquitted, and the prosecutor vented his indignation on the hapless Précorbin, who had fled the murder scene half-clothed, for "having cost Mme du Bourg her honor and then not defended her."[25]

Perhaps the most sensational celebrity trial of the era—ostensibly about separation and child custody—turned essentially on issues of male honor. Married in 1861, the Princesse de Bauffremont (née de Chimay) and Paul de Bauffrement were scions of ancient noble families. The princess seemed assured of inheriting fabulous wealth, while Bauffremont, less fortunate, was obliged to follow a military career. Despite the birth of two girls, the princess' unconventional social and intellectual independence put a strain on the marriage, and in 1867 the Bauffremonts agreed to an informal separation. This arrangement proved unsatisfactory, but the princess' application in 1869 for a formal *séparation de corps* was refused by the courts. Their personal differences were momentarily eclipsed in 1870 when Paul de Bauffremont went off to war with his regiment and the princess turned her country chateau north of Paris into a hospital for the wounded.[26]

After the war the princess renewed her quest for a separation. Certain things had happened in the interim, however, that weakened the Princess' case. First, there was another man, none other than the dashing and brave Prince Georges Bibesco, a naturalized Frenchman of Romanian royal blood; his well-known friendship with the princess goaded Bauffremont into obstinate legal resistance. Second, as Bauffremont's lawyer argued, the recent "miseries" suffered by France required Frenchmen to "re-establish social discipline, and regenerate and fortify our country's customs," in particular "paternal and conjugal authority."[27]

Despite the absence of all three principals from the proceedings, the hearing became, in effect, an investigation of the personal courage and honor of the two men, and, by extension, the sexual honor of the princess. The lawyers thus marshaled all the evidence they could bring to bear on the matter of which of the two man had, in the course of the period they had both known her, behaved most honorably. The princess' lawyer, Maître Allou, read a passage from a letter the prince had written her while serving in the Mexican campaign, giving her leave "to amuse yourself as you like, so long as you do not make me look ridiculous."[28] Having given his wife such a *carte blanche*, "a gallant man," Allou argued, would have quietly yielded to the inevitable rather than drag his family and his children through the mud. Prince Bibesco, he assured the judge, was an old family friend who had maintained decorous relations with an independent woman whose husband's interests lay elsewhere; indeed, Allou suggested, Bauffremont seemed more interested in maintaining access to his wife's dowry than in reinvigorating their moribund marriage. A distant husband and a brutal father, he had forfeited his conjugal rights by exposing the princess to a string of public humiliations that showed him to lack a "gentlemanly" and "urbane" demeanor.[29]

Bauffremont's counsel replied that the prince's behavior was that of a man trying to reestablish control of a rebellious woman under the influence of another man. Bauffremont had been deeply wounded by gossip suggesting "that if he had known the Princess well before their marriage, he would have understood that she was too superior a person to live with him and submit to his authority."[30] With this and related anecdotes about the princess' willfulness, Bauffremont's attorney hoped to capitalize on the court's clear sympathy for protecting a husband's conjugal authority.[31]

The war record of both men came up for close scrutiny. Both had been captured in 1870 and later escaped, but Bauffremont's lawyer claimed his client had then raised a new regiment in the provinces and returned to fight at Reichoffen, where he had two horses shot from under him. Maître Allou presented testimony documenting Bibesco's notable valor in battle, and implied that Bauffremont's war record was far less glorious than was claimed. As proof he introduced a deposition from a junior officer who had served with Bauffremont, describing the latter as an insufferable bully who had provoked him and then "hid behind his rank," citing the stipulation that officers of different rank were forbidden to duel.[32]

The most important testimony offered about the quality of honor possessed by these men concerned two incidents that occurred before the war. In neither of these rival narratives does the princess appear as anything other than a transparent symbol of womanhood, a pretext for the struggle between the two men. Despite the fact she had been an eyewitness, her testimony was regarded to be irrelevant to this combat on the field of honor. Bauffremont's lawyer presented one version of these events in which he attempted to characterize Bibesco as having been cowed into submission by a righteous, cane-wielding Bauffremont, insinuating that the Romanian was instinctively acknowledging his dishonorable intentions toward the princess.

In the first of these incidents, Bauffremont came to the princess' chateau in 1867 to find her entertaining Bibesco and a companion. In Bauffremont's version, he said to his wife's guests that they deserved to be chased out the windows by the servants, not being worthy of the door. He then waited for an expected visit from Bibesco's seconds that, to his surprise, never came. In the second incident, Bauffremont claimed to have confronted Bibesco on a train platform near the chateau after Bibesco had escorted the princess to her train, where he "menaced" Bibesco with his cane as he would have done to a common lackey, whereupon Bibesco retreated to the safety of the railway car.[33]

This account, as it turned out, had actually been written by Bauffremont in 1868 and circulated privately to a number of his associates to blacken Bibesco's reputation, but did not come to Bibesco's attention, as Maître Allou pointed out, until a few days before the trial. Allou then proceeded to explode Bauffremont's allegations. With respect to the first episode, he argued that no man of Bibesco's vaunted courage, "who also wore the epaulette of a French officer would have accepted the situation that de Bauffremont describes. If such remarks had really been addressed, immediate reparations would have been demanded." For the incident at the train, Allou produced someone who had witnessed the incident. The stationmaster claimed that Bauffremont did not approach Bibesco until *after* the train had departed. The two men spoke together for awhile quietly, then Bibesco made a "commanding gesture" toward Bauffremont, and tranquilly departed the platform, while Bauffremont "remained rooted to the spot as if he were petrified."[34]

Because this testimony was the occasion of the first *public* airing of Bauffremont's written libels, Allou predicted that "blood would be shed" as a consequence. As the offended party, Bibesco sent his seconds to Bauffremont on the day after the hearing ended. Being one of the best pistol shots in France, the Romanian gallantly chose the épée, but, as he was also one of its best swordsmen, Bauffremont ended up being run through on his left side and badly wounded.[35] At the trial that followed, Bauffremont chose to absent himself, and Bibesco's lawyer paraded a train of witnesses testifying that the prince was "the very ideal of the gentleman," who, unlike his slanderer, "strikes a man only in his presence."[36] For his efforts, Bibesco's lawyer got his client's sentence reduced from fifteen to six days, which Bibesco spent comfortably in the grandeur of the conciergerie.[37]

Though Bibesco won the battle of public opinion, he lost the legal war. On 17 February, the court denied the Princess' request for a separation, citing the need for inculcating a greater respect for "parental and marital authority," especially among the "high-born," who are an example to the rest of society.[38] To escape French legal jurisdiction, the princess removed herself and her daughters to Germany. After becoming a naturalized citizen of Saxe-Altenburg in 1875, she obtained a divorce there and married Bibesco. But she paid a heavy price for her fairy-tale romance. Bauffremont continued to harrass her in the courts, stripping her of her French citizenship and her entire fortune, including her beloved chateau of Menars, and laid legal claim to her children.[39]

However, if Paul de Bauffremont won the legal battle, he lost the war of reputation. The Princesse de Chimay, broken and saddened by the experience of her exile, became a tragic but sympathetic figure, while Georges Bibesco became an authentic folk hero among upper-class French men for decades to come, a veritable "mirror of chivalry," whose name was mentioned with respect and awe by men who had never known him. His rival, by contrast, who stubbornly continued to press for satisfaction at law he had been unable to obtain as a man, became an object of universal scorn.

In the face of this tide of opinion, opponents of the duel eventually abandoned the effort to abolish the duel outright. The Abbé Lemire proposed fines for dueling in a legislative proposal in 1906, but conceded that public tribunals did not offer adequate protection to a man's personal honor; perhaps private "corporations" and "syndicats" could supply juries of honor that would conciliate differences between their members.[40] A "Ligue contre le duel" founded in 1902 essentially limited its efforts to attempting to establish a system of private juries of honor whose decisions would bind both parties.[41]

Legal philosophers further undermined the sovereignty of the law by upholding the moral autonomy of private honor and proclaiming the legal impotence of the state. As Henri Marion, an otherwise vocal opponent of the duel argued, the law protects men in their interests, but leaves up to each of us the need to protect our "honor in the worldly sense of that word."[42] Moreover, the growing popularity of sociological and biological explanations of social life, prompted scholars to transform offenses against honor into natural, material qualities.[43] A convergence thus occurred in legal sociology that placed the psychosocial foundations of the law and the jural elements in human society within an identical frame of reference, an agenda made to order for theoreticians of honor.[44] For instance, students of the "laws" of honor discovered a natural continuity between a man's sentiment of honor, "rooted in the mind," and the structure of "collective thought" that linked him to his "external rights and obligations."[45] As Emile Worms put it, the right to defend one's honor was an "ethico-social right of self-conservation," whose chief "performative idea" was the newly democratized duel.[46] For Eugène Terraillon, honor was both a "sentiment" and a "psychological fact" that produced "nausea" in a man contemplating a shameful act.[47] In this kind of analysis, the links between an individual and a collectivity to which he belonged were explained by reference to the new science of collective psychology. This discipline provided an unusually deterministic account of how personal identity could be wholly subsumed within the identity of the group, suggesting the possibility that individuals are naturally unable to distinguish between them.[48] This argument in turn allowed theorists of honor to explain why individual men are personally insulted by an affront to the collective honor of their group and feel obliged to defend it with their lives.[49]

Other commentators accounted for the spread of the ideals of honor into the modern bourgeoisie by a similar appeal to group psychology. Both Georges Palante and Paul Desjardins doubted that social imitation in itself could produce in the bourgeoisie a sentiment of honor as firmly rooted (or as esthetically refined) as that of the old aristocracy, but they did not doubt the immediate effects of "herd mentality," especially when women or the family were at issue.[50] Though convinced of the superciliousness of most manifestations of bourgeois honor, Desjardins did not doubt the impact on a man whose *foyer* had been invaded by another: "Whoever has suffered the adultery of his wife or of some woman with his family blood, he is abominable; he has deserted the call of his God; if he accepts a monetary compensation for it, he is twice abominable; he has sold his God."[51] Similarly, the legal theorist Emile Beaussire held that there is a "persistence of a state of nature" in human society that binds together family, clan, and community in honorable relations.[52] Indeed, he argued, there are occasions where the "natural right" of a member of a community of honorable men takes precedence over mere "positive law." For instance, if I am a man of honor, I must be willing to risk a charge of libel to expose the dishonorable or villainous behavior of a colleague, in which case, "I will be absolved by the conscience of other men of honor."[53]

We may also trace the growth of a "natural law" theory of honor in more popular sources. Editorials in the moderately republican *Le Temps* in 1877 gave general assent to a new abolition law introduced in the Senate. The paper opined that a new bill and stronger libel laws might have some effect on reducing the number of duels produced by trivial causes, though it doubted if "serious" duels, especially those involving women, could be abated by any means.[54] But when a fresh abolitionist effort was mounted six years later, *Le Temps* was openly hostile. Until the law can protect us against the "special griefs" we feel so keenly in "our highly refined society," an editorial warned, Frenchmen will continue to duel. While our laws protect us against brutal physical attacks, we are still exposed to "impertinence, insinuation, treachery, and calumny." Thus the law punishes "consummated adultery," but men are legally "disarmed against the secret maneuvers that bring it about or the mockery that follows its publicity."[55] For these offenses men still engage "in a struggle for honor, which is nothing less than one of the forms of the struggle for existence," and the law must, in such instances, "Laissez-faire le temps et les moeurs [leave present customs alone]".[56]

In the modern struggle for existence, no less than the struggles of more primitive times, it is all to the good that the "spirit of castes" still excludes from society the man who fails to defend his honor (see Fig. 6).[57] Such a man, wrote Emile Worms in 1890, "may still physically survive, to his discredit, but he no longer exists for society, because that society will have no dealings with him in the future, nor ask him to do anything of a productive nature. He is annihilated and reduced to paralysis."[58] Rémy de Gourmont argued similarly that the same *natural* process of exclusion works on the dishonored cuckold to assure the survival of society as a whole:

> The idea of punishing the man who has been betrayed by his wife is no doubt cruel, but it is not absurd; because the infidelity of the wife is nearly always the result of the *incapacity* of the husband. From that same cause springs all the ridicule society showers on cuckolds, that is on all those who do not know how to make themselves loved, who are not up to the job either physically or emotionally. The disdain the public shows in these matters is thus extraordinarily clairvoyant.[59]

Figure 6. "Your father went bankrupt, your wife is cheating on you, your sister has lovers, and you dare to speak of your honor!"

How Many Duels?

Evidence that pays rhetorical tribute to honor is easy to find. But how many men in this era were actually moved to risk life and limb to defend their honor, and under what circumstances? We may judge the quality of honor more accurately if we can identify the situations in which men felt their personal honor to be in question, analyze the behavior of the participants, and assess the judgments made about them. I propose to do this by dividing duels into different categories, the very categories that contemporaries themselves used when they spoke or wrote about dueling. Duels were not all cut from the same material; depending on motive, the occupation of the duelers, and the degree of the offense, duels might vary in a range between "serious" duels and what contemporaries called "duels pour rire" (ridiculous duels).

First, so far as I can, I will consider the matter of absolute numbers. The documentation on dueling between 1860 and 1914 is somewhat better than the first half of the century. The mass press, hungry for sensational material, made note of many duels, and obligingly printed the official *procès-verbaux* when they were provided by the seconds. Important duels received even closer press scrutiny, as did fatal encounters, where the survivor and the friends of the combatants ended up in the assizes courts. There are a few useful inventories gathered by afficianados of the practice, compiled largely from press accounts, which reflect the inadequacies of that source. Emile Desjardins's (Ferreus) *Annuaire du duel* covers the decade of the 1880s. The author scanned the Parisian press for news and relied to some extent on word of mouth; his plan to publish volumes on the 1870s and 1890s came to naught.[60] Carl Thimm's international inventory, gathered from the *Times* of London, covers a longer period (1831–95), but was far less complete.[61]

In his 1892 study of the duel, the criminologist Gabriel Tarde used Ferreus and a few other sources to conclude that there were 598 French duels between 1880 and 1889, of which 16 were fatal.[62] He decided on the basis of this assessment that duels in Italy were far more numerous if somewhat less dangerous, producing figures between 1880 and 1888 of 2,424 duels and 43 mortalities. Knowing little else than the raw numbers, Tarde deduced that most of these were of military provenance, since the overwhelming majority were saber duels, a mistake as the saber was the weapon of choice for civilians and officers alike.[63] The numbers were reported to be about the same in this period in Austria-Hungary, but fatalities were fewer, and a large proportion of combatants appears to have been active or reserve officers.[64] The German duel, as we have seen, was far less frequent but more fatal, owing to the popularity of the pistol "barrier" duel.[65]

There is little we can reliably conclude from these figures. Even though dueling was a formal offense elsewhere in Europe, judicial statistics do not reflect *real* dueling rates anywhere, except, perhaps, the figures on fatalities. In France, where one must sample the newspapers or comb through inventories, the problems are worse still. Emile Desjardins, for instance, did not even manage to report all the public duels reported by the Parisian press, much less those that took place in the depths of the provinces which attracted only local attention.[66]

There are a number of indications that many more duels took place than were collected in dueling inventories or reported in the press. Public figures are unlikely to have slipped through the net; most of Georges Clemenceau's twenty-two duels were certainly reported in the newspapers, but many of the *affaires* of less celebrated figures may have escaped general notice. The clubman and skilled fencer Alphonse de Aldama reported in 1892 to have had eleven duels and assisted at forty-four others.[67] In connection with the investigation of a fatal duel in 1893, it emerged that a restaurant on the Grande Jatte in the outskirts of Paris was a favorite rendez-vous of duelers. Its owner proudly showed the press the covered ballroom to which swordsmen could repair in inclement weather. He claimed Georges Clemenceau was a regular client and that he booked an average of three duels a week on the premises, a figure which, if accurate, would double the number of duels Tarde held took place in a typical year in the 1880s.[68]

More important still is the very real likelihood that a large proportion of "private" duels, particularly those involving women or touching on intimate family matters, were never made public. The fencing-master Arsène Vigeant, who served as second on dozens of occasions, insisted that most duels of this kind remained secret. In such cases, seconds were sworn to silence, no *procès-verbal* delivered to the papers, and wounds were portrayed as accidents.[69] There is no reason to doubt this point. All the dueling manuals published in this period distinguish between "public" and "private" duels, recommending in the latter case no written transcript and no publicity.[70] A man who breached the veil of secrecy surrounding a private affair of honor would have committed an act of odious disloyalty instantly disqualifying him as a man of honor.

I would conclude from all this that Tarde's estimate of 60 duels per year in the 1880s is far too low. I think a conservative estimate might be 200 duels per year on the average between 1875 and 1900, with higher totals, perhaps as many as 300, in certain years. There were epidemics of dueling during each general election and in the midst of political crises such as those provoked by the Boulanger or Dreyfus affairs. During periods of a month or more there might have been a dozen duels a week in Paris alone. There are no inventories for the period after 1895, but, judging from regular press samplings, publically reported duels appear to have tailed off after 1900 or so. However, as late as 1911 one could still find as many as five duels taking place in Paris alone in a span of twenty days.[71]

Nonetheless, general inventories of publicly reported duels in the fin de siècle, such as Desjardins's *Annuaire,* do tell us a few interesting things. First, as opposed to duels elsewhere in Europe at this time, French duels were overwhelmingly a civilian phenomenon. The *Annuaire* found only nine duels where both men were in active military service in the 1880s. We have reason to suspect many more took place in the privacy of the barracks, but military observers in the period thought that dueling in the corps was in precipitous decline.[72] Second, the épée was by far the favored weapon for duelers in this era. Only 10 percent of the duels in the 1880s were pistol duels, and only 1 percent of French duelers used the saber, which further underlines the civilian flavor of the French affair of honor. Third, the *Annuaire* reports that of the 600 or so duels in its sample, a few more than 400 were actually fought. The rest were "arranged" by conscientious seconds. If all private duels were added to this number, it might slightly diminish the percentage of reconciliations, but there is no other reason to think that more than two of every three challenges was consummated in combat. Finally, duels were overwhelmingly Parisian phenomena. The *Annuaire* places 80 percent of its duels in the capital or its environs, nearly all the rest in major provincial cities. Even allowing for the Parisian bias of Desjardins's sources, the urban nature of the duel seems incontrovertible. As Tarde wrote, "the rural duel, so to speak, does not exist."[73]

Though they were all ultimately about personal or corporate honor, from the perspective of contemporaries duels fell more or less naturally into certain categories. There was considerable overlap between them, as we will see, but for analytical purposes we may identify four major kinds. Together, journalistic and political duels constituted the majority of all public duels. All these duels were public because publicity was an important part of their motive. It is not easy to distinguish between these two varieties; the subject matter over which journalists dueled was frequently the sort that provoked encounters between politicians. But unless a journalist had political ambitions of his own or edited or wrote for a paper that was the mouthpiece for a leading politician, he probably thought of himself as a professional reporter or editor in competition for news and audience with other men like himself.[74]

The "futile" duel was also frequent, but, unlike other duels, the causes of these duels were usually spontaneous. They arose not from reflective provocation but from a chance remark or insult delivered in a public place, or were the result of a misunderstanding or an overreaction to criticism that was not intended to deeply offend. Finally, there is the "serious" duel, often called the "gallant" duel, where men fought over issues that touched on intimate details of private life: family name, personal integrity, and, especially, women. In these encounters, the elaborate rituals of the duel—designed to save lives and limit damage—were often unable to contain the deep anger or desperation of the men involved, and they produced far more fatalities and serious wounds than duels with other motives at stake.

The Journalistic Duel

In the *belle époque,* journalistic duels assisted, in a very real sense, in the birth of a new profession. With the rise of the mass press in the 1860s, journalists were less often distinguished men of letters than ambitious young men anxious to make a mark in the world. Since newspapers were risky financial endeavors navigating in the troubled and uncertain waters of taste and politics, their survival depended on a high profile, a "cause," or a reputation for tenacity and fearless reporting. The reporters who gathered and wrote their news did not have reliable news services on which to base their stories. Most stories were compiled from other papers, hearsay, and rumor, and were unreliable to say the least. Editors could choose between anodyne stories that reported the obvious, or try to increase their audience share by floating unsubstantiated but more spectacular "news."

Most chose the latter route. However, to protect themselves and give the news they printed greater credibility, in the 1880s managers and editors began to insist their reporters take more responsibility by signing their own articles. In the dog-eat-dog world of the mass press, this practice became both an article of faith for ambitious reporters and a credo of journalistic integrity. I do not mean to suggest this guaranteed the truth of what was printed, but it did the next best thing by assuring readers that someone was personally willing to vouch for it. In view of the slight satisfaction provided by libel laws after 1881, this meant in practice that a journalist had to expect occasional visits from the seconds of a man who imagined himself outraged by something he had written. As the seasoned polemicist and dueler Edouard Drumont said in 1886, "Behind every signature everyone expects to find a chest."[75]

The sort of bravado this assumption inspired discouraged editors from printing anonymously written articles when they might contain something controversial. As the dueling manuals made clear, the editor himself must assume responsibility for an unsigned article unless the author voluntarily revealed himself.[76] Besides, there was something suspect, even feminine, in anonymity. As Aurelian Scholl put it, when a man authors an unsigned article, "scorn is sufficient compensation for such cowardice; when the author is not a man, there are two natural avengers: time and Saint-Lazare [the Paris prison for women].[77] This swashbuckling atmosphere simply magnified the ordinary problems women might have in making a profession of journalism. In September of 1890 the feminist journalist Séverine wrote an article in *Gil Blas* that the Boulangist Mermeix (Gabriel Terrail) deemed insulting. He issued a challenge to her editor, George de LaBruyère, who was badly wounded in the subsequent duel. Sévérine was angrily denounced by another feminist, Astié de Valsayre, for having betrayed her responsibility by acting in a way that required a man to come to her defense.[78]

Guy de Maupassant described a typical journalistic duel in his *Bel-Ami* in 1885. The novel's hero, Georges Duroy, is forging a reputation as a witty columnist for *La Vie française,* but a rival at a competitive paper contradicts an assertion Duroy had made about police intervention in a butcher shop squabble. Duroy is obliged to defend his interpretation of events, only to find a signed article by his tormenter implying he had lied. His editor informs him he must defend himself, and, by implication, the paper, since "Like Caesar's wife, a journalist must be above suspicion"; and at 7 A.M. the next morning Duroy found himself in a chilly meadow staring into the muzzle of a dueling pistol.[79]

As with the boost given here to Georges Duroy's fortunes, there is no doubt that the publicity of a duel helped a man's career, but it also cultivated in him a characteristic feeling of moral superiority that made him even more sensitive to affront, and led him into ideological battles which he was inclined to interpret through the lens of his personal honor (see Fig. 7).[80] The slightest derogation could send such a journalist in search of his seconds. When Albert Dubrujeaud characterized a piece of René Maizeroy as "yelping in a minor mode," in the *Echo de Paris,* Maizeroy responded with a challenge, as he did to Jean Lorrain after a similarly obscure insult a few months later.[81]

What is more, if a member of the journalistic corporation did not respond properly to an affront, his colleagues felt compelled to call him to account. M. Stollig, a former drama critic at *Le Gaulois,* was slapped by an actor angered over a negative review. Instead of sending his seconds, Stollig invoked his right of professional criticism and took the actor to court. Carle des Perrières, an editor at *Le Gaulois,* published a long diatribe against his former collaborator whom he characterized as a man "well-known for his flabby sentiments," reminding him that even after a court decision, "a man who has been slapped is still slapped."[82] Stollig immediately sent his seconds and was wounded by des Perrières in the ensuing duel.[83] Other journalists applauded this action. According to Henri Fouquier, des Perrières was helping enforce honorable relations between colleagues, and Francisque Sarcey imagined that Stollig was secretly pleased to trade a bad wound in return for a rehabilitation of his damaged honor.[84]

It thus seems to have been the case that if a journalist was willing to back up his words with his sword, he could write virtually whatever he wished, no matter how scurrilous or unsubstantiated it might be. More cautious men were obliged to bring their prose into alignment with their

Figure 7. "The Laurels. These are the newspapers that mention monsieur."

confidence in their skills on the dueling ground. This may be the reason that the boldest or most venomous journalists of the era were also the most frequent duelers. Arthur Ranc, Carle des Perrières, Arthur Meyer, Aurélien Scholl, Henri Bauer, Paul de Cassagnac, Georges Clemenceau, and, above all, Henri Rochefort and Edouard Drumont seldom flinched from either a polemic or a challenge. It is no coincidence that several of these men peddled rather extreme political views: radical republicanism, Bonapartism, Boulangism, royalism, or anti-Semitism. It took a bold fellow to advocate unpopular views.

For all that, the journalistic duel was perhaps the least dangerous of any kind. Using the *Annuaire* of Emile Desjardins, it appears as though there were only two deaths and about a dozen serious wounds in the 200 or so journalistic duels Desjardins lists in the decade of the 1880s.[85] Collegial seconds usually imposed minimal conditions to reduce the danger of a press polemic having a serious result. When such a duel did turn out badly, it transpired that there were often collateral, complicating factors. In July of 1889, the Boulangist Belz de Villar of the revisionist *Bulletin officiel* provoked a duel with Louis Pierotti, who wrote for the formerly Boulangist *Petit provençal*. The conditions set by the seconds were modest in the extreme: bare chests (to enable the seconds to spot even tiny scratches), and a limit of two one-minute engagements, whether or not either man was wounded.[86] Despite these precautions, Villar savagely attacked his opponent, wounding him twice before running him through and killing him instantly.

In the subsequent trial, it emerged that in the polemic leading up to the duel, Villar had not only attacked Pierotti's political views, but questioned whether a man of Italian origins was up to the mark as a French patriot, knowing full well the younger man's morbid sensitivity on this point.[87] Moreover, the prosecution obtained a letter indicating that Villar had planned the duel, hoping that the publicity surrounding his triumph would aid his candidacy in the upcoming elections.[88] Villar also displayed little remorse following the duel itself; after placing election portraits of himself in shop windows in Marseille, he appeared with his mistress at his political club, smoking and sipping insouciantly from a glass.[89]

Repelled by his behavior, his political associates demanded he leave the premises, and his seconds let it be known they would never support him again. The court, for its part, found Pierotti a sympathetic character. A novice to dueling, he wrote a touching letter to his wife the night before the duel expressing his hope that all his efforts to assimilate to French society had not been in vain. Villar was portrayed as a bully who had dueled many times and who deliberately picked a fight with an inept opponent to further his career. He was given an unusually harsh sentence of two years, a 50,000 franc fine, and was showered with obloquy by the press and by the magistrate at his trial.[90] In short, it was one thing to build a reputation as a man of firm conviction by exposing one's honor in legitimate polemics, and quite another to cynically use the duel as a means of naked personal advance.

The Political Duel

Since politicians were often quoted in the press or wrote regularly for an ideologically allied paper, it is not easy to know where the journalistic duel leaves off and the political duel begins. However, I have defined political duels as *affaires* between active public officials that arose from breaches of political correction or from ideological disputes. Many of these fights were indeed sparked by press battles, but a substantial number grew out of debates in parliament, or in municipal and administrative councils. In the ideologically charged rough and tumble of Third Republic political life, sheer competence and patience might eventually guarantee a successful career, but in a pinch association with a highly visible cause could advance a man more quickly, if not more surely, into prominence. As in the equally competitive world of journalism, however, the more extreme a man's views became, the more numerous were his detractors and the more blunt the detractions. A man's political opinions were only as good as his willingness to defend them, by force if it came to that.

Of course a man who advocated mainstream views put himself at less risk, but even a political moderate needed to express his convictions with sincerity and demonstrate loyalty to his cause for his opinion to have any force in political debate. As both Maurice Barrès and Louis Barthou later recalled, the words most often heard from the tribune of the chamber were "sincere" and "loyal."[91] It was not in the nature of this kind of loyalty to prohibit a man from changing his views, over either the long or the short run. One need only think of Aristide Briand, or even Georges Clemenceau, who traveled the better part of the political spectrum in the course of their careers. What was at stake here was the authenticity of the bond between a man and his ideals at any moment in time.[92] A politician could change his mind, but he must avoid ambiguity at all costs.

It was some time in the mid-1870s before the cautious "prudence" of the parliaments of the Second Empire was replaced with the "frankness" that characterized the tone of political discourse in the new regime.[93] Indeed, writing in 1890 the former premier Jules Simon excused his old colleague Jules Favre for having foolishly promised never to yield to Prussia a stone of the fatherland. "Would we be better advised," he asked, "to neither speak or act rashly? That is neither noble or honest [*honnête*], but it is ... prudent."[94] The tone and *ad hominum* nature of parliamentary debate simply worsened during the Boulanger and Dreyfus affairs. Newspapers deplored the degeneration of debate into personal calumny, comparing the aristocratic "finesse" of yesteryear to the more vulgar and bourgeois insult of the present.[95]

Much of this change may be due to the sheer importance of verbal oratory in the French parliaments of the period. The Chamber of Deputies did virtually all its work in those days on the floor of the chamber itself; parliamentary commissions and party caucuses had not developed sufficiently to relieve the chamber of the need to examine the details and policy implications of each piece of legislation. Debate itself was more like anarchy than a well-regulated discussion governed by established procedures.[96] Since virtually every ministerial assertion could be challenged on the spot by an unfriendly interpellation, the life of the ministry rested with the oratorical ability of the minister whose policy was under siege.

It is not without significance that the historian Charles Aubertin, his eyes fixed firmly on his own times, wrote in 1882 that "the virile age" of French parliamentary eloquence began only when the Revolution allowed Frenchmen "to freely express all their thoughts and desires from the tribune."[97] The title seems entirely appropriate to an era when fencing was one of the most commonly used metaphors for debate in the chamber.[98] As in Drumont's apostrophe about signatures and chests, it might be said equally that a man's chest lay behind the words he spoke from the tribune, since they so often provoked duels. In 1893 an editorialist for *Le Temps* lamented that parliamentary duels, which used to curb parliamentary intemperance, now served to legitimate it, "as if it were no longer one's conscience, but sheer audacity that was the arbiter of honor."[99] Louis Barthou confirmed this point when he argued many years later that a man did nothing less than "place his honor in peril" when he mounted the tribune.[100]

By the 1880s dueling had become so integral a part of political life that it was practically impossible for a parliamentarian to allow a personal affront to pass without responding. If a minister gave offense to a deputy, he was obliged to give him satisfaction, despite concern that making a man a "champion" for his faction might prove to be yet another way of overturning governments.[101] Nor was any public official likely to take refuge in the legal immunity afforded him if his personal reputation might suffer as a result. Gustave Larroumet, a functionary in the Ministry of Public Instruction, sent his seconds to Henri Bauer after an article about him in Bauer's *L'Echo de Paris*. Bauer claimed the criticism was of Larroumet in his "public function," but Larroumet badgered the paper until a staff journalist took up the challenge.[102] Incidents of a similar kind between deputies and bureaucrats and between functionaries in different corps seem to suggest that public officials might well have been afraid to permit the prosecution of their antagonists to which they were entitled by law.[103]

Most political duels reveal themselves to us only through the haze of ideological conflict, but it is important not to forget that political difference in itself was generally not sufficient cause for an affair of honor. Rather, it was the particular sensibility of the man behind the ideology that was the target of political insults and thus the efficient trigger of a dueling challenge. We see this clearly in the case of political duels that arose over matters of parliamentary precedence or correction, where ideology seems not to have been a factor at all. Speaking one day in the Chamber of Deputies on a vote on fiscal credits, M. Gaston Douville-Maillefeu was interrupted by a fellow deputy, M. Sans-Leroy, to whom the former replied, "I am not speaking to you, sir." "But I am speaking to *you*, sir," his questioner said, to which Douville-Maillefeu replied by forbidding Sans-Leroy to speak further to him. Sans-Leroy then raised the ante by calling his colleague a "drôle" (rascal) upon which the two men traded slaps and retired to the cloakroom to choose their seconds.[104]

A similar discussion in the Departmental Council of the Nord between a local notable, Alexandre Saint-Léger, and the departmental deputy, Alexandre-Antonin des Rotours, produced a duel in 1872. Saint-Léger had said of his colleague that the latter was not acting like a man "accustomed to the company of honorable men." Des Rotours, claiming he was wounded "in my personal consideration," sent his seconds forthwith. In later testimony to the Lille Correctional Tribunal, the president of the council could find nothing more damning to say about Saint-Léger remarks than they were "too vivid and scarcely parliamentary in nature." Nonetheless, as one of des Rotours's seconds put it, in view of his substantial local reputation, his client, "could not afford to simply slip such an admonition in his pocket without diminishing himself."[105]

More typically, however, insults that found a tender spot were embedded in the framework of a larger political argument. Such was the case in Paul Déroulède's celebrated provocation of Georges Clémenceau at the height of the Panama scandal in the winter of 1892. In the midst of a parliamentary session devoted to "naming names" of politicians who had profited by their aid to the defunct Panama Canal company, the ex-Boulangist Déroulède initiated his attack on the republican majority by identifying boldly the man his colleagues most feared on account of "his sword, his pistol, and his tongue."[106] He charged Clémenceau with being in the pay of a company bagman, Cornelius Herz, and of being a conscious agent for the British Foreign Office. It was this accusation of personal corruption and lack of political *independence* that made a duel inevitable, not Déroulède's general ideological brief that parliamentary republics by nature breed favoritism and self-seeking.

In the event, it appears Clémenceau himself welcomed the personal orientation of this attack, in the mistaken belief that in choosing to fight an unusually dangerous duel with his antagonist the slate against him might somehow be wiped clean.[107] Clémenceau's willingness to duel to defend his honor in this case could not forestall a temporary retirement from political life, but by conducting himself with his customary sangfroid under fire he left the door ajar for his later personal and political rehabilitation. Politicians of the era who lacked the cool resolve of "the tiger" were not so fortunate.

Political figures whose reputations rose on the strength of their willingness to back words with deeds had to be prepared for setbacks when those deeds fell short of expectations. The brilliant career of General Georges Boulanger is an instructive case in point. By the summer of 1886, Boulanger's star was rising rapidly. As war minister and darling of the radicals, Boulanger expelled the Ducs d'Aumale and de Chartres from the army, implying they were not deserving of their rank. The royalist Baron Clément-Gustave de Lareinty took exception to Boulanger's actions and provoked him into a duel, implying the cowardice of a man who insulted those not present to defend themselves. Despite the relatively safe conditions chosen for the duel—one shot at twenty-five paces—Boulanger managed to bring credit to himself by behaving with admirable calm. After the general's pistol misfired, and Lareinty's missed, Boulanger chatted amiably with his opponent, asserting gallantly, "I would have been unhappy to deprive France of one of her most precious defenders."[108]

A year later Boulanger was in temporary eclipse at a provincial command in Auvergne, on the look-out for a way to bring his name back into public view. He found his opportunity in the text of a speech Jules Ferry gave in Saint-Dié on 26 July, in which he referred to Boulanger as a "music-hall Saint-Arnaud," a witticism in fashion at the time linking the general to the compliant minister of war who supervised Louis Napoléon's *coup d'état* of 2 December, 1851.[109] Claiming an affront to his "military honor," Boulanger underscored this point by choosing two men as seconds who were not politicians, Count Arthur Dillon and General Faverot de Kerbiech, who departed for Ferry's home in the Vosges amidst great speculation and fanfare in the Parisian press.[110]

Ferry no doubt delivered this barb as part of a campaign to rebuild his own flagging political fortunes, on the wane since Clémenceau engineered the fall of his last cabinet in 1885. Hated by the right for his anticlerical program, and by the radicals on his left for his cautious foreign policy, Ferry hoped to gather enough centrist republican support to either lead another cabinet or eventually assume the presidency of the Republic. Because he drew his own support from both ends of the spectrum of political sympathies, Boulanger was, in a certain sense, a natural opponent for the former premier. Both men, in short, had far more at stake in this affair than their physical well-being or their courage, though these were precisely the terms in which their political aspirations were invariably discussed.

On 30 July Ferry received his antagonist's seconds outside his house in

Saint-Dié to assure them he would give their client satisfaction. While Boulanger's men were returning to Paris, Ferry selected two fellow politicians—Antonin Proust and David Raynal—to defend his interests, stressing thereby the purely political nature of the offense he had given the general.[111] Negotiations between the four men were lengthy and strained. Boulanger's men claimed their client had been gravely offended and demanded unusually harsh conditions for the duel: an unlimited number of shots with rifled pistols until one man had fallen. Raynal and Proust refused those conditions out of hand, upon which Dillon and Faverol countered with one shot at twenty paces, *visé*.

By the 1880s all pistol duels between politicians were of the "command" variety, where the men were placed at the agreed distance, pistols at their sides. After being given the order to fire, each man had to raise his arm, aim, and fire before the "director of combat" counted to three. Since firing *after* the director uttered "three" would have permanently dishonored a man, duelers did not really have the luxury of taking careful aim. In the "aimed" *visé* duel, however, both men had one minute to set themselves and squeeze off a shot, making it a grueling test of nerves and the most dangerous form of the French duel.[112] Boulanger's men were surely bluffing here, confident that Ferry's seconds would not expose their older, less experienced client to this danger; indeed, Raynal and Proust countered with the conventional command duel: one shot, at twenty-five paces. Dillon and Faverol accepted this distance but reintroduced the requirement that firing continue until one man was wounded, upon which Ferry's seconds broke off negotiations, claiming that Dillon and Faverol did not have the right to choose both the weapon *and* the conditions of the duel.[113]

Once it became clear no duel would take place, both principals wrote letters to their seconds, Ferry to congratulate his men for rejecting an "abnormal" duel, Boulanger to castigate the man who insults a soldier of France "from afar," then offers him only a "derisory" satisfaction.[114] There was some disingenuousness on both sides. Had they wanted a fight, Ferry's men could have taken the duel into binding arbitration, from which some kind of compromise on conditions might have emerged; and Boulanger's seconds conducted themselves throughout as if they hoped to force Ferry to refuse their conditions. Whatever the technical merits of his case, however, Ferry was the big loser in the court of opinion.

The radical press was particularly savage, aiming its invective directly at the man whose policies it so despised. *La Lanterne* wrote that Ferry's ignoble refusal to duel "disqualified" him from leadership. *Le Radical* held that "France will forget everything except ridicule; what it pardons least of all are retreats." "When one has had the honor of governing so great and valiant a nation as France and wishes to govern it again," wrote Edmond Magnier in *L'Evènement,* " . . . one must behave more proudly, respond to danger in a warlike way, and be prepared to exact of the enemy whatever revenge is required."[115] In *Le Paris,* Charles Laurent wrote:

> Those who do not believe in the duel would do well to offer no insults. Once one accepts the jurisdiction of arms, . . . to avoid dishonor one must do so boldly and completely, without looking back or considering the sacrifice. The ridiculous combination which consists of having recourse to violent means but measuring their effect, a mixture of blood-thirsty instinct and self-preservation, is the most bizarre and least prestigious thing one can imagine. One may recover from a wound, but one can rarely recover after refusing a duel to a brave man whom one has insulted.[116]

Papers better disposed to Ferry's politics nonetheless found fault with the "quibbling" stance of his seconds, blaming, by implication, the indecisiveness of their champion.[117] Others were more direct about the disgrace of "offending someone, then taking refuge in principles, crying all the while, 'I am ready to fight.' "[118] Even those in the general public who do not understand the technical usages of the duel will understand, wrote *Gil Blas,* that Boulanger wanted an "appreciable result," while Ferry wanted to "limit the dangers and useful effects," and forfeit the "honorable consequences."[119] Arthur Ranc, one of the few public figures willing to defend Ferry, recalled his bravery in the face of the Communards in 1871, and reminded his readers that those who underestimated the dangers of the duel recommended by Ferry's seconds have themselves "never dueled, never will, and have never faced danger of any sort."[120] His voice was virtually alone, however, in the swarm of observers who saw in Ferry's prevarications the death-knell to his politics and his political career. Denied the presidency of the Republic by the maneuvers of Clemenceau and his parliamentary allies only a few months later, Ferry's political influence was irretrievably dead.

If overly cautious behavior could deliver the *coup de grace* to an already weakened politician like Ferry, a resolute defense of honor helped someone like Boulanger, whose star was still on the rise. Indeed, following the duel *manqué* with Ferry, Boulanger's extraordinary popularity and his dalliance with the royalist right gave second thoughts to the republican politicians of the left who had helped engineer his reputation. To protect the foundering Republic against the campaign for an authoritarian "revision" of the constitution, Boulanger was first suspended from his duties and later expelled from the army. This stop gap merely speeded Boulanger on his political migration to the right, plunging him into spectacular electoral successes bankrolled by royalist opponents of the regime.[121]

Elected to the Chamber of Deputies in several by-elections, the ex-general was now fair game for political invective that he could not have tolerated as an active officer, such as Charles Floquet's aphorism, "Sir, at your age Bonaparte was already dead."[122] The implications of remarks of this kind, together with the charge by republicans that he was eating at both royalist and republican tables, nettled Boulanger's vanity.[123] In a rare appearance in the chamber on 12 July 1888, observers noted that Boulanger had exchanged his long, carefully coiffed locks for a close-cut military "brush," and was in fighting form.[124] As he held forth from the tribune on the need for "revision," he was heckled mercilessly by the premier, Floquet, who accused him of frequenting "sacristies" and fawning on princes to win support for his cause. Seizing on this provocation, Boulanger replied *ad hominum* that Floquet was behaving like a vulgar "pion de college," (a monitor of schoolboys), and had, moreover, "impudently lied."[125]

A duel was inevitable, and both men left the chamber to constitute their seconds. Boulanger was thus embarked on his third affair of honor in three years, which, moreover, marked his progress across the political spectrum: the first with a royalist, the second with a centrist republican, the third with a radical. The duel took place the following day on the shaded grounds of Count Dillon in Neuilly. A select group of observers, including the head of the *sûreté*, watched from within while journalists and onlookers tried to catch a glimpse of the action through the bars of the gate. Though he had just turned sixty years old and could not be sure of cutting a good figure in a sword duel, Floquet chose the épée and the two men squared off. Virtually all press reports later described Boulanger as nervous and pale and his older opponent as calm; indeed, the ex-general immediately took the offensive, backing his opponent up and inflicting a few scratches with frantic and ungainly swipes of his sword.[126] As Floquet slowly surrendered ground, parrying his every thrust, Boulanger apparently lost his patience and leapt forward, impaling himself on Floquet's sword, which penetrated seven centimeters into his neck. He was carried off the field of battle by worried supporters in a state his detractors later described as "hysterical."[127]

The postmortems of the duel produced some predictable reactions. The Boulangist paper *Le Cocarde* printed an interview with Boulanger's associate Arthur Dillon, who defended Boulanger's impetuous charge by explaining that the general could not move backward because of an old war wound. But he also claimed, in contradiction to other eyewitnesses, that Floquet had twice dropped his sword, which was twice handed back to him by the chivalrous Boulanger.[128] Republican papers, on the contrary, revelled in the aspect of an aging "pékin" giving a lesson in swordsmanship to a general. As Emmanuel Arène put it in *Le Matin*, "... for the first time M. Boulanger has found himself in combat with one of the 'idlers' [*rois fainéants*] for which he has evinced so much disdain, and has found them, no doubt, less 'idle' than he might have wished."[129] Indeed, Boulanger's inept performance stimulated more than one meditation on the irony of living in an era when civilians were better equipped to defend their honor than military men.[130]

Providentially, the day after the duel fell on 14 July, the great republican holiday commemorating the fall of the Bastille. With Floquet at his side, President Sadi Carnot reviewed the troops at Longchamps, where they were hailed enthusiastically by the crowds. They then commemorated a statue to the republican politician Léon Gambetta where Carnot praised the republican program "for knowing how to keep the most perfect calm [sangfroid] in the face of party agitations from within or without our frontiers."[131] The anti-Boulangist press was ecstatic. Many, like *Le Matin,* drew the pertinent conclusions: "Would Boulanger not lead us against the enemy as unconsciously as he precipitated himself upon the sword of M. Floquet? Has he not given us here a measure of his blindness, of his madness, of his absolute lack of *sang-froid,* . . . in throwing himself so furiously on his adversary, counting all the while on a weakness in him that never materialized?"[132] Opinion from different political quarters was less certain that the general's prestige had been irretrievably damaged, but no one seemed to doubt that the duel, by reproducing an instance of life lived *in extremis,* provided an unusually reliable representation of a man's character.[133]

The pronouncements of Boulanger's political demise that appeared in France and elsewhere following his inelegant performance were certainly premature.[134] The momentum of his movement and the depth of dissatisfaction with the "republic of pals" continued to fuel Boulanger's electoral successes well into 1889. But Boulanger's third and last duel certainly did not help his cause, not to mention his own self-confidence, and its outcome may well have imparted greater resolve to the defenders of a shaky regime. In any case, the unreliability and impulsiveness that subsequently destroyed his movement was later held by some astute observers to have been prefigured in the debacle with Floquet.[135]

I do not want to push this point too hard. Political duels were certainly not very dangerous affairs. Of the hundred-odd duels between politicians in the 1880s, for example, there were no deaths and only eleven serious wounds.[136] This does not mean politicians felt little trepidation the night before an encounter; too many stories were in circulation about men disfigured in pistol duels or brought to death's door by a sword thrust to the spleen (see Fig. 8). On the eve of his duel with Oscar Bardy de Fourtou, Léon Gambetta wrote his mistress a cool dispatch about "this monsieur who wishes to test my skill with a pistol; he will be satisfied. There is nothing to worry about." However, the exuberant letter he wrote her the next day ("what pride and what joy fill my heart!") suggests the nearly cathartic sense of relief that Gambetta felt at the duel's harmless outcome,

Figure 8. "A Glorious Wound. THE DOCTOR: 'Don't worry!... As no blood is visible, I'll just give you a little scratch with my scalpel.'"

belying the authenticity of the calm self-mastery he wished to convey to others, and perhaps to himself.[137]

The generally nonlethal results of political duels reflects, I think, both the comparatively safe conditions in which such affairs were fought and the deliberate and calculated motives that inspired them. As integral aspects of the parliamentary life of the Third Republic, however, duels were not without their *political* dangers; for it was in dueling narratives such as these that contemporaries read metaphors of courage or cowardice, self-mastery or fear, qualities that reflected significantly on a man's reputation as a leader, and, by extension, on the worthiness of his cause.

The "Serious" Duel

Though the mettle of a man was surely on display in journalistic and political duels, many contemporaries seem to have thought that what was at stake in this preeminently public act was a man's personal *consideration,* the less weighty form of honor that attached to his performance of his public function. Of course if a man behaved dishonorably in even a duel of this kind, he exposed himself to far more serious consequences. Honor was never more at stake than in the duel itself.[138] But to be provoked into a "serious" duel, a man had to be wounded in his personal *honor,* that is, by an imputation against his private integrity, his family, a woman under his "protection," or a group with which he had bonds of deep emotional solidarity.

Such duels were by nature more serious because they combined deeper feelings of outrage with more dangerous dueling conditions. As I have said, we do not know how many "serious" duels there were, since many were conducted secretly, and because duels of other kinds may have had more serious motives than were apparent on the surface. But, using the *Annuaire* for the 1880s, there were 85 duels that seem to have had serious motives or dangerous conditions, or both, producing twenty-nine life-threatening wounds and five deaths.[139] Only two deaths and twenty-four serious wounds resulted from the 200-odd journalistic–political duels listed by Desjardins in the 1880s.

Serious duels were provoked by any number of situations, but in the fin de siècle there were two categories into which most of them fell: "gallant" duels in which women were somehow involved, and the "Jewish" duel, where Jews and anti-Semites fought over the issue of whether honor was a feature of the Jewish "race." The first variety appears to have been the most frequent and the most deadly. Men fought principally to defend the honor of their wives, but there were duels in which the *causus belli* was a mistress, a mother, even a sister. In point of fact, few of the serious duels we know about were the results of an open competition for the favors of a woman, as in popular melodramas or travesties of the wild west. Much more common were situations in which an able-bodied male who was the legal guardian, husband, or closest relation of an offended woman was obliged to challenge her offender. In other cases, where women did not figure directly as the offended party, their presence served as a catalyst for the subsequent combat. As we shall see, however, in all these variations of the "gallant" duel, it is the *amour-propre* of the male and his susceptibility to the judgment of others that seems to trigger his action, not, so far as we can tell, some transcendent chivalric ideal (see Fig. 9).

One of the most celebrated duels of the era, the Olivier–Feuilerade duel, does appear to have been a struggle for possession of a woman. Olivier, who had already been in eleven duels, provoked the inexperienced Feuilerade to a duel when his ex-mistress took up with the younger man. Feuilerade killed his opponent with a sword thrust to the chest, but when the doctor loosened Olivier's shirt, he found a broad metal-backed belt around his waist, a reason, no doubt, for Olivier's notorious alacrity in matters of honor. The scoundrel's seconds denied vociferously that they had known in advance of this wicked "disloyalty," and the assizes court that acquitted Feuilerade spent most of its indignation on the crime of the dead man rather than the homicide of the survivor.[140]

Another fatal duel, which took place in Lille during Carnaval in the spring of 1885, also involved a dueling irregularity following a squabble over a woman. Eugène Deikerel, a local businessman, killed Lieutenant Chapuis after parrying the officer's sword with his left hand and running him through. The woman in question was a singer in the bar where Deikerel, Chapuis—dressed in *bourgeois*—and others were celebrating in the early hours of the morning. Asked his opinion of her looks, Chapuis said loudly enough for her to hear that she had pretty hands but he had seen prettier. The chanteuse, Louise Andouin, replied with a pleasantry, but Deikerel, though himself married, chose to interpret Chapuis's remark as an insult to the womanhood of Lille. Chapuis responded by noting Deikerel's "vulgar" tastes, and Deikerel for his part expressed his doubts about Chapuis's military status and called him a "coward." Friends of the two attempted a reconciliation, but the sticking point was Deikerel's demand for an apology, on the grounds that he had been insulted first in his capacity as champion of the women of Lille. Chapuis balked over the words, "gave his excuses," preferring "admitted his wrongs," and negotiations broke down.[141]

All four seconds agreed the duel must be serious; six shots with pistols at twenty paces was first suggested, but as both men were well-practiced fencers, the sword was chosen instead. Indeed, before he was himself run through, Chapuis had attempted at least one thrust at his opponent's mid-

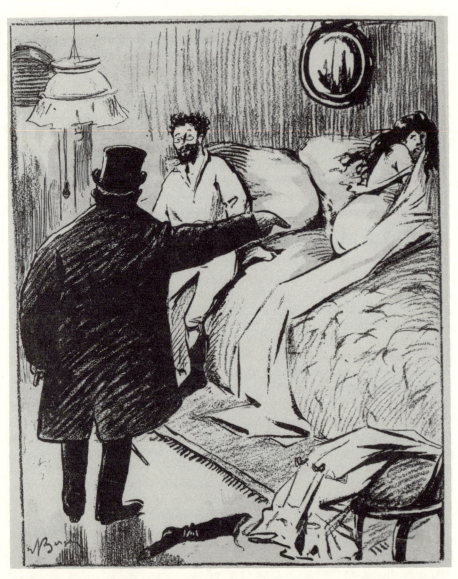

Figure 9. "The Husband's Honor. THE HUSBAND: 'You have stolen my honor, monsieur! I am within my rights to kill you, but I prefer a duel'. THE OTHER: 'Me too.'"

section, in contrast to the custom in less serious duels of trying to inflict a wound on the hand or forearm. According to witnesses, the pre-duel sentiments expressed by both men suggested that the chief issues had become the honor of Dunquerquers versus that of the 110th Regiment of the Line.[142] At the subsequent trial, however, three other main issues emerged: had Deikerel behaved honorably in the duel, was he a man of honor, and was Mlle. Andouin's honor worth defending?

To decide the first issue, fencing-masters from near and far testified to the legitimacy of the "left-handed parade," as Deikerel's maneuver was called. Though many called it patently "disloyal," they were neutralized by others who declared it acceptable.[143] On the other matters, the chief prosecutor sought to establish the point that as a married man Deikerel had no business acting the part of champion to a woman of doubtful virtue. "One does not find," he said, "proper women wearing [carnival] masks in cafés at four in the morning," and there is little honor "in the kind of man who tries to reconcile the carefree life of a bachelor with the duties of a husband and father." In response, after quoting Victor Hugo on the honor of fallen women and defending his client's right to intercede in her behalf, Deikerel's lawyer turned sententiously to the male audience in the room to ask them, "What would you have done?" Despite the Nord's reputation for straitlaced Catholic family life, the male jurors who acquitted Deikerel apparently sympathized with his gallantry, no matter how tarnished the lady who provoked it.[144]

The same mixture of defense of female honor and personal susceptibility may be found in a more traditional variation of the gallant duel that occurred in Paris in 1888. Félix Dupuis was a moderately successful academic painter in his fifties who enjoyed a local celebrity in the seventeenth arrondissement where he lived and worked. One of the regular guests at the *matinées* Dupuis and his wife held every week was Eugène Habert, a young painter who also edited a little art magazine, *Le Journal de XVII arrondissement*. Apparently bored by the adulatory atmosphere of these gatherings, Habert published some uncomplimentary remarks about a young woman who had submitted a sonnet to his magazine, suggesting that the fulsome praise the sonnet offered to Dupuis's painting was inspired by something more than esthetic admiration. Madame Dupuis responded indignantly by letter to indicate Habert would no longer be welcome at their *matinées*. Habert replied with a piece in his magazine that ridiculed the pretentiousness of the Dupuis' gatherings, referred to Mme Dupuis as "the mistress of panegyric," and to Dupuis himself as a "cherdepoul."[145]

Though Dupuis was not immediately certain of the word's meaning, and was initially more amused than angry, he felt, on reflection, that his reputation in the neighborhood would suffer if he took no action. Claiming he felt himself to have been "outraged in his person and in that of his wife," he sent his seconds to Habert.[146] It emerged that "cherdepoul" was actually "chair de poule," a common insult meaning "gooseflesh," implying Dupuis was afraid to defend his honor. Habert at first took refuge in his right of legitimate artistic criticism, but as he refused to retract the awful slander, a duel was inevitable. Habert later claimed that if he had retracted his remarks, the vindictive Mme. Dupuis would have trumpeted his ignominy in the papers, as had recently been done with such effect to Jules Ferry.

Outside observers, judging from the occupation of the two men and the duel's motive, considered it a "futile" duel.[147] The seconds knew better. Safe conditions—twenty-five paces, one shot—were chosen, but the seconds selected rifled pistols and placed the combatants in an *allée* of trees, which helped focus the aim, rather than in an open space. After he brought Dupuis down with a shot between the eyes, Habert was quoted as remarking tersely, "tant pis" (tough luck). In her own testimony at the trial, Mme Dupuis emphasized how "suffocated" her husband had been by the phrase "chair de poule," and how he needed a serious duel or would be said "to be lacking in honor."[148] Mme Dupuis's testimony about the seriousness of the duel helped, of course, to acquit Habert, but it is hard to escape the conclusion that Dupuis's sense of outrage in this matter was absurdly overdetermined by the combination of publicity, his obligation to defend two women, and the implication he was hiding behind his wife's skirts.

Similar complications marked a fatal duel in the sub-prefecture of Avesnes in the Mayenne department in the summer of 1872. In this affair the young sub-prefect, Appleton, was annoyed with the local tax collector in Avesnes, Charles Ritter, because the latter had not acknowledged calling cards he had left at Ritter's house. One evening in a crowded salon, Appleton failed to return Ritter's greeting, and Ritter thought he discerned "mocking smiles" on the faces of some of Avesnes' local notables. Appleton then ostentatiously greeted Ritter's wife, leading Ritter to conclude he was "simply drawing attention to the outrage and the insult he had just given the husband."[149] Ritter approached Appleton and demanded a formal greeting from him or risk the consequences. Appleton refused, upon which Ritter hurled his glove in the face of the sub-prefect and received a slap in return. A reconciliation was arranged on the spot, however, and the matter was apparently resolved.

Appleton, however, was worried that he had not acted decisively enough in the eyes of opinion, and a few days later he asked a friend if he should send seconds to Ritter for the provocation he had received. He was assured the affair was terminated, but news of Appleton's inquiry circulated through the women's gossip network in distorted form, to wit, that Appleton had "waited in vain" for two days for Ritter's seconds.

When Ritter heard this news from the lips of his own wife, he knew a duel was inevitable. In the eyes of "opinion" the courage of both men had been put in doubt, and in the "serious" duel that followed, Appleton was killed by a ball from Ritter's pistol at close range. In the trial that followed, Ritter, despite dueling experience and a reputation as a bully, was exonerated, amidst much praise of the importance of honor to the nation and references to the recent war.[150]

It was regarded as good form in gallant duels to not inform womenfolk until after the fact, ostensibly to spare them worry. But another reason may have been that, having no legal or personal recourse of her own, when a woman knew about an offense given her she might put extra pressure on a father or husband to stand in for her, even though his own honor or courage had not been directly impugned. Unless he possessed an unusually acute sense of gallantry, a man might be reluctant to risk his life to protect an estranged wife or avenge insults meant for her that she may have felt more keenly than him.

In 1883 the wife of Clovis Hughes, the socialist deputy from the Bouches-de-Rhône, learned her name had appeared as correspondent in a separation case brought by another woman against her own spouse. She traced the information back to a detective agency, where she demanded a retraction, but was summarily refused. Unwilling to wait for legal action to clear her name, Mme Hughes wrote her husband—who had until then done nothing at all—that she would kill the owner of the agency to exonerate herself. This finally goaded Hughes into action. He sent his seconds to both the detective and his employer, received an apology, and the matter was closed, though only temporarily.[151] Similarly, when the novelist Alphonse Daudet did not react immediately to an attack on his wife in the press, Mme Daudet tearfully complained to Edmond de Goncourt that "It is strange that Alphonse, who is always so prickly on his own account, is not sensitive over the insult to me."[152] Though his wife later reversed herself, Daudet decided reluctantly to go ahead with a duel, both because of her grief and because it was expected of him.[153]

The gallant defense of women also figured in the other category of serious duels, those between Jews and anti-Semites, though usually as a metaphor standing in for a greater collectivity. Despite official Catholic disapproval, the anti-Semite Edouard Drumont explained his own willingness to duel by saying, "Those I have defended will say about me that he had disobeyed the laws of the church only because he was too indignant about the outrages heaped upon the mother he venerated." It was precisely this chivalrous quality, according to Drumont, that distinguished Christians from Jews, "who demonstrate their courage only in their attacks on our priests, monks and nuns."[154] Indeed, the contrast between "Semites" and "Aryans" that Drumont drew in his *La France juive* in 1886 did more than anything else to initiate the epidemic of "Jewish" duels of the following twenty-five years. "The Semite," he wrote, "is mercantile, greedy, intriguing, subtle, and evasive," while the Aryan is "enthusiastic, heroic, chivalrous, disinterested, frank, and confident to the point of naiveté."[155]

Racial polemics emphasizing the "natural" cowardice of Jews, often coupled with insinuations that Jews were effeminate and inclined by nature to homosexuality, remained an integral feature of right-wing political discourse well into the twentieth century.[156] But if anti-Semites really believed in the truth of their peremptory declarations about the nonexistence of Jewish honor, they were quickly disabused. Edouard Drumont had two duels on his hands within a week of the appearance of his book, and Henri Rochefort was provoked into a duel by Camille Dreyfus, whose seconds demanded such a dangerous duel that Rochefort's seconds were obliged to appeal to less threatening precedents.[157] Indeed, until well past the turn of the century, Jews in public life were quick to take offense at anti-Semitic slights; they demanded serious dueling conditions and were noted for the unusual energy with which they pursued the combat.[158] In a sword duel in 1912 following a theater fracas with the playwright Pierre Veber, Léon Blum charged forward relentlessly, seeking his opponent's midsection. Veber was spared being run through only because Blum's sword buried itself in his sternum, knocking him on his back.[159]

The mocking tone adopted by Drumont and his acolytes when they commented on this rather vigorous response does not reveal whether they had expected their bullying tactics to have this effect. "Nothing is more touching," wrote Drumont *à propos* a duel in Algeria, "than to see a man of their race who knows how to use a sword."[160] There is a certain irony in the fact that in their Jew-baiting anti-Semites were, in effect, schooling their victims in civil equality and then legitimizing them in the subsequent duel. To duel with a man meant to acknowledge his worthiness as a man of honor, so that what anti-Semitic rhetoric denied in principle, anti-Semites acknowledged in practice.

We seem to be present here at the birth of a remarkable phenomenon in Jewish history: an effort by Jews to create a new identity for themselves that would replace old stereotypes with the image of a Jew ready to defend his rights and those of his community. It is no coincidence that the founder of Zionism, Theodor Herzl, witnessed some of the most dramatic episodes of the "Jewish" duel while a correspondent of the Neue Freie Presse in Paris in the early 1890s. As Peter Loewenberg has pointed out, Herzl arrived in France with a deep commitment to the idea that Jews must appropriate for themselves the "strictest traditions of chivalric honor," but what he saw after he arrived must have surpassed even his wildest imaginings.[161]

Once embarked on this course, there was no backing away from it for either side. Since the end result of any polemic between anti-Semite and Jew was likely to end up on the dueling ground, their combats took on a heightened significance for the sympathizers of each group and a correspondingly exaggerated ideological meaning. Because unfriendly generalizations might be drawn from any salient behavior, each detail of an affair of honor was evaluated by both sides according to the highest standards of correctness. Men who might not previously have known the regulations governing duels took pains to learn them.

When Drumont had his duel with Arthur Meyer, editor of the conservative *Le Gaulois,* Meyer twice grasped Drumont's sword with his left hand during violent *corps-à-corps.* On the second occasion, he ran his sword into Drumont's thigh, ending the duel. Meyer's immediate and thorough apologies for this "unconscious" action did not get him off the hook with his enemies, or protect him from the torrent of anti-Semitic abuse screamed at him by Drumont as his seconds pulled off his bloody trousers. Edmond de Goncourt has left us an account of the duel in which he describes how "all of Yiddom" had gathered at the offices of *Le Gaulois* to welcome back their hero, Meyer, who was obliged to report how badly he had acquitted himself.[162] Shortly thereafter, the anti-Semitic cartoonist Adolphe Willette published a drawing of Drumont in crusader's garb, wielding an axe but impervious to a hail of quill pens flying at him, one of which has embedded itself in his thigh.[163]

In the early 1890s Drumont's paper, *La Libre parole*, mounted an attack on Jewish officers in the army. Over the signature of Paul de Lamase, the paper published anonymous "information" alleging that Jews gained preferential treatment in billets and promotions through bribery and political influence, and were, furthermore, not trustworthy comrades-in-arms. There is little doubt that *La Libre parole* was simply giving voice to the deep anti-Semitic sentiment in the officers corps itself, but the insinuations of disloyalty aroused deep resentment in the Jewish community and inspired a Captain Cremieux-Foa to write Drumont, challenging him in behalf of "the three hundred Jewish officers of the army."[164] Claiming the correct procedures for choosing the "champion" of a collectivity had not been followed, Drumont nonetheless replied that Jewish officers could choose as many champions as they liked, and "we will oppose to them an equal number of *French* swords."[165]

Though both Lamase and Drumont's staff bully, the Marquis de Morès, demanded the right to defend the paper's cause, the honor fell to Lamase. Dangerous conditions were established by common consent: four shots at twenty-five paces. Emotion ran so high at the dueling ground that Morès, who was Lamase's chief second and director of combat, took open exception to Cremieux-Foa's failure to reply to the traditional, "Gentlemen are you ready," by challenging him on the spot to a duel the next day, to which

Cremieux-Foa replied fiercely, "I am your man."[166] The Lamase duel ended without injury, but on the following morning, Captain Cremieux-Foa's chief second, Captain Armand Mayer, was obliged to report to Morès that his client had been forbidden by his regimental commander to duel and was confined to barracks. Morès had another bone to pick, however. The official transcript of the previous day's duel had appeared in the morning papers, despite the prior agreement struck by the seconds that there be no publicity. Though he had not been responsible for this indiscretion, Mayer insisted on assuming responsibility for it, and a sword duel was arranged for the following morning on the Grande Jatte.[167]

Armand Mayer was the fencing-master at the Ecole Polytechnique and an excellent swordsman, but Morès met his attack with a riposte under the arm, and Mayer sank to the ground to die in the arms of his seconds, Lieutenant Trochu and Commandant Ferdinand Esterhazy, which makes this duel a prelude to the Dreyfus affair in more ways than one. After expressing his regret for his opponent's death, Morès let it be known that he saw this duel as a conflict of principles rather than men, and the first episode of the civil war to come.[168] On 26 June, the chief rabbi of France pronounced a moving oration after several thousand people marched solemnly through Paris in the wake of Mayer's flag-draped coffin. This "gentle and virile" officer, he said, embodied the finest qualities of the French officer: "rectitude, loyalty, honor, self-abnegation, a scorn for danger, and the taste for sacrifice," a noble example of a French family giving its son to the fatherland.[169]

At Morès's trial in August, it emerged that the one who had published the offending transcript, and thus the man for whom Armand Mayer had died, was Captain Cremieux-Foa's civilian brother, Ernest. Despite evidence suggesting that Morès and the anti-Semitic coterie around *La Libre parole* had willfully provoked Jewish officers in order to "have a corpse," as one testimony put it, it was Ernest Cremieux-Foa's behavior that became the chief issue in the proceedings. Edgar Demange, who later defended Alfred Dreyfus, was Morès's lawyer at the trial. Putting his own client in the chair, he asked Morès what *he* would have done if he had been in Mayer's place. Would he have denounced Ernest Cremieux-Foa as the man who had published the transcript? Morès was silent. "Your silence is as good as an answer," Demange continued; had he done so, "his situation would have been impossible in the world and in the army alike."[170]

Demange's strategy was masterful. Rather than find fault with Mayer, who had become something of a martyr to French Jews, or Captain Cremieux-Foa, whose own comportment had been irreproachable (and who had in the meanwhile died in a cavalry charge in Dahomey), he conceived a situation in which his own client could gallantly resist the temptation to reproach a Jew, who would then be made to bear the responsibility for the whole affair. Indeed, when he was called to testify on the following day, Ernest Cremieux-Foa blustered and prevaricated under Demange's questions. Asserting his brother had been ill-served by his seconds, he admitted to having overheard the seconds agree not to publish the transcript—itself an indiscretion—but published it anyway to unmask the source of the slander against Jewish officers. "Did you do it for your brother's sake?" asked Demange. "No," he replied, "for our race."[171] Why then, asked Demange, did you allow Mayer to take a responsibility that was in fact your own? To this Cremieux-Foa replied that Mayer wanted an excuse to fight Morès, and that, besides, he had told everyone he had published it. "Yes," replied Demange sententiously, "everyone except M. de Morès."[172]

Whistles greeted Cremieux-Foa as he took his seat; according to *La Libre parole* several men offered him their cards and jeered him as he left the courtroom.[173] The trial ended in the usual acquittal, but Ernest Cremieux-Foa's trials had just begun. He was universally damned in the press for his "piteous" conduct, both by the anti-Semitic press, which disingenuously "scorned" him for conduct "scarcely favorable to the Jewish race," and by republican papers like *Le Temps,* which editorialized on how badly he had served his *coreligionnaires.*[174] In his weekly column, Jules Simon, himself of Jewish origin, reproached any man who risks the life of another man rather than frighten him with the "truth." How would it be, he asked, if we all followed the "curious pretention of respecting the tranquility of those for whose security we were entirely responsible?" "One need never repent for having been prudent, but one must always blush at temerity. Having pushed temerity so far as to endanger the life of a fellow citizen is not only a shame, it is a crime."[175]

Cremieux-Foa tried desperately to avoid being the sacrificial lamb in this affair, but in his frantic efforts to rehabilitate himself, he simply confirmed the established prejudices against him, and, alas, against Jews. He gave incoherent interviews to the press. He challenged one of his brother's seconds, Lieutenant Trochu, to a duel, claiming Trochu lied about him in court. Trochu would not likely have honored the provocation anyway, but when Trochu's senior officer confined him to barracks, Cremieux-Foa made his way to his provincial garrison, burst into the officer's mess and hurled his glove in Trochu's face. This would ordinarily have been sufficient to force an opponent's hand and confirm a rehabilitating duel, but apparently Trochu and his colleagues believed Cremieux-Foa to be irredeemable, because they responded by kicking and punching the offender and hurling him out the door, at which point even his seconds abandoned him.[176] The unhappy man was left with the sole, inadequate, recourse of publishing his own version of events.[177]

According to Jean-Denis Bredin, the Dreyfus affair, which unfolded between 1894 and about 1906, produced no fewer than thirty-one duels, many of them of the "Jewish" variety.[178] Though all these duels were by nature "serious" duels, they did not produce a single casualty, perhaps because defending the cause of Dreyfusism or anti-Dreyfusism soon achieved a ceremonial status that dampened the sting of personal affront. As the affair became politicized, in other words, the affairs of honor it provoked began to resemble the highly ritualized and less dangerous form of the political duel, where personal motive was subsumed into a "higher" cause, producing a sense of outrage in duelers that burned steadily but less intensely than more intimate conflicts.

The "Futile" Duel

In the "futile" duel, to which we now turn, the motives were nearly always trivial or spontaneous in nature. The differences that pitted men against one another in such duels did not arise from noble or high-minded partisanship, but from real or imagined insults to their persons. Men who engaged in duels for what contemporaries called "futile" motives did not have, therefore, a strong sense of corporate honor or solidarity to either steel their resolve or mitigate their anger. They could depend only on their personal experiences and emotional resources to guide them through the thicket of dangers that confronted them in affairs of honor. The "futile" duel thus produced less predictable outcomes than other varieties, oscillating between the tragic and the ludicrous. If we look again at Desjardins's inventory from the 1880s, there were about 150 duels that appeared to arise from some public breach of *politesse,* a fracas, or a personal, though not serious, slight delivered in speech or in print. There was approximately the same proportion of men badly wounded in such duels as there was in political duels (12/150 as against 11/108), but the latter kind produced no deaths, while five men died in duels for futile motives.[179]

It was fashionable to mock duels with futile or contrived motives; vaudevilles that made fun of such encounters were a staple of *belle époque* stagecraft and enjoyed considerable success. One such confection, entitled "Un Duel s'il vous plaît," ("A Duel if you please") played to appreciative audiences in 1885. A young man having an affair with a friend's wife is surprised by the husband's late-night return from a trip. Thinking fast, he apologizes to the husband for his disheveled dress, explaining that he rushed over immediately after receiving a dueling challenge to find a loyal second. While his friend goes in search of an additional second, the seducer must find an adversary to fight. He begins by offering insults to perfect strangers on the sidewalk—who ignore what they take to be the ravings of a madman—and finally resorts to slapping men randomly as they leave a theater, including, to his evident horror, the man who was to have been his future father-in-law.[180]

The typical futile duel grew out of an altercation in a public setting: the races, a men's club, the theater, or even a crowded sidewalk, when one man thought it beneath his dignity to make way for another man in his path. General François de Négrier was chatting with friends one night in a box at the Opéra comique when a voice nearby demanded silence. Négrier took offense at this impertinence, cards were exchanged at the intermission, and a duel was fought the next morning. His antagonist was the well-known amateur fencer, Georges LeGrand, who was known as a bully, but since the reproach had come from a neighboring box—assuring the social credentials of his opponent—Négrier did not feel at liberty to make further discriminations.[181]

However trivial the motive, a man in the upper reaches of society who believed himself to have been insulted—especially in the presence of witnesses—was required to take up weapons in his defense. Once he did so, the matter was in the hands of his seconds, and he might be required to face conditions as dangerous as a man with a much more serious affair on his hands. It was unthinkable to bring the conditions of combat into line with the superficiality of the offense; such arrangements raised questions about a man's courage, and made the public "smile."[182] The journalist and man of letters Harry Alis (Hippolyte Percher) was run through and killed by Alfred LeChatelier, a fellow member of the pro-colonialist *Comité d'Afrique Française,* for a vague imputation LeChatelier had made in a letter about personal advantage he had gained from a railway concessions in the Congo. Alis and LeChatelier had been close friends and co-founders of the group, but neither man felt he could retreat once offense had been taken and acknowledged.[183]

A near-fatal duel in 1870 between an army officer and a young aristocrat further illustrates the power of the honor code to shape conduct. A difference of opinion about horses caused a captain of the Dragoons to follow his civilian adversary to Strasbourg to issue a challenge. In the duel that followed, Vicomte Philippe Hallez-Claparède was nearly killed by a sword thrust. Asked in court why he had agreed to fight over such a trivial difference, he replied, "I had never had an affair of honor before, and I feared that my conduct would be prejudicially judged if I backed out of a fight with an officer who had fought several duels."[184]

Backing out of a duel might not prove socially damaging providing a man acted promptly to redeem himself. He could not provoke a fresh encounter with his original antagonist—a version in the private law of the duel of double jeopardy—but he might accomplish the same end by provoking one of his opponent's friends. M. de la Poëze was standing in his club when M. de Malortie trod upon his foot. Poëze remarked politely that the gentlemen "had chosen badly the spot on which to place his foot," upon which Malortie repeated his provocation. Poëze later claimed in correctional court that he knew Malortie was simply trying to "rehabilitate" himself for failing to fight a friend of his the week before, but felt he had "no choice" but to give him satisfaction.[185] The fine points in the dueling manuals about who was "worthy" and who was not did not often hold in practice.

When a man refused to fight, he was made to pay a heavy price. A squabble at the stock exchange one day between Gaston Dreyfus and the thin-skinned editor of *Le Gaulois,* Arthur Meyer, was joined by a third party, M. Lange, who took Dreyfus's part in the dispute. Meyer sent seconds to each man. When Lange refused them satisfaction, they reconstructed his prevaricating remarks ("Please be assured, Messieurs, it was never my intention. . . . "), and published it in the papers the next day, together with their own warnings to him: "Sir, we must insist on the situation in which you are placing yourself . . . which forces us to *execute* you. You will be *executed* not only in the press, but in the world." They concluded that Lange's friend Gaston Dreyfus, behaved "as he should" by giving satisfaction to Meyer.[186]

Most upper-class men, however, apparently believed the dangers of a fight preferable to the circulation of rumors about their cowardice, the one thing a duel could lay to rest once and for all. The famous fin de siècle dandy Count Robert de Montesquiou appeared one night in June 1897 at a party given by the Baroness Alphonse de Rothschild. The elegant Montesquiou, who was later to be the model for Proust's character Charlus, had already served as the model for the passive and effeminate Duc des Esseintes in J. K. Huysmans's novel *A Rebours.* A month before the Baroness' party, a terrible fire at the Bazaar de la Charité had taken the lives of several society ladies, and some gentlemen were rumored to have used their canes to clear a path for themselves through the crowd of suffocating women.

Coincidentally, Jean Boldini's elegant portrait of Montesquiou holding a favorite cane was exhibited the same month in the Salon in the Champs de Mars. This gave rise to certain cruel speculations in connection with the count which the wife and sister-in-law of the poet Henri de Regnier repeated at the Rothschild party in the presence of Montesquiou and others. Montesquiou replied by saying it was a shame men no longer wore swords, as they were useful for chastising women. Regnier himself then responded with a remark of his own about fashion directed at the count: "It would certainly be amusing if we men were also able to make use of muffs in the winter and fans in the summer." Realizing the die was cast, Montesquiou chose Maurice Barrès and the dashing but unstable society bully Albert de Dion to represent him. Regnier, who apparently hoped the matter would end with this delicious exchange of pleasantries, finally agreed to a duel, and Montesquiou was wounded on the hand.[187]

To the evident delight of contemporaries, duels for futile motives lent themselves well to caricature. Such duels allowed opponents of the practice to heap scorn on affairs of honor with an impunity forbidden in "serious" duels, and for "men of heart" to distance serious duels from the "duels pour rire" (ridiculous duels) that futile motives often provoked. As they were often unpracticed in weapons, but easily aroused by aesthetic slights, poets and playwrights were the typical participants in such duels. When the symbolist poet Jean Moréas fought a duel with his colleague Rudolph Darzens, the swords and flowing shirts of the poets became hopelessly entangled, they wrestled at close quarters, and the duel ended amidst accusations of disloyalty on both sides.[188] In 1897 the theater director Aurelian-Marie Lugné-Poë fought the critic Catulle Mendès over a crucial matter of taste. Mendès was a practiced combatant, but Lugné-Poë's sole experience consisted of a brief lesson the previous night. Thinking it best to yield ground, Lugné-Poë retreated steadily as Mendès advanced, surrendering huge chunks of terrain to avoid injury. Furious, Mendès broke off and demanded a limit to such "cowardly" evasiveness. The seconds agreed on twenty-five meters and the duel resumed, but Lugné-Poë continued his tactic and Mendés hurled down his sword, demanding a replacement for this "poltroon." Lugné-Poë's chief second, Aristide Briand, immediately took off his coat and seized a sword, but was physically restrained from a further breach of decorum. Only after tempers calmed was it noticed that the inept Lugné-Poë had somehow managed to wound Mendès on the arm, drawing blood and ending the duel.[189]

Most men preferred the risk of cutting a bad figure on the dueling ground to charges of cowardice. A rare exception involved a dispute between the eccentric novelist Joséphin Péladan and the cabaretier and humorist, Rodolphe Salis, who took issue with Péladan for the latter's reference to him as a "lemonade salesman." Péladan refused to duel for three reasons. First, he was a Catholic. Second, on account of certain "occult" powers he possessed, he was certain to kill his opponent. Finally, an assassination would constitute a "hermetic impurity" in the order of the universe, and there was no "magic college" that could purify him. The Paris press openly mocked such arrant nonsense, but Péladan then revealed his true reason for declining the privilege of the duel:

> Your echoes give voice only to my theoretical reasons against the duel;
> but the friends of the lemonade salesman have neglected the only worthy
> reason in the present case. It is not enough to spatter mud on an out-
> standing writer to become his equal. The twenty volumes of my work

separate me decisively from a mere cabaret performer. Duelist though
he be, I refuse to fight M. Salis for the clear reason that one only duels
with one's equals.[190]

Such an artful dismissal of an affair of honor could only have been
managed by someone with a well-established reputation for lunacy. Though
the manuals devoted much space to deciding who was qualified to duel
and who was not, less eccentric men than Péladan were obliged to respect
the conventions unless there was substantial doubt about an opponent's
eligibility. In his *Les Lois du duel,* Bruneau de Laborie attempted to
demarcate the borders separating men of honor and others by arguing that
honorable men possess a "painfully nervous noble susceptibility" that bris-
tles at an insult tendered by an equal. For our social and moral inferiors
we feel only disdain, he wrote, and this "fact" will naturally discourage us
from placing our lives in the balance.[191] Such a scheme overlooked two
important points, both of which undermined the social exclusiveness of
dueling. First, any man who believed himself worthy would anticipate
experiencing the very feelings of refined susceptibility that Laborie thought
"naturally" distinguished the man of breeding, as in the self-fulfilling behavior of those marked by predestination. Second, few men had the luxury
of calmly reviewing the qualifications of someone who had just offered him
an insult. To hesitate—for even an instant—was to prevaricate, and pre-
varication was the manner of cowards.

In practice the real, indeed the only reliable, measure of the quality
that made a man eligible to invoke the *point d'honneur* was the knowledge
of its elaborate rituals and the willingness to carry them out. In the late
nineteenth century, a man from the popular classes might learn fencing or
shooting serving with his regiment or while taking recreation with his local
shooting society or fencing hall; but skill at weapons was a necessary but
not sufficient condition for full qualification for an affair of honor. The
urchins who "dueled" with nail-tipped sticks in 1892 in a Paris street over
a local beauty were not playing out a *point d'honneur* but were engaging
in an act of social imitation they had learned from the popular press.[192]
No doubt the gap between this crude version of the "gallant" duel and the
real thing was being slowly eroded by the progressive democratization of
modern life and by the ethos of equality implicit in the code of honor itself,
but there was an imperishable element of hierarchy and exclusiveness in
the code that accounts for an important element of its mystique.

We may best understand the dialectic between equality and hierarchy
in the modern affair of honor if we think of it as a kind of rite of passage.
The duel created for its participants a moment of perfect liminality, when,
in the the face of possible injury or death, men were suspended between
honor and dishonor, depending on how their nerves and luck held out.
The stakes were high, but to have survived and shown sangfroid was to

confirm a kind of corporate male solidarity that built or reaffirmed durable bonds between antagonists, who, as often as not, clasped hands warmly moments after trying to cripple or kill one another.[193] But, as the anthropologist Victor Turner has pointed out, the experience of *communitas* that accompanies the liminal *rite de passage* is offset by a reassertion of hierarchy and structure once the ordeal has run its course.[194] Some fail the rites, and are barred from the community. Others do not know the rites, and so are excluded by their ignorance, as were peasants and most men from the popular classes. Still others did not qualify *by nature* for the rite. Men with a criminal record were regarded as beyond the pale, and we have seen how Jews fought duels in the nineteenth century in the face of an often vociferous opposition. There is no record of a woman having fought one.

The same dialectic of exclusion and community was present in the early modern French duel. But, in contrast to the wholly class-based notion of honor that had confined the duel to the nobility in the Old Regime, the modern duel was far less concerned with the social qualifications of honor. The ethos of the modern duel was more egalitarian than its ancestor because it depended on a conception of masculinity that all men possessed *as males,* a birthright, as it were, conferred on them by the modern discovery of the difference between the sexes. The equality of modern men was an equality of courage, of ardor, of willingness to risk life and limb for some higher ideal.

The scientific and popular articulation of a universal and "natural" conception of masculinity helped weaken the social and cultural distinctions that had divided men historically into different social, political, and cultural categories, each with its own codes and criteria of manly comportment. Those older categories were not yet dead by 1914 or so, but they were being relentlessly supplanted by a form of male identity that was common to all men and that was rooted in male sex and in the masculine behavior appropriate to it.

10

Conclusion: Courage

On the eve of World War I, Georges Breittmayer, a Parisian socialite and fencer, was in the midst of preparing what was destined to be the last French dueling manual. When he finally brought out his little book in 1918, the terrible suffering and death he had witnessed led Breittmayer to conclude that "... after a war in which the French race has demonstrated such indomitable courage and energy, it would be truly ridiculous for the duel to continue the same practices and conditions as before."[1] If the duel was to survive in the post-war world, he wrote, it must adjudicate only the most deeply serious personal matters, not the trivial differences over which men fought before 1914. In homage to the men who had risked their lives, no duel could end before many shots were exchanged or a serious wound inflicted, and no man who had avoided action had the right to challenge an active combatant.[2]

Despite Breittmayer's effort to resuscitate the duel, it must have seemed to post-war observers a pathetic relic of a sunnier, more carefree time when men were obliged to manufacture moments of danger in lieu of the real thing. The twenty-five paces that conventionally separated men holding single-shot dueling pistols made a ludicrous contrast with the deadly terrors of no-man's land. Though a last effort to legally abolish the duel in 1920 met with the same fate as earlier efforts, the duel became very rare indeed after 1914.[3] The dubious privilege of being the last champion of the duel fell to the Socialist mayor of Marseille, Gaston Deferre, who participated in at least two sword duels after 1945, the last of them, incredibly, in 1967 with a rival deputy, René Ribière.

The duel could not avoid the fate of all historical dramas—beginning in tragedy, ending in comedy—but while it prospered it played a notable role in continuing and popularizing the usages of a warrior ethic of honor in the modern era. If I have stressed the remarkable continuities in its assumptions and rituals, I have also tried to indicate the ways the modern duel differed from its ancient ancestor. The personal qualities required by the seventeenth-century gentleman for carrying out the *point d'honneur* were wholly subsumed in his identity as a nobleman; if he thought at all

216

about courage and sangfroid, it was as a birthright indistinguishable from the other rights and obligations of men of his class. There were surely distinctions between magnitudes of bravery and acts of prowess—there could be no heroism otherwise—but men of noble blood were assumed to be endowed *by nature* with features that other men exhibited only *contingently*. The long-surviving belief in western societies that noblemen were better suited for war than non-nobles helps account for their historically disproportionate numbers in the officer corps of all modern European armies.

In the passage from hierarchical-prescriptive to democratic societies, modern states have faced the problem of inculcating the "natural" courage and sangfroid of the nobleman into the mass of men for whom military service was a consequence of their natural *rights*. As Michel Foucault has argued, the modern state has patterned its systems for training and disciplining bodies on military models, including its responsibilities for punishment and education. Depending on the aim, this "discipline" attempts to "construct individuals with a particular technique in which power treats individuals as the objects and the exercise of itself."[4] Not surprisingly, as Alain Ehrenberg has shown, this analysis works best with modern military "pedagogy" itself. In keeping with the importance of individualism in modern societies, the aim of military training since the French Revolution has not been to create "a passive being . . . , but a *combative individual,* whose power is equalled only by his obedience and *whose docility is guaranteed by his autonomy*. These procedures have aimed to destroy anything in the individual dangerous or hostile to the smooth functioning of the society, whether comportments of cowardice, indecisiveness, weakness, or uncontrolled violence, in brief anything that might gnaw away at sociability."[5]

In a sense, the bourgeois *régime* of emotional self-control and asceticism I discussed in the first part of this book was the personal and private corollary of the state's public effort to discipline the unruly masses. My point here is to emphasize once again that though an important aim of this system of personal discipline was the regulation of sexuality, this goal was imbricated in a code of honor that had inherited the military virtues through its noble ancestry. Personal courage, which was the most precious of these virtues, thus became a crucial component of the sex—the masculine identity—of men who aspired to honor. This is how it happened, I think, that the aims of the French state—seeking the most valuable psycho-social results from military training—paralleled the aims of upper-class French males in their pursuit of honor: both placed the same high value on courage and regarded it as indistinguishable from manliness.

In the context of military crisis and fear of national decline that reigned in France in the period 1890–1914, courage was a universally prized quality. As I have pointed out elsewhere, because the French lagged behind Germany in both material resources and population, they were obliged to compensate for this deficit by developing superior "spiritual" qualities, of which courage was perhaps the most important.[6] In the period 1890–1914, therefore, one is able to find considerable evidence of a self-conscious social effort to cultivate the noble flowers of courage and heroism and eradicate the weeds of cowardice and fear that inhibited their growth.

There were essentially two ways contemporaries had of thinking about courage, both of which were based on the logic of evolutionary theory. One of these was of courage as a "moral atavism," a biological instinct in each of our primitive ancestors that ensured his survival in the savage past. As Gabriel Tarde wrote in 1892 of this quality, "When a devoted and nobly generous being rises above the conflicting egoism and utilitarianism of our urban society, one must recognize in him the distant image of our ancestors, whose blood and sweat established our present state of well-being. Heroism is perhaps the finest example we have of a moral atavism."[7] Tarde's sentiments are not far different from Nietzsche's estheticized version of the "warrior" energy latent in the racial "soul" that was so popular with avant-garde French intellectuals around the turn of the century.

A complementary way of thinking about the evolution of courage was to imagine that the group itself enhanced its fitness to survive by preserving individuals with a high degree of altruism and willingness to sacrifice their individual interests to those of the larger society. To a considerable extent, the solidarist movement promoted by important radical politicians like Léon Bourgeois was undergirded by this particular vision of social evolution. Sanford Elwitt has recently portrayed solidarism as a middle-class political strategy designed to counter the disruptive effects of class warfare, which indeed it was, but it was far more than that; there was a deeper and fiercer biological logic to the argument that society should revere and cultivate the socially useful sentiments in individuals.[8] Jean-Marie Guyau, one of the chief theorists of solidarism, argued that we must counteract the unregulated egoism that is the bane of our times by stimulating the sacrificial instincts, of which courage was the principal human incarnation. As he put it in his *L'Irreligion de l'avenir* (1909 ed.), "The only way of achieving true greatness in this life is to possess the certainty that one will not retreat in the face of death."[9]

The sense of danger and decline in fin de siècle France so permeated the cultural atmosphere that courage became the obligation of all citizens. Paul Gerbod has written of the extraordinary explosion of a literature of heroism between 1870 and 1914 that was deployed in the form of a "pedagogical strategy" and applied in a variety of public domains. Military heroism was chronicled in statues to the heroes of the 1870 war, in a yearly *Almanach de Drapeau* listing the heroic exploits of soldiers and policemen, and in the revival of the cult of Joan of Arc, which celebrated the tradition of sacrifice to the fatherland.[10] Civic heroism became an aim of religious teaching, of the numerous patriotic and veteran's organizations of the period, the colonial movement, and even the nascent sporting movement. As though it were the most natural thing in the world, both civic and military heroism were incorporated into the official pedagogy of the Third Republic and served up to students in lectures and textbooks.[11]

In the discourse on heroism in the Third Republic, the bridge between the civic and military varieties was provided by a masculine conception of physical courage, which became, willy-nilly, a model for men, women, and children alike. In a book on the civic courage of French children in 1901, a military author argued that the courage that inspires a boy to save someone from drowning is the same quality which "transforms him into a man."[12] "A man," Captain Richard continued, "who devotes himself in this way to his fellow man cannot fail to be a loyal and brave soldier prepared to pay the sacred tax of his own blood."[13] Edmond Mulle, another writer on civic courage, expressed his gratitude that France was a republic so that the nation could draw equally on the courage of all its citizens. "Formerly," he wrote, "the army was the sword of the nation; today, it is correct to say, that, in the flower of its virility, the nation is a sword itself."[14]

A number of visionary contemporaries understood how this conception of the nation in arms could be implemented in modern society. We have already seen how, in the post-war reaction to the defeat of 1870, the fencing and gymnastics societies of the 1880s sought to train the young to manifest the mental and physical courage needed for revenge. These same goals later motivated the movement to introduce English sports into France and the coeval effort to revive traditional French games. Though these movements were in a certain sense competitors for participants and state patronage, they both invoked the principles of sportive chivalry, endorsed the ideal of amateurism, and strove to portray sport as the means by which courage and the martial sentiments could be instilled in young men. For the leaders of these movements, sport was far more than a means foɪ promoting fitness and health; it was "a conception of life" entailing notions of character-building and particular ethical ideals.[15]

Sport was not simply, in this view, the "moral equivalent of war"; it was the means by which the moral and psychological conditions of the battlefield could be socially produced. The model of the warrior it advocated was that of a man of honor engaged in a noble quest, a heroic knight for modern times.[16] The sportsman Davin de Champdos put it this way: "When battle is bloody it is called war, when it is pacific, fought out in stadiums or the playing field, it is called sport; but, devastating or courteous, it always includes the elements of grandeur, generosity and disinterestedness."[17]

Sporting honor was not simply a rhetorical device in a greater ideological strategy; it was also a social practice that regulated the earliest competitions of mass sport. As Guy Laurens has shown for Languedoc, before a system of leagues or divisions developed to match teams of equal strength, village or town teams issued challenges (*défis*) to one another on the model of dueling provocations.[18] As in the system of personal honor, such challenges were only accepted when the challenger—based on past performance—was of equal or greater strength. There was no glory in crushing a rival of notably weaker force. Before a renowned team would grant an opponent a match, notoriously weak teams were first obliged to comb the region for opponents of roughly equal strength and establish a victorious record.[19] This regard for the usages of honor was not just a feature of traditional southern sociability, or a continuation of the forms of traditional village games; one need only peruse the sporting magazines of the early 1890s to see how Le Racing Club de France and Le Stade Français—the principal sporting clubs of the Paris region—issued and received challenges from one another or other teams in France or in England.

Paschal Grousset was the leader of the nationwide effort to preserve traditional French rural games and establish them in the schools. Despite the peasant and village origin of these sports, Grousset believed the chief effect of their practice would be to encourage the "loyalty and rectitude naturally possessed by the man who devotes himself habitually to fatigue and danger," and to breed "self-confidence, virility, courage, and noble instincts."[20] Grousset's rival in the modern sporting movement, Pierre de Coubertin, used the same language as Grousset in describing the benefits of English sport. It would cultivate, he wrote, the ideal of amateurism, which is "the chivalry of modern sport," strengthen the will, inculcate sangfroid, and preserve young men from "discouragement and bitterness" by reaffirming "courage, bravery, perseverance, and noble sentiments."[21] Coubertin hoped to train gentlemen-warriors, Grousset to enoble the common man, but both enlisted the image of the man of honor and courage who devotes himself to an ethical and national cause that transcends his own self-interest. Ultimately, the nation would benefit. As Coubertin wrote about the virtues of football: "Whoever learns not to shrink from a football scrimmage will not retreat from the mouth of a Prussian cannon."[22]

In effect, fin de siècle sportsmen yoked the ethical ideal of an honorable amateurism—disinterestedness, the striving for "pure" goals—to a doctrine of state service in the formation of military valor. As Richard Holt has pointed out, the leaders of the turn-of-the-century sporting movement fought a rearguard and ultimately losing battle against their own rank and file, which inclined toward prizes and favored the professionalization of boxing, cycling, and team sports.[23] But, through the network of sporting magazines they edited, the columns they wrote for the big Paris dailies, and Coubertin's successful effort to revive the Olympic Games, the sporting elite nonetheless managed to control the rhetorical field in which sport was discussed and presented to competitors and their public. The codifying of rules and regulations, and the standards governing eligibility and disqualification were set up for each sport under the aegis of the principles of amateurism; invariably, the words "loyalty," "courtesy," and "generosity" functioned in these early sporting codes as talismanic guarantees that "honor" would be respected between competitors.[24] Eventually, professional sports promotors and the public fascination with times and records undermined "pure" amateur principles, but, as one commentator wrote in 1909, so long as the ideal, if not the practice of sport was guided by upper-class advocates of national revival, sport was the domain of "virile" men "who have put all their forces in the service of what seems to them noble and desirable," and for whom "virility consists of doing what is necessary without fear."[25]

Advocates were divided about whether the devotion and sacrifices of modern sport were appropriate for women too, though no one disputed the benefits exercise might have for prospective mothers.[26] But, as the contemporary admiration for Joan of Arc suggests, women could also attain to a kind of heroism and be useful to the nation, not simply in the traditional manner of selfless devotion, but in the more active sense of risking life and limb to save others.[27] When dozens of Parisian society women perished in the terrible fire of the annual charity bazaar in 1897, their courage was fulsomely praised. In the words of Paul Fesch, the women who died in the blaze were "heroines . . . , martyrs of courage, abnegation, and devotion."[28] They demonstrated that "our French soil is not sterile if it can still produce heroes who valiantly spill their blood on the battlefield and heroines who fall and die nobly on the field of honor of charity."[29] Since a number of workingmen perished trying to rescue the women, the disaster provided an opportunity for meditations on the wider meaning of sex and civic heroism. At a banquet commemorating the victims, Jules Auffray evoked the "patrimony of honor of France," and praised "Charity, the gift of one's self in an immolation unto death, which united in flames the man of the people and the woman of the world, symbolizing for us in an admirable way the setting aside of [class] prejudices and differences."[30]

We may clearly follow the growing importance of physical courage in civic life by studying the evolution of the prizes for virtue (*prix de vertu*) that were awarded under the auspices of the French Academy. The first prizes for virtue were awarded from a fund (Fonds Montyon) established in 1783 by a rich nobleman who wished to reward acts of charity. The Prix Montyon was the only prize of its kind for three-quarters of a century, until the Fondation Souriau was established in the name of a watchmaker who hoped to encourage acts of virtue, devotion, *and* courage.[31] By 1888, seven more prizes had been established, many of which explicitly indicated they should be awarded for rescues (*sauvetage*) or other notable demonstrations of courage. By 1900 there were twenty-nine such prizes, some of which went to policemen, firemen, citizens who rescued the lives of others, or to domestic servants, male or female, who braved danger to help their masters.[32] Although the more traditional concept of charity as generosity persisted, by the end of the century it was obliged to share the stage with a notion of selflessness in which an individual risked more than his purse to aid his fellow man.

This new and rather self-conscious concern with heroism had the effect of stimulating interest in the biological and human sources of courage, and in its opposite, fear. As it happened, this particular French concern flowed smoothly into a larger set of general European anxieties expressed in fin de siècle industrial societies about decadence and decline. As Anson Rabinbach has recently argued, these worries about the future of material progress were inseparable in this era from concerns about the strength and endurance of the human body. The corporeal economy became, in short, a metaphor for the larger problem of the vitality and prospects of the industrial order, and for the fragile and still larger cosmic balance of indestructible energy and irreversible decline (entropy) proposed in nineteenth-century thermodynamics.[33]

Fatigue studies became the empirical point of entry into this set of issues. As Rabinbach puts it, "In fatigue the physical horizon of the body's forces was identified with the moral horizon of the species; the moral infirmity of the populace was directly proportional to the debilitating effects of fatigue."[34] The "Galileo" of fatigue studies, the Italian physiologist Angelo Mosso, wrote that fatigue "seems to consume our noblest qualities" by diminishing the power of reason and the will to govern the passions, a view already anticipated in France by Théodule Ribot and others concerned with "will pathology" from a clinical point of view.[35] Formulated in this synoptic way, fatigue seemed to explain a number of the neurological disorders of modernity whose most prominent symptoms were exhaustion—psychasthenia, neurasthenia, aboulia—and also to suggest the direction that therapy might take: exercise and strengthening of the will.

Fear was believed to be the most prominent emotional residue of exhaustion and the other pathologies of modern life and was accorded close attention by the leading psychologists and physiologists of the era. Alfred Binet studied the effects of fear on his own daughters in his laboratory in the Sorbonne, and Charles Richet, a Nobel prizewinner for medicine, speculated that fear was a reflex that was designed to augment our physiological forces unless present in paralyzing quantity.[36] Other scientists studied timidity, the milder form of fear that manifested itself in social life. They found that the "embarrassment, tentativeness, . . . scruples and modesty" of the timid man—in short, his timidity—were symptoms linked to the principal *emotions* of shame and fear, which manifested themselves in disorders of the will.[37] As Ludovic Dugas explained it, timid individuals are *naturally shameful (honteuse)*. They lead lives of "complicated dissimulation, full of subtleties and detours . . . ," which are lacking in "cordiality, spontaneity, and frankness."[38]

The link these studies forged between shame and fear, and the physiological status they accorded to shameful emotions helped provide a modern scientific discourse for the historic honor/shame binary. As Dr. Paul Hartenberg argued, men bedeviled by timidity or fearfulness were proportionately enfeebled in "their sentiments of personal dignity and masculine honor, which corresponds to the opinion they have of themselves and that others have of them. That is why men are so angered at the appearance of an emotion that robs them of their force, lessening them in their own eyes and weakening them against their rivals in the struggle for life and in sexual conquests."[39] The irony of fear, Dugas pointed out, is that it leads to more not less conflict, and therefore to greater "discouragement" and "impotence."[40] The frankness of a man of courage, on the other hand, announces to those around him where he stands, enabling him to avoid misunderstandings a more timid man would provoke.

In keeping with the new interventionist therapeutic spirit of the turn of the century, all such studies proposed some *régime* that might counteract the baneful influences of fear, which would, in Binet's words, "toughen the character, . . . and progressively stimulate the habit of courage."[41] The guiding principle for any rehabilitation was a pragmatic variation of the well-known "James–Lange" theory, based on the work of William James and the philosopher Friedrich Lange. The James–Lange theory advanced the paradoxical notion that we experience the physiological reaction of fear because we are afraid, not the other way around. The power of the mind was such, in other words, that mental states often gave rise to corporeal sensation, even the most extreme convulsions of rage or terror. If a man followed a "cerebral gymnastic," in which he adopted "the attitude and allure of decision and energy," he would be able to "raise up his head, throw out his chest, look his interlocutor squarely in the eye and speak in a strong and sonorous voice."[42] Ludovic Dugas suggested that a man could build his courage by seeking the company of other men and measuring himself against them in an atmosphere of "familiarity," and Charles Richet recommended that fearful men should spurn pusillanimous egoism by "habituating themselves to danger, envisaging as often as possible, without bravado, but without sadness, the image of death that awaits us all."[43]

As Anson Rabinbach has shown, suggestions of this order were typical of the contemporary European fascination with will pathology as a biomedical explanation of individual and social exhaustion.[44] There was a veritable industry in France of popular self-help books on will therapy, led by the many late nineteenth-century editions of Jules Payot's influential *L'Education de la volonté*. Books of this kind tended to emphasize the lucrative advantages in strengthened willpower, but many of them directed their attention to the education of courage in particular, a quality additionally useful to the nation. One popular writer transposed Descartes' famous dictum to "I am what I think," hoping to convince his readers that men of action who were supremely "loyal, sincere, and frank" could be formed by a "mental gymnastic" that would transform the "pygmies of today" into the "men of tomorrow."[45] The most intellectually serious work in this genre, the psychologist Paul Souriau's *L'Entrainement au courage* (1926), was also the most specific about how courage and personal bravery were the most distinctive features of the male, as was "beauty" for women.[46] Cowardice was not so much a character trait as the "vile and odious" behavior of a man whose personal energy and force had fallen below a certain limit. This defect obliged him to forfeit his "honor" and "reputation," the very qualities on which his identity as a man depended; he could only regain them by exposing himself to danger and through arduous physical and mental therapy.[47] It is reasonable to assume that reducing manly honor to a quantitative measurement might have deprived the concept of a portion of its *mystique,* but the traditional requirement that courage could only be revealed in conspicuous behavior remained intact in these will therapies, as did the ancient link between honor, courage, and manliness.

The problem of fear and its cures drew unusual public interest as international tensions escalated on the eve of World War I. The journalist Fernand Mazade conducted an inquiry with twenty distinguished scientists, doctors, politicians, generals, and men of letters to whom he asked the following questions: "Have you ever been afraid?" and "How does one combat fear?" To appreciate the uniqueness of such an inquiry, one must imagine a similar survey in the contemporary United States with respondants such as C. Everett Koop, Robert Gallo, Bruno Bettelheim, Arthur Sacks, Gore Vidal, Arthur Miller, John Updike, Steven J. Gould, Willard Quine, Teddy Kennedy, George Bush, and Norman Schwartzkopf. Mazade did not report the answers of all the respondents to the first question, but he notes that eight of them denied ever having experienced fear as adults; those who assented pleaded mitigating or unusual circumstances, or, like the novelist Victor Margueritte, admitted to occasional fear while denying fearfulness in general.[48] Only one candid individual, Dr. Etienne Lancereaux, acknowledged retaining a childhood fear of the dark; most proudly boasted, as did Frédéric Passy, of having "conquered" unworthy terrors.[49]

More to the point, every one of Mazade's interlocutors believed that all but the most preternatural upheavals of instinctive fear could be, indeed must be, dominated by the will. Doctors (Gilbert Ballet, Edouard Toulouse, Joseph Grasset) employed all the fashionable therapeutic termi-nology about educating the will, but the non-medical men also showed an intimate familiarity with the clinical language of will pathologies.[50] Some recommended strengthening the body, reading about acts of heroism, or schooling the populace in its civic duty; others advocated the tonic effects of cultivating a scorn for death (Emile Boutroux, Charles Richet, Edouard Toulouse); all endorsed the efficacy of conducting oneself courageously in all circumstances in order to habituate the mind and body to bravery, whether on the battlefield (General Percin) or while making speeches to a crowded Chamber of Deputies (Raymond Poincaré).

The extraordinary emphasis French scientists, intellectuals, and other public figures placed on courage and physical heroism in the years before 1914 was the consequence of a number of related developments. As we have seen, courage seemed to many thoughtful contemporaries an indis-pensable quality that French men *and* women must possess if a numerically weakened fatherland was to survive future conflict with a stronger military adversary. The numerous panegyrics—both biological and lyrical—in this era to the altruism of individual sacrifice suggests the presence of both a widespread sense of national inferiority *and* a deeply felt reaction of col-lective guilt to the egoism and selfishness of modern consumer culture. Even the buoyant new culture of sport might be interpreted as a kind of symbolic ritual of self-sacrifice, despite our conventional notions of sport as pleasure or as a socially narcissistic cult of heroes. As David Sansome has provocatively argued, the Greek athlete "sacrificed" his energy to the gods so that the life of the community could continue. In his words, "The exhilaration that accompanies sport is precisely parallel to that which ac-companies sacrifice: by a traumatic and enervating act, the sacrificer has given birth to renewed life and restored vigor."[51] Indeed, it is the ideal of amateur sport, with its emphasis on the "useless gesture" of competition in and for itself that contrasts so forcefully with the individualistic values of professional sport.[52]

Second, as Robert Wohl and others have pointed out, in the decade or so before the war a generation of young men posed a powerful critique of the materialist and positivist founders of the Third Republic that con-trasted the putative intellectualism, rationalism, and determinism of the older generation with its own activism, vitality, and spontaneity.[53] Abetted by their elders to a far greater extent than they were willing to concede, this cadre of writers and intellectuals believed that their decadent nation could only be saved by a revival that was at once physical and moral in nature. They dreamed of a disciplined and courageous France reaffirming her warlike identity and her historic mission; they saw themselves—as did Henri de Montherlant and Ernest Psichari—in chivalric terms as "the knights of nothingness" or "the knights of death."[54] Another member of this generation, Edmond de Rostand, captured perfectly the spirit of contemporary chivalry in the most popular play of the fin de siècle, *Cyrano de Bergerac* (1897). The play's famously disfigured hero—a Don Quixote for modern times—nobly devotes his wit and his sword to art, unrequited love, and other hopeless causes for the sake of his "panache." That Rostand took this ideal seriously as a social philosophy is revealed in his acceptance speech to the French Academy in 1912, where he praised the glories of French "panache," which he called the "modesty of heroism," in which "to make jokes in the face of danger is the supreme act of politeness [*politesse*], a delicate refusal to yield to the tragic. . . ."[55]

Third, the homage paid to courage at this time was part of a complex male reaction to the crisis of masculinity provoked by the challenge of feminism and by the first signs of the twentieth-century gender revolution. No less an observer than Henry Miller regarded the "loss of sex polarity" in these developments to be a major source of the world's problems.[56] In France, part of this reaction entailed the elaboration of a new, "scientific" misogyny that could be used as a shield against women's suffrage and female admission to male-monopolized professions.[57] Another part, as I have argued, involved the fabrication by doctors and intellectuals of a deeply unflattering identity for homosexuals that incorporated insulting caricatures of the female sex. The positive side of these negative representations of women and "effeminate" males was the expression of an ideal of physical courage toward which men might strive, and by means of which they could both shore up traditional notions of masculinity and rearticulate the boundaries of traditional sexual difference. It would appear that on the eve of the Great War courage was absurdly overdetermined and performed an astonishingly wide variety of ideological tasks.

When the war finally arrived, this burden of courage proved more than many men were able to bear. The shell-shocked victims who overwhelmed field hospitals manifested symptoms of paralysis and motor disorders similar to the cases of male hysteria that the French neurologist Jean-Martin Charcot identified in the Salpétrière clinic in the 1880s and 1890s.[58] This reaction to the horrors of death and trench warfare was believed by contemporary medical observers to be an involuntary escape from the overwhelming terrors of the war. As Elaine Showalter has put it, "Placed in intolerable and unprecedented circumstances of fear and stress, deprived of their sense of control and expected to react with outmoded and unnatural 'courage,' thousands of men reacted instead with symptoms of hysteria; soldiers lost their voices and spoke through their bodies."[59] Furthermore, the nearly universal association of sexual impotence with severe shell-shock reveals the direct links between shattered masculine identity and sexual dysfunction in the "language" of the shell-shocked body, a connection anticipated in nineteenth-century French medicine, as I have tried to show in previous chapters.

While continuing to follow the path laid down by the scientific study of fear before the war, the major French wartime study of military courage underscored this relationship between potency and masculine courage.[60] According to Doctors Louis Huot and Paul Voivenel, the bravery of fighting men was at its height during the physiological "tumescence" soldiers experienced during battle; when the guns fell silent, a "detumescence" occurred which returned them to their "normal" condition.[61] Episodes of cowardice most often occurred, they wrote, when men were "exhausted" or had suffered some sudden "surprise" or unanticipated shock, which allowed "fear" and the natural "instinct of conservation" to dominate the organism.[62] Huot and Voivnel believed they could make no more telling point about the link between sexuality and courage than to remind their readers of the renowned cowardice of eunuchs, and to credit the "common fighting man with a vividly imaginative phrase for anatomically expressing the chief quality of a warrior."[63] It followed that "one loves one's country as one loves a woman, and fights for it as one would fight for a woman. It is a point of sexuality [*point de sexualité*] to love one's country."[64]

Overwhelmed by the enormous flood of shell-shocked victims, whom they were under pressure to return to action as soon as possible, doctors in all European armies improvised therapies based on these medical shibboleths. Doctors "shamed" soldiers for abandoning their comrades, appealed to their "manly" honor, or, as in the "therapy" W.H.R. Rivers used on Siegfried Sassoon, "embarked on a delicate and subtle intensification of his fears that pacifism was unmanly and cowardly. . . ."[65] The cure for lack of manliness, in other words, was a dose of more manliness, best administered by awakening a man's shocked, dormant, or underdeveloped sense of honor. The trick, wrote Huot and Voivenel in 1917, was for the doctor to treat a man's identity as an instrumentality of being, because "none of us sees things exactly as they are, but as they appear to us in the mirror that we are. The true is what we believe."[66] Thus, they decided, "one must adopt the *attitude* of heroism: it is by means of this *gesture* that we will experience the sentiment of which it is the sign."[67]

The notion that a man's identity was rooted in the sex of his body—and was therefore an aspect of his organic being—was still in vigor in France in 1918, as was masculinity as a quality of a man of honor guided by a code that was an open book to all honorable men. But a new psychological sophistication and the characteristic moral detachment taught by pragmatism had loosened the bonds between biology and identity, so that one could now conceive of men as organic artifacts composed of some permanent "hardware" but also "software" that could be modified at will, strengthened or weakened as the need required. Because the war brought masculinity into clear focus by putting so high a premium on courage and the virile sentiments, one may easily find evidence of these beliefs among the fighting men. The historian Marc Bloch was a sergeant and platoon commander in the first years of war, and, though unusually well-educated for a *poilu,* provides a clear example of the prevailing outlook. He concluded his brief memoirs of the war with the following excursis on courage:

> Military courage is certainly widespread, . . . but often it is the result of effort, an effort that a healthy individual makes without injury to himself and which rapidly becomes instinctive. I have always noticed that by some fortunate reflex, death ceases to appear very terrible the moment it seems close: it is this, ultimately, that explains courage. Most men dread going under fire and especially returning to it. Once there, however, they no longer tremble. Also, I believe that few soldiers, except the most noble or intelligent, think of their country while conducting themselves bravely; they are much more often guided by a sense of personal honor, which is very strong when it is reinforced by the group. If a unit consisted of a majority of slackers, the point of honor would be to get out of any situation with the least harm possible. Thus I always thought it a good policy to express openly the profound disgust that the few cowards in my platoon inspired in me.[68]

NOTES

Chapter 1

1. Marcel Rouet, *Virilité et puissance sexuelle* (Paris: Editions J'ai Lu, 1971), 87–92. The same themes may be found in texts on premature ejaculation and in standard male sex manuals from the first decade of this century. See Dr. Brennus, *L'Acte bref: Traité de l'incontinence spasmodique* (Paris, 1907), 20–21; Dr. Paul Fauconney, *Histoire de l'homme (physiologie du mâle)* (Paris, 1903), 27.

2. For this argument see the "Introduction," by Pat Caplan, in Pat Caplan, ed., *The Cultural Construction of Sexuality* (London: Tavistock, 1987), 1–30; also Jeffrey Weeks, *Sexuality and its Discontents: Meanings, Myths, and Modern Sexualities* (London, 1985), 67–76.

3. The best politico-epistemological discussion of these issues is still John Boswell, "Revolutions, Universals, and Sexual Categories," in *Hidden From History. Reclaiming the Gay and Lesbian past,* ed. Martin Duberman, Martha Vicinus, and George Chauncey, Jr. (New York: NAL, 1989), 17–36. See also the discussion of these issues in Sharon Sievers, "Gay and Lesbian Research in the 1980's: History and Theory," *Radical History Review* 50 (1991): 204–12.

4. Diana Fuss, *Essentially Speaking. Feminism, Nature and Difference* (New York: Routledge, 1989), xi–xii, 1–22.

5. Denise Riley, *"Am I That Name?" Feminism and the Category of "Women" in History* (Minneapolis: University of Minnesota Press, 1988), 4–5.

6. Joan Scott, *Gender and the Politics of History* (New York: Columbia University Press, 1988), 29.

7. Georges Bataille, *Erotism. Death and Sensuality,* trans. Mary Dalwood (San Francisco: City Light, 1986), esp. 11–17.

8. Scott, *Gender and the Politics of History,* 32.

9. Harriet Whitehead, "The Bow and the Burden Strap: A New Look at Institutionalized Homosexuality in Native North America," in *Sexual Meanings. The Cultural Construction of Gender and Sexuality,* ed. Sherry Ortner and Harriet Whitehead (Cambridge: Cambridge University Press, 1981), 83.

10. Ortner and Whitehead, "Accounting for Sexual Meanings," in ibid., 13.

11. An anthropological illustration of this point may be found in Yvonne Verdier, *Façons de dire, façons de faire. La Laveuse, la couturière* (Paris: Gallimard, 1979), 339–40. For a contemporary sociological study see Christine L. Williams, *Gender Difference at Work: Women and Men in Non-Traditional Occupations* (Berkeley, Calif.: University of California Press, 1989).

12. Martine Segalen, *Love and Power in the Peasant Family* (Chicago: University of Chicago Press, 1983), 37–47, 157–60. See also Henri Rey-Flaud, *Le*

Charivari. Les rituels fondamentaux de la sexualité (Paris: Payot, 1985), 126–54, 203–40.

13. Verdier, *Façons de dire,* 338–39.

14. Pierre Bourdieu, *The Logic of Practice,* trans. Richard Nice, (Stanford, Calif.: Stanford University Press, 1990), 68.

15. Ibid., 71.

16. Ibid., 73. Bourdieu's emphasis.

17. Ibid., 79.

18. Ibid., 78.

19. Norbert Elias, *The Civilizing Process,* vol. 3, *The Court Society,* trans. Edmund Jephcott (New York: Pantheon, 1983), 103.

20. Michel Foucault, *The History of Sexuality. An Introduction,* trans. Robert Hurley vol. 1 (New York: Random, 1980), 124–25.

21. Julian Pitt-Rivers, *The Fate of Schechem. Essays in the Anthropology of the Mediterranean* (Cambridge: Cambridge University Press, 1977), 36; see also J. K. Campbell, *Honour, Family and Patronage. A Study of Moral Values and Institutions in a Greek Mountain Village* (Oxford: Oxford University Press, 1964), 274–91. I have discussed these issues elsewhere in "Honor Codes in Modern France. A Historical Anthropology," *Ethnologia Europea* 21 (1991): 5–17.

22. J. G. Peristiany, *Honour and Shame. The Values of Mediterranean Society* (Chicago: University of Chicago Press, 1961), 22.

23. Stanley Brandes, "Like a Wounded Stag: Male Sexual Ideology in an Andalusian Town," in *Sexual Meanings*, 230; Campbell, *Honour, Family and Patronage*, 270. David Gilmore summarizes the Andalusian ideal of *machismo* in similar terms: "A macho, then, is a virile, sexually insatiable stud. Potent as a bull, lascivious as a billy-goat, he unhesitatingly obeys the commands of the *cojones* [testicles]" (*Aggression and Community. Paradoxes of Andalusian Culture* [New Haven, Conn.: Yale University Press, 1987], 132).

24. There has been some interesting historical and anthropological work in France using folklore collections, testamentary records, and oral history. These provide some information about the way systems of honor, vengeance, and the sexual division of labor operated in traditional society. Though not directly germane, as I have said, to aristocratic and bourgeois concepts of honor, they clearly reveal that France has until recent times shared in the Mediterranean honor and shame tradition. See Segalen, *Love and Power* and Verdier, *Façons de dire;* Yves Castan, *Hônneteté et relations sociales en Languedoc (1715–1780)* (Paris, 1974); Elisabeth Claverie and Pierre Lamaison, *L'Impossible mariage. Violence et parenté en Gévaudan au 17e, 18e et 19e siècles* (Paris: Hachette, 1982). For Corsica see Stephen Wilson, "Infanticide, Child Abandonment and Female Honour in Nineteenth-Century Corsica," *Comparative Studies in Society and History* 30 (1988): 762–83.

25. David Gilmore, *Manhood in the Making. Cultural Concepts of Masculinity* (New Haven, Conn.: Yale University Press, 1990), 4–5.

26. Julian Pitt-Rivers, "Honor," in *International Encyclopedia of the Social Sciences* (New York: Macmillan, 1968), 510; Hans Speier, *Social Order and the Risks of War* (Cambridge: Cambridge University Press, 1969), 37–39.

27. On these points see Scott, *Gender and the Politics of History,* 5–6; Lynn Hunt, "Introduction: History, Culture, and Text," in *The New Cultural History,* ed. Lynn Hunt, (Berkeley, Calif.: University of California Press, 1989), 12–17; Patricia O'Brien, "Michel Foucault's History of Culture," in ibid., 25–46; for an appraisal of the application of Emile Durkheim's notion of collective representations to the new cultural history, see Jeffrey Alexander, ed., *Durkheimian Sociology: Cultural Studies* (Cambridge: Cambridge University Press, 1988).

28. Roger Chartier, *Cultural History. Between Practices and Representations* (Ithaca, N.Y.: Cornell University Press, 1988), 9.

29. The difficulties of breaking with the old tradition is illustrated by Scott, *Gender and the Politics of History,* 15–27.

30. Peter Gay, *The Bourgeois Experience: Victoria to Freud,* vol. 1, *The Education of the Senses* (New York: Oxford University Press, 1984), 144.

31. Thomas Laqueur, *Making Sex. Body and Gender from the Greeks to Freud* (Cambridge, Mass.: Harvard University Press, 1990), 22. For an extended evaluation of this view and on the virtues of the "one-sex," "two-sex" model, see Katharine Park and Robert A. Nye, "Destiny is Anatomy," *The New Republic,* 18 Feb. 1991, 53–57.

32. Alain Corbin, "Le 'Sexe en deuil' et l'histoire des femmes au XIXe siècle," in *Une Histoire des femmes est-elle possible?* ed. Michelle Perrot, (Paris: Rivages, 1984), 148.

33. Robert J. Stoller, *Sex and Gender: On the Development of Masculinity and Femininity* (New York: Science House, 1968), 263–68; Nancy Chodorow, *The Reproduction of Mothering: Psychoanalysis and the Sociology of Gender* (Berkeley, California: University of California Press, 1978).

34. Walter J. Ong, *Fighting for Life. Contest, Sexuality, and Consciousness* (Ithaca, N.Y.: Cornell University Press, 1981), 98.

35. Michel Leiris, *Manhood. A Journey From Childhood Into the Fierce Order of Virility,* trans. Richard Howard (New York: Grossman Publishers, 1963), 158. Originally published as *L'Age d'Homme* (Paris: Gallimard, 1946).

Chapter 2

1. This is the phraseology of François Billacois in *Le Duel dans la société française des XVIe–XVIIe siècles. Essai de psychosociologie historique* (Paris: Editions de l'École des Hautes Études en Sciences Sociales, 1986), 82; Arlette Jouanna has argued similarly that for honorable men, "the virtue which is proposed to them as a model, like the quality which allows them to conform themselves to it are equally called 'honor,' a usage which suggests a freely-accepted constraint and a vigorous endorsement of conformism" (*Ordre social. Mythes et hiérarchies dans la France du XVIe siècle* [Paris: Hachette, 1977], 56). See also Jouanna, "La notion d'honneur au XVIe siècle," *Revue d'histoire moderne et contemporaine,* 1968, 597–623.

2. Frédéric Godefroy, ed., *Dictionnaire de l'ancienne langue française et de tous ses dialectes du ix au xv siècle,* vol. 4 (Paris, 1885), 224–25.

3. Edmond Huguet, *Dictionnaire de la langue française du seizième siècle,* vol. 4 (Paris: Didier, 1980), 497–98.

4. Emile Littré, *Dictionnaire de la langue française,* vol. 3 (Paris: Hachette, 1863), 2040–45.

5. *Grande Larousse de la langue française,* vol. 3 (Paris, 1973), 2449–50. Strictly speaking, Kristen Neuschel's excellent study of the sixteenth-century nobility contains an anachronism in the title. It is unlikely that the phrase "word of honor" was ever uttered by any of the nobles in her study, despite the obsession with honor in their largely verbal culture. See Kristen B. Neuschel, *Word of Honor. Interpreting Noble Culture in Sixteenth-Century France* (Ithaca, N.Y.: Cornell University Press, 1989).

6. Ibid., 2452.

7. Georges Duby, "Lineage, Nobility, and Chivalry in the Region of Mâcon During the Twelfth Century," in *Family and Society. Selections from the Annales Economies, Sociétés, Civilisations,* ed. Robert Forster and Orest Ranum; trans. Elborg Forster and Patricia M. Ranum (Baltimore: Johns Hopkins University Press, 1976), 26.

8. Pierre Bourdieu, "Marriage Strategies as Strategies of Social Reproduction," in ibid., ed. Forster and Ranum, 141. E. A. Wrigley remarks in the same vein that marital strategies flow from the requirements of social reproduction. See Wrigley's "Marriage, Fertility and Population Growth in Eighteenth-Century England," in *Marriage and Society. Studies in the Social History of Marriage,* ed. R. B. Outhwaite (New York: St. Martins Press, 1981), 182. David Sabean discusses the analytical utility of property for the social history of the family in *Property, Production, and Family in Neckarhausen, 1700–1870* (Cambridge: Cambridge University Press, 1990), 17–19; see also Hans Medick and David Sabean, "Interest and Emotion in Family and Kinship Studies: A Critique of Social History and Anthropology," in *Interest and Emotion: Essays on the Study of Family and Kinship* (Cambridge: Cambridge University Press, 1984), 9–27.

9. Bourdieu, ibid., 141.

10. Jack Goody, *Production and Reproduction. A Comparative Study of the Domestic Domain* (Cambridge: Cambridge University Press, 1976), 7–8, 89.

11. Bourdieu, "Marriage Strategies," 122–23.

12. See also Duby, "Lineage, Nobility, and Chivalry," 34.

13. As Goody puts it, the purity demanded of women in Mediterranean societies, the "concern for their honor, cannot be divorced from the position of women as carriers of property" (*Production and Reproduction,* 15).

14. James Casey, *The History of The Family* (Oxford: Basil Blackwell, 1989), 38.

15. Bourdieu discusses this function of the family in "Marriage Strategies," 129–30. For the way this process worked in the Gévaudan in the seventeenth and eighteenth centuries, see Claverie and Lamaison, *L'Impossible mariage. Violence et parenté en Gévaudan 17e, 18e, et 19e siècles,* 89–132.

16. Casey, *History of the Family,* 38. On this internalization process, Emmanuel Todd has written, "The power of the reproductive mechanism springs from the fact that it does not need to be conscious or expressed: it is automatic and has

its own internal logic" (*The Explanation of Ideology. Family Structures and Social Systems,* trans. David Garrioch [New York: Basil Blackwell, 1988], 12).

17. Bourdieu, "Marriage Strategies," 137–38. It is perhaps for this reason that the overwhelming majority of marriage contracts between wealthy families insisted on equality of contribution if at all possible. On the dangers of female adultery to family heritage, see also Maxime Kovalevsky, *Coutume contemporaine et loi ancienne. Droit coutumier ossétien éclairé par l'histoire comparée* (Paris: Larose, 1893), 255.

18. Duby, "Lineage, Nobility, and Chivalry," 39.

19. Maurice Keen, *Chivalry* (New Haven, Conn.: Yale University Press, 1984), 177.

20. Ibid., 163.

21. Duby, "Lineage, Nobility, and Chivalry," 39.

22. Keen, *Chivalry,* 2.

23. From Honoré Bonet, *L'Arbre de batailles,* 1390, as quoted in Philippe Contamine, "Mourir pour la patrie, Xe–XXe siècle," in *Les Lieux de mémoire,* ed. Pierre Nora, vol. 2, *La Nation* (Paris: Gallimard, 1986), 16.

24. On this aspect of chivalric love, see Keen, *Chivalry,* 14–15.

25. Domna Stanton discusses this aspect of the function of courtly love in a later period. "Submission to women was but the sexualized analog to the *complaisance* that the *honnête homme* artfully displayed to his peers." Women were "an instrumentality of competence" (*The Aristocrat as Art. A Study of the Honnête Homme and the Dandy in Seventeenth and Nineteenth-Century French Literature* [New York: Columbia University Press, 1980], 138–39).

26. Casey, *History of the Family,* 20–21.

27. Ellery Schalk, *From Valor to Pedigree. Ideas of Nobility in France in the Sixteenth and Seventeenth Centuries* (Princeton: Princeton University Press, 1986), esp. 3–36.

28. Jouanna, *Ordre social,* 17.

29. Ibid., 39–41.

30. Ibid., 49.

31. Jouanna explains that the Latin root for the word *généreux* ("generous"), which as we have seen is a noble quality, is *genus,* i.e., *race,* which noblemen naturally inherited. But "celui qui degénéré" has failed to exercise this aptitude, or, literally, fallen away from his race. Ibid., 50.

32. Ibid., 50–52.

33. As Jouanna writes, nobles were thought to project a "beauty and a luster, ... an elegance and a grace which were entirely natural" (Ibid., 29; also 90).

34. Ibid., 73.

35. See Elias, *The Court Society, passim;* also Roger Chartier, *Cultural History. Between Practices and Representations* (Ithaca, N.Y.: Cornell University Press, 1988), 85–91.

36. The best survey of the content of these books is still Maurice Magendie, *La Politesse mondaine et les théories de l'honnêteté en France au XVIIe siècle, de 1600 à 1660,* 2 vols. (Paris, 1925). On their aims, Domna Stanton has written that "Rather than ennoble the bourgeois intellectual, the seventeenth-century was bent

on intellectualizing or civilizing the noble" (*Aristocrat as Art,* 48). It appears Hans Speier misunderstands this point, arguing as he does that "honnêteté" was a bourgeois invention designed to endow *roturiers* with the moral equivalent of noble honor ("Honor and Social Structure," in *Social Order and the Risks of War* [Cambridge: M.I.T. Press, 1969], 44–45).

37. Jouanna, *Ordre Social,* 65. See also Stanton, *Aristocrat as Art,* 79.

38. Jouanna, ibid., 64.

39. This passage is quoted, with emendations, from Schalk, *From Valor to Pedigree,* 116–17.

40. Stanton, *Aristocrat as Art,* 165. Chartier, commenting on Elias, makes the same point in *Cultural History,* 85–86.

41. V. G. Kiernan, *The Duel in European History. Honour and the Reign of Aristocracy* (Oxford: Oxford University Press, 1988), 38–41; see also Keen, *Chivalry,* 200–212.

42. Keen, ibid., 206.

43. See on this point, Henri Morel, "La Fin de duel judiciaire en France et naissance du point d'honneur," *Revue historique du droit français et étranger,* 1964, 574–639.

44. Billacois, *Le Duel dans la société française des XVIe–XVIIe siècles,* 89.

45. Ibid., 83–94.

46. There is some sentiment for dating the cleavage between honor and victory to the remark of Henri II's predecessor, François I, who is said to have proclaimed after the French defeat at the battle of Pavia in 1525, "All is lost save honor." For the history and attribution of this phrase see Léon-E Halkin, "Pour une histoire de l'honneur," *Annales E.S.C.* 4 (1949): 433–44.

47. Billacois, *Le Duel dans la société française des XVIe–XVIIe siècles,* 7.

48. Kristen Neuschel, *Word of Honor. Interpreting Noble Culture in Sixteenth-Century France* (Ithaca, N.Y.: Cornell University Press, 1989), 15–17. The anthropologist Julian Pitt-Rivers has made the point that "The man of honor is a law, but a law unto himself. Wherever the authority of law is questioned or ignored, the code of honor reemerges to allocate the right to precedence and dictate the principles of conduct" ("Honor", in *International Encyclopedia of the Social Sciences* [New York: Macmillan, 1968], 510).

49. This standard of loyalty was present in the regional noble resistance to Tudor state building. As Mervyn James has argued, there was no conception of "unconditional obedience" in this era; " 'faithfulness' implied a response to 'good lordship'," that is, a response in keeping with signs of appreciation displayed by the leader (Mervyn James, *Society, Politics and Culture. Studies on Early Modern England* [Cambridge: Cambridge University Press, 1986], 357).

50. Neuschel, *Word of Honor,* 18.

51. Ibid., 197–208; Billacois, *Le Duel dans la société française des XVIe–XVIIe siècles,* 218–19.

52. On the effort at repression see Robert A. Schneider, "Swordplay and Statemaking. Aspects of the Campaign Against the Duel in Early Modern France," in *Statemaking and Social Movements. Essays in History and Theory,* ed. Charles Bright and Susan Harding (Ann Arbor: University of Michigan Press, 1984), 265–

96. Cardinal Richelieu confided to his "political testament" that "Frenchmen hold their lives in contempt. . . . They have fancied that it was more glorious to violate such edicts, demonstrating by so extravagent a gesture that they valued honor above life itself" (*Political Testament,* trans. Henry B. Hill [Madison: University of Wisconsin Press, 1961], 22).

53. Billacois, *Le Duel dans la société française des XVIe–XVIIe siècles,* 209. The term "aristocratic romanticism" is Elias's from *The Court Society,* 109–12. Schneider points out ("Swordplay and Statemaking," 272) that there was a decline in this era in the importance and the prestige of the cavalry, which had been a reserve of noble *cavaliers* from feudal times. As they were excluded from a primary role in the enterprise that was their chief source of corporate and professional identity, they tried to compensate psychologically by engaging in an activity that recapitulated the conditions of individual (though mostly unhorsed) combat.

54. The best source for these codes is still Frank R. Bryson, *The Sixteenth-Century Italian Duel: A Study in Renaissance Social History* (Chicago: University of Chicago Press, 1938).

55. On this development see Micheline Cuénin, *Le Duel sous l'ancien régime* (Paris: Presses de la Renaissance, 1982), 60.

56. Ibid., 30.

57. Billacois, *Le Duel dans la société française des XVIe–XVIIe siècles,* 98–107.

58. Ibid., 321–33. Also Cuénin, *Le Duel sous l'ancien régime* 143–44.

59. Billacois, *Le Duel dans la société français des XVIe–XVIIe Siècles,* 361. Billacois's emphasis.

60. Ibid., 114–15.

61. Ibid., 331–34.

62. Billacois surveys the comparative settings for the duel in his chapter "Un phénomène français," 41–82 in Ibid., 46.

63. James, *Society, Politics and Culture,* 310. James discusses the evolution of the concept of honor in his lengthy chapter, "English Politics and the Concept of Honor, 1485–1642," 308–415.

64. Alan Macfarlane emphasizes how, in distinction with continental patterns, English marriages more frequently crossed class lines (*Marriage and Love in England. Modes of Reproduction 1300–1840,* [Oxford: Basil Blackwell, 1986], 252–53).

65. Francis Bacon's *Charge Touching Duels. . .* (1614), as quoted by Billacois, *Le Duel dans la société français des XVIe–XVIIe siècles,* 58, n. 70.

66. James, *Society, Politics and Culture,* 375.

67. Schalk, *From Valor to Pedigree,* 115–22.

68. Billacois, *Le Duel dans la société français des XVIe–XVIIe siècles,* 243–45; Cuénin, *Le Duel sous l'ancien régime,* 227–40.

69. Peter Burke, "Popular Culture Between History and Ethnology," *Ethnologia Europaea* 14 (1984): 5–13.

70. Yves Castan, *Honnêteté et relations sociales en Languedoc (1715–1780)* (Paris: Plon, 1974), 17–18.

71. Ibid., 23.

72. Ibid., 184.

73. Ibid., 182–85.

74. Ibid., 164.

75. Stephen Wilson "Infanticide, Child Abandonment, and Female Honour in Nineteenth-Century Corsica," *Comparative Studies in Society and History* 30, no. 4 (Oct. 1988): 762–83.

76. For a striking example from early modern Wurttemburg, see Sabean, *Property, Production, and Family in Neckerhausen* and, in addition, *Power in the Blood. Popular Culture and Village Discourse in Early Modern Germany* (Cambridge: Cambridge University Press, 1984).

77. Thomas Brennan, *Public Drinking and Popular Culture in Eighteenth-Century Paris* (Princeton: Princeton University Press, 1988), 29–30, 59–63, 68–69. Mervyn James has noted a culture of honor in English towns in connection with guild rivalries in Corpus Christi processions and dramas ("Ritual, Drama and the Social Body in the Late Medieval English Town," in *Society, Politics and Culture,* 16–47). James Casey discusses the relation of honor and the quality of guild work in *History of the Family,* 21.

78. Ibid., 67.

79. Ibid., 63.

80. Ibid., 74.

Chapter 3

1. Honoré de Balzac, *Le Cabinet des antiques* in *Oeuvres complètes* (Paris: Editions de la Pleiade, 1947), 459.

2. Pierre Bourdieu, *Distinction. A Social Critique of the Judgement of Taste,* trans. Richard Nice (Cambridge, Mass.: Harvard University Press, 1984), xi.

3. These are the words of George Armstrong Kelley, "Duelling in Eighteenth-Century France: Archaeology, Rationale, Implications," *The Eighteenth Century* 21, no. 3 (1980): 241. On the critiques of Rousseau and D'Alembert, see John Pappas, "Le Campagne des philosophes contre l'honneur," *Studies in Voltaire and the Eighteenth Century* 205 (1982): 38–40.

4. Montesquieu, *Lettres Persanes,* ed. Paul Vernière (Paris, 1960), 188.

5. Montesquieu, *L'Esprit des lois,* vol. 1 (Paris, 1973), 32.

6. The phrase of Pappas in "Campagne des philosophes," 35.

7. On this point see Carol Blum, *Rousseau and the Republic of Virtue. Th Language of Politics in the French Revolution* (Ithaca, N.Y., Cornell University Press, 1986), 25–27, 133–52.

8. Schalk, *From Valor to Pedigree,* 117.

9. Quoted in Blum, *Rousseau and Republic of Virtue*, 144.

10. Robespierre, as quoted in Norman Hampson, "The French Revolution and the Nationalization of Honour," in *War and Society. Historical Essays in Honour of J.R. Western,* ed. M. R. D. Foot, (New York: Barnes and Noble, 1973), 209. See also Hampson, "La Patrie," in *The Political Culture of the French Revolution,* ed. Colin Lucas, (Oxford: Pergamon Press, 1988), 134–36.

11. Kelley, "Duelling in Eighteenth-Century France," 249–50.

12. Hampson, "La Patrie," *passim;* Kelley, "Duelling in Eighteenth-Century France," 251–53; Geoffrey Best, *Honour Among Men and Nations. Transformations of an Idea* (Toronto: University of Toronto Press, 1982), 18–36.

13. Colin Lucas, "Introduction," in *The Political Culture of the French Revolution,* ed. Lucas, xv. See also Hampson, "La Patrie," 134.

14. Lynn Hunt, "The Sacred and the French Revolution," in *Durkheimian Sociology: Cultural Studies,* ed. Jeffrey Alexander (Cambridge: Cambridge University Press, 1988), 36; see also Hunt, *Politics, Culture and Class in the French Revolution* (Berkeley, Calif.: University of California Press, 1984), 87–119. On fraternity and the religion of *patrie,* see Philippe Contamine, "Mourir pour la patrie," in *Les Lieux de mémoire,* ed. Pierre Nora, vol. 2, *La Nation,* 30–32.

15. As quoted in Contamine, "Mourir pour la patrie," 36.

16. There is much evidence that, despite a general fall in the dueling rate in the eighteenth century (so far as we can tell), the practice ramified within the non-noble elite and even spread to lower domains. Kelley, "Duelling in Eighteenth-Century France," 240; Cuénin, 227–40; Billacois, "La Duel dans la société français des XVe–XVIe siècles," 243–45.

17. Colin Lucas, "Nobles, Bourgeois, and the Origins of the French Revolution," in *French Society and the Revolution,* ed. Douglas Johnson (Cambridge: Cambridge University Press, 1976), 94.

18. F. Bluche, "Les Magistrats du Parlement de Paris au XVIIIe siècle," as extracted in Guy Chaussinand-Nogaret, *Une Histoire des élites, 1700–1848* (Paris: Mouton, 1975), 52.

19. Lucas, 107.

20. Guy Chaussinand-Nogaret, *The French Nobility in the Eighteenth Century,* trans. William Doyle (Cambridge: Cambridge University Press, 1985), 34–35.

21. As quoted in Lucas, "Nobles," 123.

22. Christophe Charle reminds us that the term "meritocracy" may not be used in the modern sense of a fully competitive and "open" service class for elite civil servants in the early nineteenth century. These positions were very much "venal" and "hereditary" in the sense of Old Regime venal office, that is, they were passed from father to son by exploiting the advantages of wealth and influence; see Charle, *Les Hauts fonctionnaires en France au XIXe siècle* (Paris: Gallimard, 1980), 11–14. For the Napoleonic period see Louis Bergeron, *L'Episode napoléonien: aspects intérieurs* (Paris: Editions du Seuil, 1972). For the Restoration and July Monarchy see A. Jardin and A. J. Tudesq, *La France des notables (1815–1848)* (Paris: Editions du Seuil, 1973) and A. J. Tudesq, *Les Grands notables en France sous la Monarchie de Juillet,* 2 vols. (Paris: Presses Universitaires de France, 1964). On the practice and legal status of ennoblement under successive nineteenth-century regimes see Adeline Daumard, "Noblesse et aristocratie en France au XIXe siècle," in *Les Noblesses Européenes au XIXe siècle,* vol. 107 (Rome: Collection de l'Ecole Française de Rome, 1988), 89–104.

23. Christophe Charle, "Noblesse et élites en France au début du XXe siècle," in *Les Noblesses Européenes au XIXe siècle,* 407–37.

24. On the exclusive and distinctive features of the modern nobility see, in particular, Ralph Gibson, "The French Nobility in the Nineteenth Century," in

Elites in France: Origins, Reproduction, Power, ed. Jolyon Howorth and Philip
Cerny (New York: St. Martin's Press, 1981), 5–45; André-Jean Tudesq, "L'Elar-
gissement de la noblesse en France de XIXe siècle," in *Les Noblesses Européenes
au XIXe siècle,* 121–35; David Higgs, *Nobles in Nineteenth-Century France. The
Practice of Inegalitarianism* (Baltimore: Johns Hopkins University Press, 1987),
passim.

25. James F. Traer puts it this way: "The rule of primogeniture applied
throughout France, wherever land was held by feudal tenure. In medieval times it
had been important to keep the fief undivided in order not to reduce the fighting
capacity of the vassal who held it, but in the seventeenth and eighteenth centuries
the only justification for primogeniture was that it maintained intact the property,
and hence the status, of illustrious families" (*Marriage and the Family in Eighteenth-
Century France* [Ithaca, N.Y.: Cornell University Press, 1980], 42).

26. On this point see the summary of Ralph Giesey, "Rules of Inheritance
and Strategies of Mobility in Prerevolutionary France," *American Historical Review*
82, no. 2 (April 1977): 272–76; also Traer, ibid., 42–44.

27. Alan Macfarlane is most eloquent on this difference; see *Marriage and
Love in England, 1300–1840,* esp. 321–44.

28. Giesey, "Rules of Inheritance," 281.

29. Ibid.

30. See the examples cited by Margaret Darrow from the Montauban
bourgeoisie: *Revolution in the House. Family, Class, and Inheritance in Southern
France, 1775–1825* (Princeton: Princeton University Press, 1989), 102–107; also,
Giesey, "Rules of Inheritance," 276–79; Traer, *Marriage and the Family in Eighteenth-Century France,* 44–47.

31. On this point see Bourdieu, "Marriage Strategies," 136–41; also Gérard
Duplessis-LeGuéland, *Les Mariages en France* (Paris: Colin, 1954), 11–12; Darrow,
Revolution in the House, 107–17.

32. E. A. Wrigley, "Marriage, Fertility and Population Growth in Eighteenth-
Century England," in *Marriage and Society,* ed. R. B. Outhwaite, 176–78.

33. E. A. Wrigley gives a figure of 19 percent for the decline of overall fertility
in the eighteenth century in ibid., 178. Jacques Depauw has shown that bourgeois
men had largely broken off illegitimate relations with lower-class women by the
end of the century, apparently confining sexual relations to their marriages or to
women of their own class, but in any case employing contraception to limit the
births they had not much worried about with women of the people. See Jacques
Depauw, "Illicit Sexual Activity and Society in Eighteenth-Century Nantes," in
Family and Society, ed. Forster and Ranum, 145–91.

34. André Burguière, "From Malthus to Max Weber, Belated Marriage and
the Spirit of Enterprise," in ibid., ed. Forster and Ranum, 250.

35. On bourgeois ancestor worship, see Elinor G. Barber, *The Bourgeoisie
in 18th Century France* (Princeton: Princeton University Press, 1955), 59–60.

36. Giesey, "Rules of Inheritance," 284. Elinor G. Barber has discussed the
criterion of *vivre noblement* in connection with bourgeois ambition in several areas,
including offices, patents, the army and the church, the professions, and "life style"
in ibid., esp. 55–74, 99–140.

37. This material is surveyed in *The History of Manners,* vol. 1, *The Civilizing Process,* trans. Edmund Jephcott (New York: Pantheon, 1978), esp. 84–160.

38. See here *The Court Society,* vol. 3, *The Civilizing Process* (New York: Pantheon, 1983).

39. *Power and Civility,* vol. 2 *The Civilizing Process* (New York: Pantheon, 1982), 292–300.

40. Elias, *The Court Society,* 3: 292.

41. Ibid., 298.

42. Ibid., 319.

43. Pierre Bourdieu also notes that the public/private division arose in opposition to the wholly *public* nature of court society: "Thus, whereas the court aristocracy made the whole of life a continuous spectacle, the bourgeoisie has established the opposition between what is paid for and what is free, the interested and the disinterested, in the form of the opposition, which Weber saw as characterizing it, between place of work and place of residence, working days and holidays, the outside (male) and the inside (female), business and sentiment, industry and art, the world of economic necessity and the world of artistic freedom . . . " (*Distinction,* 55).

44. Elias, *The Court Society,* 307.

45. Bernard Groethuysen, *The Bourgeois. Catholicism vs. Capitalism in Eighteenth-Century France,* trans. Mary Ilford (London: Barrie & Rockliff, 1968), 161.

46. The phrase of Adeline Daumard, *Les Bourgeois et la bourgeoisie en France depuis 1815* (Paris: Aubier, 1987), 244. My emphasis.

47. Ulf Pernö, as quoted in Jonas Frykman and Orvar Löfgren, *Culture Builders. A Historical Anthropology of Middle-Class Life,* trans. Alan Crozier (New Brunswick, N.J.: Rutgers University Press, 1987), 115. My emphasis.

48. A. M. Dupin, *Profession d'avocat. Recueil de pièces concernant l'exercice de cette profession* (Paris: B. Warée, 1830–32). Agénor Bardoux mixes together noble and bourgeois traits in his remarks on the lawyers of the Old Regime corporation, saying they possessed "passion, generosity and audacity," but also "probity, independence, and honor" (*La Bourgeoisie Française, 1789–1848* [Paris: Calmann Lévy, 1886], 8, 99).

49. As quoted in Régine Pernoud, *Histoire de la bourgeoisie en France,* vol. 2, *Les Temps modernes* (Paris: Editions du Seuil, 1981), 181.

50. Adeline Daumard, *Les Bourgeois de Paris au XIXe siécle* (Paris: Presses Universitaires de France, 1979), 165–66.

51. Todd, *The Explanation of Ideology,* 14.

52. Daumard, *Les Bourgeois et la bourgeoisie,* 242–43. As Todd writes, "It was a question of giving each individual an equal start; after this some could be promoted, preferably according to individual merit. This is an exact transposition of the familial mechanism which requires equality between sons in dividing up the inheritance, but later tolerates a divergence of fortune without thinking that fraternal solidarity should continue beyond adolescence" (ibid., 110). Margaret Darrow writes that after the revolutionary settlement, "fathers continued to plan and worry over their son's careers, but now more depended on the son's ambitions and

abilities. One could no longer automatically give the eldest son pride of place; it might prove to be a younger son who would ensure the family's prestige in the next generation" (*Revolution in the House*, 128).

53. Tronchet, as quoted in Bardoux, *La Bourgeoisie Française, 1789–1848*, 33.

54. Burgière, "From Malthus to Max Weber: Belated Marriage and the Spirit of Enterprise," 239.

55. Jean-Paul Aron and Roger Kempf, *La Bourgeoisie, le sexe, et l'honneur* (Paris: Editions complexe, n.d.), 166–67. My emphasis. This book originally appeared as *Le Pénis et la démoralisation de l'occident* (Paris: Grasset, 1978).

56. Foucault, *The History of Sexuality*, 124.

57. Ibid., 124–25.

58. Ibid., 122–23.

59. Ibid., 57–58; 70–71.

60. Ibid., 34–35.

61. Jean-Louis Flandrin, *Le Sexe de l'occident. Evolution des comportements et des attitudes* (Paris: Editions du Seuil, 1981), 84–89.

62. Etienne Van de Walle, "Motivations and Technology in the Decline of French Fertility," in *Family and Sexuality in French History,* ed. Tamara Harevan and Robert Wheaton (Philadelphia: University of Pennsylvania Press, 1980), 190–91.

63. Jean-Louis Flandrin, *Families in Former Times. Household and Sexualty,* trans. Richard Southern (Cambridge: Cambridge University Press, 1979), 224–25.

Chapter 4

1. Jean-Pierre Machelon, *La République contre les libertés? Les Restrictions aux libertés de 1879 à 1914* (Paris: Presses de la Fondation Nationale des Sciences Politiques, 1976), 17–18.

2. André-Jean Arnaud, *Essai d'analyse structurale du code civil français. La Règle du jeu dans la paix bourgeoise* (Paris: R. Pichon et R. Durand-Auzias, 1973), 55.

3. The best account of this long-term relation is in Laqueur, *Making Sex.*

4. Joel Schwartz, *The Sexual Politics of Jean-Jacques Rousseau* (Chicago: University of Chicago Press, 1984), 10–73. *Emile* contains most of the prescriptions for the rearing of citizens.

5. Ibid., 38–39. This section is in *Emile,* bk. 5.

6. On this latter point see the discussion in Leonore Davidoff and Catherine Hall, *Family Fortunes. Men and Women of the English Middle Class, 1780–1850* (London: Hutchinson, 1987), 28–35.

7. This passage is quoted from Sergio Moravia, "From *homme machine* to *homme sensible:* Changing Eighteenth-Century Images of Man," *Journal of the History of Ideas* 39 (1978): 56. See on this issue in general, Karl Figlio, "The Metaphor of Organization: An Historiographical Perspective on the Bio-Medical Sciences of the Early Nineteenth Century," *History of Science* 25 (1987): 111–46.

And on Bordeu, Elizabeth L. Haigh, "Vitalism, the Soul, and Sensibility: The Physiology of Théophile Bordeu," *Journal of the History of Medicine* 31 (1976): 30–41.

8. On Bichat's physiological work in the 1790s, see William R. Albury, "Experiment and Explanation in the Physiology of Bichat and Magendie," *Studies in the History of Biology,* ed. William Coleman and Camille Limoges (Baltimore: Johns Hopkins University Press, 1977), 47–131; and more briefly, Russell C. Maulitz, *Morbid Appearances. The Anatomy of Pathology in the Early Nineteenth Century* (Cambridge: Cambridge University Press, 1987), 14–17, 25–35.

9. It is easy to see here an analogy with contemporary doctrines of political economy in which individuals following their own aims fulfill general laws that sustain the welfare of the whole. There is here, as John Pickstone has pointed out, a kind of "mapping" on the body of the ideals of the French Revolution in which bureaucratic efficiency was of particular importance; see "Bureaucracy, Liberalism and the Body in Post-Revolutionary France: Bichat's Physiology and the Paris School of Medicine," *History of Science* 19 (1981): 115–42.

10. P.-J.-G. Cabanis, *Rapports du physique et du moral de l'homme* in *Oeuvres philosophiques de Cabanis,* ed. Claude Lehec and Jean Cazeneuve (Paris: Presses Universitaires de France, 1956), 188. See in general on this aspect of Cabanis's thought, Martin S. Staum, *Cabanis. Enlightenment and Medical Philosophy in the French Revolution* (Princeton: Princeton University Press, 1980), 189–99.

11. See on this issue, Elizabeth Williams, " 'Limited Energy' and Physiological Types in French Medicine of the Revolutionary Era" (unpublished work).

12. Dorinda Outram, *The Body and the French Revolution. Sex, Class and Political Culture* (New Haven, Conn.: Yale University Press, 1989), 48, 55–61; See also Williams, "Limited Energy," ibid.; Harvey Mitchell, "Rationality and Control in French Eighteenth-Century Views of the Peasantry," *Comparative Studies in Society and History* 21 (January 1979): 82–112; Frykman and Löfgren, *Culture Builders,* 174–75.

13. Laqueur, *Making Sex,* 26–34, 149–54.

14. On some of this science see Londa Schiebinger, *The Mind Has No Sex? Women in the Origins of Modern Science* (Cambridge: Cambridge University Press, 1990), 160–88.

15. Laqueur, *Making Sex,* 43–52; Schiebinger, ibid., 180; Roy Porter, " 'The Secrets of Generation Display'd': *Aristotle's Master-piece* in Eighteenth-Century England," in *'Tis Nature's Fault. Unauthorized Sexuality During the Enlightenment,* ed. Robert Maccubbin (Cambridge: Cambridge University Press, 1987), 1–22.

16. Schiebinger, *The Mind Has No Sex?* 191–213.

17. Yvonne Knibiehler and Catherine Fouquet, *La Femme et les médecins* (Paris: Hachette, 1983), 94–96.

18. Geneviève Fraisse argues that to understand the nature of a particular woman, this medicine needed to know the balance she maintained between the "two poles" of her being: her reproductive apparatus and her brain. She quotes J. J. Virey saying that the "abuse of one will lead to the destruction of the other" (*Muse de la raison. La Démocratie exclusive et la différence des sexes* [Paris: Alinea, 1989], 95).

19. Knibiehler and Fouquet, ibid., 87–94. Also Williams, "Limited Energy." See in general on this totalistic construction of women's nature by science and medicine, Maurice Bloch and Jean H. Bloch, "Women and the Dialectics of Nature in Eighteenth-Century French Thought," in *Nature, Culture and Gender,* ed. Carol P. MacCormack and Marilyn Strathern (Cambridge: Cambridge University Press, 1980), 25–41; Paul Hoffmann, *La Femme dans la pensée des lumières* (Paris: Ophrys, 1977); Ludmilla Jordanova, *Sexual Visions. Images of Gender in Science and Medicine Between the Eighteenth and Twentieth Centuries* (Madison: Wisconsin University Press, 1989), 19–42.

20. On how French biologists from Lamarck to Cuvier understood the nature of these "internal correlations," see Camille Limoges, "Darwinisme et adaptation," *Revue des questions scientifiques* 141 (July 1970): 358–61. On the nature and limits of these correlations, see Jordanova, *Sexual Visions,* 26–28.

21. This is the phrase of Ludmilla Jordanova in "Naturalizing the Family: Literature and the Bio-Medical Sciences in the Late Eighteenth Century," in *Languages of Nature. Critical Essays on Science and Literature* (New Brunswick, N.J.: Rutgers University Press, 1986), 93–94.

22. As Geneviève Fraisse has written also *à propos* Cabanis, "One passes here a bit too easily from the natural function of an organ to a social role. One should note the ease of terminological confusion between organic function and social role, because this feminine role of a maternity which is both domestic and social becomes in effect a social function in contemporary society" (*Muse de la raison,* 88).

23. Ibid., 82–83.

24. Jordanova, "Naturalizing the Family," 113.

25. Laqueur, *Making Sex,* 181–92.

26. See Rousseau's *Contrat social,* bk. 3, ch. 8, and bk. 4, ch. 4.

27. On official Old Regime "populationism," see Marcel Reinhard, *Histoire de la population mondiale de 1700 à 1948* (Paris: Editions Domat Montchrestien, n.d.), 78–83.

28. Catherine Gallagher, "The Body Versus the Social Body in the Works of Thomas Malthus and Henry Mayhew," in *The Making of the Modern Body. Sexuality and Society in the Nineteenth Century,* ed. Gallagher and Thomas Laqueur (Berkeley, Calif.: University of California Press, 1987), 83. See Schiebinger, *The Mind Has No Sex?,* 218–20, for an argument about the relation between populationism and concern about women's fertility and their child-rearing practices.

29. Jordanova, "Naturalizing the Family," 112.

30. William Sewell, "Le citoyen/la citoyenne: Activity, Passivity, and the Revolutionary Concept of Citizenship," in *The Political Culture of the French Revolution,* ed. Colin Lucas (London: Pergamon Press, 1988), 114.

31. On feminist movements in revolutionary Paris, see Jane Abray, "Feminism in the French Revolution," *American Historical Review* 80 (1975): 43–62; Darlene Gay Levy, Harriet Applewhite, and Mary Johnson, eds., *Women in Revolutionary Paris, 1789–1795* (Urbana: University of Illinois Press, 1979).

32. On this general point see Blum, *Rousseau and the Republic of Virtue,* 133–52.

33. Outram, *The Body and the French Revolution,* 79.

34. Ibid., 83.

35. On the emergence of a critical Old Regime discourse which coupled loss of political mastery with sexual exhaustion, impotence, and depravity in the person of Louis XV, and also alleged the political and physical impotence of Louis XVI, see Robert Darnton, "The High Enlightenment and the Low-Life of Literature in Prerevolutionary France," *Past and Present,* no. 51 (May 1971): 81–115, and "Reading, Writing, and Publishing in Eighteenth-Century France. A Case Study in the Sociology of Literature," *Daedalus,* Winter 1971, 214–56; Jean-Pierre Guicciardi, "Between the Licit and the Illicit: The Sexuality of the King," in *'Tis Nature's Fault,* ed. Maccubbin, 88–97.

36. As quoted in Outram, *The Body and the French Revolution,* 126.

37. As quoted in Sewell, "Le citoyen/la citoyenne," 117–18.

38. Ibid., 117. See also on this point, Outram, *The Body and the French Revolution,* 124–29.

39. For the revolutionary legislation on civil rights, marriage, and divorce, see Traer, *Marriage and the Family in Eighteenth-Century France,* 79–136; Marcel Garaud and Romuald Szramkiewicz, *La Révolution française et la famille* (Paris: Presses Universitaires de France, 1978).

40. Arnaud, *Essai d'analyse structurale du code civil français,* 80–81. See also Yvonne Kniebiehler, *Les Pères aussi ont une histoire* (Paris: Hachette, 1987), 157–65.

41. For these measures see Traer, *Marriage and the Family in Eighteenth-Century France,* 174–75, 189; Arnaud, ibid., 71–74.

42. Kniebiehler, *Les Pères aussi ont une histoire,* 218.

43. Arnaud, *Essai d'analyse structurale du code civil français,* 71.

44. Ibid., 130.

45. Traer, *Marriage and the Family in Eighteenth-Century France,* 49, 56–58; Copley, *Sexual Moralities in France, 1780–1980,* 13–14.

46. Louis de Bonald, *Du divorce considéré au XIXe siècle relativement à l'état public de société* (Paris, 1801), 43. My emphasis.

47. Fraisse, *Muse de la raison,* 94.

48. Ibid., 86–89.

49. Georges Canguilhem, *Le Normal et le pathologique* 3d ed. (Paris: Presses Universitaires de France), 19–25.

50. Ibid., 25. My emphasis.

51. Georges Canguilhem, *La Connaissance de la vie,* 2d ed. (Paris: Vrin, 1985), 155.

52. Ibid., 157.

53. Canguilhem, *Le Normal et le pathologique,* 34–40.

54. J. J. Virey, *De la femme* (Paris: Crochard, 1825), 195.

55. S. A. A. D. Tissot, the eighteenth-century Jeremiah of masturbation, who published his *L'Onanisme . . .* in Lausanne in 1760, argued that semen was at the summit of the "precious humors" in the body's natural hierarchy of humors. Valuable in itself as an agent of fertilization, it was the catalyst that also invigorated the movements of all the baser humors. Jean Stengers and Anne Van Neck, *Histoire*

d'un grande peur: la masturbation (Bruxelles: Editions de l'université de Bruxelles, 1984), 81–83; Théodore Tarczylo, *Sexe et liberté au siècle des lumières* (Paris: Presses de la Renaissance, 1983), 114–18.

56. Virey, *De la Femme*, 181.

57. Ibid., 86.

58. In Virey's words, "It would appear, therefore, that in this sort of fencing, a woman is the equivalent of two and half men" (ibid., 159).

59. Ibid., 74. Elsewhere Virey praises the coquettishness of women as their natural defense against particularly aggressive males. Women prefer valiant men over the meek of their sex, but enjoy holding them at arm's length while simultaneously provoking them. He warns of a tactic sexually experienced women use to "subjugate" men: they "praise your athletic superiority to insure their domination." In urging men on to ever greater feats of sexual prowess, "they thus triumph in our defeats, for the truly most adorable king in their eyes is the one who has succumbed to the greatest number of temptations" (p. 419).

60. Ibid., 86. See pp. 186–87 for an extensive number of such binary terms contrasting men and women.

61. Ibid., 141.

62. Ibid., 194.

63. Ibid., 199. See in general pp. 187–210. Virey here continues a tradition that was a part of both medical and popular culture in the Old Regime, and would remain vigorous throughout the nineteenth century. The aim was to have healthy boys. Thus, true manliness consisted, Tarczylo has argued, not in the "varieties of erotic expression, but in the capacity to engender, and to engender boys" (*Sexe et liberté au siècle des lumières,* 83). For more on the dangers of disharmony and procreation, see Virey's *De la puissance vitale considéré dans ses fonctions physiologiques* (Paris: Crochard, 1823), 71–73.

64. Virey, *De la femme,* 193. Virey argues that in polygamous societies, where men were sexually exhausted, a preponderance of girls are born, in contrast to the greater number of boys in monogamous societies. The polygamous societies of the East were also notably "cowardly and effeminate," while in the monogamous West, "courage, spirit, and enterprise" prevailed (pp. 146–48).

65. On the issues at the basis of this debate, see Toby A. Appel, *The Cuvier-Geoffroy Debate. French Biology in the Decades Before Darwin* (New York: Oxford University Press, 1987).

66. Katherine Park and Lorraine Daston, "Unnatural Conceptions: The Study of Monsters in Sixteenth Century France and England," *Past and Present* 92 (1981): 43.

67. Canguilhem, *La Connaissance de la vie,* 172–73.

68. Isidore Geoffroy Saint-Hilaire, *Histoire générale et particulière des anomalies de l'organisation chez l'homme et les animaux, des monstruosités, des variétés et vices de conformation, ou traité de tératologie,* 3 vols. (Paris: J. B. Baillière, 1832–37), 36–37, 206–207. See on Geoffroy and the new science of teratology, Appel, *The Cuvier-Geoffroy Debate,* 125–30.

69. Geoffroy Saint-Hilaire, ibid., 53–58, 116, 279.

70. Ibid., 182–83. For other comments on dwarves and giants, see pp. 246–50, 279.

71. As he says in his final volume, every "teratological law has its corresponding law in the order of moral facts" (Ibid., 3: 611).

72. On the epigenetic tradition in French embryology, see Georges Canguilhem, Georges Lapassade, Jacques Piquemal, and Jacques Ulmann, *Du développement à l'évolution au XIXe siècle* (Paris: Presses Universitaires de France, 1985), 10–18; Appel, *The Cuvier-Geoffroy Debate*, 49–50, 75–77.

73. Geoffroy Saint-Hilaire, *Histoire générale et particulière des anomalies,* 2:42.

74. Ibid., 44.

75. Ibid., 169–71.

76. Ibid., 3: 573.

77. Gabriel Tourdes, "Hermaphrodisme. Tératologie" in *Dictionnaire encyclopédique des sciences médicales,* 4th ser., vol. 13 (Paris, 1888), 643. On the similar relations of law and medicine in the Old Regime tradition of civil law, see Lorraine Daston and Katherine Park, "Hermaphrodites in Renaissance France," *Critical Matrix. Princeton Working Papers in Women's Studies* 1, no. 5 (1985): 1–18. For mid nineteenth-century medical commentaries on the famous case of Herculine Barbin, see Michel Foucault, *Herculine Barbin, dite Alexina B.* (Paris: Gallimard, 1978), 135–56.

78. J. B. F. Descuret, *La Médecine des passions considerées dans leurs rapports avec les maladies, les lois et la religion* (Paris, 1860), 5–6. I have reversed Descuret's columns of vices.

79. Gabriel Tourdes, "Aphrodisie," in *Dictionnaire encyclopédique des sciences médicales,* 1st ser., 5 (1866): 661; Bouchereau adds flushed complexion and vigorous nervous system: "Satyriasis," in *Dictionnaire encyclopédique des sciences médicales,* 3d ser., 7 (1879): 67. According to the system, women afflicted with "aphrodisia" or nymphomania had the same qualities, though to a slightly lesser extent, reflecting the fact that their abnormal sexual appetites situated them at the upper end of the female scale where they had more in common with hermaphrodites than with "typical" plump, white, and smooth-skinned women (Tourdes, "Aphrodisia," 661; Bouchereau, 67).

80. Tourdes, Ibid., 662.

81. Another danger, to which men were particularly susceptible, was "general paralysis," a progressive and incurable syndrome, the first symptoms of which were various expressions of "genital furor" (*fureur génitale*) (Dr. J. Christian and Dr. Antoine Ritti, "Paralysie générale," in *Dictionnaire encyclopédique des sciences médicales* 2d ser. 20 [1884]: 740–41, 754).

82. See George David, "La Stérilité masculine: le déni du mâle," *Le Genre humain* 10 (1984): 23–38. As Pierre Darmon points out, at least 5 percent of the "impotence" trials in the Old Regime were brought against women by their husbands (*Le Tribunal de l'impuissance. Virilité et défaillances conjugales dans l'ancienne France* [Paris: Editions du Seuil, 1979], 49).

83. See, in general, Darmon, ibid. Guy Richard provides the example of a seventeenth-century peasant, divorced by his wife for impotence, who remarried

and bore children by his second wife. A court annulled his second marriage (and his first wife's subsequent one) and forced them to remarry (*Histoire de l'amour en France* [Paris, 1985], 53–54).

84. Dr. Gabriel Tourdes, "Paternité," in *Dictionnaire encyclopédique des sciences médicales* 2d ser., 21 (1885): 557 (my emphasis); Tourdes argues elsewhere that men with vices of genital conformation are invariably impotent and should be forbidden to marry; see "Hermaphrodisme. médecine légale," in *Dictionnaire encyclopédique des sciences médicales,* 4th ser., 13 (1888): 652. Dr. G. Herrmann reveals that Geoffroy Saint-Hilaire's criteria for (sexual) "error on the person" are still in vigor in 1888 ("Hermaphrodisme. Tératologie," 614).

85. Darmon, *Le Tribunal de l'impuissance*, 233–49.

86. Ibid., 15, 242–45.

87. Gay, *The Bourgeois Experience. Victoria to Freud*, 1: 146–57.

88. Dr. Rauland, *Le Livre des époux. Guide pour la guérison de l'impuissance, de la stérilité et de toutes les maladies des organes génitaux* (Paris: private printing, 1852), 3. See also the discussion of female sexuality and her need for orgasm in order to be "physiologically complete," in Dr. Félix Roubaud, *Traité de l'impuissance et de la stérilité chez l'homme et chez la femme,* 2 vols. (Paris: J.B. Baillière, 1855), 1: 33–34. In his preface to Octave de Saint Ernest's book on the wedding night, Dr. Morel de Rubempré wrote that women expect to find in their new spouses "that vigor and procreative potency" that is the stuff of happy marriages (*Physiologie de la première nuit de noces*, Paris: Terry, 1842, vii).

89. Dr. Jean-Alexis Belliol, *Conseil aux hommes affaiblis. Traité des maladies chroniques de l'impuissance prématurée ou épuisement nerveux des organes générateurs,* 12th ed. (Paris: Dentu, 1877), 86.

90. Rauland, *Le Livre des époux*, 75.

91. Ibid., 75–76. In a rather less decisive case, Dr. Roubaud tells a story in which a patient, despairing of being able to manage vaginal penetration attempted to "safeguard his honor" by having his mistress masturbate him to orgasm, and who thereby "honorably avoided an act he knew himself unequipped to carry out" (*Traité de l'impuissance*, 220).

92. Belliol, *Conseil aux hommes affaiblis,* 95–96.

93. Roubaud, *Traité de l'impuissance,* 3.

94. Connections between sexual excess and the threat of impotence, dishonor, and shame were endemic in the prescriptive medical literature on male sexuality. Thus the "shameful leprosy" of masturbation provoked shame in its victims, facilitating their identification (downcast eyes, shiftiness, etc.); on the other hand, the appearance of shame provided ironically hopeful signs to a therapist because it suggested that appeals to the masturbator's sense of honor and decency might yet prove effective. See Stenger and Van Neck, *Histoire d'un grande peur,* 14, 132. Kempf and Aron also note a number of these connections in *La Bourgeoisie, le sexe, et l'honneur,* 18, 40–42, 78, 171. At least one early nineteenth-century physician believed it was possible to distinguish between the blushing of simple modesty and the pathological suffusion of blood that accompanied shame. See Roy Porter, "Love, Sex, and Madness in Eighteenth-Century England," *Social Research* 53 (Summer 1986): 221–22.

95. Belliol, *Conseil aux hommes affaiblis*, 87–94; Roubaud, *Traité de l'impuissance*, 135–36; Rauland, *Le Livre des époux*, 127–52. In her review of the standard nineteenth-century marriage manuals, Laure Adler found a widespread concern with vital equilibrium, exhaustion, and male impotence (*Secrets d'alcôve: histoire du couple de 1830 à 1930* [Paris: Hachette, 1983], 67–99).

96. Rauland, *Le Livre des époux*, 90; Belliol, *Conseil aux hommes affaiblis*, 77; Roubaud, *Traité de l'impuissance,* 121, 138.

97. Roubaud, ibid., 162.

98. Rauland, *Le Livre des époux*, 345–49.

99. Belliol, *Conseil aux hommes affaiblis,* 62.

100. Roubaud, *Traité de l'impuissance,* 130.

101. Laurent Martin, *Les Dangers de l'amour, de la luxure, et du libertinage,* 2d ed. (Paris: Lebigre-Duquesne frères, 1866), 276–77.

102. See the preface by Dominique Fernandez to the reprinted edition of Charles Ancillon, *Traité des eunuques* (Paris: Editions Ramsay, 1978), 13–16.

Chapter 5

1. Benoiston de Châteauneuf, "Sur la durée des familles nobles en France," *Annales d'hygiène publique et de médecine légale* 35 (Jan. 1846): 27–56.

2. Ibid., 41–44.

3. Daniel Pick, *Faces of Degeneration. A European Disorder, c.1848–c.1918* (Cambridge: Cambridge University Press, 1989), 59.

4. Prosper Lucas, *Traité philosophique et physiologique de l'hérédité naturelle* 2 vols. (Paris, 1847–50), as quoted in Jean Borie, *Mythologies de l'hérédité au XIXe siècle* (Paris: Editions Galilée, 1981), 13.

5. Lucas, ibid., 1: 5, as quoted in Borie, 70. On Lucas's career and reputation see Borie, ibid., 70–75; Jacques Postel and Claude Quetel, *Nouvelle histoire de la psychiatrie* (Paris: Privat, 1983), 670–71.

6. On Morel's career and early writing on cretinism, which became the model of the degenerate condition, see Pick, *Faces of Degeneration,* 44–50.

7. On the "bifurcation" in the first half of the century between a "moral" therapy that treated the mind, and a diagnostics that searched for organic "signs," see Robert Castel, *L'Ordre psychiatrique: L'âge d'or d'aliénisme* (Paris, 1976), 108–18.

8. On the role Bernard played in the laboratory medical revolution of the 1850s and 1860s, see Georges Canguilhem, *Etudes d'histoire et de philosophie des sciences,* 5th ed. (Paris: Vrin, 1989), 127–62. On the notion of the internal milieu and how it was related to judgments of the normal and the pathological, see Canguilhem, *Le Normal et le pathologique,* 34–40.

9. On this and related issues, see Ian Dowbiggin, *Inheriting Madness. Professionalization and Psychiatric Knowledge in Nineteenth-Century France* (Berkeley, Calif.: University of California Press, 1991), 116–43.

10. I have discussed these developments in *Crime, Madness and Politics in Modern France: The Medical Concept of National Decline* (Princeton: Princeton

University Press, 1984), 121–24. See also Ruth Harris, *Murders and Madness: Medicine, Law, and Society in the Fin-de-Siècle* (Oxford: Oxford University Press, 1989), 25–79; Dowbiggin, ibid., 144–61.

11. On this development in particular and on the important role that Lamarckian *transformisme* played in the nineteenth-century sciences of life, see Yvette Conry, *L'Introduction du Darwinisme en France au XIXe siècle* (Paris: Vrin, 1974), 39–44. One might say that Lamarckism and neo-Lamarckian theories of inheritance differed from Darwinian and neo-Darwinian theories in one important respect. In general, Darwinians believed that the variations any species exhibited were part of a *natural* process inherent in reproduction. Natural selection then accounted for which of these randomly occurring variations managed to survive long enough to be passed to descendants. Lamarckians held, by contrast, that variations in nature were a product of the self-willed changes provoked in the organism by the "challenge" of adaptation. In this view, the success of the adaptation—and therefore the survival of the species—depended on whether the new variation was strongly enough rooted in the organism to be passed on to offspring. In the Lamarckian tradition, then, the whole weight of successful evolutionary outcomes fell on an adaptational variation as a "force" of reproduction, which may explain, in part, the preoccupation with French biology with the epigenetic *circumstances* surrounding reproduction.

12. On this point see Canguilhem, *Connaissance de la vie,* 135–36.

13. As it was explained by the foremost (non-Darwinian) theoretician of evolutionary theory, Felix LeDantec, "vivre, c'est habituer" in *Science et conscience* (Paris: Flammarion, 1908), 76. See on this point Canguilhem, ibid., 134–35; Conry, *L'Introduction du Darwinisme* 317–23. Henri Milne-Edwards sums up the mid-century thinking of French biologists on the potential variability in species in *Rapport sur les progrès récents des sciences zoologiques en France* (Paris, 1867), 426–27.

14. Charles Letourneau, "Hérédité," in *Dictionnaire encyclopédique des sciences médicales,* 4th ser., 13 (1888): 589.

15. Valentin Magnan and Paul-Maurice LeGrain, *Les Dégénérés* (Paris: Rueff, 1895), 95.

16. Joseph Moreau de Tours, *La Psychologie morbide dans ses rapports avec la philosophie de l'histoire ou de l'influence des névropathies sur le dynamisme intellectuel* (Paris: Masson, 1859), 255. Other major psychiatric works in this tradition were Henri Le Grande du Saulle, *La Folie héréditaire* (1873); Théodule Ribot, *L'Hérédité psychologique* (1873); J. Déjérine, *L'Hérédité dans les maladies du système nerveux* (1886); and Charles Féré, *La Famille névropathique. Théorie tératologique de l'hérédité et de la prédisposition morbide et de la dégénérescence* (1899).

17. Jacques Donzelot, *The Policing of Families,* trans. Robert Hurley (New York, 1979), 173. Also, Pick, *Faces of Degeneration,* 72–73.

18. Ulysse Trélat, *La Folie lucide étudiée et considerée au point de vue de la famille et de la société* (Paris, 1861); B. A. Morel, in the séance of the Société Médico-Psychologique of 25 May 1868, *Annales médico-psychologiques* 11 (1868): 290. See also Dowbiggin, *Inheriting Madness,* 138–41.

19. On Italy, see Pick, *Faces of Degeneration*, 109–32; Nye, *Crime, Madness and Politics*, 98–110; and Pierre Darmon, *Médecins et assassins à la belle époque. La Médicalisation du crime* (Paris: Editions du Seuil, 1989). On England, Pick, *Faces of Degeneration*, 155–221; Gareth Stedman Jones, *Outcast London: A Study in the Relationship Between Classes in Victorian Society* (Oxford: Oxford University Press, 1971); Richard Soloway, "Counting the Degenerates: The Statistics of Race Deterioration in Edwardian England," *Journal of Contemporary History* 17 (1982): 137–62.

20. Pick, ibid., 133.

21. For example, Nye, *Crime, Madness, and Politics;* Harris, *Murders and Madness;* William Schneider, *Quality and Quantity. The Quest for Biological Regeneration in Twentieth-century France* (Cambridge: Cambridge University Press, 1990).

22. I am indebted to the image of the diseases of degeneracy as a dance *au ronde* to Jean Borie in *Le Célibataire français* (Paris: Le Sagittaire, 1976), 92. See also Nye, ibid., 142–44.

23. See the charts for France, Sweden, Great Britain, Italy, and Germany in Pierre Guillaume, *Individus, familles, nations. Essai d'histoire démographique XIXe–XXe siècles* (Paris: Société d'Edition d'Enseignement Supérieur, 1985), 26–31.

24. André Armengaud, *La Population française au XIXe siècle* (Paris: Presses Universitaires de France, 1971), 47–51. The fullest demographic treatment of the downturn in fertility may be found in Jean-Pierre Bardet and Hervé LeBras, "La Chute de la fécondité," in *Histoire de la population française,* vol. 3, *De 1789 à 1914* (Paris: Presses Universitaires de France, 1988), 351–402.

25. Jean-Pierre Bardet discusses the "ordinary" Malthusianism of the nineteenth-century bourgeoisie, its early mastery of birth control techniques, and motives to limit family size in Bardet and LeBras, ibid., 368–72. On the effort to spread neo-Malthusian advice to the proletariat, and its general lack of success, see Francis Ronsin, *La Grève des ventres: Propagande néo-malthusienne et baisse de la natalité française (XIX–XXe siècles)* (Paris: Aubier, 1980).

26. Paul Leroy-Beaulieu, *La Question de la population* (Paris: Alcan, 1911), 350–51. Martine Segalen has discussed the monopoly held on population discourse by bourgeois commentators in "Les Structures familiales," in *Histoire de la Population française,* 3: 414–15.

27. Claude Digeon, *La Crise allemande de la pensée française, 1870–1914* (Paris: Presses Universitaires de France, 1959), 431. See on this point of analysis Victor Nguyen, "Situation des études maurrasiennes: Contribution à l'histoire de la presse et des mentalités," *Revue d'histoire moderne et contemporaine* 18 (1971): 503–38. On the question of French "decadence" and its popularity as a philosophical and literary theme, see A. E. Carter, *The Idea of Decadence in French Literature, 1830–1900* (Toronto: University of Toronto Press, 1958) and Konraad Swart, *The Sense of Decadence in Nineteenth-Century France* (The Hague: Nijhoff, 1964).

28. André Armengaud, *L'Opinion publique en France et la crise nationale allemande en 1866* (Paris: Société les Belles Lettres, 1962), 93–94.

29. An account of the debate appeared in the *Revue des cours scientifiques* 4

(13–20 April 1967): 305–11, 320–31, under the title, "Sur la prétendue dégénérescence de la population française." See also the remarks of Dr. Félix-Henri Boudet in *Revue des cours scientifiques* 4 (29 June 1867): 494–96.

30. Lucien Prevost-Paradol, *La France nouvelle* (Paris: Michel Lévy Frères, 1868), 410.

31. Ibid., 395. My emphasis.

32. See on these themes, Ouriel Reshef, *Guerre, mythes et caricature. Au Berceau d'une mentalité française* (Paris: Presses de la Fondation Nationale des Sciences Politiques, 1984), 27–49.

33. Ernest Renan, *La Réforme intellectuelle et morale* (Paris: Calmann Lévy, 1871), 47.

34. Ibid., 304.

35. In Clemenceau's words, "The treaty does not require the French to have a lot of children, but I might have wished it to be the first thing it mentioned. Because if France refuses to have families with numerous children, you can put the most magnificent clauses in all the treaties you wish, take away all the cannons the Germans possess, in short, do all you please, but France will nonetheless be lost because there will be no more French. It is a misfortune, a terrible misfortune, and an act of cowardice" (*Journal officiel,* 11 Oct. 1919, as quoted in André Armengaud, *Les Français et Malthus* [Paris: Presses Universitaires de France, 1975], 64).

36. For this part of the text of Petain's speech, see Philippe Pétain, *Quatre années au pouvoir* (Montréal, 1949), 49.

37. Charles DeGaulle, as quoted in Armengaud, *Les Français et Malthus,* 70.

38. Alfred Sauvy, *Richesse et population,* 2d ed. (Paris: Payot, 1944), 320.

39. See on this point Armengaud, *Les Français et Malthus,* 52–53.

40. Richard Tomlinson, "The 'Disappearance of France', 1896–1940: French Politics and the Birth Rate," *The Historical Journal* 28, no. 2 (1985): 407–408. For the texts and parliamentary debate on these laws, see Louis Boucoiran, *La Famille nombreuse dans l'histoire et de nos jours* (Bourg: Imprimerie Nouvelle, 1921), 104–253. Rachel Fuchs has discussed related legislation in *Abandoned Children. Foundlings and Child Welfare in Nineteenth-Century France* (Albany: SUNY Press, 1984), 45–61. Mary Lynn Stewart has discussed how women's labor protection legislation in the Third Republic was aimed squarely both at protecting the male workplace and supporting the family in *Women, Work, and the French State. Labour Protection and Social Patriarchy, 1879–1919* (Montreal: McGill-Queen's University Press, 1989), esp. 3–17, 41–57.

41. Marie-Monique Huss, "Pronatalism in the Inter-War Period in France," *Journal of Contemporary History* 25 (1990): 39–68; Tomlinson, ibid., 410–11.

42. Tomlinson, ibid., 412–13. Medical doctors had urged heavy penalties for bachelors from the early 1870s; see Borie, *Le Célibataire français,* 90–92 and Schneider, *Quality and Quantity.*

43. See *Statistique annuelle du mouvement de la population pour 1899–1900 XXIX–XXX* Ministère du Commerce (Paris: Imprimerie Nationale, 1901), lvii. Consanguinary marriages decreased slightly as a percentage of total marriages during the early Third Republic. But, in an astonishing reversal, medical opinion,

which had once condemned consanguinary marriages as hereditarily suspect, began to take a more positive point of view. On this new literature, see Emile Laurent, *Mariages consanguins et dégénérescences* (Paris: Maloine, 1895), 24–29.

44. Copley, *Sexual Moralities in France, 1780–1980,* 114–16. The strict rule forbidding a divorced person from marrying the correspondent in an adultery case was overturned in 1903 (see p. 129). See also Roderick Phillips, *Putting Asunder. A History of Divorce in Western Society* (Cambridge: Cambridge University Press), 422–28, and Edward Berenson, "The Politics of Divorce in France of the Belle Epoque: The Case of Joseph and Henriette Caillaux," *American Historical Review* 93, no. 1 (Feb. 1988): 31–55.

45. Tomlinson, "Disappearance of France," 405–406; Huss, "Pronatalism in the Inter-War Period in France," 43–53.

46. Nye, *Crime, Madness and Politics,* 165–70.

47. Karen Offen, "Depopulation, Nationalism, and Feminism in Fin-de-Siécle France," *American Historical Review* 89 (June 1984): 648–76; see also Steven Hause and Anne C. Kenney, *Women's Suffrage and Social Politics in the French Third Republic* (Princeton: Princeton University Press, 1984), 101–31; Huss, "Pronatalism in the Inter-War Period in France," 64; Agnès Fine, "Enfant et normes familiales," *Histoire de la population française,* 3: 451–58.

48. Richard J. Evans, *The Feminist Movement in Germany, 1894–1933* (London and Beverly Hills: Sage Publications, 1976), 158–70.

49. On the critical response, see William Logue, *Léon Blum. The Formative Years, 1872–1914* (DeKalb, Ill.: Northern Illinois University Press, 1973), 189–201.

50. "Rapport des deux sexes," *Statistique de la France. Statistique annuelle II,* new ser. (1872) (Paris: Imprimerie Nationale, 1875), xxxv.

51. Ministère du Commerce, *Statistique annuelle du mouvement de la population pour 1899–1900* (Paris: Imprimerie Nationale, 1901), lxxxiv.

52. E. Maurel, "Etude sur la masculinité," *Revue scientifique,* no. 12 (21 March 1903): 353–60. See also Arsène Dumont, "Natalité et masculinité," *Revue scientifique,* 4th ser., no. 24 (16 June 1894): 752–56.

53. René Worms, *La Sexualité dans les naissances françaises* (Paris: M. Giard et E. Brière, 1912), 55–60.

54. On the first stages of success of this development, see John Farley, *Gametes and Spores. Ideas About Sexual Reproduction, 1750–1914* (Baltimore: Johns Hopkins University Press, 1982), 185–88. On France, see Denis Buican, "La Génétique classique en France devant le néo-Lamarckisme tardif," *Revue de synthèse* 95–96 (1979): 301–24, and, in general, *Histoire de la génétique et de l'evolutionnisme en France* (Paris: Presses Universitaires de France, 1984), 17–226; on the institutional context of these developments in French biology, see Harry W. Paul, *From Knowledge to Power. The Rise of the French Empire in Science, 1860–1939* (London: Cambridge University Press, 1985), 93–133.

55. Sabatier was professor at the College de France. See his statement of these issues in *Essai sur la vie et la mort* (Paris: V. Babé, 1892), esp. 161–64, 235–76. For the continuation of the ideas of internal equilibria in physiology, see Henri Beaunis, *Les Sensations internes* (Paris: Alcan, 1889), and Eugène Gley, *Etudes de psychologie physiologique et pathologique* (Paris: Alcan, 1903). A clear popu-

larization of these ideas may be found in Alfred Fouillée, "Le Tempérament physique et moral d'après la biologie contemporaine," *Revue des deux mondes* 63 (15 July 1893): esp. 285–304.

56. Sabatier, ibid., 161.

57. Maurice Caullery, France's most eminent early twentieth-century embryologist, summed up French objections to Weismannian notions of heredity by noting that organisms are ruled by an "indivisible" equilibrium, not the artificial distinction between germ and soma (*Les Problèmes de la sexualité* [Paris: Alcan, 1913], 130–32).

58. On this experimental tradition and its relation to international developments, see J.-L. Fischer, "Yves Delage (1854–1920): L'Epigénèse néo-Lamarckienne contre la prédétermination Weismanienne," *Revue de synthèse* 95–96 (1979): 443–61; Camille Limoges, "Natural Selection, Phagocytosis and Pre-adaptation: Lucien Cuenot, 1886–1902," *Journal of the History of Medicine* 31 (1976): 178–84; Jane Maienschein, "What Determines Sex? A Study of Convergent Research Approaches, 1880–1916," *Isis* 75 (Sept. 1984): 457–80.

59. Joseph Spengler, *France Faces Depopulation* (Durham, N.C.: Duke University Press, 1938), 138–40. I have discussed this matter in *Crime, Madness and Politics in Modern France,* 141–44.

60. On the English models see Roy Porter, " 'The Secrets of Generation Display'd': *Aristotle's Master-piece* in Eighteenth-Century England," in *'Tis Nature's Fault. Unauthorized Sexuality During the Enlightenment,* ed. Maccubin, 1–21.; on a major French text, see Roy Porter, "Spreading Carnal Knowledge or Selling Dirt Cheap? Nicholas Venette's *Tableau de l'amour conjugal* in Eighteenth-Century England," *Journal of European Studies* 14 (1984): 233–55. On France in the eighteenth-century, see Tarczylo, *Sexe et liberté au siècle des lumières,* 71–83.

61. On the popularity of such literature throughout the nineteenth century, see J.-C. Bénard, "Fille ou garçon à volonté: Un aspect du discours médical au 19e siècle," *Ethnologie française* 11 (1981): 63–76; also Adler, *Secrets d'alcôve. Histoire du couple de 1830 à 1930,* 80–90, 103–106.

62. On the forms taken by scientific vulgarization since the eighteenth century, see Terry Shinn and Richard Whitley, eds., *Expository Science: Forms and Functions of Popularization* (Dordrecht, 1985).

63. For this view, see Charles Robin, "Fécondation," in *Dictionnaire encyclopédique des sciences médicales,* 4th ser., 1 (1877): 464–65; Dr. Armand Sabatier, *Recueil des mémoires sur la morphologie des éléments sexuels et sur la nature de la sexualité* (Montpellier 1886), 202–203; Dr. Augustin Cleisz, *Recherches des lois qui président à la création des sexes* (Paris: Rougier, 1889), 24–28; Jean-Charles Houzeau, *Etudes sur les facultés mentales des animales comparées à celles de l'homme,* 2 vols. (Paris: Hector Manceau, 1872), 2: 409–410. As John Farley points out in *Gametes and Spores,* the French scientist J.-B. Dumas was the first to articulate this view in the 1820s, as part of his argument that the sperm contributed directly to the fertilization of the egg (pp. 39–43).

64. On this point see Farley, ibid., 125–27.

65. The term of André Sanson, *L'Hérédité normale et pathologique* (Paris: Asselin et Houzeau, 1893), 5; 102.

66. Léonce Manouvrier, "Sexe," in *Dictionnaire des sciences anthropologiques* (Paris: Doin, 1884), 993–97; Charles Letourneau, "Hérédité," in *Dictionnaire encyclopédique des sciences médicales,* 4th ser., 13 (1888): 592–93; Houzeau, *Etudes sur les facultés mentales,* 2: 410–13; Dumont, "Natalité et masculinité," 753; Dr. Serge-Paul, *Physiologie de la vie sexuelle chez l'homme et chez la femme, suivie d'une étude sur la procréation des sexes à volonté* (Paris: Bibliothèque Populaire des Sciences Médicales, 1910), 233–39; Dr. A. Corivaud, *Le Lendemain du mariage,* 2d ed. (Paris: Baillière, 1889), 61–70; Worms, *La Sexualité dans les naissances françaises,* 174–212.

67. Sanson, *L'Hérédité normale et pathologique,* 104–105.

68. These are the words, respectively, of Charles Letourneau, "L'Hérédité," 593, of an unnamed colleague of René Worms, quoted in *La Sexualité . . . ,* 78, and of Coriveaud, *Le Lendemain du mariage,* 224.

69. For this view, see Dr. Louis Bernard, *Contribution à l'étude de la question du déterminisme sexuel* (Trévoux: Imprimerie Jeanin, 1909), 44.

70. See on the period around mid-century, Frederick Churchill, "Sex and the Single Organism: Biological Theories of Sexuality in the Mid-Nineteenth Century," *Studies in the History of Biology* 3 (1979): 139–78.

71. Farley, *Gametes and Spores,* 160–68.

72. Henri Milne-Edwards, *Eléments de zoologie* (Paris, 1834); *Leçons sur la physiologie et l'anatomie comparée de l'homme et des animaux,* vol. 8 (Paris, 1863).

73. Sabatier, *Recueil des mémoires sur la morphologie des éléments sexuels et sur la nature de la sexualité,* 163–64.

74. Alfred Fouillée, "La Psychologie des sexes et ses fondements physiologiques," *Revue des deux mondes* 119 (Sept. 1893): 400. My emphasis.

75. J. L. de Lanessan, "preface" to L. Tillier, *L'Instinct sexuel chez l'homme et chez les animaux* (Paris: Doin, 1889), ix–xi, also, 2–11. An excellent summary of the argument may be found in Dr. René Koehler, "Pourquoi ressemblons-nous à nos parents? Essai sur la fécondation, sa nature et son origine," *Revue philosophique* 35 (April 1893): 267–70. For a more cautious view about the evolutionary *order* of forms of reproduction, see Maurice Caullery, *Les Problèmes de la sexualité* (Paris: Flammarion, 1913), 57–62.

76. Tillier, *L'Instinct sexuel,* 51–70.

77. Fouillée, "La Psychologie des sexes . . . ", 401. See Patrick Geddes and J. A. Thomson, *The Evolution of Sex* (London, 1889).

78. Fouillée, ibid., 401.

79. Ibid., 405–406. One of the most innovative French cytologists, G. Balbiani, wrote of "selection" and "struggle" between spermatozoa: " . . . it is the most agile ones which arrive first at the egg and are able to complete its fertilization. Selection does not content itself with individuals alone, but works as well through the sexual elements" (*Leçons sur la génération des vertébrés* [Paris: Doin, 1879], 160).

80. Sabatier, *Recueil . . . ,* 183–87; Beaunis, *Les Sensations internes,* 52; André Cresson, *L'Espèce et son serviteur (sexualité, moralité)* (Paris: Alcan, 1913), 39–41; R. Koehler, "Pourquoi ressemblons-nous à nos parents?", 359–60; Rémy de Gourmont, *Physique de l'amour. Essai sur l'instinct sexuel* (Paris: Société du Mer-

cure de France, 1903), 107–108. For other studies of contemporary science, see Emily Martin, "The Egg and the Sperm: How Science has Constructed a Romance Based on Stereotypical Male–Female Roles," *Signs: Journal of Women in Culture and Society* 16, no. 3 (1991): 485–501; Nancy Tuana, "The Weaker Seed: The Secret Bias of Reproductive Theory," in *Feminism and Science,* ed. Nancy Tuana (Bloomington: Indiana University Press, 1989), 147–91.

81. A good instance of this is the treatment of the evidence of craniology, see Elizabeth Fee, "Nineteenth-Century Craniology: The Study of the Female Skull," *Bulletin of the History of Medicine* 53 (1979): 415–33.

82. This is not to say that women were not still in some sense "sick" from childbearing and from the trauma of the menstrual cycle; see the collection of articles in Jeffrey Moussaieff Masson, *A Dark Science. Women, Sexuality and Psychiatry in the Nineteenth Century,* trans. Jeffrey Masson and Marianne Loring (New York: Farrar, Straus and Giroux, 1986); Kniebiehler and Fouquet, *La Femme et les médecins,* 203–98; Ann-Louise Shapiro, "Disordered Bodies/Disorderly Acts: Medical Discourse and the Female Criminal in Nineteenth-Century Paris," *Genders,* no. 4 (Spring 1989): 68–85. On Michelet, see Jean Borie, "Une gynécologie passionnée," in *La Femme du XIXe siècle,* ed. J.-P. Aron (Paris: Editions Complexe, 1980), 153–90); Jordanova, *Sexual Visions,* 66–86.

83. On sexual selection, see Cynthia Eagle Russett, *Sexual Science. The Victorian Construction of Womanhood* (Cambridge, Mass.: Harvard University Press, 1989), 78–89; Robert J. Richards, *Darwin and Emergence of Evolutionary Theories of Mind and Behavior* (Chicago: University of Chicago Press, 1987), 187–93.

84. L. Tillier, *L'Instinct sexuel,* 87–155; Alfred Espinas, *Des Sociétés animales,* 2d ed. (Paris: Baillière, 1878), 321–25; Gourmont, *Physique de l'amour,* 165–70.

85. For other criticism of sexual selection, see Russett, *Sexual Science,* 89–94.

86. Fouillée, "La Psychologie des sexes . . . ," 404.

87. Caullery, *Les Problèmes de la sexualité,* 322.

88. See Schneider, *Quality and Quantity, passim.*

89. Dr. Henri Thulié, *La Femme. Essai de sociologie physiologique* (Paris: Delahaye, 1885), iv, 161–63.

90. Ibid., 238–41.

91. Ibid., 104–105, 145.

92. Ibid., 167; 247–52.

93. Ibid., 510, 516. Free choice will allow the fulfillment of the "social contract" which the republican social theorist Renouvier wrote marriage should be, *and* ensure the proper relation of tradition and "progress" in the biological perfection of the race.

94. Ibid., 247.

95. François Maupas, "Recherches expérimentales sur la multiplication des infusoires ciliés," *Archives zoologiques expérimentales générales* 6 (1888): 261. On this experiment and its subsequent history, see Farley, *Gametes and Spores,* 204–206. Much earlier, another French microscopist, G. Balbiani, was the first to alert scientists to the "sexual" reproduction of infusoria, which he described as an "intimate adherence" (*Recherches sur les phénomènes sexuels des infusoires* [Paris:

Masson, 1861], 58). On the experimental history of this phenomenon, see Graham Bell, *Sex and Death in Protozoa. The History of an Obsession* (New York: Cambridge University Press, 1989), and Jacques Ruffié, *Le Sexe et la mort* (Paris: Editions du Seuil, 1986), 28–44.

96. Alfred Binet, "La Vie psychique des micro-organisms," *Revue philosophique* 24 (Dec. 1887): 585. This quotation should be compared with the entry on "sexe" in the *Grande encyclopédie,* vol. 29, written by the anthropologist Zaborowski around 1914, who described the evolution of sexual reproduction as having brought about the present state of sexual dimorphism in men and women. " . . . one must understand that it is inevitable that a civilization that procures for women such complete security and leisure, also develops her sexual characteristics, her grace, the roundness of her forms, and even favors a mental differentiation through her exclusive cultivation of sentiment, her great attention to coquetry, her search for whatever it is that charms or seduces, all of which relieves her intelligence of the efforts that are necessary to maintain its vigor."

97. Sabatier, *Recueil des mémoires sur la morphologie des éléments sexuels et sur la nature de la sexualité,* 163–93, 232–35.

98. Balbiani, *Leçons sur la génération des vertébrés,* 159–60.

99. Beaunis, *Les Sensations internes,* 52. See also Binet, "La Vie psychique," 592–93.

100. Koehler, "Pourquoi ressemblons-nous à nos parents?", 378.

101. Sabatier, *Recueil des mémoires sur la morphologie des éléments sexuels et sur la nature de la sexualité,* 172.

102. Espinas, *Les Sociétés animales* (Paris: 1887), 314–15.

103. Jacques Delboeuf, "Pourquoi mourrons-nous?" *Revue philosophique* 31 (March 1891): 257. My emphasis.

104. See the feminist tract of Jean Finot, *Préjugé et problèmes des sexes,* 3d ed. (Paris: Alcan, 1913); A feminist work expressing similar sentiments is Pierre Bonnier, *Sexualisme* (Paris: Giard, 1914); anti-feminist positions are expressed in Jacques Lourbet, *Le Problème des sexes* (Paris: Giard, 1900); Dr. Jules Roger, *Etude psycho-physiologique sur l'amour* (Paris: Baillière, 1899), 13–14.

105. Roger, ibid., 30; Lourbet, ibid., 287.

106. Gaston Danville, "L'Amour, est-il un état pathologique?", *Revue philosophique* 35 (March 1893): 261–83.

107. The most important works in this genre are Paul Bourget, *Physiologie de l'amour moderne. Fragments posthumes d'un ouvrage de Claude Larcher* (Paris: Lemerre, 1891); Gourmont, *Physique de l'amour;* Léon Blum, *Du Mariage* (Paris: Ollendorf, 1907); Jules Soury, "La psychologie physiologique des protozoaires," *Revue philosophique* 31 (Jan. 1891):1–44.

108. Blum, ibid., 37–38.

109. Ibid., 88–89, 158–67, 179.

110. Ibid., 307–11.

111. Jean Finot, "Les Femmes et le Darwinisme," *Revue des revues* 8 (May 1894): 328. See also his *Préjugé et problèmes,* 424–92 for his discussion that dimorphism will prevail and a feminist "equality in difference" will triumph.

Alfred Fouillée also believed that for the good of the "race" it behooved women not to upset their "grace" and their natural complementarity with men by working or engaging to any greater extent in the "struggle for life." It is necessary, he wrote, "that her energies be employed in a manner that conforms to the interests and to the natural relations of the two sexes, as well as to the interests of children and the race." ("La Psychologie des sexes," 426–28).

112. Gourmont, *Physique de l'amour*, 68.

113. This is the argument of Dr. Sicard de Plauzolles, *La Fonction sexuelle au point de vue de l'éthique et de l'hygiène social* (Paris: Giard, 1908), 36–37.

114. On this point, see Dr. Edouard Toulouse, *La Question sexuelle et la femme* (Paris: Charpentier, 1918), 242; Sicard de Plauzolles, ibid., 44, 56, 75.

115. Dr. Edouard Toulouse, ibid., 271. For similar, pre-war views contrasting coquettish and sprightly French women with languorous and submissive German women, see Sanson, *L'Hérédité normale et pathologique*, 417.

116. Bourget, *Physiologie de l'amour moderne*, 347.

117. Ibid., 80–81.

118. Ibid., 27–40.

119. Ibid., 375–78. Bourget did not entirely exonerate French women. Following a lecture tour to America in 1895, he returned with open admiration for American women, who, in contrast to their Gallic sisters, were "robust, gay, fresh, . . . free of false modesty, and perfectly suited to assure the happiness of their husbands and the perpetuity of their race" (*Le Temps*, 7 April 1895).

120. Dr. Sicard de Plauzolles put it this way: "From the national point of view, if military readiness demands the force represented by numerous armies, the real force of a country does not reside alone in the number of men it can mobilize, but also in the physical, intellectual and moral quality of the whole of the population" (*La Fonction sexuelle*, 285).

121. Fernand Boverat, *Patriotisme et paternité* (Paris: Grasset, 1913), 99, 135.

122. Ibid., 143–45. As he puts it, man must seek to become a "beautiful animal" (p. 144).

123. Sicard de Plauzolles, *La Fonction sexuelle*, 90.

124. Cresson, *L'Espèce et son serviteur*, 187.

125. For instance, Espinas says men must measure up to the "power" of women's collective representations of them (*Les Sociétés animales*, 285); Fouillée argues that women are naturally attracted to the "intellectual and corporeal power" of men ("La Psychologie des sexes," 412); also E. Dally, "Femmes," in *Dictionnaire des sciences médicales*, 4th ser., 1 (1877): 427–38; Charles Letourneau, "Femmes," in *Dictionnaire des sciences anthropologiques*, 476–78. On the role of the family in this effort, Dr. Armand Marie wrote in 1910, "In the social order, the progress, the fluctuations and the regressions of human groups are in a cause and effect relation with the modifications in the status of the family; marriage, birthrate, depopulation, and the variable preponderance of numbers depends on the variations in the essential social element that constitutes the conjugal relationship" ("preface" to Dr. Anton Nystrom, *La Vie sexuelle et ses lois* (Paris: Vigot, 1910), vi.

126. Fouillée, "La Psychologie des sexes," 429. My emphasis.

127. Jacques Bertillon, "Mariage," in *Dictionnaire des sciences médicales,* 2d ser., 5 (1872): 67.

Chapter 6

1. Charles Robin, "Sexe. Sexualité. Sexuels," in *Dictionnaire encyclopédique des sciences médicales,* 3d ser., 9 (1883): 479. Robin's emphasis.

2. Barrett Wendell, *La France d'aujourd'hui* (Paris: Fleury, 1910), 174.

3. Jesse Pitts, "Continuity and Change in Bourgeois France," in *In Search of France,* ed. Stanley Hoffman (New York: Harper and Row, 1965), 254.

4. See the cross-cultural discussion in the "Introduction" by Pat Caplan in Caplan, ed., *The Cultural Construction of Sexuality* (London: Tavistock, 1987), 22–24.

5. Sander Gilman, *Difference and Pathology. Stereotypes of Sexuality, Race, and Madness* (Ithaca, N. Y.: Cornell University Press, 1985), 20.

6. See Jack D. Ellis, *The Physician-legislators of France. Medicine and Politics in the Early Third Republic, 1870–1914* (Cambridge: Cambridge University Press, 1990).

7. On this theme, see in particular Jan Goldstein, *Console and Classify. The French Psychiatric Profession in the Nineteenth Century* (Cambridge: Cambridge University Press, 1987); Ian Dowbiggin, *Inheriting Madness. Professionalization and Psychiatric Knowledge in Nineteenth-Century France* (Berkeley, Calif.: University of California Press, 1991).

8. Stengers and Van Neck, *Histoire d'une grande peur: la masturbation,* 139–61.

9. The classic distinction is made by Richard Von Krafft-Ebing in his *Psychopathia sexualis,* trans. Harry Wedeck (first ed., 1886; New York: Putnam, 1965), 108.

10. See especially Jules Christian, "Onanisme," in *Dictionnaire des sciences médicales,* 2d ser., 15 (1881): 368–69. Also Stengers and Van Neck, *Histoire d'une grande peur,* 138–39.

11. Christian, ibid., 380.

12. Dr. Pierre J. C. Debreyne, *Essai sur la théologie morale considerée dans ses rapports avec la physiologie et la médecine,* as quoted in Stengers and Van Neck, *Histoire d'une grande peur,* 130.

13. Christian, "Onanisme," 377.

14. Théodore Tarczylo has done a bibliographic survey of the frequency of negative medical publications on masturbation between 1740 and 1900. He has found that in France, as in the rest of Europe and America, after a high point in the last decade of the eighteenth century, the number of medical texts hostile to the practice reached its highest historical crest in the two decades prior to 1900. See *Sexe et liberté au siècle des lumières,* 297–98.

15. For the argument that the "organic" nosology was qualitative, a system of signs that signified autonomous states, see Georges Lantéri-Laura, *Lecture des*

perversions: histoire de leur appropriation médicale (Paris: Masson, 1978), esp. 26–29. Psychiatrists committed to degeneration theory regularly warned against this simple translation, preferring to see symptoms as the fluctuating representations of a fluid organic substratum, which produced signs in correlation with the progression of a *general* degenerative syndrome. See, for example, Jean-Martin Charcot and Valentin Magnan, "Inversion de sens génitale," *Archives de neurologie* 4 (Nov. 1882): 320.

16. Eugène Gley, "Les abérrations de l'instinct sexuel," *Revue philosophique* 17 (1884): 92.

17. Foucault, *The History of Sexuality,* 1: 44.

18. The importance of a terminology of sexual identity is, to my mind, an indisputable fact that few scholars of the history of medical discourse would doubt. There is a vigorous debate, as I mentioned in the introduction, however, about the meaning of the notion of invention, not to mention that of identity, in the literature on the history of sexuality. See Caplan, ed., *The Cultural Construction of Sexuality,* and the appropriate sections of Martin Duberman, Martha Vicinus, and George Chauncey, Jr., eds., *Hidden From History: Reclaiming the Gay and Lesbian Past* (New York: NAL, 1989), and David F. Greenberg, *The Construction of Homosexuality* (Chicago: University of Chicago Press, 1988), 1–25, 482–500.

19. For example, Frank Sulloway, *Freud, Biologist of the Mind* (New York: Basic Books, 1979), 277–319; Lawrence Birkin, *Consuming Desire. Sexual Science and the Emergence of a Culture of Abundance* (Ithaca, N.Y.: Cornell University Press, 1988); Cynthia Eagle Russett, *Sexual Science. The Victorian Construction of Womanhood* (Cambridge, Mass.: Harvard University Press, 1989).

20. Sigmund Freud, *Three Essays on the Theory of Sexuality,* trans. James Strachey (New York: Basic Books, 1975). French authors are cited elsewhere in particular connections: Alfred Binet, p. 105, n.; Eugène Gley and Jules Chevalier, p. 9, n.

21. Arnold Davidson, "How to do the History of Psychoanalysis. A Reading of Freud's *Three Essays on the Theory of Sexuality,*" *Critical Inquiry* 14 (Winter 1987): 267–73; also "Sex and the Emergence of Sexuality," *Critical Inquiry* 14 (Autumn 1987): 16–48.

22. This view is also maintained by Lawrence Birkin, who formulates it correctly as an ambivalent aim: "Thus, from its inception, sexology in its different forms represented (even as it struggled against) the dissolution of heterogenitality as a universal 'species need' in favor of the emancipation of idiosyncratic desire in the form of 'fetishes' " (*Consuming Desire,* 50).

23. On Carpenter and his connection to British socialism, see Jeffrey Weeks, *Coming Out. Homosexual Politics in Britain From the Nineteenth Century to the Present* (London: Quartet Books, 1977), 68–84. For Hirschfeld's activities, see John Lauritsen and David Thorstad, *The Early Homosexual Rights Movement, 1864–1935* (New York: Times Change Press, 1974), 10–31; and Charlotte Wolff, *Magnus Hirschfeld. A Portrait of a Pioneer in Sexology* (London: Quartet Books, 1986). On Havelock Ellis, see Phyllis Grosskurth, *Havelock Ellis. A Biography* (London: Allen Lane, 1980); Paul Robinson, *The Modernization of Sex* (New York: Harper and Row, 1976).

24. The Harden–Eulenberg trials were the setting for impassioned arguments in behalf of legal reform, but the short-term results were far from positive for homosexuals. These trials are discussed in James D. Steakley, "Iconography of a Scandal: Political Cartoons of the Eulenberg Affair," *Studies in Visual Communication* 9 (March 1983): 20–51, also reprinted in Duberman, Vicinus, and Chauncey, eds., *Hidden from History,* 233–64. See also Isabel Hull, *The Entourage of Kaiser Wilhelm II, 1888–1918* (Cambridge: Cambridge University Press, 1982), 109–45.

25. Greenberg, *Construction of Homosexuality,* 408–11; George Mosse, *Nationalism and Sexuality. Respectability and Abnormal Sexuality in Modern Europe* (New York: Fertig, 1985), 28–29.

26. Krafft-Ebing, *Psychopathia Sexualis,* 587–88. He advises doctors on how they might give expert testimony in trials favorable to defendants accused of homosexual acts (pp. 462–63).

27. On this legislation, see Weeks, *Coming Out,* 11–18, and *Sex, Politics, and Society. The Regulation of Sexuality Since 1800* (London: Longmans, 1981), 99–108; also Frank Mort, *Dangerous Sexualities. Medico-Moral Politics in England Since 1830* (London: Routledge and Kegan Paul, 1987), 126–30; Greenberg, *Construction of Homosexuality,* 400–401, 411.

28. Havelock Ellis, *Sexual Inversion,* vol. 2, *Studies in the Psychology of Sex* (New York: Random House, 1936), 345–56; Krafft-Ebing, *Psychopathia Sexualis,* 589–90.

29. Ellis, ibid., 287–89; Krafft-Ebing, ibid., 385–402.

30. Ellis, ibid., 318–19; Krafft-Ebing, ibid., 464.

31. Krafft-Ebing, ibid., 464.

32. Freud, *Three Essays,* 8–9.

33. Ibid., 14. It is this passage that Arnold Davidson indicates as marking the decisive breach with the older tradition of sexual identity and reproduction. Davidson, "How to do the History of Psychoanalysis . . ." 264–65.

34. The literature on this subject is now abundant. For the United States, see Charles Rosenberg, *The Trial of the Assassin Guiteau. Psychiatry and Law in the Gilded Age* (Chicago: University of Chicago Press, 1968); for England, Roger Smith, *Trial by Medicine: Insanity and Responsibility in Victorian Trials* (Edinborough: Edinborough University Press, 1981); for Germany, Knut Engelhardt, *Psychoanalyze der Strafenden Gesellschaft* (Frankfurt, 1976); On France, see Jan Goldstein, *Console and Classify. The French Psychiatric Profession in the Nineteenth Century* (Cambridge: Cambridge University Press, 1987); Nye, *Crime, Madness and Politics in Modern France*; Harris, *Murders and Madness;* Pierre Darmon, *Médecins et assassins à la belle époque. La Médicalisation du crime* (Paris: Editions du Seuil, 1989).

35. The picture in the United States is complicated, owing in part to the overlapping and occasionally contradictory structures of local and state law, and the varied patterns of local advocacy and resistance to legal reform in behalf of homosexuals, in which doctors took roles on both sides. Bert Hansen and George Chauncey have surveyed the early medical literature and found doctors often congenial to the notion of "inversion" as a "natural anomaly," though the older notion

of same-sex acts continued to persist. See Bert Hansen, "American Physicians' Earliest Writings About Homosexuals, 1880–1900," *The Milbank Quarterly* 67, suppl. 1 (1989): 92–108; and George Chauncey, "From Sexual Inversion to Homosexuality: Medicine and the Changing Conception of Female Deviance," *Salmagundi* 58–59 (1982–83): 114–46; "Christian Brotherhood or Sexual Perversion? Homosexual Identities and the Construction of Sexual Boundaries in the World War I Era," in *Hidden From History,* ed. Duberman et. al., 294–317. Also see Greenberg, *Construction...,* 420–21.

36. Lauritsen and Thorstad, *The Early Homosexual Rights Movement,* 10. The pro-homosexual writings of Edward Carpenter were translated into every European language except French, a revealing fact in view of the fact that French was the language par excellence of pornography in the late nineteenth century (p. 34).

37. See in general on this point Jacques Girard, *Le Mouvement homosexuel en France, 1945–1980* (Paris: Editions Syros, 1981).

38. The French criminal law code was much admired by sexologists elsewhere. See Ellis, *Sexual Inversion,* 347–48. It has been alleged that the responsibility for keeping homosexuality out of the *civil* code lay with the openly homosexual jurist, Jean-Jacques Cambacérès, who was one of its principal authors. But Cambacérès had nothing to do with the criminal code, which also failed to identify same-sex acts as offenses. See on this point Greenberg, *Construction...,* 352, n. and Copley, *Sexual Moralities in France,* 24–25.

39. Robert Aldrich, "Homosexuality in France," *Contemporary French Civilization* 7 (Fall 1982): 6; and Girard, *Le Mouvement homosexuel,* 14–15.

40. William Monter argues that the sodomy statutes in France were used to justify the burning of "sodomites" long after executions for heresy (with which sodomy had often been confounded in practice) had ceased in the seventeenth century, though these, too, ceased after 1700 or so. William Monter, *Ritual, Myth, and Magic in Early Modern Europe* (Brighton: Harvester Press, 1983), 107–108, 117.

41. On this point see Claude Courouve, *Vocabulaire de l'homosexualité masculine* (Paris: Payot, 1985), 169–78, 191–98.

42. See Randolph Trumbach, "Sodomitical Subcultures, Sodomitical Roles and the Gender Revolution of the Eighteenth Century: The Recent Historiography," and Michel Rey, "Parisian Homosexuals Create a Lifestyle," in *'Tis Nature's Fault'. Unauthorized Sexuality in the Enlightenment,* ed. Maccubbin, 109–21, 179–91.

43. On these activities in the Second Empire, see Pierre Hahn, *Nos Ancêtres les pervers: la vie des homosexuels sous le sécond empire* (Paris: Olivier Orban, 1979), 41–63; See also Copley, *Sexual Moralities in France,* 100–101; and Benjamin F. Martin, "Sex, Property, and Crime in the Third Republic," *Historical Reflections, Réflexions Historiques* 11 no. 3 (Fall 1984): 323–50.

44. Eugene Weber, *France Fin-de-Siècle* (Cambridge, Mass.: Harvard University Press, 1986), 37–39.

45. Courouve, *Vocabulaire de l'homosexualité masculine,* 129–33.

46. See the standard forensic definition in Dr. Pierre Reydellet, "Pédérastie,"

in *Dictionnaire des sciences médicales,* 60 vols. (Paris: Panckoucke, 1812–1822), 40: 44. On Gide, see Courouve, *Vocabulaire de l'homosexualité masculine,* 176–77.

47. Courouve, ibid., 198.

48. Greenberg, *Construction*..., 410–11.

49. Courouve, *Vocabulaire de l'homosexualité masculine,* 214–15. Courouve notes Valentin Magnan's resistance to the German usage. For an example of the French outlook, see the comment by Dr. Camuset in 1895 on a discussion of hermaphrodism in ancient Greece, in which he writes that such creatures still existed, but were now called "infantile" and "effeminate" ("Deux Cas d'hermaphrodisme antique," *Archives de Neurologie* 30 [Sept. 1895]: 153).

50. See, in general, Ambroise Tardieu, *Etude médico-légale sur les attentats aux moeurs* (Paris, 1857). On Tardieu, see Aron and Kempf, *Le Bourgeoisie, le sexe et l'honneur,* 45–87, and Hahn, *Nos Ancêtres les pervers,* 65–70.

51. Dr. Jean Masbrenier, "Péderastie et assassinat," *Annales d'hygiène publique et de médecine légale,* 3d., ser., 1 (1879): 254–56.

52. The paper most responsible for this revision was Paul Brouardel's "Etude critique sur la valeur des signes attribués à la pédérastie," *Annales d'hygiène publique et de médecine légale,* 3d ser., 4 (1880): 282–89.

53. This is the observation of F. Carlier, Louis Napoleon's prefect of police, in *Les Deux prostitutions (1860–1870),* (Paris: Dentu, 1887), 276.

54. Etienne Esquirol, *Des Maladies mentales,* vol. 2 (Paris, 1838), 182–98.

55. From Dr. Jean-Louis Alibert, *Nouveaux éléments de thérapeutique et de matière médicale,* 2d ed., vol. 2, p. 556, as quoted in Roubaud, *Traité de l'impuissance,* 223–26.

56. Roubaud, ibid., 226–29.

57. Foucault, *The History of Sexuality,* 1: 154.

58. Henri Le Grand Du Saulle, Séance of the Société Médico-Psychologique, 27 March 1876 in *Annales médico-psychologiques* 15 (May 1876): 446.

59. For a contemporary and roughly similar analysis, which attempted to analyse a case of homosexual attraction as a form of "circular" madness (alternation of periods of delusion and lucidity), and which also threw in an analogy of the attraction of the same sexes to a reversed electrical current, see Dr. Antoine Ritti, "De l'attraction des sexes semblables (Perversion de l'instinct sexuel)," *Gazette hebdomadaire de médecine et de chirurgie,* 2d ser., 15 (4 June 1878): 1–3.

60. *Archives de neurologie* 3 (Jan.–Feb. 1882): 53–60; 4 (Nov. 1882): 296–322.

61. Ibid., 4: 305.

62. In his preface to a recently reprinted version of Charcot and Magnan's paper, Gérard Bonnet makes no mention of this point; see J.-M. Charcot and Victor (sic) Magnan, *Inversion du sens génital et autres perversions sexuelles* (Paris, 1987), v–xxv. Charcot and Magnan do not deserve credit for the medical "invention" of the homosexual; that credit usually goes to the German psychiatrist Carl Westphal, for his 1870 article, "Die conträre Sexualempfindung: Symptom eines neuropathischen (psychopathischen) Zustandes," *Archiv für Psychiatrie* 2 (1870): 73–108.

63. Charcot and Magnan, ibid., 54–57.

64. For instance, William A. Hammond, M.D., *Sexual Impotence in the Male* (New York, 1883), esp. 32–35, 40–52, 59–66.

65. Charcot and Magnan, *Inversion du sens génital*, 54.

66. On this connection, see Dr. Edmond Dupouy, *Médecine et moeurs de l'ancienne Rome d'après les poètes latins* (Paris, 1885).

67. Alfred Binet, "Le Fétichisme dans l'amour. Etude de psychologie morbide," *Revue philosophique* 24 (1887): 166.

68. Ibid. His exact words are that fetishism is "pathologique, c'est-à-dire exagérée" (p. 143).

69. Ibid., 164.

70. Ibid., 165.

71. Ibid., 170.

72. Ibid., 164–65. My emphasis.

73. See, on these phenomena, Dr. Benjamin Ball, *La Folie érotique* (Paris: Baillière, 1888), esp. 82–84, 116–24, 130–39, 140–48; Dr. Paul-Emile Garnier, *Les Fétichistes, pervertis, et invertis sexuels; observations médico-légales* (Paris: Baillière, 1896), *passim;* Dr. Emile Laurent, *L'Amour morbide: étude de psychologie pathologique,* 3d ed. (Paris, 1895), 154–230.

74. Laurent, ibid., 76.

75. Tarde uses the example of a general or someone else in a high station wishing to marry a prostitute in "Amour morbide," *Etudes pénales et sociales,* 145–47.

76. Charles Féré, *The Evolution and Dissolution of the Sexual Instinct,* 2d rev. ed. (London: Charles Carrington, 1904), 31.

77. Dr. Joanny Roux, *Psychologie de l'instinct sexuel* (Paris: Baillière, 1899), 87–91.

78. Laurent, *Fétichistes,* 44. See also, on this point, Binet, "Le Fétichisme dans l'amour," *passim.*

79. See the variations on this point in Ludovic Dugas, "L'Inversion sexuelle," *Archives de l'anthropologie criminelle* 10 (1895): 327; Dr. Georges Saint-Paul (pseudonym, Dr. Laupts), *Perversion et perversités sexuelles: une enquête médicale sur l'inversion* (Paris: Georges Carré, 1896), 202–205; Paul Moreau de Tours, *Des Aberrations du sens génésique* (Paris: A. Helm, 1880), 172; Laurent, *L'Amour morbide,* 11; Garnier, *Les Fétichistes,* 18–19.

80. Julien Chevalier, *L'Inversion sexuelle: une maladie de la personnalité* (Lyon: Storck, 1893), 414–15.

81. Garnier, *Les Fétichistes,* 22; Saint-Paul, *Perversion,* 20–31.

82. Paul-Emile Garnier, *La Stérilité humaine et l'hermaphrodisme* (Paris: Garnier Frères, 1883), 497.

83. Dr. Henri Legludic, *Notes et observations de médecine légale: attentats aux moeurs* (Paris: Masson, 1896), 224–25; Dr. Louis Reuss, "Des Abérrations du sens génésique chez l'homme," *Annales d'hygiène publique et de médecine légale,* 3d ser., 16 (1886): 311; Garnier, *Fétichistes,* 144–45; Chevalier, *Inversion,* 343.

84. Dr. Louis Thoinot, *Attentats aux moeurs et perversions du sens génital*

(Paris: Doin, 1898), 308. Féré, *Evolution and Dissolution of the Sexual Instinct,* 191.

85. Dr. Antoine Luyt, *Les Fellatores* (Paris, 1885); Paul Brouardel wrote of passive pederasts in 1880 that they lacked the normal "ardor" of males, and so "they undergo rather than provoke the genital activity in which they participate" ("Etude Critique," 189); Chevalier writes in *Inversion* that "active" pederasts become by degrees, "passive" ones, and descend finally to "oral onanism, the last stage of depravity and the termination of all genital potency" (p. 173).

86. Chevalier, ibid., 377.

87. Ibid., 203–21; Saint-Paul, *Perversion,* 30, 78–79; Dugas, "L'Inversion," 328–29.

88. Dugas, ibid., 330.

89. Emile Laurent, *Les Bissexués, gynecomastes et hermaphrodites* (Paris: Georges Carré, 1894), 103.

90. Paul-Emile Garnier, *Impuissance physique et morale chez l'homme et la femme,* 3d ed. (Paris: Garnier Frères, 1882), 124.

91. Thoinot, *Attentats au moeurs,* 309; Chevalier, *Inversion,* 194.

92. Laurent, *Les Bissexués,* 18; Reuss, "Des Abérrations," 131.

93. Saint-Paul, *Perversion,* 14–20.

94. Ibid. 207. My emphasis.

95. Carroll Smith-Rosenberg has persuasively documented the misogynous impulses that informed the medical descriptions of "mannish" lesbians in this same period in Britain and the United States, suggesting that the same factors were at work in the construction of all "pathological" sexual identities; see "The New Woman as Androgyne: Social Disorder and Gender Crisis, 1870–1936," in *Disorderly Conduct: Visions of Gender in Victorian America* (New York: Oxford University Press, 1985), 259–65.

96. Davidson, "Sex and the Emergence of Sexuality," 23.

97. Emile Littré, *Dictionnaire de la langue française* (Paris: Hachette, 1882); *Le Grand Robert* (Paris, 1985); the *Grand Larousse* lists a similar definition from 1845.

98. "Sexualité" in *Le Grand Robert* and *Grand Larousse.*

99. Emmanuel Régis, *Précis de psychiatrie,* 5th ed. (Paris: Doin, 1914), v–vi, 178–86, 220–39, 950–59; Copley discusses French "resistance" to Freud in *Sexual Moralities,* 147–52.

100. Elizabeth Roudinesco, *La Bataille de cent ans. Histoire de la psychanalyse en France,* vol. 1 (Paris: Ramsay, 1982), 405–406.

101. Dr. Angelo Hesnard, *Traité de sexologie normale et pathologique* (Paris: Payot, 1933), 29.

102. Ibid., 90–110, 50, 127, 176, 190, 423.

103. Ibid., 296.

104. Ibid., 303.

105. Ibid., 425. The most important survey of research on the physico-chemical foundations of sexual life published in the interwar period in France reached similar conclusions about the reproductive aims of libido, though not from a Freudian point of view. It is also obvious that the model of the hermaphrodite is still being

employed as a way of discussing the intermediary zone of sexual types; see Albert Hogge et. al., *Physiologie sexuelle normale et pathologique* (Paris: Doin, 1931), esp. 22–25, 32, 42–46.

106. Freud, *Three Essays,* 5 n.

107. Ibid., 15 n.

108. John Addington Symonds, *Studies in Sexual Inversion* (private printing, 1928 ed.), 13.

109. Ibid., 153.

110. Ellis, *Sexual Inversion,* 58–59.

111. See, respectively, Ball, *La Folie érotique,* 142; Toulouse, *La Question sexuelle,* 278; Saint-Paul, *Perversion,* 206.

112. Hesnard, *Traité,* 441.

113. See Alain Corbin, "Backstage," in *From the Fires of Revolution to the Great War,* ed. Michelle Perrot, vol. 4, *A History of Private Life,* trans. Arthur Goldhammer (Cambridge, Mass.: Harvard University Press, 1990), esp. 578–82; 591–622.

114. See on this point, and in general for the way women were represented in paint and in print, Bram Dijkstra, *Idols of Perversity. Fantasies of Feminine Evil in Fin-de-siècle Culture* (Oxford: Oxford University Press, 1986), 210–402.

115. Annelise Mauge, *L'Identité masculine en crise au tournant du siècle, 1871–1914* (Paris: Rivages, 1987), 103. See also Jennifer Waelti-Walters, " 'New Women' in the Novels of *Belle Epoque* France," *History of European Ideas* 8, nos. 4–5 (1987): 537–48.

116. See on these themes, Mauge, ibid., 85–142; Michelle Ouerd, "Homosexuelles, représentations culturelles, (per)-version décadente," *Masques,* no. 4 (Spring 1980): 49–53; Isabelle de Courtivon, "Weak Men and Fatal Women: The Sand Image," in *Homosexualities and French Literature: Cultural Contexts, Critical Texts* ed. George Stambolian and Elaine Marks, (Ithaca, N.Y.: Cornell University Press, 1979), 210–27. Bertholet, *Le Bourgeois dans tous ses états,* 79–109.

117. An excellent source for Huysmans, Louys, Péladan, Lorrain, Rachilde, and Gourmont and the ways they deployed sexual variation in their work is Jennifer Birkett, *The Sins of the Fathers. Decadence in France, 1870–1914* (London, 1986).

118. Jean-Pierre Joecker has been able to find only one francophone novelist who was willing to risk the legal and critical storms that greeted positive representations of homosexuality before 1914. Georges Eekhoud was a Belgian author who went on trial in Bruges in 1900 for publishing *Escal-Vigor* in 1899 ("Georges Eekhoud, un buveur de vie et de sang," *Masques,* no. 16 (Winter 1982–83): 18–24).

119. Joris-Karl Huysmans, *A Rebours* (Paris: Fasquelle, n.d.), 140.

120. Ibid., 141.

121. Ibid., 144.

122. Ibid., 146. In an example that demonstrates the ease with which these ideas were exchanged between the literary and medical realms, Alfred Binet, writing three years after the appearance of Huysmans's novel wrote about how impotent men "seek rare sensations" to provide "the new source of energy and pleasure" that will sustain erections, including "luxury . . . , the risk of being caught

in flagrante delicto . . . , all these refinements invented by the subtle imaginations of the jaded attests to an unconscious search for sensory excitations which are able, by stimulating the subject, to augment the physical pleasure of love" (Binet, "Le Fetichisme dans l'amour," 160).

123. Ibid., 147. I have discussed the matter of sexual fetishism in greater detail in "The Medical Origins of Sexual Fetishism," in *Fetishism as Cultural Discourse: Gender, Commodity, and Vision,* ed. Emily Apter and William Pietz (Ithaca, N.Y.: Cornell University Press), forthcoming.

124. André Raffalovitch, "Quelques observations sur l'inversion," *Archives d'anthropologie criminelle* 9 (1894): 216.

125. Emile Zola, "preface" to Saint-Paul, *Perversion,* 3–4.

126. André Gide, *Corydon,* trans. Richard Howard (New York: Farrar, Straus & Giroux, 1983), 17.

127. Ibid., 119.

128. Ibid., 115.

129. Ibid., 118.

130. Ibid., xx n.

131. On this incident see Jean Delay, *La Jeunesse d'André Gide,* 5th ed., 2 (Paris: Gallimard, 1957), 517–20; See also Gide's autobiographical *Si le grain ne meurt* and his *Journals;* also Gerald H. Storzer, "The Homosexual Paradigm in Balzac, Gide, and Genet," in *Homosexualities and French Literature,* 186–210; also Wallace Fowlie, "Sexuality in Gide's Self-Portrait," in ibid., 243–61.

132. J. E. Rivers, *Proust and the Art of Love: The Aesthetics of Sexuality in the Life, Times, and Art of Marcel Proust* (New York: Columbia University Press, 1980), 73; see in addition, Serge Béhar, *L'Univers médical de Proust* (Paris: Gallimard, 1970), and Bernard Straus, *Maladies of Marcel Proust: Doctors and Disease in his Life and Work* (New York: Holmes and Meier, 1980).

133. Marcel Proust, *Cities of the Plain* (Fr. title, *Sodome et Gomorrhe*), trans. C. K. Scott Moncrief (New York: Vintage, 1970), 5.

134. Ibid., 13.

135. Rivers, *Proust and the Art of Love,* 188–89.

136. Proust, *Cities of the Plain,* 13.

137. Ibid., 22.

138. Rivers comments on this as a "mode of selfhood" and a "category" of (homosexual) identity in Proust's novel, *Cities of the Plain,* 198.

139. Béhar, *L'Univers médical de Proust,* 32.

140. Rivers, *Proust and the Art of Love,* 33–37.

141. Quoted in ibid., 32.

142. Jules Huret, *Le Temps,* 13 April, 1895. The press coverage of the trial was rather short on specifics, but long on expressions of indignation at the "unspeakable habits" and the "ignoble spectacle" of this "shameful affair" (*Le Temps,* 5 and 7 April, 1895). Other papers began by treating the matter lightly, but turned to invective when testimony revealed Wilde's relations with homosexual prostitutes (*Le Figaro,* 5, 6, 11 April, 1895). On 7 April a columnist for *Le Figaro* warned against the danger in France of the decadent style in literature, equating it with a noxious odor to which one ends by being attracted. *Gil Blas* described Oscar as

an "effeminate Dandy" and heaped abuse on him (11 April, 1895), as *Le Temps* did on his "pale and exhausted [*épuisée*] lover," Lord Alfred Douglas (6 April 1895). Raul Roche's interview with Max Nordau in *Le Gaulois* allowed the self-appointed critic of decadent literature to trot out his vocabulary of medical pathology to brand Wilde and his ilk "anti-social," and "unnatural parasites" (10 April 1895).

143. *Le Temps*, 18 April 1895.

144. Ibid., 19 April 1895.

145. Ibid., 18 April 1895.

146. Ball, *La Folie érotique*, 84.

147. Garnier, *L'Impuissance physique et morale*, 4–5; Laurent, *L'Amour morbide*, 205–206, 215–16, 231; Saint-Paul, *Perversion*, 208.

148. Ball, *La Folie érotique*, 47. In his *Les Psychonévroses et leur traitement moral* (Paris: Masson, 1904), Dr. Dubois wrote about the doctor searching for a shred of the "sentiment of honor" on which to base his therapy (p. 518).

149. Dr. Alfred Fournier, "Simulation of Sexual Attacks on Young Children," originally from a paper in the *Annales d'hygiène publique* (1880), reprinted in Jeffrey Masson, *A Dark Science. Women, Sexuality and Psychiatry in the Nineteenth Century* (New York: Farrar, Straus and Giroux, 1986), 107, 118.

150. On the homosexual scandals in Germany, see Hull, *The Entourage of Kaiser Wilhelm II, 1888–1918*, 109–45; James D. Steakley, "Iconography of a Scandal: Political Cartoons of the Eulenberg Affair," in *Hidden From History*, ed. Duberman et. al. 233–63; Mosse, *Nationalism and Sexuality*, 1–47.

151. Smith-Rosenberg, "New Woman as Androgyne," 287–96.

152. Saint-Paul, *Perversion*, 232.

153. Ernest Charles, *La Grande revue*, 25 July 1910.

154. Hahn, *Nos Ancêtres les pervers*, 82.

155. Roudinesco, *La Bataille de cent ans*, 2: 47.

Chapter 7

1. Eugène Terrailon, *L'Honneur. Sentiment et principe moral* (Paris: Alcan, 1912), 42–43.

2. On these points see Maurice Agulhon, *Pénitents et Francmaçons de l'ancienne provence* (Paris: Fayard, 1968), 185–86, 210; Ran Halevi has shown how the themes of "harmony," "peace," and "brotherhood" were dominant in the titles chosen by lodges to identify themselves ("Les Représentations de la démocratie maçonnique au xviiie siècle," *Revue d'histoire moderne et contemporaine* 31 [1984], 582–84).

3. Agulhon, ibid., 208–18.

4. Ibid., 179; Halevi, ibid., 594–96.

5. On the salon/circle distinction, see Maurice Agulhon, *Le Cercle dans la France bourgeoise, 1810–1848. Etude d'une mutation de sociabilité* (Paris: Colin, 1977), 52–54.

6. Edmond Goblot, *La Barrière et le niveau. Etude sociologique sur la bourgeoisie française moderne* (Paris: Alcan, 1925), 14.

7. Pierre Rosanvallon, *Le Moment Guizot* (Paris: Gallimard, 1985), 97.

8. Michael Curtin, "A Question of Manners: Status and Gender in Etiquette and Courtesy," *Journal of Modern History* 57 (Sept. 1985): 409–10.

9. Louis-Damien Emeric, *Nouveau guide de la politesse*, 2d ed. (Paris: Roret et Roussel, 1821), 23.

10. Edouard Alletz, *De la démocratie nouvelle. Ou des moeurs et de la puissance des classes moyennes en France*, vol. 1 (Paris: F. Lequieu, 1837), 107. My emphasis.

11. Horce Raisson, *Code civil. Manuel complet de la politesse, du ton, des manières de la bonne compagnie*, 14th ed. (Paris: R. Renault, 1853), 6–8.

12. Goblot, *La Barrière et le niveau*, 91.

13. Raisson, *Code civil*, 58; see on this same point Alletz, *De la démocratie nouvelle*, 85–86; Emeric, *Nouveau guide de la politesse*, 18–22, 25.

14. Raisson, ibid., 80; M. Cholet de Chavanges, *L'Art de se présenter dans le monde, ou miroir de l'homme de bonne compagnie* (Paris: Librairie Universelle, 1828), 35; Emeric is far more disapproving, finding no justification for the duel (*Nouveau guide*, 97–105).

15. Goblot, *La Barrière et le niveau*, 96.

16. Ibid., 99.

17. Ibid., 100.

18. See, for example, the language in article one of the statutes of the literary circle of the town of Parthenay (1840) cited in Agulhon, *Le Cercle dans la France bourgeoise*, 40.

19. Quoted in Jean-Luc Marais, *Les Sociétés d'hommes. Histoire d'une sociabilité du 18ᵉ siècle à nos jours. Anjou, Maine, Touraine* (Monchrétien: Ivan Duny, 1986), 19.

20. As quoted in Agulhon, *Le Cercle dans la France bourgeoise*, 42.

21. Marais, *Les Sociétés d'honneur*, 20, 23, 25–28, 69–70.

22. See the "Règlement intérieur" of the Cercle de l'Union Artistique, reprinted in its *Annuaire de 1898* (Paris: Paul Dupont, 1898).

23. Marais, *Les Sociétés d'honneur*, 70–71.

24. Ibid., 23–25, 71.

25. For an example of some of this wit, see Jules Claretie, "La vie à Paris," *Le Temps*, 25 January 1881.

26. Ibid., 15 Feb. 1884; and 25 Jan. 1881.

27. Ibid., 25 Jan. 1881.

28. Commandant Pierre Chalmin, "La Pratique du duel dans l'armée française au xixᵉ siècle," in *Actes du 80ᵉ Congrès des Sociétés Savantes* (Lille, 1955), 330–34; Vigéant, *Un Maître d'armes sous la restauration* (Paris: Motteroz, 1883), 41–43; V. G. Kiernan, in *The Duel in European History*, discusses the spread of the practice through all the European armies during the Napoleonic wars (pp. 191–196).

29. Chalmin, ibid., 330. On the unfashionable civilian duel, see *Aventures parisiennes. Avant et depuis la Révolution*, vol. 3 (Paris: Maugeret, 1808), 306–17.

30. Chalmin, ibid., argues that this practice died out after 1870 (pp. 348–49), but other commentators disagree. See Dr. Charles Teissier, *Du Duel au point de vue médico-légal et particulièrement dans l'armée* (Lyon: Storck, 1890), 30–33;

Général Bourelly, in his *Le Duel et l'escrime dans l'armée en France et à l'étranger. Les Tribuneaux d'honneur* (Paris: A. Pedonc, 1900) shows convincingly how civilian and military authorities ensured this tradition did not die (esp. pp. 27–60). See also William Serman, *Les Officiers français dans la nation, 1848–1914* (Paris: Aubier, 1982), 137–43.

31. Kiernan, *The Duel in European History,* 194–95.

32. For England, see the figures compiled by Antony Simpson in "Dandelions on the Field of Honor: Dueling, the Middle Classes, and the Law in Nineteenth-Century England," *Criminal Justice History* 9 (1988): 106–107; for Germany, see Kevin McAleer, "The Last Teutonic Knights: The German Duel in Comparative Perspective, 1871–1918" (Ph.D. diss., University of California at San Diego, 1990), 29–30. For Austria-Hungary, see Istvan Deak, "Latter-Day Knights: Officers, Honor and Duelling in the Austro-Hungarian Army," *Oesterreichischen Osthefte* 28 (Wien, 1986).

33. McAleer, ibid., 60–64, 80, 182–90.

34. See on the phenomenon of the bourgeois duel in Germany, Ute Frevert, "Bourgeois Honor: Middle-Class Duellists in Germany From the Late Eighteenth to the Early Twentieth Century," in *The German Bourgeoisie. Essays on the Social History of the German Middle Class from the Late Eighteenth to the Early Twentieth Century,* ed. David Blackbourn and Richard J. Evans, (London: Routledge, 1991), 255–92.

35. Simpson, "Dandelions on the Field of Honor," 106–107.

36. Ibid., 116–21; McAleer discusses the impact of middle class integration into the *Landwehr* after 1870, in "The Last Teutonic Knights," 176–95.

37. See, for example, Chalmin, "La Pratique du duel," 349–50; Billacois, *Le Duel,* 312–13.

38. Simpson, "Dandelions on the Field of Honor," 139–40.

39. Frevert, "Bourgeois Honor," 282–84.

40. Simpson, "Dandelions on the Field of Honor," 122; McAleer, "The Last Teutonic Knights," 36–42.

41. Simpson, ibid., 123, found that of 172 known English duels fought between 1762 and 1821, 69 resulted in deaths, of which 18 were brought to trial and only 10 found guilty. On Germany, see Frevert, "Bourgeois Honor," 268–69.

42. As Emile Garçon pointed out in a review of European law codes between the wars, virtually all nations punished dueling and its consequences by "special" legislation condemning the act itself, rather than attempting to prosecute it under assault or murder statutes (*Code pénal annoté,* new ed., vol. 2 [Paris: Sirey, 1956], 17).

43. On this legend, see Gabriel Tarde, "Le Duel dans le présent," *Etudes pénales et sociales* (Paris: Masson, 1892), 32.

44. *Table analytique des arrêts de la cour de cassation rendus en matière criminelle,* vol. 2 (Paris, 1857), 444.

45. Ibid., 444–45.

46. For the text of Dupin's circular to state prosecutors, see *Gazette des tribuneaux,* 1 July 1836.

47. For an account of the Baron-Pessen duel, see the appendix in A. Croab-

bon, *La Science du point d'honneur* (Paris: Librairies des Imprimeries, 1894), 465–66. Pessen's defense lay in his assertion that the insult (a slap) given him by M. Baron was "the worst one a man of honor can undergo," and required a "spontaneous and personal" apology by Baron himself, not one tendered by proxy.

48. For the major jurisprudence after 1837, see Garçon, *Code pénal annoté,* 18–22; *Table analytique,* 445–46.

49. These figures appear in Tarde, "Le Duel dans le présent," 33.

50. *La Sentinelle,* 24 June 1845, 189.

51. Raymond Duplantier, "Les Duels à Poitiers et dans la Vienne au cours de la première moitié du dix-neuvième siècle," in proceedings of *Société des antiquaires de l'ouest,* 22 Jan. 1950, 1, 17–18.

52. Gabriel Desert, "Pour une relecture de la notion du duel," [A review of Yves Baron's *Les Duels dans le Calvados au xixe siècle,* mémoire de maitrise, Caen, 1982], *Annales de Normandie* 33, no. 3 (1983): 181, 184.

53. Ibid., 181–84; Duplantier, "Les Duels à Poitiers," 14.

54. Desert, ibid.; Duplantier, ibid., 5–6.

55. Chalmin, *La Pratique du duel,* 336–37.

56. Jean-Claude Chesnais, *Histoire de la violence* (Paris: Robert Lafont, 1981), 126. For a similar judgment on official statistics presenting only the "tip of the iceberg" of *real* dueling rates, see Frevert, "Bourgeois Honor," 267–69.

57. Chatauvillard also claimed to have received a multitude of letters from ministers, prefects, and other government officials, who could not, for legal reasons, affix their signatures to the document (*Essai sur le duel* [Paris: Bohaire, 1836], 87–90).

58. Ibid., 5.

59. *Journal des débats,* 27 Jan. 1834.

60. This account appears in the *Journal de Paris,* 2 Feb. 1834. Dulong's seconds managed to acquire all the printed copies, and these were presented ceremoniously to Dulong and to Bugeaud's chief second moments before the duel.

61. A version of the "barrier" duel in which both men stood at forty paces, advancing on command and firing at will. The danger here lay in the full frontal target each man offered to his opponent's aim, in distinction to the immobile "signal" duel, which became axiomatic in the Third Republic, in which each man presented a side profile, which protected the heart. The neck and face were partly shielded by the high arm and shoulder position required to sight down the pistol. For details on the duel, see *Le Constitutionnel,* 30 Jan. 1834.

62. *Gazette de France,* 31 Jan. and 1, 2, 3 Feb. 1834. This duel is often referred to with reverence by *belle époque* parliamentary duelers as an example of the impossibility of distinguishing between public and private honor.

63. For the texts of Carrel's Chamber of Deputies speech, see *Gazette de France,* 3 Feb. 1834, and *Le National,* 1, 2 Feb. 1834.

64. *Le National,* 20, 21 July 1836.

65. *La Presse,* 21 July 1836.

66. *Journal de Paris,* 23 July 1836.

67. See *Le Constitutionnel,* 23 July 1836.

68. *La Presse,* 31 July 1836.

69. M. de Chaix-d'Est in the trial transcript reprinted in the *Gazette des tribuneaux,* 27 Aug. 1836. The transcripts I use here appeared in the *Gazette des tribuneaux,* of 8, 27, 28, and 29 Aug. 1836.

70. This emerged from the testimony of an innkeeper in Limoges, where Durepaire often took his meals. *Gazette des tribuneaux,* 27 Aug. 1836.

71. Sirey was alleged to have demanded a pistol duel in which only one of the pistols was loaded. *Gazette des tribuneaux,* 28 Aug. 1836.

72. *Gazette des tribuneaux,* 27 Aug. 1836.

73. *Guet-apens,* punished in the criminal code by the death penalty.

74. *Gazette des tribuneaux,* 28 Aug. 1836.

75. On the trial and Crémieux's role in it, see Daniel Amson, *Adolphe Crémieux. L'oublie de la gloire* (Paris: Editions du Seuil, 1988), 167–71.

76. *Gazette des tribuneaux,* 29 Aug. 1836.

77. Ibid., 28 Aug. 1836.

78. Chatauvillard, *Essai sur le duel,* 7–9.

79. Ibid., 71.

80. Ibid., 123.

81. Ibid., 53–57.

82. Ibid., 120–22.

83. As he put it, "All doctors agree that it is easier to save the life of a man wounded by a sword than one struck by a ball" (Augustin Grisier, *Journal de Paris,* 2 Dec. 1829).

84. Chatauvillard, *Essai sur le duel,* 120–22.

85. Augustin Grisier, *Les Armes et le duel* (Paris, 1847), 133.

86. Ibid., 135.

87. See McAleer, "The Last Teutonic Knights," 74–139, 317–52; Robert Baldick, *The Duel. A History of Dueling* (London: Chapman and Hall, 1965), 144–45; Tarde, *Etudes pénales et sociales,* 36.

88. Chatauvillard, *Essai sur le duel*, 91–92, 105–106.

89. Ibid., 99.

90. Ibid., 104.

91. Ibid., 10.

92. Ibid., 9–12.

93. As quoted in Adeline Daumard, "Noblesse et aristocratie en France au xixᵉ siècle," in *Les Nobelesses au xixᵉ siècle,* vol. 107 (Rome: Ecole Française de Rome, 1988), 82. On the selfconscious effort of the politicians and theorists of this era to encourage and justify the emergence of a new "aristocracy" of merit and "capacity," see Rosanvallon, *Le Moment Guizot,* 98–120.

94. André-Marie Dupin, as quoted in his summation of the Baron-Pessen trial, *Gazette des tribuneaux,* 16 Dec. 1837.

95. Ibid., 26 March 1845. This case involved a fatal duel over a young woman between a medical student and a student at the Ecole polytechnique, who carried a sword as part of his school uniform. Acquitted by a jury in Orléans, the young *polytechnicien*'s verdict was overturned (broken) by the Cour de Cassation in a case argued by Dupin himself. The student's lawyer was none other than the later

quarante-huitard Alexandre-Auguste Ledru-Rollin. For the account of the trial, see the *Gazette des tribuneaux,* 5 Jan. 1845, and 26, 27 March 1845.

96. Alphonse Signol, *Apologie du duel. Ou quelques mots sur le nouveau projet de loi* (Paris: Chaunerot, 1828), 22.

97. Anatole France, "La Vie à Paris," *Le Temps,* 18 July 1886.

98. The source of this original quotation is unknown to me. It has been, however, widely reproduced. This translation is from Georges Bibesco and Féry d'Esclands, *Conseils sur les duels* (Paris, 1900), 131–32. It is small wonder that, given the ferocity of these views, proponents of the duel whispered at the time, and repeated years later, that Procureur-General Dupin was full of rage at the duel because he had himself once been obliged to make his excuses in a particularly humiliating way, choosing to make a virtue out of a personal failure of nerve; see Georges Bibesco, *Recueil, politique, religion, duel* (Paris: Plon, 1888), 268. For another account of Dupin's renowned cowardice, Alexis de Toqueville records that Dupin's failure to take his presidential seat at the assembly on the day of Louis-Napoleon's coup of 2 December 1852 "surprised no one as his cowardice was known" (Alexis de Toqueville, *Selected Letters on Politics and Society,* trans. James Toupin [Berkeley, Calif.: University of California Press, 1985], 271).

99. See Chalmin, "La Pratique du duel dans l'armée française," 345. As Augustin Grisier quotes Guizot, "The barbarian uses the armed ambush to avenge himself. . . . The Frenchman has the duel. . . . You will legislate against it in vain, men of heart will never support it" (*Les Armes et le duel,* 92). Guizot was even quoted by dueling proponents in the German Reich. See Robert Berdahl, *The Politics of the Prussian Nobility* (Princeton: Princeton University Press, 1988), 343.

100. Signol, *Apologie du duel,* 11.

Chapter 8

1. The play "Le Maître des forges" premiered at the *Gymnase* in December 1883. See Francisque Sarcey's review in *Le Temps,* 24 Dec. 1883. See, on Ohnet, Pierre Abraham and Roland Desné, *Histoire littéraire de la France,* vol. 10 (1873–1913) (Paris: Editions Sociales pour Culture, Arts et Lettres, 1978), 56.

2. We come upon Philippe hunting as the novel opens, fully at one with the natural world around him. *Le Maître des forges* (Paris: Ollendorff, 1882), 1–10. For other descriptions of him, see pp. 54–64, 146.

3. Ohnet, *Maître,* 156.

4. Ibid., 22, 149.

5. An important legal expert on the duel thought the fictional account of this duel so important that he listed it in his inventory of dueling precedents in 1894. His comment was that the duke had behaved correctly in addressing Philippe, "Are you ready to make your excuses?" rather than asking him if he was ready to make excuses for his *wife,* acting thereby "as if Mme Derblay did not exist, and as if the offense had been committed by her husband" (Croabbon, *La Science du point d'honneur,* 451).

6. Ohnet, *Maître,* 450–51.

7. Ibid., 483–86.

8. Mark Girouard, *The Return to Camelot. Chivalry and the English Gentleman* (New Haven, Conn.: Yale University Press, 1981), 33, 130–33.

9. See ibid., for a discussion of the Eglinton tournament of 1839 (pp. 88–95); Arno Mayer discusses the tournament sponsored by the industrial magnate, Krupp, in *The Persistence of the Old Regime* (New York: Vintage, 1981), 100. For the political consequences of these developments in Germany, see George Mosse, *The Crisis of German Ideology* (New York, 1964); Fritz Stern, *The Politics of Cultural Despair. A Study in the Rise of the Germanic Ideology* (Berkeley, 1961).

10. Stanley Mellon, "Introduction," to François Guizot, *Historical Essays and Lectures* (Chicago: University of Chicago Press, 1972), xxiii. See also Linda Orr, *Headless History. Nineteenth-Century Historiography of the Revolution* (Ithaca, N.Y.: Cornell University Press, 1990).

11. Léon Gautier, *La Chevalerie* (Paris: Victor Palmé, 1884), 98. See also pp. 782–83. In his introduction to Gautier's volume, Victor Palmé characterized chivalry as contrary to the modern economic spirit, but nonetheless the key to French survival in a hostile world: "What a madness of ardor, courage and pride is necessary to nations worthy of the name; I prefer a race that produces scores of Don Quixotes to one that produces nothing but industrialists or merchants" ("préface," to ibid., xi). See also Philippe Contamine, "Mourir pour la Patrie—X–XXe siècles," in *Les Lieux de mémoire. La Nation* ed. Pierre Nora, vol. 1 (Paris: Gallimard, 1986), 11–43.

12. Guizot, "The History of Civilization in France," in *Historical Essays and Lectures,* ed. Mellon, 393.

13. Ibid., 375. For Guizot's views on the importance of "honnêteté" and "dignité" in public life, see *Meditations et études morales,* new ed. (Paris: Didier, 1857), 18–22. His views on the need for romantic love, tempered by devotion and self-mastery, in marriage are expressed in *L'Amour dans le mariage,* 11th ed. (Paris: Hachette, 1879), 21–26, 91–92.

14. Elias, *The History of Manners,* 7.

15. Alain Plessis, *De la fête impériale au mur des fédérés, 1852–1871* (Paris: Editions du Seuil, 1973), 130–31.

16. See, on this development, Herman Lebovics, *The Alliance of Iron and Wheat in the Third French Republic, 1860–1914. Origins of the New Conservatism* (Baton Rouge, La.: Louisiana University Press, 1988).

17. Christophe Charle, *Les Elites de la République* (Paris: Fayard, 1987), 30–31, 255–56.

18. This is the formulation of Mme Le Cocq de Montborne, *Noblesse et bourgeoisie* (Paris: Charles Dounial, 1862), 19.

19. Bourdieu, *Distinction. A Social Critique of the Judgement of Taste,* 70–71.

20. Quoted in Alain Guillemin, "Nobles oisifs, bourgeois laborieux et rentiers honorables: loisirs et classes sociales dans 'Le Gendre de Monsieur Poirier,' " in *Les Noblesses Européenes au XIXe siècle,* 69.

21. Claude Digeon, *La Crise allemande de la pensée française* (Paris: Presses Universitaires de France, 1959), 31.

22. Lucien Prevost-Paradol, *La France Nouvelle* (Paris: Michel Lévy, 1868), 352–53.

23. Ibid., 357–58.

24. Ibid., 393.

25. Ibid., 360, 410.

26. Michel Mohrt, *Les Intellectuels devant la défaite. 1870* (Paris: Editions Corrêa, 1942), 77.

27. *Le Petit journal,* 1 Jan. 1871. Both Thomas Grimm and the philosopher Elme Caro contrast "honorable" French soldiers with the enemy's willingness to engage in espionage activity. Drawing out this comparison as an aspect of national honor, they concluded that the French had pursued "glory" and high ideals, and the Germans a utilitarian ethic of power and force.

28. Ernst Renan, *La Réforme intellectuelle et morale* (Paris: Calmann Levy, 1871), 25, 52, 67, 92, 326–27. See, on this subject, Henriette Psichari, *Renan et la guerre de 70* (Paris, Albin Michel, 1947). Claude Digeon quotes Renan's belief that France's historic royal decapitation had cost her most dearly, "leaving her a mere commoner, understanding neither the privilege of the spirit or of the sword" (*La Crise allemande,* 195).

29. See the account of this episode in Daniel Halévy, *La Fin des notables. La République des ducs* (Paris: Bernard Grasset, 1937), 253–54. Sanford Elwitt has discussed this "progressive" conservatism in the social policy of the early Third Republic. As he puts it, "Bourgeois construction of the social question . . . easily could accommodate both counter-revolution against socialism and progressive reform" (*The Third Republic Defended. Bourgeois Reform in France, 1880–1914* [Baton Rouge, La.: Louisiana State University Press, 1986], 40).

30. Quoted in Pierre Nora, "Lavisse, Instituteur National. Le petit Lavisse, évangile de la République," in *Les Lieux de mémoire* ed. Pierre Nora, vol. 1, *La République,* 253.

31. Katherine Auspitz, *The Radical Bourgeoisie. The Ligue de l'Enseignement and the Origins of the Third Republic* (Cambridge: Cambridge University Press, 1982), 19–20. The whole aim of the republican agenda, as Marie-Christine Kirk-Escalle has written, was "to create a new kind of competence, that of the republican man" (*Instaurer une culture par l'enseignement de l'histoire de France, 1876–1912. Contribution à une sémiotique de la culture* [Berne: Peter Lang, 1988], 33).

32. Charles Bigot, *Questions d'enseignement secondaire* (Paris: Hachette, 1886), 15.

33. *Le Temps,* 2 Aug. 1887.

34. The number of Masonic *ateliers* increased between 1858 and 1870 from 244 to 392. See Auspitz, *The Radical Bourgeoisie,* 78.

35. Ibid., 50.

36. Ibid., 89.

37. Ernest LeGouvé, *Un Tournoi au XIXe siècle* (Paris: Lemerre, 1872), 10.

38. Ernest LeGouvé, *La Femme en France au XIXe siècle* (Paris: Librarie de la Bibliothèque Democratique, 1873), 158–60.

39. Ibid., 178.

40. Ibid., 167–69.

41. Ibid., 190.

42. Karen Offen, "Depopulation, Nationalism, and Feminism in Fin-de-siècle France," *American Historical Review* 89 (June 1984): 648–76; "Ernest LeGouvé, A Case of Male Feminism in Nineteenth-Century French Thought," *Journal of Modern History* 58 (June 1984): 452–84. See also Steven Hause and Anne C. Kenny, *Women's Suffrage and Social Politics in the French Third Republic* (Princeton: Princeton University Press, 1984).

43. These phrases are from the feminist tract of Maugis-Ramel, *De la liberté sociale de la femme et de son égalité avec l'homme devant la loi* (Paris: Philippe Cordier, 1862), 24–45. Of all the countries in modern Europe, Maugis-Ramel held, France had best preserved the traditions of "gallantry and chivalry in its national character" (p. 27).

44. For example, Linda Clark, *Schooling the Daughters of Marianne. Textbooks and the Socialization of Girls in Modern French Primary Schools* (Albany: State University of New York Press, 1984).

45. As Auspitz puts it, "honest men sensed the parallel deficiencies of the marital and social bond," and, believing that "education does not unsex . . . ," concluded that a better education for women would reach "perfection achieved through complementarity of roles" (*The Radical Bourgeoisie,* 40–45).

46. *Le Temps,* 5 Sept. 1881.

47. Paul LaCroix, *L'Ancienne France. Le Chevalerie et les croisades* (Paris: Firmin Didot, 1886), 87–88; Emile Duvernay and René Harmand, *Le Tournoi de Chauvency en 1205. Etude sur la société et les moeurs chevaleresques au XIII siècle* (Paris: Berger-Levrault, 1905), 48.

48. After praising the sword as the "first instrument of civilization," Anatole France wrote in 1886 that "if man should become entirely pacific, he will no longer be a man, but something presently unknown to us" ("La Vie à Paris," *Le Temps,* 18 July 1886). The conflation here of man in general and man in particular was a rhetorical convention irresistible to males at this time.

49. Henri de Pène, "Les Métamorphoses du duel," preface to Brantôme, *Discours sur les duels* (Paris, 1887), iii.

50. Reported in *L'Escrime française,* 5 Oct. 1891.

51. See the breakdown of these numbers in *L'Escrime française,* 5, 22 March 1889.

52. The best source for the fortunes of the société are the memoires of Hebrard de Villeneuve, a prominent career bureaucrat, who was its president from 1882 to 1894: *Propos d'épée. 1882–1894* (Paris: Lahure, 1894).

53. See for the organization of this group the *Annuaire des maîtres d'armes français* (Paris: Bureau de l'Escrime Française, 1889), 20–28. As was the case with all the other French academies of the era, the "statutes" of the original group of thirty masters stipulate that the members must all be French and reside in Paris. Provincial masters could only have honorary memberships. Emile André discusses the original aim of the group to set standards for the trade that would eventually raise the level of teaching and the comportment of the provincial "masters" flooding into Paris (pp. 62–68).

54. See, for a description of the 1882 assault, *L'Escrime,* 22 Jan. 1882.

55. *Annuaire des maitres d'armes français,* 89–91.

56. *L'Escrime,* 19 Feb. 1882.

57. The Parisian master Camille Prévost has left an account of the assaults of 1884–86 in his *Escrimeurs et duellistes. Souvenirs et anecdotes* (Paris: Aristide Quillet, s.d.), 97–101.

58. Reported in the *Annuaire des maîtres d'armes français,* 82.

59. Daniel Cloutier, "La Rentrée—L'Escrime," *Le Moniteur officiel de la gymnastique et de l'escrime* 1, no. 2 (5 Nov. 1886): 1.

60. Louis de Caters, "L'Assaut public," *L'Escrime française,* 20 April 1889.

61. LeGouvé, *Un Tournoi au XIXe siècle,* 4–10.

62. Ibid., 8. Another contemporary, the sports journalist Henri Vallée, described him as "every bit a fencer of honor and courtesy, . . . a paladin" (*La Vie sportive en 1874* [Paris, 1874], 90–95.

63. A wine merchant who denies touches must, LeGouvé alleges, sell spoiled wine (*Un Toast à l'escrime* [Paris, 1864], 9). See also, "Coups de bouton" where one writer suggests electrifying the foils to expose those who refuse to admit their touches (*L'Escrime,* 13 Nov. 1881, 64). It is deplored also by Captain Robaglia, *Le Duel et l'escrime* (Paris: Kolb, 1890), 195; Hebrard de Villeneuve and Daniel Cloutier, two fencing purists, deplore any emphasis on touches at all. As both say, the emphasis "should be on the fashion of touching, not on the touch itself"; see de Villeneuve, *L'Escrime française,* 5 April 1891; and Cloutier, who accuses the Italians of preferring effect to form, *Deux écoles d'armes. L'Escrime et le duel en Italie et en France,* 4th ed. (Paris: Charles Lavauzelle, 1896), 112–13. The famed master Lucien Merignac had an effective way of dealing with any refusal to acknowledge his touch: "He drew back on guard, as though waiting for his opponent to announce the touch that had passed by unacknowledged"; see Louis Perrée, *Silhouettes d'escrimeurs* (Paris: Pierre Lafitte, 1901), 120. Verbally chaffing an opponent for his reticence was also bad form; the gentleman simply breaks off the engagement and shows his back to the offender; see Robaglia, *Le Duel et l'escrime,* 206.

64. LeGouvé, ibid, 10. After five minutes in an assault, he wrote, a man's worldly manner crumbles away, and "instead of a polished man of the world in yellow gloves, speaking conventional formulas, you have before you the real man, heedless or reflective, weak or firm, cunning or naive, sincere or faithless. The soul is never more visible than through the fine grill-work of the fencing mask" (p. 8).

65. Arsène Vigeant, *Ma Collection de l'escrime* (Paris: Quantin, 1892), iv–v.

66. Emile André, "A Propos d'un annuaire," in *Annuaire des maîtres d'armes Français,* 63–64.

67. Féry d'Esclands, "Les Temps en escrime," *L'Escrime française,* 5 July, 1890.

68. See on these points Georges Robert, *La Science des armes. L'assaut et les assauts publics. Le Duel et la leçon du duel* (Paris: Garnier Frères, 1887), 195–96; Villeneuve, *Propos d'épée,* 26–30.

69. See on this point generally the argument of the physical culturist Georges Hebert in *La Code de la force* (Paris: Lucien Laveur, 1911), 5–6, 15. In his preface to the *Annuaire des maîtres d'armes français,* Emile André traces the evolution

of the rapier into the lighter, contemporary épée, which, in combat, favors "*adresse over force*, and allows one to demonstrate courage and cleverness" (pp. 3–4).

70. Prince Georges Bibesco and Duc Féry d'Esclands, *Conseils pour les duels* (Paris: Alphonse Lemerre, 1900), 22.

71. Villeneuve, *Propos d'épée*, 54–55.

72. Robaglia, *Le Duel et l'escrime*, 18.

73. These themes appear regularly in the textbooks of the new republic, often with a chivalric inflection. Thus, this warning from Paul Bert, "Look, and remember this well: whoever insults the fatherland insults your mother. And if someone insults your mother you will be like a little lion, I am sure. Whoever takes one of your fellow citizens by force of arms steals your brother, and your duty is to prepare yourself for his deliverance if you are not yet strong enough to defend him" (*L'Instruction civique à l'école* [Paris: Picard-Bernheim, 1883], 29). See also Mona Ozouf, "La Tour de la France par deux enfants. Le petit livre rouge de la République," in *Les Lieux de mémoire*, ed. Nora, 299–304.

74. A verse of a song written in 1891 for the "scholarly batallions" goes, "We are the little soldiers of the batallion of hope. We are exercising our little arms to avenge the honor of France" (quoted in Kirk-Escalle, *Instaurer une culture par l'enseignement*, 132). On the batallions, see Albert Bourzac, "Les bataillons scolaires en France. Naissance, développement, disparition," and Pierre Arnaud, "Un exemple de militantisme municipal. Les bataillons scolaires à Lyon et dans le département du Rhône," in *Les Athlètes de la République. Gymnastique, sport et idéologie républicaine, 1870–1914,* ed. Pierre Arnaud (Paris: Privat, 1987), 41–62, 63–86. Jean-Louis Gay-Lescot discusses the *sociétés de tir* in "les sociétés scolaires et post-scolaires de tir dans le département de l'Ille-et-Vilaine (1907–1914)," ibid., 125–40.

75. LeGouvé, *Un Tournoi au XIXe siècle*, 16–19.

76. Adolphe Corthey, "Français et allemands. Armes blanches et armes à feu," *Le Moniteur officiel de la gymnastique et de l'escrime*, no. 42 (20 Nov. 1886): 7. Also Robert, *La Science des armes*, 214–15.

77. Féry d'Esclands, as quoted in *L'Escrime française*, 20 Feb. 1889.

78. Corthey, "Français et allemands...," 5–6; also Villeneuve, *Propos d'épée*, 53.

79. E. Cardeillac, "Duel au regiment," *L'Escrime française*, 20 Aug. 1890.

80. Dr. Watrin, "Physiologie de l'escrime," *L'Escrime*, no. 3 (23 Oct. 1881): 60–62.

81. The phrase of Anatole de la Forge in his preface to Emile André, *Le Jeu d'épée. Leçons de Jules Jacob* (Paris: Ollendorff, 1887), xxxvi. Practically the same phrase is used by Villeneuve, *Propos d'épée*, 98.

82. Cloutier, *Deux écoles d'armes*, 110.

83. G. Fradin, *Le Duel* (Chalons-sur-Marne, 1886), 3–4.

84. "Fencers of talent are pacific men," wrote the fencing-master Camille Prevost in his memoirs, *Escrimeurs et duellistes*, 270. This point is also made by Bibesco and d'Esclands in *Conseils pour les duels*, 22–23.

85. Pierre d'Hughes, *Bruneau de Laborie* (Paris: Société d'Editions Geographique, Maritimes et Coloniales, 1939), 30.

86. A typical set of rules is printed in *L'Escrime,* 30 Oct. 1881; For another see *L'Escrime française,* 5 Jan. 1890.

87. Prévost, *Escrimeurs et duellistes,* 269–70.

88. *L'Escrime française,* 20 Aug. 1890; 20 April 1891.

89. Descriptions of this transitional period in the history of the fencing hall may be found throughout the periodical press. See Adolphe Tavernier, "L'Escrime Actuelle," *Annuaire des maîtres d'armes français,* 37–42; also Albert de Saint Albin, *A Travers les salles d'armes* (Paris: A La Librarie Illustré, 1887), *passim;* Jacques Thibault has also noted this evolution in the art in *L'Influence du mouvement sportif sur l'évolution de l'éducation physique dans la France bourgeoise* (Paris: Colin, 1977), 87–88. Georges Ohnet has left us a description of these remodeled *salles* in his novel, *Six heures. La Salle d'armes* (Paris: Société d'Editions Litteraires et Artistiques, 1902). In this account, men of high standing bring their valets, who gossip in the dressing rooms while their masters fence (see esp. pp. 70–75).

90. This loss of authority by the masters was deplored by many observers, because it encouraged the hiring of inexperienced and less polished instructors. It appears many of the most famous of them managed to retain considerable reputations, and many retired comfortably on the profits from the sales of their halls. See, for example, Robaglia, *Le Duel et L'escrime,* 24–25; d'Hughes, *Bruneau de Laborie,* 30–31; Saint-Crispin, "Chronique," *L'Escrime française,* 20 Jan. 1890; Hebrard de Villeneuve, "preface" to Perrée, *Silhouettes d'escrimeurs,* vii.

91. On the different clienteles of the *salles,* see Saint-Albin, *A Travers les salles d'armes,* 62–175.

92. Richard Holt has argued that sport was seldom successful in erasing class distinctions because sporting groups were organized in the first instance on class foundations. It may be that fencing, which was not considered a sport but a traditional discipline or an esthetic, does not fit into this rubric until after the turn of the century. See *Sport and Society in Modern France* (Hamden, Conn: Archon Books, 1979), 189.

93. Hugh LeRoux, "La Vie à Paris," *Le Temps,* 21 March 1889. The worker had learned to fence in the army. LeRoux explains this incident in the standard way: "The fencing hall is a house of perfect equality. One enters here into a society that has its own conventions of honor, its code, and its bearing."

94. Cloutier, *Deux écoles d'armes,* 74. See also Louis de Caters, "Autrefois et aujourd'hui," *Annuaire des maîtres d'armes français,* 44–55; In his memoirs the fencing-master Camille Prévost tells a story that, for all his celebrated *savoir-vivre,* illustrates the view serious fencers had of upper-class dilettantes. The writer and critic Henry de Varigny hosted an assault for upper-crust "men of the world" in his elegant townhouse. In Prévost's account, the only genuine fencer present was the amateur Georges Audoin, whom Varigny had selected as his opponent for the first assault of the evening. Varigny made his appearance in a sexually ambiguous white silk outfit, complete with skirt, of "an extreme elegance." The stolid Audoin, "who disapproved of the pretentiousness of this sort of affair," thoroughly humiliated the host in their skirmish, and that was the last of such reunions in Paris, according to Prévost (*Escrimeurs et duellistes,* 114–15).

95. Villeneuve, *Propos d'épée,* 50–51.

96. Aurelian Scholl, "preface" to *Annuaire des maîtres'd'armes français*, 3.

97. Quoted in Thibault, *L'Influence du mouvement sportif*, 70.

98. Johan Huizinga, *The Waning of the Middle Ages* (New York: Doubleday, 1954), 63–64.

99. Inevitably, Thomeguex was wounded in the ensuing duel. This account is given by Camille Prévost, who had tried to mediate the fracas (*Escrimeurs et duellistes*, 212).

100. Albert de Saint-Albin tells this story in *A Travers les salles d'armes*, 19–25. As Saint-Albin tells it, San Malato shouted less often at assaults in the future, and Pons learned better to hold his tongue.

101. These duels are discussed in *L'Escrime*, 22 Nov. 1881, and in *Le Temps*, 23 Dec. 1895.

102. These are the expressions of the master-at-arms Jules Jacob, quoted in Emile André, *Le Jeu d'épée. Leçons de Jules Jacob* (Paris: Ollendorff, 1887), 12.

103. See Saint-Albin, *A Travers les salles d'armes*, 93–96. Emile André published the essence of Jacob's lessons in *Le Jeu d'épée*. An approving article appeared in *L'Escrime*, 12 Feb. 1882.

104. See the comment on this point in *L'Escrime*, 8 Jan. 1882. Camille Prévost and other masters refused to believe épée deserved a *jeu* of its own, but as the master Georges Robert put it, training in the *fleuret* alone did not prepare a man for combat on the dueling grounds. One must, he wrote, "consider the *fleuret* as a means and the *épée* as an end" (*La Science des armes*, 26). Hebrard de Villeneuve puts it somewhat differently: "The foil has an undistinguished renown; the family name, the great name, is the sword." Indeed, he argued elsewhere, to make a new science of épée combat is "to rediscover a particularly virile version of the art" (*Propos d'épée*, 50, 174). Diehards like Adolphe Corthey held the line against this innovation. See his *L'Escrime à travers les ages* (Paris: Charles DuPont, 1898), 53. As Corthey points out, the *fleuret* is the arm par excellence of defense, the *riposte* being its most effective tactic, while the épée was most useful in the offensive and might unjustly reward the aggressor.

105. See on this point, Claretie, "La Vie à Paris," *Le Temps*, 15 Feb. 1884, who also discusses the remodeling of the fencing halls into *cercles*.

106. Georges Ohnet, *Six heures, la salle d'armes* (Paris: Ollendorff, 1902), 85.

107. Carle des Perrières, "Duels d'autrefois," *L'Escrime*, no. 8, 23 Nov. 1882 120.

108. Claretie, "La Vie à Paris," *Le Temps*, 20 June 1884.

Chapter 9

1. Georges LeTainturier-Fradin, *Le Duel* (Chalons-sur-Marne, 1886), 5.

2. Georges LeTainturier-Fradin quotes from Léon XIII's injunction against the duel, arguing that, "as the church has always done, his eminence misunderstands the aim of the duel" (*Les Jurys d'honneur et le duel* [Nice: Imprimerie Spéciale, 1895], 46–50). Proponents of the duel's abolition were discouraged to learn that

Spanish Catholics were pressing the Holy See for special exemptions from the ban, from fear of losing their souls in an unavoidable duel; Henri Prudhomme, "Une Préface de M. F. Lastres," *Revue pénitentiaire* 24 (July–Nov. 1900): 1375–6.

3. Gabriel Tarde, *Etudes pénales et sociales* (Paris: Masson, 1892), 29.

4. Quoted in *Le Figaro,* 1 Dec. 1904.

5. Ibid., 2 Dec. 1904.

6. Jaurès left 100 francs in the local charity. Déroulède handed money to the farmer on whose land they had fought, to the parish church, and bought tobacco for some locals in a café where he took refreshment before crossing back to Spain. Ibid., 7, 8 Dec. 1904.

7. *Le Temps,* 6 June 1869. His seconds, who were reproached by the judge for not having tried harder to reconcile the two men, received fines of a few hundred francs. There was no additional jurisprudence on the duel after 1862, which means that the courts after that date effectively ceased their efforts to interpret new violations of the general principle. For the last item, see the ruling from 25 Nov. 1862 in *Table des vingt-deux années du M.D. Dalloz. Recueil périodique* (Paris: Dalloz, 1867), 534.

8. The words of the judge in the case of the Duc de Gramont-Caderousse, who had killed M. Dillon over a slur Dillon had made about one of the Duke's racehorses in his periodical *Le Sport.* See *Le Temps,* 26, Nov. 1862.

9. Albert Faivre and Edmond Benoit-Lévy, *Code manuel de la presse* (Paris: A. Cotillon, 1881), 146.

10. By 1881 there were forty-two separate laws regulating the press on the books. One particularly draconian law, dating from 1868, punished with a fine of 500 francs any mention in the press of an individual's private life. See Faivre and Benoit-Lévy, ibid., 170.

11. The best summary of the law and its provisions is in ibid.

12. In order to allow judges and prosecutors to weigh the seriousness of the offense, the law had to distinguish between the two different qualities of the offended man, honor and consideration. These distinctions followed legal principles in use since the seventeenth century. Honor pertained to "probity or loyalty," and touched particularly on "self-esteem, . . . the principles of conscience possessed innately by all men." Consideration, on the contrary, "is relative, and not the same for all men." Consideration was the "esteem a man acquires in the function [*état*] he exercises." This is also a precious thing, "but one may be a man of honor, and not be defamed as such, and yet suffer slander in the other moral qualities that make him a good businessman, a good lawyer, or a good doctor" (ibid., 125–27).

13. This is clear from the debate on the law reprinted by Faivre and Benoit-Lévy, ibid., 170–75.

14. In the debate in 1881, Jules Simon lamented that in the old days newspapers were serious enough that one could carry them to the tribune of the Chamber of Deputies, but the "new school of journalists see the news everywhere, in the theaters, war, the various ministries, the courts, even the racing track, looking for any facts, big or small" (*Le Temps,* 13 July 1881).

15. Quoted in Louis Rivière, "La Repression des outrages aux bonnes moeurs," *Revue pénitentiaire* 29 (June 1905): 837.

16. Yves Chartier, *La Réparation du préjudice dans la responsibilité civile* (Paris: Dalloz, 1983), 263

17. Michael B. Palmer, *Des Petits journaux aux grandes agences. Naissance du journalisme moderne* (Paris: Aubier, 1983), 83–85.

18. Guy de Maupassant, *Bel-Ami,* trans. Douglas Parmée (New York: Penguin, 1975), 149.

19. *Le Temps,* 28 April 1886.

20. See on this point, Bruneau de Laborie, *Les Lois de duel* (Paris: Manzi Joyant, 1906), 8–14; Prince Georges Bibesco and Duc Féry d'Esclands, *Conseils pour les duels* (Paris: Alphonse Lemerre, 1900), 16–19. See also the remarks of the abolitionist Ferdinand Pelletier who wrote that, under the present legal regime, "a man who seeks reparation in the courts finds himself classed among the cowards of this world, and if he should have the honor of wearing a sword [an officer], one will reward him by breaking it" ("A propos du duel," *Revue pénitentiaire* 21 [July–Aug. 1897], 1204).

21. This was precisely the argument of Deputy Arthur Ballue, who had proposed in the debate over the press law of 1881 that the court be required to ascertain the truth of a slander. As he argued, one must consider the situation of a blameless citizen who has been falsely accused of theft by a journalist. He might have a sentence passed against his accuser, but the journalist might leave the courtroom saying, "I have been condemned, because the law dictates I may not speculate on the private life of a citizen, but this conviction in no way proves the falsity of my charge, and I continue to maintain that he is a thief" (Faivre and Benoit-Lévy, *Code manuel de la presse*, 172).

22. Ruth Harris, *Murders and Madness. Medicine, Law, and Society in the Fin-de-Siècle* (Oxford: Oxford University Press, 1989), 288.

23. Ibid., 291. As an example of the latter, Harris cites the case of a wine merchant who felt obliged to seek personal vengeance on an adulterous rival when he received a signal proof of his wife's infidelity in the form of a lamb's head crowned with stag horns (p. 289).

24. *Gazette des tribuneaux,* 15 June 1872. As Harris has reminded us, this case inspired the notorious essay, *Tue-la* (Kill her) of Alexandre Dumas *fils,* which urged the same punishment on other adulterous wives. Harris, ibid., 289.

25. *Gazette des tribuneaux,* 16 June 1872. It seems likely that the "honor defense," like the duel, was more or less restricted to bourgeois milieux or above. Working-class men seem to have preferred to defend themselves by appeal to extreme states of passion; or it may be that—a more subtle point—they realized that magistrates would find the language of honor inappropriate to them. See, for instance, *Gazette des tribuneaux,* 10 April 1878.

26. My account of this case is drawn from newspaper accounts of this celebrated affair and from the transcripts published in the *Gazette des tribuneaux* from February 1872.

27. Ibid., 3 Feb. 1872.

28. Ibid., 4 Feb. 1872.

29. Ibid., 8 Feb. 1872. Among these charges was his verbal abuse of the

princess, and a vulgar altercation with a ticket-taker in 1861 about a seat reservation on a train.

30. Ibid., 4 Feb. 1872.

31. In this connection, Maître Allou read from a letter of the princess to her husband that quoted her as saying neither of them were suited for marriage, and that books, and the arts and sciences were adequate company for her. Instead of helping her case, by establishing her qualities as a *person* unsuited for subordination, it hurt her by indicating how unusual she was as a *woman*. See *Le Gaulois,* 8 Feb. 1872.

32. See *Gazette des tribuneaux,* 3, 8 Feb. 1872. There was indeed a formal stipulation against duels between officers of different ranks, but senior officers often chose to overlook this rule unless the ranks were widely separated.

33. Ibid., 8 Feb. 1872. See also the clearly skeptical account of this testimony in *Le Gaulois,* 8 Feb. 1872.

34. The fullest account of this testimony is reprinted in Bibesco's *Notes du Prince Bibesco relative à l'affaire de Bauffremont* (private printing, 1872), 30–32. Allou also called a friend of Bibesco who ascertained that Bibesco was not the sort of man who would have retreated under the menace of a caning. See *Gazette des tribuneaux,* 8 Feb. 1872.

35. See *Le Figaro,* 20 Feb. 1872, and *Le Gaulois,* 20, 22 Feb. 1872.

36. *Gazette des tribuneaux,* 20 June 1872.

37. Bibesco followed this up by publishing his *Notes du Prince Bibesco relative à l'affaire de Bauffremont,* a kind of private legal brief on the quality of his honor and the absence of Bauffremont's. The frontispiece of his pamphlet reads, "The sword punishes the calumniator, the pen confounds his calumny."

38. *Gazette des tribuneaux,* 11, 17 Feb. 1872.

39. See ibid., 26 Feb. and 4, 11 March 1876. The courts declared themselves horrified at the "challenge" the princess had thrown down to French "honor" and institutions, deploring the danger of a "contagion" of women defying the *tutelle* (legal guardianship) of their husbands. In arguing to strip the princess of her legal rights to her inheritance, the prosecutor declared it unthinkable that an "inexperienced woman be allowed the right to administer a patrimony that was intended for the welfare of her husband and children" (ibid., 4 March 1876).

40. Lemire chronicles prior legislative failures, including the most recent effort of Gustave-Paul Cluseret in 1892. See Abbé Lemire, *Proposition de loi relative au duel* (Paris: Motterez et Martinet, 1906). Some proponents of the duel also hoped to refine a system of juries of honor. The most elaborate plan for such a system was that of LeTainturier-Fradin's *Les Jurys d'honneur et le duel.* However, for the most ardent partisans of the duel, even honor juries were an unwelcome intrusion on privacy. Alfred Jarry, the iconoclastic creator of *père Ubu,* disapproved of LeTainturier-Fradin's suggestions because " . . . the great advantage of the duel is precisely that it is one of few things left for us in which we are free to manage our own affairs." ("Le Duel moderne," in *La Chandelle verte* [Paris: Livre de Poche, n.d.], 1 May 1901).

41. "Ligue contre le duel," *Revue pénitentiaire* 26 (March 1902): 485–86.

42. Henri Marion, "Duel," in *La Grande Encyclopédie* (Paris: H. Lamirant, n.d.), 9.

43. See on these themes, Harris, *Murders and Madness,* 80–124; Nye, *Crime, Madness, and Politics in Modern France,* 97–131.

44. See the general discussion in Georges Gurvitch, *Sociology of Law* (London: Routledge and Kegan Paul, 1973), esp. 1–52; and, for the French tradition, pp. 83–115.

45. Emile Worms, *Les Attentats à l'honneur* (Paris: Perrin, 1890), 10–11.

46. Ibid., 80.

47. Eugène Terraillon, *L'Honneur. Sentiment et principe moral* (Paris: Alcan, 1912), 7–11.

48. On collective psychology see, *inter alia,* Robert A. Nye, *The Origins of Crowd Psychology. Gustave LeBon and the Crisis of Mass Psychology in the Third Republic* (London: Sage Publications, 1975).

49. See Terraillon, *L'Honneur* 73–78. For a particularly unfriendly account of this phenonenon see Augustin Hamon, *Psychologie du militaire professionnel* (Paris: Bureau de La Revue Socialiste, 1894). The sociologist René Worms, in *Organicisme et société* (Paris: V. Giard, 1896), 127, distinguished between "natural" family honor, and the more "artificial" sort that defines professions and corporate groups.

50. Citing Strindberg as his primary example, Georges Palante argues that since "conjugal honor" is the model for all other types, women in the modern era have gained the the upper hand in manipulating the honorable sentiments of men; see "L'Embourgeoisement du sentiment de l'honneur," *La Plume* 14 (1 July 1902): 774–75.

51. Paul Desjardins, "L'Empreinte de noblesse," *La Grande Revue* 13, no. 19 (10 Oct. 1909): 518.

52. Emile Beaussire, *Les Principes du droit* (Paris: Alcan, 1888), 4–8.

53. Ibid., 371–72. See on individual defense of honor leading to public benefit, Terraillon, *L'Honneur*, 47. Beaussire also explains convincingly why French slander suits do not produce large monetary awards for the plaintiffs. Judges and juries, he writes, will not repair more than the "material" damage suffered by someone publically libeled. The "moral" damage one experiences is, by nature, irreparable by material compensation. Unlike the way British civil suits amalgamate the moral and the material damages in large awards, the legal process in France presumed that one would seek moral redress on one's personal account (see pp. 387–88).

54. See *Le Temps,* 2 Feb.; 6 April; 9 May 1877. The paper expressed hope that a recent downturn in dueling incidents might mean it would naturally disappear.

55. Ibid., 27 Feb. 1883.

56. Ibid., 27 Feb. and 12 March 1883.

57. Terraillon, *L'Honneur*, 228.

58. Worms, *Les Attentats à l'honneur*, 146. The key to understanding the phenomenon of exclusion, as Paul Hervieu pointed out in 1888, lay in a society's willingness to give public voice to a widely felt disdain that would ordinarily be kept secret. He quoted Schopenhauer to demonstrate that "honor does not consist of the opinion others have of our merit, but uniquely in the manifestations of that

opinion. As a result, the world may scorn us as much as it desires, but our honor is in no way affected so long as no one permits himself to utter it openly." However, once " . . . one person has announced his disdain for us, in one stroke our honor has been damaged, perhaps lost, unless we find some way to retrieve it" ("L'Enschopenhauerderie," *Le Monde illustré* [20 Oct. 1888], 243).

59. Rémy de Gourmont, *Le Dépêche de Toulouse,* 15 Nov. 1908. My emphasis.

60. Ferreus, *Annuaire du duel* (Paris: Perrin, 1891). Desjardins called it the "dossier of honor of my contemporaries" (p. v).

61. Carl A. Thimm, *A Complete Bibliography of Fencing and Dueling* (London: John Lane, 1896), 291–313.

62. Tarde, *Etudes pénales et sociales,* 34.

63. Ibid., 36. Robert Baldick supplies similar figures for Italy for the period 1875–89. He claims there were 2,759 duels in that period with a mortality rate of less than 2 percent. Military duels made up 30 percent of the total; see *The Duel. A History of Dueling* (London: Chapman and Hall, 1965), 144.

64. See McAleer, "The Last Teutonic Knights," 317–25. He cites a figure of 2,500 between 1880 and 1893; Istvan Deak, *Beyond Nationalism. A Social and Political History of the Hapsburg Officer Corps* (New York, Oxford University Press, 1990), 126–38.

65. McAleer, ibid., 195–97. As Ute Frevert has said in her study of the German duel, "The great majority of duels, indeed, went unreported either in autobiographies or in police and court records or in the press" ("Bourgeois Honor," 269).

66. I have found references in the press to dozens of duels in the 1880s not mentioned in the *Annuaire du duel.* This was particularly the case during dueling epidemics, such as in the late spring of 1888. One writer noted eleven duels between 25 April and 3 May, complaining that "one will end by indicating one's *affaires* on an agenda like a young girl her dance partners in a *carnet de bal*" (*Le Petit journal,* 3 May 1888). Ferreus lists only six duels in this period (*Annuaire du duel,* 220–22).

67. *La Libre parole,* 27 Aug. 1892.

68. Th. Sisson, "Restaurant pour duels," *Le Temps,* 8 Aug. 1893.

69. Vigeant is quoted in LeTainturier-Fradin, *Les Jurys d'honneur et le duel,* 119.

70. See, for instance, Adolphe Tavernier, *L'Art du duel,* new ed. (Paris: Marpon et Flammarion, 1885), 156; Croabbon, *La Science du point d'honneur,* 270–71; Bibesco and Féry d'Esclands, *Conseils pour les duels,* 16–17.

71. See *Le Journal* for 8, 23, 24, 25, 28 Nov. 1911.

72. See Tarde, *Etudes pénales et sociales,* 40–46; also Général Bourelly, *Le Duel et l'escrime dans l'armée en France et l'étranger* (Paris: A. Pedone, 1900), 19–25; Dr. Charles Teissier, *Du Duel au point de vue médico-légal et particulièrement dans l'armée* (Lyon: Storck, 1890).

73. Tarde, *Etudes pénales et sociales,* 39.

74. On this distinction see Palmer, *Des Petits journaux aux grandes agences,* 70–71.

75. From an interview in *Le Temps,* 23 April 1886.

76. Laborie, *Les Lois du duel,* 124–26; Croabbon, *La Science du point d'honneur,* 89–99; Bibesco and Féry d'Esclands praise the editor who steps in when the actual author is indisposed. They cite the case of Edouard Hervé, editor of the *Journal de Paris,* who fought Edmond About on account of a text he had never even seen (*Conseils pour les duels,* 11–12).

77. Aurelian Scholl, *L'Esprit du boulevard,* 3d ed. (Paris: Victor Havard, n.d.), 1.

78. This incident was widely reported in the press. See the extended account in *L'Escrime française,* 5 Sept. 1890.

79. Maupassant, *Bel-Ami,* 173–79.

80. Maupassant astutely describes the effect of the duel on *Bel-Ami:* " . . . he made it his specialty to rail against the lowering of moral standards, the general weakening of character, the decline of patriotism and the anemia that was sapping the French sense of honour!" (p. 194). Aurélien Scholl portrays this aspect of journalism in his collected articles from *Le Figaro.* The journalist, he wrote, was not the advocate of a mere "cause," but a disinterested defender of an "idea!" (*L'Esprit du boulevard,* 54). In a post-duel trial in 1872, Arthur Ranc defended his actions by invoking the political outlook of his paper, *La République française,* and his "corporation" of fellow journalists (*Le Temps,* 1 Aug. 1872). In another trial the same year, Paul de Cassagnac explained his duel with Edouard Lockroy as a defense of the emperor against Lockroy's slanders (*Gazette des tribuneaux,* 3 July 1872).

81. See *Le Temps,* 2 Feb. and 20 April 1887.

82. Carle des Perrières, *Le Gaulois,* 12 June 1887. Des Perrières argued vigorously that the right to slap another man, once reserved for the aristocracy, was "one of the conquests of the democratic world." No one may hide behind some superior principle when he has been struck by another man, however humble he may be. I will not, he averred, leave to someone else the responsibility of defending my civil or private status; "and I will never inquire [of someone who strikes me] if he has a criminal record [which would disqualify him]; if I know his name, that is enough."

83. *Le Temps,* 16 June 1887.

84. See *Le XIXe siècle,* 16 June 1887; *République française,* 16 June 1887.

85. The actual numbers are 183 duels, of which 15 resulted in serious injury. As I have said, these are estimates based on the motives and affiliations of duelers listed in the *Annuaire du duel.* They do not include all the duels that occurred in these years, and my description of these as journalistic duels rather than political or some other kind must be regarded as provisional, lacking as we do more detailed evidence. These figures do, however, probably give a rough estimate of the proportions of kinds of duels and their dangers.

86. *Le Temps,* 17 July 1889.

87. Ibid., 14 Dec. 1889.

88. In the letter, sent after the duel to a friend, Belz wrote that "I have done an abominable thing in killing a friend. But I have done a fine thing for my party

and for my forthcoming candidacy. Ah, the press and public opinion! What a send-off! (ibid., 16 Dec. 1889).

89. Ibid., 14 Dec. 1889.

90. Ibid., 15, 16 Dec. 1889.

91. For Barrès's "livre de parlement," see Jean Bécarud, *Maurice Barrès et le parlement de la belle époque (1906–1914)* (Paris: Plon, 1987), 89. As Louis Barthou wrote in 1923, in the tribune, "What was required was to be sincere, to lie neither to others or to oneself." Or, more subtly, "It is necessary to be loyal: in politics as in everything else, the supreme cleverness lies in being honest" (*La Politique* [Paris: Hachette, 1923], 48, 52).

92. This is not "party" loyalty in the more narrow modern sense of being lined up by the party whip for a crucial vote. Parties in the modern British, American, or even French sense did not exist at this point in the history of French parliaments. A man was not required to adhere to all the positions of the radical socialist party, for instance, but he must be "sure" or have "given his guarantees" about any particular issue. Pierre Guiral and Guy Thullier, *La Vie quotidienne des députés en France de 1871–1914* (Paris: Hachette, 1980), 170.

93. Jean-Pierre Rioux, "Le Palais-Bourbon de Gambetta à de Gaulle," *Les Lieux de mémoire,* ed. Pierre Nora, vol. 2, *La Nation,* 500.

94. Jules Simon, "Mon petit journal," *Le Temps,* 21 May 1890.

95. Hughes LeRoux, "La Vie de Paris," ibid., 22 May 1890; "L'Evolution de l'injure en politique," ibid., 28 Dec. 1896. Gugliemo Ferrero wrote that the "violent emotions" expressed in parliamentary debates were a neurotic condition of the fin de siècle in "Les Névroses parlementaires," *Revue des revues* 8 (Jan. 1894): 6.

96. Guiral and Thullier, *La Vie quotidienne des députés,* 244–46.

97. Aubertin expressed these views in *L'Eloquence politique et parlementaire en France avant 1789,* as quoted in Jean-Pierre Rioux, "Le Palais-Bourbon," 500.

98. The editorialist of "Moeurs parlementaires," deplored the "rigid etiquette of political fencing" (*Le Temps,* 22 Feb. 1896). As the political commentator Bosq wrote of Clemenceau, he was "fierce in his attack, terrible in his ripost, he senses and touches you through the chinks in your armor with a marvelous dexterity" (*Nos chers souverains* [Paris: Juvan, 1898], 60).

99. *Le Temps,* 4 Sept. 1893.

100. Barthou, *La Politique,* 45. As Guiral and Thullier put it, "[deputies] were often obliged to continue their oratory duels on the dueling ground" (*La Vie quotidienne des députés,* 304).

101. In an incident in July of 1895, the minister of agriculture, Antoine Gadaud, was challenged by Léon Mirman. The editorial writer from *Le Temps* doubted he could refuse to duel for fear of encouraging the parliamentary opposition; see *Le Temps,* 1 July 1895.

102. Larroumet used the usual successful phrase: "I leave to public opinion the right to judge the behavior of Henri Bauer" (*Le Temps,* 17 Feb. 1891).

103. On 12 Nov. 1884, *Le Temps* reported the case of three functionaries of the ministry of the interior who challenged Deputy Georges Laguerre after ques-

tions had been raised about their work. For another episode of functionaries settling their differences by means of the duel, see Guy Thullier, *Bureaucratie et bureaucrates en France au XIXe siècle* (Genève: Droz, 1980), 549.

104. *Le Temps,* 31 March 1887. The duel did not take place immediately, since the chamber speaker placed M. Douville-Maillefeu under house discipline for his intemperate overreaction to a colleague. But the chamber, fearing a precedent that would limit the independence of members, overturned this ruling, permitting the duel to take place; see *Le Temps,* 1, 4, 6, 7 April 1887.

105. Saint-Léger was fined 200 francs for his provocation. See the trial transcript in the *Gazette des tribuneaux* 18 Jan. 1872.

106. Denis Brogan has an excellent account of this political imbroglio in which he appreciates fully the role that Clemenceau's reputation as a duelist played in veiling his involvement in the fiasco. *The Development of Modern France. 1870– 1939* (New York: Harper, 1966), 269–95.

107. Clémenceau was quoted as saying about the incident on the chamber floor: "Good, this makes it an affair between the two of us." The combatants exchanged three shots at twenty-five paces with no result, but Déroulède's seconds had hoped for an even more dangerous variety: three shots followed by a sword duel if no balls found their mark. When this was rejected by Clémenceau's men, Déroulède replied, "I have agreed to expose myself to the pistol of M. Clémenceau, but he has refused to expose himself to my sword. The public will judge" (*Le Temps,* 23, 25 Nov. 1892).

108. *Le Gaulois,* 18 July 1886. Lareinty, concerned about appearances, questioned whether Boulanger's pistol had misfired or whether he had simply fired in the air, which would have given the general the moral advantage. The *Le Temps* of 19 July 1886 hinted more darkly that the official transcript left that issue open, allowing Boulanger's friends to draw conclusions generous to him: "It is thus that legends are born; but take care that they do not turn against their object." Several radical papers published special editions highlighting the general's courageous behavior. See *Le Radical, Le Rappel,* and *Le Soleil* of 18 July 1886. See in general on this episode, William D. Irvine, *The Boulanger Affair Reconsidered. Royalism, Boulangism, and the Origins of the Radical Right in France* (New York: Oxford University Press, 1989), 35.

109. *Le Temps,* 27 July 1887. Realizing this would be a pretext for a duel, some of the press announced Ferry's speech as an "outrage" (*Petit Parisien,* 28 July 1887). In *La Justice,* 27 July 1887, Camille Pelletan wrote of the "incredible violence" of Ferry's language.

110. *Le Gaulois* saw it as a battle between two republican factions, the one favoring "all-out peace," the other "all-out war" (30 July 1887). Anatole de la Forge, a renowned expert on the duel, said flatly that Boulanger was defending his officer's epaulettes, and should "spit in Ferry's face" if the latter refused him satisfaction (*Le Gaulois,* 31 July 1887).

111. *Le Gaulois,* 31 July 1887.

112. Both varieties were admitted by Chatauvillard (*Essai sur le duel,* 111–20) in the 1830s. Croabbon still recognized both in the fin de siècle: Croabbon, *La Science du point d'honneur,* 201–21. Paul de Cassagnac, who was perhaps the fairest

and most dependable judge of these matters in the era, argued that the "aimed" duel was only appropriate nowadays for outraged husbands, not for the less important offenses of political life (*Le Gaulois,* 3 Aug. 1887).

113. Most handbooks on the duel confirm Proust and Raynal's point. The choice of both weapons and conditions falls only to the man who has received a *voie de fait* (blow). See Croabbon, ibid. 46–48. Boulanger's men published an official *procès-verbal* vindicating their actions; Ferry's men wrote their champion a letter explaining their actions that was also published. See *Le Gaulois,* 2, 3 Aug. 1887, or *Le Temps,* 3 Aug. 1887.

114. *Le Gaulois,* 5 Aug. 1887; *Petit Parisien,* 10 Aug. 1887.

115. *La Lanterne,* 3 Aug. 1887; *Le Radical,* 3 Aug. 1887; *L'Evènement,* 3 Aug. 1887.

116. Charles Laurent, *Le Paris,* 4 Aug. 1887. For similar sentiments, see also Clemenceau's *Le Justice,* 3, 4, 5 Aug. 1887.

117. For example, *La République française, Le Soleil, Liberté,* 3 Aug. 1887.

118. "Le réculade," *Petit Parisien,* 4 Aug. 1887.

119. *Gil Blas,* 4 Aug. 1887.

120. Arthur Ranc, *Le Temps,* 6 Aug. 1887.

121. See on Boulanger's new ties to royalists, Irvine, *The Boulanger Affair Reconsidered,* 73–106.

122. Quoted in Brogan, *The Development of Modern France,* 203. This rebuke was delivered in the Chamber of Deputies on 4 June 1888.

123. Camille Pelletan, "Monsieur Boulanger," *La Justice,* 13 July 1888.

124. *Le Petit journal,* 13 July 1888.

125. The latter phrase was italicized in the transcript printed in *Gil Blas,* 14 July 1888.

126. *Le Petit Parisien,* 15 July 1888; *Le Matin,* 14 July 1888.

127. *Le Petit Parisien,* 16 July 1888. The *procès-verbal* of the duel may be found in all the papers on 15 July.

128. *La Cocarde,* 14 July 1888.

129. Emmanuel Arène, "Série à la blanche," *Le Matin,* 16 July 1888.

130. See, for example, "Duels entre civils et militaires," *Le Gaulois,* 16 July 1888; Jules Delafosse, "Choses d'hier," *Le Matin,* 17 July 1888.

131. *Le Petit journal,* 16 July 1888. The same story reported that many in the crowd at Longchamps were heard to say of Boulanger, "Just two years ago he was here on his black horse, and today there he is in his bed." See also the description of the crowd's acclaim of Floquet in *La Justice,* 14 July 1888.

132. *Le Matin,* 16 July 1888.

133. *Le Gaulois,* 18, 19 July 1888.

134. *Le Matin,* 14, 16 July 1888.

135. Charles Benoist wrote in 1891 that Boulanger had been killed "by a sword stroke in Neuilly" (*Croquis parlementaires* [Paris: Perrin, 1891], xvii); Gabriel Tarde, a mordant critic of the duel, admitted in 1892 that "the sword thrust the General received, in the face of all expectations, was the first serious blow to this pseudo-Caesar, and dimmed his star to a considerable degree" (*Etudes pénales et sociales,* 15).

136. Computed from the *Annuaire du duel* of duels where both men were active politicians.

137. Gambetta to Léonie Léon, letters nos. 393 and 394, 20, 21 Nov. 1878. Daniel Halévy and Emile Pilléas, eds., *Lettres de Gambetta, 1868–1882* (Paris: Grasset, 1938). The conditions of the duel were extremely safe, one shot at thirty-five paces. See J. P. T. Bury, *Gambetta's Final Years. The Era of Difficulties, 1877–1882* (London: Longman, 1982), 95–97. For a mocking account, see *Le Temps,* 22 Nov. 1878.

138. A duel between two journalists in Grenoble in 1887 was the occasion for the wounding of one and the dishonor of the other. Directly violating the rules of the sword duel, Gustave Nacquet seized the sword of his opponent, M. Menvielle, with his left hand, and ran him through with his own weapon. Menvielle cried, "Coward, it's a *coup de juif.*" Nacquet's editor, who was his second on this occasion, declared to him, "In one second you have lost the fruit of thirty years of honesty [*honnêteté*]. There is now nothing left for you but to retire" (*Le Temps,* 20 July 1887). In the subsequent trial, Nacquet got less a penalty than he might have partly because in his six previous duels, he had conducted himself irreproachably (*Gazette des tribuneaux,* 1, 2, 4, 11 Aug. 1887).

139. *Annuaire du duel.*

140. The trial was reported in *Le Temps,* 4, 5 Aug. 1876. The case echoed down the years as an exemplar of *déloyauté. Le Temps* noted Feuilerade's death on 20 April 1886.

141. *Gazette des tribuneaux,* 30, 31 May 1885. One of Chapuis's seconds made it clear that his client "simply did not want the word 'excuses' to be publicly pronounced."

142. After the duel had been decided on, one Dunquerquer recalled a conversation with Chapuis in which the lieutenant boasted of having killed men and of being the best blade in his regiment, to which the local responded, "Yes, but the other men you have killed were not Dunquerquers" (*Gazette des tribuneaux,* 30 May 1885).

143. The prickly sensitivity of Dunquerquers was revealed in indignant remarks about the "honor" of local fencing halls by the chief magistrate at the suggestion that Deikerel's *gaffe* was the result of inexpert training that was somehow not up to Parisian standards (ibid.).

144. Ibid., 31 May and 4 Aug. 1885. On the Catholic moral environment of the Nord, see Bonnie G. Smith, *Ladies of the Leisure Class. The Bourgeoises of Northern France in the Nineteenth Century* (Princeton: Princeton University Press, 1981).

145. *Gazette des tribuneaux,* 26 June 1888.

146. The testimony of one of Dupuis's seconds, ibid.

147. This was the opinion of Féry d'Esclands, who testified at the trial; see *Gazette des tribuneaux,* 26 June 1888.

148. *Gazette des tribuneaux,* 26, 27 June 1888.

149. This was Ritter's testimony in the trial that followed Appleton's death (ibid., 2 April 1873).

150. The chief prosecutor, whose job it was to find holes in the honor defense

of Ritter bravely admitted that "under my magistrate's robe one will find the sentiments of a man of the world" (ibid., 3 April 1873).

151. *Le Temps,* 3 Sept. 1883. Mme Hughes later shot the detective in the back after a subsequent trial, and was later acquitted. For a similar example of feminine initiative, see Edward Berenson, *The Trial of Madame Caillaux* (Berkeley: University of California Press, 1992).

152. Edmond de Goncourt, *Paris and the Arts, 1851–96: From the Goncourt Journal,* ed. and trans. George J. Becker and Edith Philips, vol. 2 (Ithaca, N.Y.: Cornell University Press, 1971), 256.

153. Ibid., 256–60.

154. These quotations are from a letter Drumont published in the Catholic paper, *Le Monde,* reprinted in *Le Temps,* 23 April 1886. Jewish champions also rose to defend their women. Camille Dreyfus provoked a duel with Drumont over a remark Drumont had made in *La Libre parole* that upper-class Jewish women were "sluts," by calling him the "son of a madman" (*Le Temps,* 31 Aug. 1893).

155. Edouard Drumont, *La France juive,* vol. 1 (Paris: Marpon, 1886), 9.

156. Jules Soury made the point in 1906 by speaking of dogs: "The Jew . . . is to the aryan what an ignoble and degenerate mutt, which is noisy and impudent, cruel to beings weaker than itself, but cowardly and servile under the whip, is to a noble Scotch greyhound" (*La Libre parole,* 4 July 1906). On the general theme of Jewish sexual perversions, see Pierre Birnbaum, *Un Mythe politique: "La République juive" de Léon Blum à Pierre Mendès-France* (Paris: Fayard, 1988), 196–230.

157. Dreyfus's polemic with Rochefort illustrates the way that the word "Jew" was used as an insult in this era, and the preference for members of the Jewish community for the term "Israelite." "Which of us is more Jewish?" Dreyfus asked of Rochefort, "No merchant of Venice or second-hand clothes dealer from Francfort ever showed himself more greedy than that man of letters" (*Le Temps,* 29 April 1886). For Drumont's duels with Charles Laurent and Arthur Meyer, see *Le Temps,* 20, 26 April 1886.

158. Pierre Birnbaum has noted the number of unusually bitter affairs of honor in this era which appear to have been the result of anti-Semitic slander. He lists Camille and Maxime Dreyfus, Bernard Lazare, Maurice Schwob, Henry Bernstein (who had at least six duels), Catulle Mendès, Joseph Reinach, and many others (*Un Mythe politique,* 230–36).

159. *Le Journal,* 15 Oct. 1912.

160. *La Libre parole,* 13 Aug. 1892. Drumont's colleague, Félicien Pascal, wrote sarcastically about Jews "who imagine themselves our equals in all things, playing at being gentlemen by posing as swordsmen" (*La Libre parole,* 28 Aug. 1892).

161. In Loewenberg's analysis of Herzl's writings and fantasy life, he finds much evidence of Herzl's identity with the image of the gallant knight, the man of honor, and the courageous warrior. See *Decoding the Past. The Psychohistorical Approach* (Berkeley, Calif.: University of California Press, 1969), 101–35. George Mosse discusses the parallel efforts by Max Nordau and others in the 1890s to

encourage the development of the "muscled" Jew who would replace the wizened, shrunken Jew of the stereotype. See *Nationalism and Sexuality,* 42.

162. Goncourt, *Paris and the Arts,* 234–36. Goncourt also describes the preliminaries on Drumont's side. He entertained dozens of well-wishers, heard that some Carmelite nuns were praying for him, and was in ebullient spirits generally.

163. This print is reproduced in Phillip Dennis Cate, "The Paris Cry: Graphic Artists and the Dreyfus Affair," in *The Dreyfus Affair. Art, Truth, Justice,* ed. Norman L. Kleeblatt (Berkeley, Calif.: University of California Press, 1987), 66.

164. *Le Temps,* 1 June 1892. Charles Laurent later attempted to flush out the anonymous officer who was the source of this "information" by publishing a violently insulting open letter in *Le Matin:* "I wish to speak about the French officer, who, if he exists at all, is a coward . . . " (24 June 1892). See on this episode and on the rise of anti-Semitism in the army, William Serman, *Les Officiers français dans la nation* (Paris: Aubier, 1982), 102–03.

165. Quoted in *Le Temps,* 1 June 1892. My emphasis.

166. Ibid., 22 June 1892.

167. Ibid., 25 June 1892.

168. Quoted from *L'Echo de Paris* in ibid., 25 June 1892.

169. Ibid., 27 June 1892. See also the editorial in *Le Temps* of 25 June for a stern disapproval of those who would divide us into "races." See also the column of Jules Simon and the interview of Mayer's commander at the Ecole Polytechnique (who had authorized the duel) on the young man's irreproachable conduct in defense of his honor in *Le Temps,* 28 June 1892.

170. Ibid., 30 Aug. 1892.

171. Ibid., 31 Aug. 1892. The assizes president intervened at this point to rebuke Cremieux-Foa, telling him he might have spared Mayer's life "by one less indiscretion."

172. Ibid., 31 Aug. 1892.

173. *La Libre parole,* 30 Aug. 1892.

174. See Henri Rochefort in *L'Intransigéant* and *Le Temps,* 2 Sept. 1892.

175. *Le Temps,* 3 Sept. 1892.

176. Ibid., 2 Sept. 1892. In interviews he accorded the press, Trochu claims he responded to Cremieux-Foa's insults by telling him he would perhaps merit being given satisfaction now "if he had put his chest between Captain Mayer and the sword of the Marquis de Morès."

177. *La Campagne Antisémitique. Les duels. Les résponsabilités. mémores avec pièces justificatives* (Paris: Alcan-Lévy, 1892). Cremieux-Foa saves most of his invective here for the "Judas" in the officer corps who refused to come forth and admit he was the author of anti-Jewish slanders (p. 73).

178. Bredin, *The Affair,* 483.

179. Desjardins, *Annuaire du duel.*

180. Albert Carré, Maurice Desvilliers, "Un Duel s'il vous plaît," produced 16 Nov. 1885 at the Théatre de la Renaissance. See the review by Francisque Sarcey, *Le Temps,* 16 Nov. 1885.

181. See the report of the incident in ibid., 25 April 1891. LeGrand was in the habit of going to the theater with his fencing comrades Alphonse de Aldama and

Jacques Abbatucci and behaving pretty much as he pleased. In an earlier incident at the Théâtre de Chateau-D'Eau, LeGrand was admonished by another patron, and responded by exchanging cards with the man, later wounding him in three places (ibid., 14 Oct. 1886). See also the account of a theater fracas in Menton in ibid., 1 Jan. 1894.

182. See the remarks of Arsène Vigeant in *L'Echo de Paris,* 13 Aug. 1889.

183. For the news accounts and trial of this case see *Le Temps,* 2, 3, 4, 5, 6 March and 16 May 1895. The morning of the combat, Alis took his chocolate as usual with his wife, who later claimed to have noticed nothing amiss in her husband's manner. The seconds took special precautions to make the sword duel a harmless one, stationing the men at close quarters to prevent the kind of headlong charge that sometimes caused amateurs serious harm, but to no avail.

184. Reported in ibid., 7 Jan. 1870.

185. Ibid., 6 Feb. 1870.

186. Ibid., 5 Oct. 1882. My emphasis. This duel is interesting because it shows that the "Jewish" duel was not a sole matter of Jews responding with sword and pistol to anti-Semitic affront, but a function of their appropriation of a ritual common to bourgeois society in general.

187. For an account of the incident see ibid., 9, 10 June 1897, and *Le Matin,* 10 June. There is also an account in Philippe Jullian, *Prince of Aesthetes. Count Robert de Montesquiou,* trans. Jon Haylock and Francis King (New York: Viking, 1965), 169–72. In his memoirs Montesquiou passed the whole incident off as a matter of social climbing on Regnier's part; see Robert de Montesquiou, *Mémoires,* vol. 1 (Emstre-Paul Frères, 1923), 279.

188. See *Le Temps,* 22 May 1888.

189. Ibid., 22 July 1897.

190. See Péladan's original letter in *La France,* 29 April 1891, and his subsequent comments in *Le Temps,* 2, 5 May 1891.

191. Laborie, *Les Lois du duel,* 14–25.

192. See *Le Temps,* 3 July 1892. This episode occurred during a veritable frenzy of duels, including the first set of "Jewish" duels.

193. The theme of two friends fighting a duel, but deepening their friendship as a result was a common one. See the example from a story of Jules Janin in *Contes et nouvelles,* vol. 1 (Paris: Librairie du Bibliophile, 1876), 141–55.

194. Victor Turner, *The Ritual Process. Structure and Anti-Structure* (Ithaca, N.Y.: Cornell University Press, 1969), 94–97.

Chapter 10

1. Georges Breittmayer, *Code de l'honneur et du duel. Après guerre août 1914* (Paris: Devambez, 1918), 5.

2. Ibid., 9–17.

3. M. Garrigues, *Propos sur le duel* (Toulouse, 1971), 10–17. See also Billacois, *Le Duel,* 309–15.

4. Michel Foucault, *Surveiller et punir. Naissance de la prison* (Paris: Gallimard, 1975), 175.

5. Alain Ehrenberg, *Le Corps militaire. Politique et pédagogie en démocratie* (Paris: Aubier, 1983), 10. Ehrenberg's emphasis.

6. Nye, *Crime, Madness, and Politics in Modern France,* 310–29; Eugene Weber, *The Nationalist Revival in France, 1905–1914* (Berkeley, Calif.: University of California Press, 1959).

7. Gabriel Tarde, "L'Atavisme moral," in *Etudes pénales et sociales,* 141. Dominique Maingueneau discusses the strengths and defects of this "survival" of "Gaulish savagery" in the school textbooks of the Third Republic; see, in general, *Les Livres d'école de la République, 1870–1914: Discours et idéologie* (Paris: Le Sycomore, 1979).

8. See Sanford Elwitt, *The Third Republic Defended. Bourgeois Reform in France, 1880–1914* (Baton Rouge, La.: Louisiana State University Press, 1986), 10–12. See also on solidarism, John A. Scott, *Republican Ideas and the Liberal Tradition in France* (New York, 1966), and especially William Logue, *From Philosophy to Sociology. The Evolution of French Liberalism* (DeKalb, Ill.: Northern Illinois University Press, 1983), 185–201. Of modern commentators, Linda Clark has appreciated most thoroughly the biological underpinnings of solidarism; see *Social Darwinism in France* (Tuscaloosa, Ala.: University of Alabama Press, 1984), 45–75.

9. Jean-Marie Guyau, *L'Irreligion de l'avenir* (Paris: Alcan, 1909), 352. See also his *Esquisse d'une morale sans obligation ni sanction* (Paris, 1884), where he roots the idea of moral obligation in organic life.

10. Paul Gerbod, "L'Ethique héroique en France (1870–1914)," *Revue historique* 268, no. 2 (1983): 409–12.

11. Ibid., 412–18.

12. Capitaine Richard, *Le Courage civique chez les enfants de France* (Paris: Combet, 1901), 11–13.

13. Ibid., 13.

14. Edmond Mulle, *Le Courage et la charité dans la France contemporaine* (Paris: Firmin-Didot, n.d.), 9.

15. Thibault, *L'Influence du mouvement sportif sur l'évolution de l'éducation physique dans l'enseignement secondaire français,* 13. Richard Holt discusses the rivalry between Pierre de Coubertin's *Union des sociétés français des sports athlétiques* and Paschal Grousset's *Ligue national d'éducation physique* in the early 1890s in *Sport and Society in Modern France,* 63–67.

16. Commenting on sport at the college of La Flèche in 1891, G. Strely observed that that "male" education in sport being given now at the school provided a generation of young men to be "initiated into the sublime laws of modern chivalry" ("Au prytanée de la flèche," *Revue athlétique,* 25 Feb. 1891, 68 [65–75]).

17. Quoted in *Sports athlétiques,* 21 Jan. 1893, 7. For a similar emphasis, see Jean Izoulet, *La Cité moderne et la métaphysique de la sociologie* (Paris: Alcan, 1894), 211.

18. Guy Laurens, "Qu'est-ce qu'un champion? La Compétition sportive en

Languedoc au début du siècle," *Annales E.S.C.,* no. 5 (Sept.–Oct. 1990): 1051–54.

19. Ibid., 1062–64.

20. Paschal Grousset, "La Morale et le physique," *L'Education physique,* May 1889, 1.

21. Pierre de Coubertin, *Revue athlétique* 1, no. 6 (25 July 1890): 389–91. The *Revue athlétique* was Coubertin's chief propaganda organ in the 1890s. His colleague, General Lewal, explicitly linked the ideals of amateur sport to the military virtues of "honor," "absolute rectitude," "a horror of intrigue, egoism, or underhanded means for gaining success"; see "La Carrière militaire et le service obligatoire," *Revue athlétique* 1, no. 3 (25 March 1890): 139–53. On Coubertin and his obsession with the ideals of amateurism and aristocratic "prowess," see John J. MacAloon, *This Great Symbol. Pierre de Coubertin and the Origins of the Modern Olympic Games* (Chicago: University of Chicago Press, 1981), 14–17 and *passim.* On Coubertin and the psychology and hygiene of modern sport, see John Hoberman, *Sport and Political Ideology* (Austin: University of Texas Press, 1984), 129–36.

22. "Causerie du samedi," *Sports athlétiques,* 13 Feb. 1892, 3.

23. Holt, *Sport and Society in Modern France,* 53.

24. This process may be followed through individual sports. In cycling, for instance, the pioneer amateur cycling association was the *Union vélocipédique de France,* which published an *Annuaire* with the rules gentlemen must observe in cycling competitions. It was assumed that a competitor's individual sense of honor would preserve the integrity of the competition in contests that were not yet officially refereed. See the *Annuaire de 1887* of the *Union* for an example of these early regulations, esp. pp. 6–13 and 34–50. For further example of the conflict of professional and amateur principles in the early cycling movement, see *Les Sports athlétiques* between January 1892 through early 1893.

25. Gaston Raphael, "L'Allemagne et l'éducation virile," *La Grande revue* 13, no. 9 (10 Oct. 1909): 566.

26. In his inaugural speech to the *Ligue nationale d'éducation physique* in 1888, Marcellin Berthelot said, "If brothers must be men, citizens, and energetic soldiers, . . . sisters ought to be the mothers of robust families, capable of fulfilling completely the sacred duty of maternity" (*Bulletin de la ligue nationale d'éducation physique,* no. 1 [Nov. 1888]: 2–3). P. d'Aliste, on the other hand, deplored the "deformation" of women's bodies in cycling competitions, and the loss of "dignity" to the sport as a whole at the "pitiable" spectacle of a race-ending sprint of women, "their hair blowing in the wind or plastered on their foreheads" (*Sports athlétiques,* 14 Jan. 1893).

27. Mulle, *Le Courage et la charité,* 74–90.

28. Paul Fesch, *Mortes au champ d'honneur. Bazar de la charité* (Paris: Flammarion, 1897), 3.

29. Ibid., 5. Fesch evokes here the parallel to Joan of Arc (p. 6). For numerous examples of this chivalric rhetoric, see the press inventory at the end of the book (pp. 300–309).

30. Ibid., 260.

31. *Discours, Académie Française, Institut Impérial de France,* (Paris: Firmin Didot, 1866), 30. In the *séance* of 20 December 1866, the Prix Montyon was described as honoring, "charity in all its forms, the active and disinterested devotion of man to his own kind" (p. 163).

32. See "Rapport sur les prix de vertu," (11 Nov. 1875) *Discours,· Académie Française, Institut de France* (Paris: Firmin Didot, 1875), 63–80; and ibid. (1888), 60–92; (1900), 65–83. As the *académicien* Sully Prudhomme expressed it in 1888, the prizes should reward acts of courage notable for their "spontaneous élan," and "pure distinterestedness" (1888, p. 80).

33. Anson Rabinbach, *The Human Motor. Energy, Fatigue, and the Origins of Modernity* (New York: Basic Books, 1990), 61–64.

34. Ibid., 43.

35. Ibid., 38–44.

36. Alfred Binet and J. Courtier, "L'Influence de la vie emotionelle sur le coeur, la respiration, et la circulation capillaire," *L'Année psychologique* (1896), 70–82; Charles Richet, "La Peur: étude psychologique," *Revue des deux mondes* 76 (July 1886): 87.

37. Dr. Paul Hartenberg, *Les Timides et la timidité* (Paris: Alcan, 1901), 3–5.

38. Ludovic Dugas, *La Timidité. Etude psychologique et morale* (Paris: Alcan, 1898), 99, 114.

39. Hartenberg, *Les Timides,* 129. As Hartenberg argues, the timidity that is so injurious to men is, by contrast, an accessory to women in their coquetry and lovemaking. Thus the blush, charming in a young virgin, is of "morbid consequence" for the male (pp. 129–30).

40. Dugas, *La Timidité,* 130–31.

41. Alfred Binet, "La Peur chez les enfants," *L'Année psychologique* (1896), 254.

42. Hartenberg, *Les Timides,* 234.

43. Dugas, *La Timidité,* 153; Richet, "La Peur," 117; Binet recommends intensive "training" in acts of courage in "La Peur chez les enfants," 251. See also Camille Méliland, "La Sentiment de peur," *Revue des revues* 38 (Dec. 1901): 520–35.

44. Rabinbach, *The Human Motor,* 163–71.

45. G. A. Mann, *L'Initiative, le courage et l'audace* (Paris: Librairie Internationale de la Pensée Nouvelle; 1913), 9, 20, 109–21.

46. Paul Souriau, *L'Entraînement au courage* (Paris: Alcan, 1926), 114.

47. Ibid., 105–109, 115–45.

48. Fernand Mazade, "Ce qu'est la peur," *La Revue,* 6th ser., 84 (15 Feb. 1910): 449–67.

49. Ibid., 456, 459.

50. For example, Alfred Capus, Louis Leger, Théodore Reinach. Ibid., 452, 456, 461.

51. David Sansone, *Greek Athletics and the Genesis of Sport* (Berkeley, Calif.: University of California Press, 1988), 130.

52. Ibid., 64–66.

53. Robert Wohl, *The Generation of 1914* (Cambridge, Mass.: Harvard University Press, 1979), 214–17.

54. Ibid., 26. On the anti-Semitic aspects of Montherlant's literary chivalry, see John M. Hoberman, "Montherlant's Moral Derelictions: A Postwar Interpretation," unpublished manuscript.

55. Quoted in Léon-E. Halkin, "Pour une histoire de l'honneur," *Annales E.S.C.* 4 (1949): 443.

56. Henry Miller, *The Cosmological Eye* (1939), as quoted in Stephen Kern, *Anatomy and Destiny. A Cultural History of the Human Body* (New York: Bobbs-Merrill, 1975), 194.

57. Michelle Perrot, "The New Eve and the Old Adam: French Women's Condition at the Turn of the Century," in *Behind the Lines. Gender and the Two World Wars,* ed. Margaret Higonnet (New Haven, Conn.: Yale University Press, 1987), 57.

58. On male hysteria, see Mark Micale, "Charcot and the Idea of Hysteria in the Male: Gender, Mental Science, and Medical Diagnosis in Late Nineteenth-Century France," *Medical History* 34 (1990): 363–411; and Ruth Harris, "Introduction," to J.-M. Charcot, *Clinical Lectures on Diseases of the Nervous System* (London and New York: Routledge, 1991), xx–xxxiii.

59. Elaine Showalter, "Rivers and Sassoon: The Inscription of Male Gender Anxieties," in *Behind the Lines,* ed. Higonnet, 64; see also Eric J. Leed, *No Man's Land. Combat and Identity in World War I* (Cambridge: Cambridge University Press, 1979), 164–66; and Mark Micale, "Hysteria and Its Historiography: The Future Perspective," *History of Psychiatry* 1 (1990): 99–100.

60. Huot and Voivenel adhered to the notion that courage was a product of the highest level of social evolution, an altruistic instinct to sacrifice oneself on behalf of the group. The chief secular manifestation of the presence of this "instinct," they averred, was a "chivalrous" patriotism. Dr. Louis Huot and Dr. Paul Voivenel, *Le Courage* (Paris: Alcan, 1917), 35–50, 285–93.

61. Ibid., 310–28.

62. Ibid., 138–56.

63. Ibid., 135, 246–48.

64. Ibid., 299. In his post-war writings, Voivenel continued to explore the relationship of cowardice and perverse sexuality. Both chaste and overly lubricious males, Voivenel believed, were likely to manifest a high degree of timidity and personal insecurity. See especially, *La Chasteté perverse* (Paris: La Renaissance du Livre, 1928), 10–17, 27–29, 77; and *Du Timide au satyre* (Paris: Librairie des Champs-Elysées, 1933), 7–10.

65. Showalter, "Rivers and Sassoon," 66; Leed, *No Man's Land,* 169–75.

66. Huot and Voivenel, *Le Courage,* 15.

67. Ibid., 127. My emphasis.

68. Marc Bloch, *Memoirs of War, 1914–15,* translated and introduced by Carole Fink, (Ithaca, N.Y.: Cornell University Press, 1980), 166.

BIBLIOGRAPHY OF SELECTED
SECONDARY WORKS

Abray, Jane. "Feminism in the French Revolution." *American Historical Review* 80 (1975): 43–62.

Adler, Laure. *Secrets d'alcôve: histoire du couple de 1830 à 1930*. Paris: Hachette, 1983.

Agulhon, Maurice. *Pénitents et francmaçons de l'ancienne provence*. Paris: Fayard, 1968.

———. *Le Cercle dans la France bourgeoise, 1810–1848*. Paris: Colin, 1977.

Albury, William R. "Experiment and Explanation in the Physiology of Bichat and Magendie." *Studies in the History of Biology*. Edited by William Coleman and Camille Limoges. Baltimore: Johns Hopkins University Press, 1977: 47–131.

Alexander, Jeffrey, ed. *Durkheimian Sociology: Cultural Studies*. Cambridge: Cambridge University Press, 1988.

Amson, Daniel. *Adolphe Crémieux. L'Oublie de la gloire*. Paris: Editions du Seuil, 1988.

Appel, Toby A. *The Cuvier–Geoffroy Debate. French Biology in the Decades Before Darwin*. New York: Oxford University Press, 1987.

Apter, Emily, and Pietz, William, ed. *Fetishism as Cultural Discourse: Gender, Commodity, and Vision*. Ithaca, N.Y.: Cornell University Press, 1993.

Armengaud, André. *L'Opinion publique en France et la crise nationale allemande en 1866*. Paris: Société des Belles Lettres, 1962.

———. *La Population française au XIXe siècle*. Paris: Presses Universitaires de France, 1971.

———. *Les Français et Malthus*. Paris: Presses Universitaires de France, 1975.

Arnaud, André-Jean. *Essai d'analyse structurale du code civil français. La Règle du jeu dans la paix bourgeoise*. Paris: R. Pichon et R. Durand-Auzias, 1973.

Arnaud, Pierre, ed. *Les Athlètes de la République. Gymnastique, sport et idéologie républicaine, 1870–1914*. Paris: Privat, 1987.

Aron, J. P., ed. *La femme du XIXe siècle*. Paris: Editions Complexe, 1980.

———. and Kempf, Roger. *La Bourgeoisie, le sexe, et l'honneur*. Paris: Editions Complexe, n.d.

Auspitz, Katherine. *The Radical Bourgeoisie. The Ligue de l'Enseignement and the Origins of the Third Republic*. Cambridge: Cambridge University Press, 1982.

Baldick, Robert. *The Duel. A History of Dueling*. London: Chapman and Hall, 1965.

Barber, Elinor G. *The Bourgeoisie in Eighteenth-Century France.* Princeton: Princeton University Press, 1955.

Bardet, Jean-Pierre, and LeBras, Hervé. "La Chute de la fécondité." *Histoire de la population française,* vol. 3. Paris: Presses Universitaires de France, 1988: 351–402.

Bataille, Georges. *Erotism. Death and Sensuality.* San Francisco: City Light, 1986.

Becarud, Jean. *Maurice Barrès et le parlement de la belle époque (1906–1914).* Paris: Plon, 1987.

Béhar, Serge. *L'Univers médical de Proust.* Paris: Gallimard, 1970.

Bénard, J. C. "Fille ou garçon à volonté: Un Aspect du discours médical au 19e siècle." *Ethnologie française* 11 (1981): 63–76.

Berenson, Edward. "The Politics of Divorce in France of the Belle Epoque: The Case of Joseph and Henriette Caillaux." *American Historical Review* 93, no. 1 (1988): 31–55.

———. *The Trial of Madame Caillaux.* Berkeley, Calif.: University of California Press, 1992.

Bertholet, Denis. *Le Bourgeois dans tous ses états.* Paris: Olivier Orban, 1987.

Best, Geoffrey. *Honour Among Men and Nations. Transformations of an Idea.* Toronto: University of Toronto Press, 1982.

Billacois, François. *Le Duel dans la société française des XVIe–XVIIe siècles. Essai de psychosociologie historique.* Paris: Editions de l'École des Hautes Études en Sciences Sociales, 1986.

Birkett, Jennifer. *The Sins of the Fathers. Decadence in France, 1879–1914.* London: Quartet Books, 1986.

Birkin, Lawrence. *Consuming Desire. Sexual Science and the Emergence of a Culture of Abundance.* Ithaca, N.Y.: Cornell University Press, 1988.

Birnbaum, Pierre. *Un Mythe politique: 'La République juive' de Léon Blum à Pierre Mendès-France.* Paris: Fayard, 1988.

Bloch, Marc. *Memoirs of War, 1914–15.* Translated and introduced by Carole Fink. Ithaca, N.Y.: Cornell University Press, 1980.

Blum, Carol. *Rousseau and the Republic of Virtue. The Language of Politics in the French Revolution.* Ithaca, N.Y.: Cornell University Press, 1986.

Borie, Jean. *Le Célibataire français.* Paris: Le Sagittaire, 1976.

———. *Mythologies de l'hérédité au XIXe siècle.* Paris: Editions Galilée, 1981.

Bourdieu, Pierre. *Distinction. A Social Critique of the Judgement of Taste.* Translated by Richard Nice. Cambridge, Mass.: Harvard University Press, 1984.

———. *The Logic of Practice.* Stanford, Calif.: Stanford University Press, 1990.

Bredin, Jean-Denis. *The Affair.* New York: Braziller, 1986.

Brennan, Thomas. *Public Drinking and Popular Culture in Eighteenth-Century Paris.* Princeton: Princeton University Press, 1988.

Brogan, Denis. *The Development of Modern France.* New York: Harper, 1966.

Bryson, Frank. *The Sixteenth-Century Italian Duel: A Study in Renaissance Social History.* Chicago: University of Chicago Press, 1938.

Buican, Denis. *Histoire de la génétique et de l'évolutionnisme en France.* Paris: Presses Universitaires de France, 1984.

Burke, Peter. "Popular Culture Between History and Ethnology." *Ethnologia Europaea* 14 (1984): 5–13.

Bury, J. P. T. *Gambetta's Final Years. The Era of Difficulties, 1877–1882.* London: Longman, 1982.

Campbell, J. K. *Honour, Family and Patronage. A Study of Moral Values in a Greek Mountain Village.* Oxford: Oxford University Press, 1964.

Canguilhem, Georges. *Le Normal et le pathologique.* Paris: Presses Universitaires de France, 1975.

———. *La Connaissance de la vie.* Paris: Vrin, 1985.

———. *Etudes d'histoire et de philosophie des sciences.* Paris: Vrin, 1989.

———. Piquemal, Jacques; and Ulmann, Jacques. *Du Développement à l évolution au XIXe siècle.* Paris: Presses Universitaires de France, 1985.

Caplan, Pat, ed. *The Cultural Construction of Sexuality.* London: Tavistock, 1987.

Casey, James. *The History of the Family.* Oxford: Basil Blackwell, 1989.

Castan, Yves. *Honnêteté et relations sociales en Languedoc (1715–1780).* Paris: Presses Universitaires de France, 1974.

Castel, Robert. *L'Ordre psychiatrique: L'âge d'or d'aliénisme.* Paris: Minuit, 1976.

Chalmin, Pierre. *La Pratique du duel dans l'armée française au XIXe siècle. Actes du 80e Congrès des sociétés savantes.* Lille: Presses Universitaires de France, 1955: 327–50.

Charle, Christophe. *Les Hauts fonctionnaires en France au XIXe siècle.* Paris: Gallimard, 1980.

———. *Les Elites de la République.* Paris: Fayard, 1987.

Chartier, Roger. *Cultural History. Between Practices and Representations.* Ithaca, N.Y.: Cornell University Press, 1988.

Chartier, Yves. *La Réparation du préjudice dans la responsibilité civile.* Paris: Dalloz, 1983.

Chauncey, George Jr. "From Sexual Inversion to Homosexuality." *Salmagundi* 58 (1982): 114–46.

Chaussinand-Nogaret, Guy, ed. *Une Histoire des élites, 1700–1848.* Paris: Mouton, 1975.

———. *The French Nobility in the Eighteenth Century.* Cambridge: Cambridge University Press, 1985.

Chesnais, Jean-Claude. *Histoire de la violence.* Paris: Robert Lafont, 1981.

Chodorow, Nancy. *The Reproduction of Mothering: Psychoanalysis and the Sociology of Gender.* Berkeley, Calif.: University of California Press, 1978.

Churchill, Frederick. "Sex and the Single Organism: Biological Theories of Sexuality in the Mid-Nineteenth Century." *Studies in the History of Biology* 3 (1979): 139–78.

Clark, Linda. *Schooling the Daughters of Marianne. Textbooks and the Socialization of Girls in Modern French Primary Schools.* Albany: State University of New York Press, 1984.

———. *Social Darwinism in France.* Tuscaloosa: University of Alabama Press, 1984.

Claverie, Elisabeth, and Lamaison, Pierre. *L'Impossible mariage. Violence et parenté en Gévaudan au 17e, 18e, et 19e siècles.* Paris: Hachette, 1982.

Conry, Yvette. *L'Introduction du Darwinisme en France au XIXe siècle*. Paris: Vrin, 1974.

Copley, Antony. *Sexual Moralities in France, 1780–1980*. London: Routledge, 1988.

Courouve, Claude. *Vocabulaire de l'homosexualité masculine*. Paris: Payot, 1985.

Cuénin, Micheline. *Le Duel sous l'ancien régime*. Paris: Presses de la Renaissance, 1982.

Curtin, Michael. "A Question of Manners: Status and Gender in Etiquette and Courtesy." *Journal of Modern History* 57 (1985): 395–423.

Darmon, Pierre. *Le Tribunal de l'impuissance. Virilité et défaillances conjugales dans l'ancienne France*. Paris: Editions du Seuil, 1979.

Darnton, Robert. "The High Enlightenment and the Low-Life of Literature in Prerevolutionary France." *Past and Present* 51 (1971): 81–115.

———. "Reading, Writing and Publishing in Eighteenth-Century France." *Daedalus* (Winter 1971): 214–56.

Darrow, Margaret. *Revolution in the House. Family, Class, and Inheritance in Southern France, 1775–1825*. Princeton: Princeton University Press, 1989.

Daston, Lorraine, and Park, Katharine. "Hermaphrodites in Renaissance France." *Critical Matrix. Princeton Working Papers in Women's Studies* 1, no. 5 (1985): 1–18.

Daumard, Adeline. *Les Bourgeois et la bourgeoisie en France depuis 1815*. Paris: Aubier, 1987.

———. "Noblesse et aristocratie en France au XIXe siècle." *Les Noblesses Européenes au XIXe siècle*. Edited by Ecole Française de Rome, vol. 107. Rome: Ecole Française de Rome, 1988: 89–104.

David, George. "La Stérilité masculine: le déni du mâle." *Le Genre humain* 10 (1984): 23–38.

Davidoff, Leonore, and Hall, Catherine. *Family Fortunes. Men and Women of the English Middle Class, 1780–1850*. London: Hutchinson, 1987.

Davidson, Arnold. "How to do the History of Psychoanalysis. A Reading of Freud's *Three Essays on the Theory of Sexuality*." *Critical Inquiry* 14 (1987): 252–77.

———. "Sex and the Emergence of Sexuality." *Critical Inquiry* 14 (1987): 16–48.

Deak, Istvan. *Beyond Nationalism. A Social and Political History of the Hapsburg Officer Corps*. New York: Oxford University Press, 1990.

Delay, Jean. *La Jeunesse d'André Gide*. 2 vols. Paris: Gallimard, 1957.

Desert, Gabriel. "Pour une relecture de la notion du duel." *Annales de Normandie* 33, no. 3 (1983): 181–84.

Digeon, Claude. *La Crise allemande de la pensée française, 1879–1914*. Paris: Presses Universitaires de France, 1959.

Donzelot, Jacques. *The Policing of Families*. New York, 1979.

Dowbiggin, Ian. *Inheriting Madness. Professionalization and Psychiatric Knowledge in Nineteenth-Century France*. Berkeley, Calif.: University of California Press, 1991.

Duberman, Martin; Vicinus, Martha; and Chauncey, George Jr., eds. *Hidden From History: Reclaiming the Gay and Lesbian Past*. New York: NAL, 1989.

Duplantier, Raymond. "Les Duels à Poitiers et dans le Vienne au cours de la première moitié du dix-neuvième siècle." *Société des antiquaires de l'ouest.* 1950: 1–21.

Ehrenberg, Alain. *Le Corps militaire. Politique et pédagogie en démocratie.* Paris: Aubier, 1983.

Elias, Norbert. *The Civilizing Process.* 3 vols. New York: Pantheon, 1983.

Ellis, Jack D. *The Physician-Legislators of France. Medicine and Politics in the Early Third Republic, 1870–1914.* Cambridge: Cambridge University Press, 1990.

Elwitt, Sanford. *The Third Republic Defended.* Baton Rouge, La.: Louisiana State University Press, 1986.

Farley, John. *Gametes and Spores. Ideas About Sexual Reproduction, 1750–1914.* Baltimore: Johns Hopkins University Press, 1982.

Figlio, Karl. "The Metaphor of Organization: An Historiographical Perspective on the Bio-Medical Sciences of the Early Nineteenth Century." *History of Science* 25 (1987): 111–46.

Fischer, J-L. "Yves Delage (1854–1920): Epigénèse néo-Lamarckienne contre la prédéterminisme Weismanienne." *Revue de synthèse* 96 (1979): 443–61.

Flandrin, Jean-Louis. *Families in Former Times. Household and Sexuality.* Cambridge: Cambridge University Press, 1979.

———. *Le Sexe de l'occident. Evolution des comportements et des attitudes.* Paris: Editions du Seuil, 1981.

Forster, Robert, and Ranum, Orest, eds. *Family and Society. Selections from the Annales Economies, Sociétés, Civilisations.* Baltimore: Johns Hopkins University Press, 1976.

Foucault, Michel. *Surveiller et punir. Naissance de la prison.* Paris: Gallimard, 1975.

———. *Herculine Barbin, Dite Alexina B.* Paris: Gallimard, 1978.

———. *The History of Sexuality. An Introduction.* New York: Random, 1980.

Fraisse, Geneviève. *Muse de la raison. La Démocratie exclusive et la différence des sexes.* Paris: Alinea, 1989.

Frevert, Ute. "Bourgeois Honor: Middle-Class Duellists in Germany From the Late Eighteenth-Century to the Early Twentieth Century." *The German Bourgeoisie. Essays on the Social History of the German Middle Class from the Late Eighteenth to the Early Twentieth Century.* Edited by Richard J. Evans and David Blackbourn. London: Routledge, 1991: 255–92.

Fuchs, Rachel. *Abandoned Children. Foundlings and Child Welfare in Nineteenth-Century France.* Albany: State University of New York Press, 1984.

Fuss, Diana. *Essentially Speaking. Feminism, Nature and Difference.* New York: Routledge, 1989.

Gallagher, Catherine, and Laqueur, Thomas, eds. *The Making of the Modern Body. Sexuality and Society in the Nineteenth Century.* Berkeley, Calif.: University of California Press, 1987.

Garçon, Emile. *Code pénal annoté.* New ed. Paris: Sirey, 1956.

Gay, Peter. *The Bourgeois Experience: Victoria to Freud.* 2 vols. New York: Oxford University Press, 1984–86.

Gerbod, Paul. L'Ethique héroique en France (1870–1914). *Revue historique* 268, no. 2 (1983): 409–29.

Gibson, Ralph. "The French Nobility in the Nineteenth Century." *Elites in France: Origins, Reproduction, Power.* Edited by Jolyon Howorth, and Philip Cerny. New York: St. Martin's Press, 1981: 5–45.

Gide, André. *Corydon.* New York: Farrar, Straus and Giroux, 1983.

Giesey, Ralph. "Rules of Inheritance and Strategies of Mobility in Prerevolutionary France." *American Historical Review* 82, no. 2 (1977): 271–89.

Gilman, Sander. *Difference and Pathology. Stereotypes of Sexuality, Race, and Madness.* Ithaca, N.Y.: Cornell University Press, 1985.

Gilmore, David. *Aggression and Community. Paradoxes of Andalusian Culture.* New Haven, Conn.: Yale University Press, 1987.

———. *Manhood in the Making. Cultural Concepts of Masculinity.* New Haven, Conn.: Yale University Press, 1990.

Girard, Jacques. *Le Mouvement homosexuel en France, 1945–1980.* Paris: Editions Syros, 1981.

Girouard, Mark. *The Return to Camelot. Chivalry and the English Gentleman.* New Haven, Conn.: Yale University Press, 1981.

Goblot, Edmond. *La Barrière et le niveau. Etude sociologique sur la bourgeoisie française moderne.* Paris: Alcan, 1925.

Goldstein, Jan. *Console and Classify. The French Psychiatric Profession in the Nineteenth Century.* Cambridge: Cambridge University Press, 1987.

Goody, Jack. *Production and Reproduction. A Comparative Study of the Domestic Domain.* Cambridge: Cambridge University Press, 1976.

Greenberg, David F. *The Construction of Homosexuality.* Chicago: University of Chicago Press, 1988.

Groethuysen, Bernard. *The Bourgeois. Catholicism vs. Capitalism in Eighteenth-Century France.* London: Barrie and Rockliff, 1968.

Guillaume, Pierre. *Individus, familles, nations. Essai d'histoire démographique XIXe–XXe siècles.* Paris: Société d'Editions d'Enseignement Superieur, 1985.

Guiral, Pierre, and Thullier, Guy. *La Vie quotidienne des députés en France de 1871–1914.* Paris: Hachette, 1980.

Hahn, Pierre. *Nos Ancêtres les pervers: la vie des homosexuels sous le sécond empire.* Paris: Olivier Orban, 1979.

Haigh, Elizabeth A. "Vitalism, the Soul, and Sensibility: The Physiology of Théophile Bordeu." *Journal of the History of Medicine* 31 (1976): 30–41.

Halkin, Léon-E. "Pour une histoire de l'honneur." *Annales E.S.C.* 4 (1949): 433–44.

Hampson, Norman. "The French Revolution and the Nationalization of Honor." *War and Society. Historical Essays in Honour of J.R. Western.* Edited by M. R. D. Foot. New York: Barnes and Noble, 1973: 199–212.

———. "La Patrie." *The Political Culture of the French Revolution.* Edited by Colin Lucas. Oxford: Pergamon Press, 1988: 130–138.

Hansen, Bert. "American Physicians' Earliest Writings About Homosexuals, 1880–1900." *The Milbank Quarterly* 67 (1989): 92–108.

Harevan, Tamara, and Wheaton, Robert, eds. *Family and Sexuality in French History*. Philadelphia: University of Pennsylvania Press, 1980.

Harris, Ruth. *Murders and Madness: Medicine, Law, and Society in the Fin-de-Siècle*. Oxford: Oxford University Press, 1989.

Harris, Ruth, ed. Jean-Martin Charcot, *Clinical Lectures on Diseases of the Nervous System*. London: Routledge, 1991.

Hause, Steven, and Kenny, Anne C. *Women's Suffrage and Social Politics in the French Third Republic*. Princeton: Princeton University Press, 1984.

Higgonet, Margaret, ed. *Behind the Lines. Gender and the Two World Wars*. New Haven, Conn.: Yale University Press, 1987.

Higgs, David. *Nobles in Nineteenth-Century France. The Practice of Inegalitarianism*. Baltimore: Johns Hopkins University Press, 1987.

Hoberman, John. *Sport and Political Ideology*. Austin: University of Texas Press, 1984.

Hoffman, Paul. *La Femme dans la pensée des lumières*. Paris: Ophrys, 1977.

Holt, Richard. *Sport and Society in Modern France*. Hamden, Conn.: Archon Books, 1979.

Huizinga, Johan. *The Waning of the Middle Ages*. New York: Doubleday, 1954.

Hull, Isabel. *The Entourage of Kaiser Wilhelm II, 1888–1918*. Cambridge: Cambridge University Press, 1982.

Hunt, Lynn. *Politics, Culture and Class in the French Revolution*. Berkeley, Calif.: University of California Press, 1984.

———, ed. *The New Cultural History*. Berkeley, Calif.: University of California Press, 1989.

Huss, Marie-Monique. "Pronatalism in the Inter-War Period in France." *Journal of Contemporary History* 25 (1990): 39–68.

Irvine, William D. *The Boulanger Affair Reconsidered. Royalism, Boulangism, and the Origins of the Radical Right in France*. New York: Oxford University Press, 1989.

James, Mervyn. *Society, Politics and Culture. Studies on Early Modern England*. Cambridge: Cambridge University Press, 1986.

Jordanova, Ludmilla, ed. *Languages of Nature. Critical Essays on Science and Literature*. New Brunswick, N.J.: Rutgers University Press, 1986.

———. *Sexual Visions. Images of Gender in Science and Medicine Between the Eighteenth and Twentieth Centuries*. Madison: University of Wisconsin Press, 1989.

Jouanna, Arlette. "La Notion de l'honneur au XVI siècle." *Revue d'histoire moderne et contemporaine* 15 (1968): 597–623.

———. *Ordre social. Mythes et hiérarchies dans la France du XVIe siècle*. Paris: Hachette, 1977.

Keen, Maurice. *Chivalry*. New Haven, Conn.: Yale University Press, 1984.

Kelley, George Armstrong. "Duelling in Eighteenth-Century France: Archeology, Rationale, Implications." *The Eighteenth Century* 21, no. 3 (1980): 236–54.

Kern, Stephen. *Anatomy and Destiny. A Cultural History of the Human Body*. New York: Bobbs-Merrill, 1975.

Kiernan, V. G. *The Duel in European History. Honour and the Reign of Aristocracy.* Oxford: Oxford University Press, 1988.

Kirk-Escalle, Marie-Christine. *Instaurer une culture par l'enseignement de l'histoire
de France, 1876–1912. Contribution à une sémiotique de la culture.* Berne:
Peter Lang, 1988.

Kleeblatt, Norman L., ed. *The Dreyfus Affair. Art, Truth, Justice.* Berkeley, Calif.:
University of California Press, 1987.

Kniebiehler, Yvonne. *Les Pères aussi ont une histoire.* Paris: Hachette, 1987.

———, and Fouquet, Catherine. *La Femme et les médecins.* Paris: Hachette, 1983.

Kovalevsky, Maxime. *Coutume contemporaine et loi ancienne. Droit coutumier
ossétien éclairé par l'histoire comparée.* Paris: Larose, 1893.

Lantéri-Laura, Georges. *Lecture des perversions: histoire de leur appropriation
médicale.* Paris: Masson, 1978.

Laqueur, Thomas. *Making Sex. Body and Gender from the Greeks to Freud.* Cambridge, Mass.: Harvard University Press, 1990.

Lauritsen, John, and Thorstad, David. *The Early Homosexual Rights Movement,
1864–1935.* New York: Times Change Press, 1974.

Leed, Eric J. *No Man's Land. Combat and Identity in World War I.* Cambridge:
Cambridge University Press, 1979.

Leiris, Michel. *Manhood. A Journey From Childhood Into the Fierce Order of
Virility.* New York: Grossman, 1963.

Levy, Darlene Gay, and Applewhite, Harriet, eds. *Women in Revolutionary Paris,
1789–1795.* Urbana: University of Illinois Press, 1979.

Loewenberg, Peter. *Decoding the Past. The Psychohistorical Approach.* Berkeley,
Calif.: University of California Press, 1984.

Logue, William. *Léon Blum. The Formative Years, 1872–1914.* DeKalb: Northern
Illinois University Press, 1973.

———. *From Philosophy to Sociology. The Evolution of French Liberalism.* Dekalb: Northern Illinois University Press, 1983.

Lucas, Colin. "Nobles, Bourgeois, and the Origins of the French Revolution."
French Society and the Revolution. Edited by Douglas Johnson. Cambridge:
Cambridge University Press, 1976: 88–131.

MacAloon, John J. *This Great Symbol. Pierre de Coubertin and the Origins of the
Modern Olympic Games.* Chicago: University of Chicago Press, 1981.

Macfarlane, Alan. *Marriage and Love in England. Modes of Reproduction, 1300–
1840.* Oxford: Basil Blackwell, 1986.

Machelon, Jean-Pierre. *La République contre les libertés? Les Restrictions aux
libertés de 1879 à 1914.* Paris: Presses de La Fondation Nationale des Sciences
Politiques, 1976.

Magendie, Maurice. *La Politesse mondaine et les théories de l'honnêteté en France
au XVIIe siècle, de 1600 à 1660.* 2 vols. Paris, 1925.

Maienschein, Jane. "What Determines Sex? A Study of Convergent Research
Approaches, 1880–1916." *Isis* 75 (1984): 457–80.

Marais, Jean-Luc. *Les Sociétés d'hommes. Histoire d'une sociabilité du 18e siècle
à nos jours. Anjou, Maine, Touraine.* Monchrétien: Ivan Duny, 1986.

Martin, Emily. "The Egg and the Sperm: How Science has Constructed a Romance

Based on Stereotypical Male–Female Roles." *Signs* 16, no. 3 (1991): 485–501.

Masson, Jeffrey, ed. *A Dark Science. Women, Sexuality and Psychiatry in the Nineteenth Century.* New York: Farrar, Straus, and Giroux, 1986.

Mauge, Annelise. *L'Identité masculine en crise au tournant du siècle, 1871–1914.* Paris: Rivages, 1987.

Maulitz, Russell C. *Morbid Appearances. The Anatomy of Pathology in the Early Nineteenth Century.* Cambridge: Cambridge University Press, 1987.

Mayer, Arno. *The Persistence of the Old Regime.* New York: Vintage, 1981.

McAleer, Kevin. "The Last Teutonic Knights: The German Duel in Comparative Perspective, 1871–1918." Ph.D. Dissertation, University of California, San Diego, 1990.

Medick, Hans, and Sabean, David, eds. *Interest and Emotion: Essays on the Study of Family and Kinship.* Cambridge: Cambridge University Press, 1984.

Micale, Mark. "Charcot and the Idea of Hysteria in the Male: Gender, Mental Science, and Medical Diagnosis in Late Nineteenth-Century France." *Medical History* 34 (1990): 363–411.

Morel, Henri. "La Fin du duel judiciaire en France et naissance du point d'honneur." *Revue historique du droit français et étranger* 30 (1964): 574–639.

Mort, Frank. *Dangerous Sexualities. Medico-Moral Politics in England Since 1830.* London: Routledge and Kegan Paul, 1987.

Mosse, George L. *Nationalism and Sexuality. Respectability and Abnormal Sexuality in Modern Europe.* New York: Fertig, 1985.

Neuschel, Kristen. *Word of Honor. Interpreting Noble Culture in Sixteenth-Century France.* Ithaca, N.Y.: Cornell University Press, 1989.

Nora, Pierre, ed. *Les Lieux de mémoire.* 2 vols. Paris: Gallimard, 1986.

Nye, Robert A. *The Origins of Crowd Psychology. Gustave LeBon and the Crisis of Mass Democracy in the Third Republic.* London: Sage, 1975.

———. *Crime, Madness and Politics in Modern France: The Medical Concept of National Decline.* Princeton: Princeton University Press, 1984.

———. "Honor, Impotence, and Male Sexuality in Nineteenth-Century French Medicine." *French Historical Studies* 16 (1989): 48–71.

———. "Sex Difference and Male Homosexuality in French Medical Discourse, 1830–1930." *Bulletin of the History of Medicine* 63 (1989): 32–51.

———. "Honor Codes in Modern France. A Historical Anthropology." *Ethnologia Europaea* 21 (1991): 5–17.

Offen, Karen. "Depopulation, Nationalism, and Feminism in Fin-de-siècle France." *American Historical Review* 89 (1984): 648–76.

———. "Ernest LeGouvé, a Case of Male Feminism in Nineteenth-Century French Thought." *Journal of Modern History* 58 (1984): 452–84.

Ong, Walter J. *Fighting for Life. Contest, Sexuality, and Consciousness.* Ithaca, N.Y.: Cornell University Press, 1981.

Ortner, Sherry, and Whitehead, Harriet, eds. *Sexual Meanings. The Cultural Construction of Gender and Sexuality.* Cambridge: Cambridge University Press, 1981.

Outhwaite, R. B., ed. *Marriage and Society. Studies in the Social History of Marriage.* New York: St. Martins Press, 1981.

Outram, Dorinda. *The Body and the French Revolution. Sex, Class and Political Culture* New Haven, Conn.: Yale University Press, 1989.

Palmer, Michael B. *Des Petits journaux aux grandes agences. Naissance du journalisme moderne.* Paris: Aubier, 1983.

Pappas, John. "Le Campagne des philosophes contre l'honneur." *Studies in Voltaire and the Eighteenth Century* 205 (1982): 37–44.

Park, Katharine, and Daston, Lorraine. "Unnatural Conceptions: The Study of Monsters in Sixteenth-Century France and England." *Past and Present* 92 (1981): 20–57.

———, and Nye, Robert A. "Destiny is Anatomy." *The New Republic* (18 Feb 1991): 53–57.

Paul, Harry. *From Knowledge to Power. The Rise of the Science Empire in France, 1860–1939.* Cambridge: Cambridge University Press, 1985.

Peristiany, J. G. *Honour and Shame. The Values of Mediterranean Society.* Chicago: University of Chicago Press, 1961.

Pernoud, Régine. *Histoire de la bourgeoisie en France.* Paris: Editions du Seuil, 1981.

Pernö, Ulf, and Löfgren, Orvar. *Culture Builders. A Historical Anthropology of Middle-Class Life.* New Brunswick, N.J.: Rutgers University Press, 1987.

Perrot, Michelle, ed. *Une Histoire des femmes, est-elle possible?* Paris: Rivages, 1984.

———, ed. *From the Fires of Revolution to the Great War.* Vol. 4 of *A History of Private Life.* Cambridge, Mass.: Harvard University Press, 1990.

Phillips, Roderick. *Putting Asunder. A History of Divorce in Western Society.* Cambridge: Cambridge University Press, 1990.

Pick, Daniel. *Faces of Degeneration. A European Disorder, c.1848–c.1918.* Cambridge: Cambridge University Press, 1989.

Pickstone, John. "Bureaucracy, Liberalism and the Body in Post-Revolutionary France: Bichat's Physiology and the Paris School of Medicine." *History of Science* 19 (1981): 115–42.

Pitt-Rivers, Julian. "Honor." *International Encyclopedia of the Social Sciences.* New York: Macmillan, 1968.

———. *The Fate of Schechem. Essays in the Anthropology of the Mediterranean.* Cambridge: Cambridge University Press, 1977.

Plessis, Alain. *De la fête impériale au mur des fédérés, 1852–1871.* Paris: Editions du Seuil, 1973.

Porter, Roy. "Spreading Carnal Knowledge Dirt Cheap? Nicholas Venette's Tableau de l'amour conjugal in Eighteenth-Century England." *Journal of European Studies* 14 (1984): 233–55.

———. " 'The Secrets of Generation Display'd': Aristotle's Masterpiece in Eighteenth-Century England." *'Tis Nature's Fault.' Unauthorized Sexuality During the Enlightenment.* Edited by Robert Maccubin. Cambridge: Cambridge University Press, 1987: 1–22.

Rabinbach, Anson. *The Human Motor. Energy, Fatigue, and the Origins of Modernity.* New York: Basic Books, 1990.

Reshef, Ouriel. *Guerre, mythes et caricature. Au berceau d'une mentalité française.* Paris: Presses de la Fondation Nationale des Sciences Politiques, 1984.

Rey-Flaud, Henri. *Le Charivari. Les Rituels fondamentaux de la sexualité.* Paris: Payot, 1985.

Richard, Guy. *Histoire de l'amour en France.* Paris, Hachette, 1985.

Richards, Robert J. *Darwin and The Emergence of Evolutionary Theories of Mind and Behavior.* Chicago: University of Chicago Press, 1987.

Riley, Denise. *"Am I That Name?" Feminism and the Category of "Women" in History.* Minneapolis: University of Minnesota Press, 1988.

Rivers, J. E. *Proust and the Art of Love: The Aesthetics of Sexuality in the Life, Times, and Art of Marcel Proust.* New York: Columbia University Press, 1980.

Robinson, Paul. *The Modernization of Sex.* New York: Harper and Row, 1976.

Ronsin, Francis. *La Grève des ventres: propagande néo-malthusienne et baisse de la natalité française (XIX–XXe siècles).* Paris: Aubier, 1980.

Rosenvallon, Pierre. *Le Moment Guizot.* Paris: Gallimard, 1985.

Roudinesco, Elizabeth. *La Bataille de cent ans. Histoire de la psychanalyse en France.* 2 vols. Paris: Ramsay, 1982.

Ruffié, Jacques. *Le Sexe et la mort.* Paris: Editions du Seuil, 1986.

Russett, Cynthia. *Sexual Science. The Victorian Construction of Womanhood.* Cambridge, Mass.: Harvard University Press, 1989.

Sabean, David. *Power in the Blood. Popular Culture and Village Discourse in Early Modern Germany.* Cambridge: Cambridge University Press, 1984.

———. *Property, Production, and Family in Neckarhausen, 1700–1870.* Cambridge: Cambridge University Press, 1990.

Sansone, David. *Greek Athletics and the Genesis of Sport.* Berkeley, Calif.: University of California Press, 1988.

Schalk, Ellery. *From Valor to Pedigree. Ideas of Nobility in France in the Sixteenth and Seventeenth Centuries.* Princeton: Princeton University Press, 1986.

Schiebinger, Londa. *The Mind Has No Sex? Women in the Origins of Modern Science.* Cambridge: Cambridge University Press, 1990.

Schneider, Robert A. "Swordplay and Statemaking. Aspects of the Campaign Against the Duel in Early Modern France." *Statemaking and Social Movements. Essays in History and Theory.* Edited by Charles Harding and Susan Bright. Ann Arbor: University of Michigan Press, 1984.

Schneider, William. *Quality and Quantity. The Quest for Biological Regeneration in Twentieth-Century France.* Cambridge: Cambridge University Press, 1990.

Schwartz, Joel. *The Sexual Politics of Jean-Jacques Rousseau.* Chicago: University of Chicago Press, 1984.

Scott, Joan W. *Gender and the Politics of History.* New York: Columbia University Press, 1988.

Segalen, Martine. *Love and Power in the Peasant Family.* Chicago: University of Chicago Press, 1983.

Serman, William. *Les Officiers français dans la nation, 1848–1914*. Paris: Aubier, 1982.

Sievers, Sharon. "Gay and Lesbian Research in the 1980s: History and Theory." *Radical History Review* 50 (1991): 204–12.

Simpson, Antony. "Dandelions on the Field of Honor: Dueling, the Middle Classes and the Law in Nineteenth-Century England." *Criminal Justice History* 9 (1988): 99–155.

Smith-Rosenberg, Carroll. *Disorderly Conduct: Visions of Gender in Victorian America*. New York: Oxford University Press, 1985.

Soloway, Richard. "Counting the Degenerates: The Statistics of Race Deterioration in Edwardian England." *Journal of Contemporary History* 17 (1982): 137–62.

Speier, Hans. *Social Order and the Risks of War*. Cambridge: Cambridge University Press, 1969.

Stambolian, George, and Marks, Elaine, eds. *Homosexualities and French Literature: Cultural Contexts, Critical Texts*. Ithaca, N.Y.: Cornell University Press, 1979.

Stanton, Domna C. *The Aristocrat as Art. A Study of the Honnête Homme and the Dandy in Seventeenth and Nineteenth-Century French Literature*. New York: Columbia University Press, 1980.

Staum, Martin S. *Cabanis. Enlightenment and Medical Philosophy in the French Revolution*. Princeton: Princeton University Press, 1980.

Steakley, James. "Iconography of a Scandal: Political Cartoons of the Eulenberg Affair." *Studies in Visual Communication* 9 (1983): 20–51.

Stengers, Jean, and Van Neck, Anne. *Histoire d'un grande peur: la masturbation*. Bruxelles: Editions de Université de Bruxelles, 1984.

Stearns, Peter. *Be a Man! Males and Modern Society*. New York: Holmes and Meier, 1979.

Stewart, Mary Lynn. *Women, Work, and the French State, Labour Protection and Social Patriarchy, 1879–1919*. Montreal: McGill-Queens University Press, 1989.

Stoller, Robert. *Sex and Gender: On the Development of Masculinity and Femininity*. New York: Science House, 1968.

Straus, Bernard. *Maladies of Marcel Proust: Doctors and Disease in his Life and Work*. New York: Holmes and Meier, 1980.

Sulloway, Frank. *Freud, Biologist of the Mind*. New York: Basic Books, 1979.

Swart, Konrad. *The Sense of Decadence in Nineteenth-Century France*. The Hague: Nijhoff, 1964.

Szramkiewicz, Romuald. *La Révolution française et la famille*. Paris: Presses Universitaires de France, 1978.

Tarczylo, Théodore. *Sexe et liberté au siècle des lumières*. Paris: Presses de la Renaissance, 1983.

Thibault, Jacques. *L'Influence du mouvement sportif sur l'évolution de l'éducation physique dans la France bourgeoise*. Paris: Colin, 1977.

Thimm, Carl A. *A Complete Bibliography of Fencing and Dueling*. London: John Lane, 1896.

Thullier, Guy. *Bureaucratie et bureaucrates en France au XIXe siècle*. Genève: Droz, 1980.

Todd, Emmanuel. *The Explanation of Ideology. Family Structures and Social Systems*. New York: Basil Blackwell, 1988.

Tomlinson, Richard. "The 'Disappearance of France', 1896–1940: French Politics and the Birth Rate." *The Historical Journal* 28, no. 2 (1985): 5–15.

Traer, James F. *Marriage and the Family in Eighteenth-Century France*. Ithaca, N.Y.: Cornell University Press, 1980.

Tuana, Nancy. "The Weaker Seed: The Secret Bias of Reproductive Theory." *Feminism and Science*. Edited by Nancy Tuana. Bloomington: Indiana University Press, 1989: 147–91.

Tudesq, A. J. *Les Grands notables en France sous la Monarchie de Juillet*. 2 vols. Paris: Presses Universitaires de France, 1964.

Turner, Victor. *The Ritual Process. Structure and Anti-Structure*. Ithaca, N.Y.: Cornell University Press, 1969.

Verdier, Yvonne. *Façons de dire, façons de faire. La Laveuse, la couturière, la cuisinière*. Paris: Gallimard, 1979.

Waelti-Walters, Jennifer. " 'New Women' in the Novels of Belle Epoque France." *History of European Ideas* 8 (1987): 537–48.

Weber, Eugene. *France Fin-de-Siècle*. Cambridge, Mass.: Harvard University Press, 1986.

Weeks, Jeffrey. *Coming Out. Homosexual Politics in Britian from the Nineteenth Century to the Present*. London: Quartet Books, 1977.

———. *Sex, Politics and Society. The Regulation of Sexuality Since 1800*. London: Longmans, 1981.

———. *Sexuality and its Discontents: Meanings, Myths, and Modern Sexualities*. London: Quartet Books, 1985.

Williams, Christine. *Gender Difference at Work: Women and Men in Non Traditional Occupations*. Berkeley, Calif.: University of California Press 1989.

Wilson, Stephen. "Infanticide, Child Abandonment, and Female Honour in Nineteenth-Century Corsica." *Comparative Studies in Society and History* 30 (1988): 762–83.

Wohl, Robert. *The Generation of 1914*. Cambridge, Mass.: Harvard University Press, 1979.

Wolff, Charlotte. *Magnus Hirschfeld. A Portrait of a Pioneer in Sexology*. London: Quartet Books, 1986.

Index